101 Hikes in the Majestic Mount Jefferson Region

Matt Reeder

Dedications and acknowledgements:

For Ted, because this is the book I wish we had when we lived in Salem. You're the best!

For Wendy: thank you for putting up with me writing this book for so long. You knew that I wouldn't accept anything less than the best, and you put up with that for three years.

For Grandpa Lee and Uncle Ol, both of whom passed away while I was writing this book: you taught me to stand up for myself, to be myself and to pursue my independence, even if you didn't realize it. I'll miss you both for the rest of my life.

Special thanks go to the following individuals:

To Gene Blick, Keith Dechant, Mike Kacmar, Ria Kotzé, Karl Langenwalter, Cabe Nicksic and Anna Revolinsky: Thank you for accompanying me on some of my crazy adventures, and even more, for giving me random ideas that had never occurred to me before. It is because of you that I was able to realign and refine the scope of this project, in many ways. Thank you for driving some of the roughest roads, putting up with some of the roughest trails and sticking by me every step of the way. I respect and admire your fearless spirits. Please don't ever change!

I wish to extend my appreciation and gratitude to my fellow friends who made my life so much easier during the process of writing this book by coming with me and offering many helpful suggestions. Thank you to Mana Amadon, Marcum Bell, Reena Clements, Krista Collins, Heather Cristia, Joe G, Paul Kallman, Jaime Kulbel, Matt Lyon, Cristin O'Brien, Rebecca Olsen, Lauren Sankovitch, Reed Scott-Schwalbach and, oh goodness, Richard Stellner.

I'd also like to thank the following individuals for their expertise in the Mount Jefferson area, which made my life so much easier even if they maybe didn't realize it: Tim Burke, Karl Helser, Cheryl Hill, Tom Kloster, Greg Lief, Don Nelson, Brad Rasmussen, John Sparks, Sean Thomas, Zach Urness, Rob Williams, and last but definitely not least, Kevin Wright.

And of course, my friends and family back in Illinois, and in France and elsewhere: your love and support continues to make all of this possible. Even if you weren't there in person, you were always there in spirit.

Thank you to the Mazamas for their continued support and encouragement. I feel honored to represent the organization as a hike leader and committee member.

Thank you to the Olallie Lake Resort, the Opal Creek Ancient Forest Center and the Marion Forks Restaurant for helping me get through some of the logistical hurdles I encountered writing this book. To Olallie Lake: thank you for letting me stay in your cabins and for your work keeping Olallie Lake the rustic and pristine place it is. To Opal Creek: thank you for your tireless dedication to preserving this most special of places. To Marion Forks: Thank you for your kindness and excellent food, which made my life easier after many long hikes.

Finally, I'd like to thank Pearl Jam, whose consistently brilliant live performances often served as the soundtrack for many long drives to and from the trailheads in the Majestic Mount Jefferson Region.

MAJESTIC MOUNT JEFFERSON!

SECTION 6: MOUNT JEFFERSON EAST

Photo on opposite page: Henline Falls (Hike 21)

Majestic Mount Jefferson!

Mount Jefferson is an enigma to many and a cherished destination to others. If you live near the great glaciated mountain, you've probably visited it at least a few times, and you know to look for it while driving through the area. And yet, despite its popularity, what makes this area great is its uniform beauty. For every popular destination, there are five that see few visitors. Most hikers have never heard of Baty Butte, Phantom Bridge, Bugaboo Ridge, Ruddy Hill, Bear Point or Table Lake. It honestly does not get better than this – these are the wildest places in Western Oregon.

I grew up in Salem. I lived in a house in the southern part of Salem, with a view that looked out towards Mount Hood and Mount Jefferson. Every day I would sit at our dinner table and look out the window at the area around Mount Jefferson, only somewhat knowing about the incredible outdoor opportunities that awaited my stepdad and I when we started exploring the area. We only scratched the surface, because we didn't even know most of the trails were there. Hiking guides touched only on the most popular hikes in the area, and this was before the days of the internet when almost every hike out there can be discovered sitting at your computer at night, beer by your side and your head full of dreams. We had to discover places the hard way, by getting stuck in the snow on the road to Crown Lake in April, by discovering just how truly terrible the Skyline Road is on a rare trip to the Olallie Lake area, and by hiking to Canyon Creek Meadows long after the wildflowers had died for the year. I wouldn't trade a single moment of it for anything in the world. And my stepdad, Ted – he was the best. He loved discovering new places, and he drove his truck up and down roads I wouldn't even dream of taking my little blue Subaru.

But what we truly needed was a detailed guidebook for the wildlands starting at the Little North Santiam River and extending east to the Olallie Plateau and south to the Old Cascades, and down past Mount Jefferson to Santiam Pass. I moved back to Illinois in high school but the imprint left by this area of wilderness was permanent. I collected magazine photos, bought hiking guides and dreamed of moving back to Oregon just so I could see

Opal Creek and Mount Jefferson again. I did return to Oregon for grad school, this time to Portland, where I've lived ever since. I quickly returned to the place where I'd spent much of my childhood, and since I moved back to Oregon in 2005 I've visited Opal Creek at least a dozen times and the Jefferson Park area almost as frequently (which is impressive, considering the fact the area is buried under snow for nine months every year). Slowly, the idea of writing the definitive guide to this area began to materialize, and I've spent the past several years making it a reality. It didn't come easy, but it was well worth it. Call it a labor of love.

Me hiking at the foot of Table Rock, July 1994. We ended up hiking about 30 of the 101 hikes covered in this book between 1991 and 1997, and all of them were memorable. This hike to the summit of Table Rock's summit was one of our favorites.

Mount Jefferson rises above a small, unnamed lake near Ruddy Hill.

Human history of the area:

I am, of course, not the only person who knows and loves the Majestic Mount Jefferson Region. The mountains both west and east of Mount Jefferson have been traveled and inhabited for millennia by various Indian tribes. Many of the area's trails are in fact remnants of longer trails used by the Indians. Trails that fit this description include the Baty Butte Trail, the Crag Trail, the Triangulation Trail and, most notably, the connector trail from Cathedral Rocks to Table Lake.

The local tribes made great use of the area. Jawbone Flats (where Battle Ax Creek and Opal Creek meet to form the Little North Santiam River) is believed to be the site of a summer camp for the Santiam tribe. The Warm Springs tribes would spend the last few weeks of summer in the Olallie area collecting huckleberries, and both Breitenbush Hot Springs were visited by countless bands of Indians throughout the years.

When the white man arrived in the 19th Century, many things changed. The various tribes were driven out of their territory, and many settled on the land that is now the Warm Springs Reservation. The reservation was the site of a long-running dispute over boundaries. In 1855, the tribes that inhabited the Mount Jefferson region signed a treaty with the United States government ceding control of the Oregon territory before the area could be overrun with white settlers; in return, they were driven onto an area that became the modern-day Warm Springs Reservation. When the area was surveyed in 1871, surveyor T.B. Handley drew up boundaries that were considerably further south and east from what the Indians requested. A second survey by a man named McQuinn came up with boundaries more in line with the request of the tribes, and the boundaries would be disputed for nearly a century. After years of pressure, the Warm Springs prevailed, and the lands in the so-called McQuinn Strip (the land contained in the McQuinn survey but not in the Handley survey) were returned to the Warm Springs. Today, these lands (including Russ and Jude Lakes, Olallie Butte and the lakes east of Olallie Lake) can be visited provided you have a valid fishing license, a Warm Springs tribal fishing permit and provided you do not spend the night.

After the arrival of the white man, recreation in the mountains became increasingly popular. Trappers, miners and mountain men built scores of trails and explored the lands in the area, and many of the landmarks in the modern-day Bull of the Woods Wilderness and Mount Jefferson Wilderness areas bear the names of these explorers. John Minto was a surveyor employed to help determine if there was a pass over the Cascades east of Salem, and he helped build the Minto Trail, which exists even today as a connector trail between Marion and Wasco Lakes. Today, many landmarks in the area near Marion Forks bear Minto's name, including the pass just north of Wasco Lake he discovered. Judge Waldo, another explorer who spent summers in the Cascades near Mount Jefferson, wrote extensively about the area. Today, his name lives on in many places in Oregon, among them the Waldo Glacier on the southeast slopes of Mount Jefferson, as well as Waldo Lake southeast of Oakridge. Other noteworthy individuals include Robert Bagby, a trapper and miner who prospected extensively in what is now the Bull of the Woods Wilderness area, and after whom Bagby Hot Springs and the Bagby Trail is named; many other prospectors, trappers and hunters helped explore and map the area throughout the years.

In the early part of the 20th Century, the United States government helped build a network of trails that crisscrossed the area (many of them old Indian trails), and in time, fire lookouts, roads and even buildings were constructed. Many of the trails in the area of this book were constructed in the 1920s and 1930s, when only a few roads existed and rangers roamed the forests. Fire lookouts were common then, and today, only a handful survive. Those currently standing are Pechuck Lookout, Bull of the Woods, Sisi Buttes, Gold Butte, Coffin Mountain, Black Butte and Green Ridge.

Although the Skyline Road dates back to the 1920s, most of the roads in the area were not constructed until the 1950s and 1960s. As logging increased in the 1970s and 1980s, many miles of new roads were constructed, and logging was a major flashpoint in the environmental battles that shaped the 1970s, 1980s and 1990s. Opal Creek became a household name when a battle over the logging of old-growth forests became a national controversy. While logging on federal lands has been drastically cut back, logging on private, state and BLM lands continues to this day. In many cases it is possible to discern the wilderness boundaries just by looking to see where the clearcuts begin. So it goes.

Equally noteworthy and historically significant is the large number of forest fires that have plagued the area between Opal Creek, the Olallie Plateau and Mount Jefferson. Since 2000, seven major fires have scarred much of the terrain in the area:

- The Olallie Lake Complex Fire of 2001: This fire burned much of the land east of Olallie Lake. The Olallie Lake Loop and the lakes east of here on the Warm Springs Reservation are now a sea of white snags.
- The B+B Fire of 2003: Two separate fires, the Booth Lake Fire and Bear Butte Fire,

Looking over the damage from the B+B Fire at Eight Lakes Basin.

combined to burn an area from the Warm Springs Reservation all the way to Mount Washington in what would become Oregon's largest and costliest fire. The scars left by the B+B fire are long-lasting, with almost 20% of the hikes in this book showing some sort of damage from the event.

- The Puzzle Creek Fire of 2006: This huge fire burned the terrain around and north of Marion Lake. The Lake of the Woods Trail and Bingham Ridge Trails both burned heavily during this fire.
- The View Lake and Mother Lode Fires, 2010-2011: These fires are lumped together because they both burned a large swath of the northeast corner of the Bull of the Woods Wilderness Area. The Mother Lode, Welcome Lake and Schreiner Trails were incinerated in this fire, and the Elk Lake Creek area shows scars from the event. The View Lake Fire also burned a portion of the Olallie Plateau from View Lake south towards Pyramid Butte, including two miles of the Pacific Crest Trail.
- The Waterfalls 2 Fire of 2012 burned a corner of the Warm Springs Reservation near Breitenbush Lake, narrowly missing Jefferson Park.
- The Bridge 99 Complex Fire of 2014, which incorporated the Bear Butte 2 Fire and the Bridge 99 fire, narrowly missed the Green Ridge lookout, burning a long swath of the ridges on both sides of the Metolius River. The Bear Butte 2 Fire in particular threatened the Table Lake area before being doused just one mile from the lake.
- The Bingham Ridge Fire of 2014, which started the same day as the Bridge 99 Complex after a lightning storm struck the area, burned the Bingham Ridge Trail for a second time in less than ten years as well as parts of Minto Peak, Lizard Ridge and the ridge above Hunts Cove.

Although fire is a natural part of the life cycle in the wilderness, we can only hope the

Mount Jefferson area is done burning for a long time. At this point, nearly half the terrain in this book has burned in the last fifteen years. Hikers planning on visiting this area in the summer should keep an eye out for any sign of fire, and be willing to put out campfires and small fires if needed. Hikers should equally be vigilant and keep an eye on the weather; lightning storms should be avoided at all costs.

A brief geologic history of the area:

Volcanic activity has shaped the land in this book. The Old Cascades are the remnants of the area's first volcanoes, and as such are both more rounded and more eroded than many other area volcanoes. Mount Jefferson appeared later, several hundred thousand years ago. It is believed that the mountain's most recent eruption was about 35,000 years ago, and is unlikely to ever erupt again. Three-Fingered Jack has been dormant for far longer than that. The geologically recent lava flows from Forked Butte, which date back to 4500 BC, shows that volcanic activity is still possible in the area. As you visit the area, look for signs of the area's volcanic past – they are everywhere and fascinating to note.

Where Everything Is:

This book covers seven federally-designated wilderness areas: the Table Rock Wilderness, the Big Bottom Wilderness, the Bull of the Woods Wilderness, the Opal Creek Wilderness, the Middle Santiam Wilderness, the Menagerie Wilderness and the Mount Jefferson Wilderness. Along with these protected areas is the Olallie Scenic Area, the wildly scenic lake-dotted plateau north of Mount Jefferson; the so-called Old Cascades, a series of craggy, meadow-dotted peaks and ridges between Sweet Home and Santiam Pass; the rugged cliffs and peaks north of Detroit Lake, where you will find some of the scariest roads in the state; and the wide and beautiful canyon of the Metolius River, about twelve miles southeast of Mount Jefferson. Together, these wildlands comprise the heart of this part of the Oregon Cascades.

This book covers everything from the Table Rock area to the northwest to the upper reaches of the Clackamas canyon on the northeast, and from Green Peter Lake on the southeast to Black Butte on the southeast. While all of these places may seem to be different, and while many of the approaches to these places differ due to the location of the roads, they are in fact one compact area approximately forty miles north to south by forty miles east to west.

What to see:

Nowhere in Oregon will you find more diversity of terrains, forests, lakes, meadows, and deep canyons. It simply does not get any better than this!

Ancient Forests: Opal Creek. Big Bottom. Dickey Creek. Elk Lake Creek. Cheat Creek. The Middle Santiam River Wilderness. Few if any places in Oregon can match the collection of ancient forest remaining in the steep slopes on both sides of the Cascade Crest near Mount Jefferson. The Bull of the Woods and Opal Creek Wilderness areas combine to form one of the largest continuous bands of ancient forest left in western Oregon, and there are isolated pockets of tremendous old-growth in every corner of the area covered in this guidebook, particularly in the Old Cascades. Hikers venturing off trail can discover groves of trees so large and tall and so old that they defy comprehension – provided you are willing to spend entire days exploring in rugged, unknown terrain. Doing this is very fun but not

Butterflies and Cascade lilies - two common sights in the Majestic Mount Jefferson Region.

recommended for anyone not used to off-trail exploration.

Waterfalls: You may have heard of a few waterfalls in the Mount Jefferson region but chances are you've never visited the tallest and most impressive cataracts in the area. Many of the tallest waterfalls in Oregon are hidden away in the backcountry north of Mount Jefferson, while some of the most beautiful waterfalls in the Pacific Northwest are tucked away deep in the backcountry throughout the region. Here's the catch: most of these falls are very difficult to get to, and many of the most impressive require substantial off-trail exploration through some of the most rugged terrain in the state. With that being said, there are many beautiful and impressive waterfalls that require a minimal effort to visit. Among these are Henline Falls, Sullivan Creek Falls, House Rock Falls, Sahalie and Koosah Falls, the upper tiers of Breitenbush Cascades and Marion Falls. For those with the time, energy and fortitude to trek into the backcountry, you will be rewarded with up-close and personal views of seldom-visited and very impressive waterfalls. Beware – cross-country travel is inherently dangerous, particularly when visiting cliffy terrain. Do not attempt to bushwhack to waterfalls unless you know what you are doing, have a very good map and the good sense to turnaround when you need to do so.

Hot Springs: Despite being a hotbed of volcanic activity, the Mount Jefferson area has very few hot springs. You've heard of the two that do exist, however: Bagby Hot Springs near the Bull of the Woods Wilderness Area and Breitenbush Hot Springs are perhaps the two most famous hot springs in the state. Both are well worth visiting and require minimal effort beyond a short hike (to Bagby) and some money (for Breitenbush). There is a third, lesser-known hot springs just downstream from Breitenbush's bustling new age resort that is an interesting visit (see Hike 65). Just outside the terrain covered in this book, Austin Hot

Springs is located on private property and requires a ford of the Clackamas River to visit. Don't bother, as the springs are so hot it can be dangerous to soak and the area is quite run-down. It is unknown if more hot springs exist deep in the backcountry, but given the area's long history of inhabitation, I doubt it.

Lakes: This is a land of lakes. Indeed, there are more lakes than I could possibly list, and most of the hikes in this book visit at least one lake. In addition to the dozens of lakes with trails to them, there are hundreds more off-trail in the area, and particularly in the Olallie Scenic Area and the west slopes of the Mount Jefferson Wilderness. With a map, compass and an altimeter (or a really good GPS), you can visit these lakes on your own to find excellent campsites and peace and quiet.

Meadows and wildflowers: Some of Oregon's finest wildflower meadows are located in the Mount Jefferson area. The most famous such meadows are found at Jefferson Park (Hikes 63, 70, 73 and 74) and Canyon Creek Meadows (Hikes 87 and 92). While both of these destinations are rightly lauded for their copious floral displays, there are many other hikes in this book with excellent flower shows. Virtually every peak in the Old Cascades is home to incredible flower displays, and many of the ridges in the Bull of the Woods and Mount Jefferson Wilderness Areas feature outstanding flower shows in June and July.

Mountains and peaks: There are only two glaciated peaks in the region covered in this book: Mount Jefferson and Three-Fingered Jack. Mount Jefferson officially has five glaciers: the Russell, the Jefferson Park, the Whitewater, the Waldo, and the Milk Creek. The first two drape the shadowy north side of the peak, while the Whitewater is a massive sheet of ice covering nearly the entire eastern face of the mountain. It is difficult to get a good view of the Whitewater Glacier from any place covered in this book as the best views are from inside the Warm Springs Reservation. The Waldo Glacier descends down the southeast slopes of the mountain, ending at a moraine complete with glacial lake at about 7,200 feet. The fifth and final glacier, the Milk Creek, may no longer even be considered a glacier — more than half of this former sheet of ice calved off during the massive "Pineapple Express" rainstorm in November 2006, flooding out the Pamelia Creek Valley. Today, only fragments of this glacier remain, and in late summer the west face of Mount Jefferson appears barren, in various shades of grey and brown. As for Three-Fingered Jack, a small and unnamed glacier resides in the shadows beneath the summit pinnacle on the north side of the peak, just above Canyon Creek Meadows (Hikes 87 and 92). Both Mount Jefferson and Three-Fingered Jack are heavily eroded volcanoes, and as such take on significantly different profiles from every angle from which you see them.

Unglaciated and much shorter but no less impressive are a number of peaks that cover the area presented in this book. Among the most noteworthy, impressive and photogenic are Table Rock, Battle Ax, Iron Mountain, Dynah-Mo Peak, Olallie Butte, North Cinder Peak, Black Butte and Forked Butte. Many of these mountains have trails to their summits, but most of these mountains are just as photogenic and imposing from the bottom as they are from the top.

Fauna: Last but not least, no discussion of the area would be complete without discussing the animals who inhabit it. In the many years I've spent traveling in the area, I've seldom seen more than deer, elk and various birds and amphibians. Many of the animals who in-

I nearly tripped over this Pacific Giant Salamander in the Opal Creek area.

habit the area covered in this book are seldom seen, and tend to avoid humans whenever possible. Many others are nocturnal, and are not out when humans tend to be traveling in the wilderness. In terms of larger fauna in the area, black bears and cougars are the most common and most noteworthy. You are unlikely to see either, but they will almost certainly see you. Both are to be respected but fear not, as bear and cougar attacks are extremely rare, rarer even than being struck by lightning. If you see a cougar, try to make yourself look tall and imposing, as cougars are unlikely to attack anything that will put up a fight. Make lots of noise and throw rocks and sticks. If you see a bear, it will most likely be running away from you as fast as it can. If you encounter a bear, try not to look him or her in the eyes, do not try to climb trees, and back slowly away, speaking in a firm voice and trying to stay upwind. Coming between a mother and cubs is a potentially dangerous situation, and the only thing you can do is to slowly back away and let mother bear find her cubs while ensuring that you are not a threat. In the case of both a bear or cougar encounter, **DO NOT RUN** – both animals may see this as an invitation to chase, and you cannot outrun either.

As for other large mammals, grizzly bears have been extinct in the Mount Jefferson area since the early 20th Century and wolves for even longer (though it is possible that wolves may return to the area in coming years, as they have been increasingly sighted in the Cascades). Mountain goats were recently reestablished into the area, but you are unlikely to see any unless you plan to climb either Mount Jefferson or Three-Fingered Jack. Deer and elk are very common, however, and with enough visits you will likely see both.

The area is prime owl habitat, particularly for Spotted Owls. These reclusive animals were the center of a fierce debate over old-growth logging in the Opal Creek area and elsewhere in the 1980s and 1990s, and today their numbers are in retreat. If you are lucky, you may see one or another type of owl if you backpack in the area. I once heard a pair of spotted owls calling to each other while camped out in the Breitenbush area one summer night. While it spooked me at first, when I figured out what it was I considered myself very fortunate to have had such an experience. The more time you spend out in the Mount Jefferson area, the more likely you are to have a similar experience.

When to visit:
Winter snows blanket the vast majority of the Mount Jefferson area, closing off access to most of the high country from November until June. Although it is sometimes possible to visit the area in the winter with snowshoes or skis, most of the area remains inaccessible on a practical level for much of the typically long winters.

Despite this lack of access, there are a decent number of places that are open year-round, or at least almost year-round. Among these places, the canyon of the Little North Santiam River is the best place to visit in the winter due to its scenic beauty and very low elevation. Those seeking snowshoe and ski trips head to the Santiam Pass area, which is plowed in the winter and allows access to the Pacific Crest Trail. In general, should you plan on traveling in the winter, remember a good rule of thumb: only state and county highways are plowed in the winter, so be very careful if you plan on driving forest roads above 2,000 feet of elevation in the winter. It is very easy to get stuck in the snow, miles from cell phone service and without anybody to find you for days on end.

While on the topic of winter driving, please do not rely on online mapping websites for directions into the Mount Jefferson area, and in particular to anywhere in the Bull of the Woods Wilderness area. Sites show Forest Service Road 46 as closed all winter, when in fact the road never closes — it is just never plowed or maintained for winter travel. In fact, most of this road is open all winter, and is frequently snow-free to the junction with FR 63, the road to Bagby Hot Springs. Similarly, online maps show the only way to Bagby Hot Springs in the winter is via a long series of forest roads — which is a very, very bad idea. Just stick to the main roads, and be prepared to turn around if you hit impassible snowdrifts. The mountain snows begin to melt starting in April, and hikers are able to keep moving uphill as spring turns to summer. Here is a simple guide to when hikes are usually open and snow-free:

- Under 2,000 feet: open year-round except during winter cold snaps
- 2,500 feet: April 1, but often open during warmer periods in winter
- 3,500 feet: May 15
- 4,500 feet: June 15
- 5,500 feet: July 15
- 6,500 feet: August 1

Naturally, some areas are more pleasant to visit at some times than at others. Of the six regions in the book, here are the ideal times to visit each:

Table Rock and Bull of the Woods North: The lower elevations are nice year-round, while the higher elevations are lovely in June when rhododendrons bloom profusely in the area. The lakes in this region are also lovely in October, when all of them have excellent displays of fall color. The higher elevations are reasonably easy to reach in the winter for energetic hikers with snowshoes, as there are numerous trailheads at very low elevations.

Walking towards Mount Jefferson on the Woodpecker Ridge Road.

Opal Creek and Bull of the Woods South: The canyon of the Little North Santiam River, as mentioned, is an ideal destination in the winter. Its scenic beauty makes the area an ideal destination in every other season, too. On the other hand, the higher elevations in this area are snowbound until June, and many of them are reached by roads many drivers would consider terrifying when snow-covered and icy. The ideal season to visit the rugged peaks north of Detroit is July, when the ridges are covered in wildflowers and the roads recently maintained. In general, fall is also a great time to visit this area, as the fall colors along the Little North Santiam River are fantastic and the huckleberry leaves up in the mountains turn red. Summer is crowded as many people come to this area to cool off from Valley heat.

The Old Cascades: Although US Highway 20 and Oregon Highway 22 cut through the Old Cascades, the hikes in this area are generally inaccessible in the winter due to the long approaches required on forest roads. The ideal time to visit the Old Cascades, without a doubt, is in June and July when the hillsides are blanketed with copious and fantastic displays of wildflowers. Make it a point to visit at this time. By fall, many of the hillsides turn brown and many of the area streams are so low that they cease to be photogenic.

The Olallie Plateau: September is the time to visit the Olallie Plateau. While the area melts out typically by mid to late June, voracious mosquitoes and huge crowds can make overnight stays in the area a chore in the summer months. The long drive to Olallie Lake (two hours or more from both Portland and Salem) makes overnight stays the way to visit the area. With all that being said, by September the mosquitos are gone, the weather is crisp and clear, the huckleberries are ripe and the crowds non-existent. October brings cold nights and spectacular fall color, as the huckleberry leaves turn many brilliant shades of red. Check the weather forecast if you plan on coming to the area in the fall.

Mount Jefferson West: Most of the Mount Jefferson Wilderness is inaccessible in winter, and some places are unreachable until at least mid-July. July and August are the perfect time to visit the area, when the wildflowers are blooming, the weather beautiful and the days long. There are caveats, though; the mountain lakes support an incredible population of mosquitoes, many of the area's trails are very crowded, and lightning storms and the resulting forest fires are a very real threat. It is worth dealing with all of these, however, as there are few things finer in life than a summer weekend spent in the Mount Jefferson backcountry. September brings uncrowded trails, cool nights and ripe huckleberries to the area; hikers without an interest in wildflowers will find September to be quite agreeable. October brings blustery and occasionally snowy weather. This is often the most dramatic time to visit the wilderness, but plan ahead and expect the unexpected. Sunny 70 degree days and snowy 30 degree days are equally likely.

Mount Jefferson East: Much of what I wrote for the western side of the Mount Jefferson Wilderness also applies to the eastern half of the wilderness, but a few notes are nevertheless necessary. Just as on the western side of the wilderness, most of the eastern side is almost inaccessible in the winter. Most of the trailheads in the area are located at the end of long, gravel forest roads that are not drivable in the winter. Cross-country skiing and snowshoeing are possible from Santiam Pass northeast towards Square Lake and Canyon Creek Meadows, but plan ahead and bring a good map and compass (or a GPS). The high mountain lakes and meadows do not melt out until mid-July in most years.

The Metolius River is accessible throughout the year, however, and is ideal for visiting in almost all seasons. You will need to call the Sisters Ranger District to see if the area is snow-free (the roads are not plowed beyond Camp Sherman) if you are planning a winter visit. In general, you can get into the Metolius River Canyon almost year-round. The Metolius area is always gorgeous, but never more so than in June, when wildflowers blanket the banks of the river, and October, when the area has magnificent displays of fall color. As elsewhere in the area covered in this book, September is a great time to visit the east side of the Mount Jefferson Wilderness, but this is also hunting season! If you plan to head out at this time, make sure to wear orange and hike in groups.

How to prepare:
Before we get started, a disclaimer is necessary. Hiking is a joyous, wonderfully fun activity. Without taking proper precautions, it can also be very dangerous. Please be prepared wherever you go, whether it's to Table Rock or Table Lake. Always tell somebody where you are going, and be sure to check in with them (if possible) should your plans change once you head out the door.

The amount of preparation required to visit the area covered in this book differs based on where and when you are going, and how long you plan to stay. If you are planning a short summer outing to a place like Sahalie and Koosah Falls (Hike 50), you will need little besides a water bottle, a windbreaker, a snack and a first-aid kit. If you are planning a trip into the backcountry or if you are traveling anywhere in this book at any point from November to May, please be sure to carry with you the Ten Essentials. They are:

1. A map of the area (preferably topographic and highly-detailed)
2. Compass and/or GPS (bring extra batteries)

Seen on the Old Cascades Crest Trail. I used nearly all of my 17 essentials on this trip, which proved to me again the importance of good preparation.

3. Extra food
4. Extra water (especially in the summer)
5. Extra clothing (no cotton!)
6. A headlamp or flashlight
7. First Aid Kit
8. Waterproof matches or a reliable lighter (or both)
9. Sunglasses and sunscreen
10. Knife and/or multitool with knife

There are seven more items I highly recommend bringing to supplement the ten essentials:

11. A Water filter or water purification tablets
12. An extra pair of warm socks wrapped in a waterproof plastic bag
13. Gloves, preferably waterproof
14. Duct tape (useful for repairing tears and emergency waterproofing)
15. A whistle
16. An emergency space blanket
17. A camera (photos of junctions and landmarks can help you find your way back if you get lost. Plus, this place is beautiful!)

These seventeen items, most of them lightweight and easy to pack, will save your life in an emergency. Make a small kit with as many of these items as possible in an emergency and keep it in your pack. You might curse the extra weight on occasion but they can and will save your life in an emergency.

Since we are talking about emergency situations, please remember that your phone will not work in most of the area covered in this book. Most of the Opal Creek and Mount Jefferson area does not have any phone or wireless service, and leaving your phone on will quickly drain your battery. You should never rely on your phone in an emergency – being prepared to deal with it on your own is the best strategy. Reception is improving throughout the area but you should always assume that you will not have reception. Self-reliance is your best strategy. While writing this book I encountered a number of very serious situations, among them car troubles, forest fires, hypothermia, disorientation and inclement weather. There is no substitution for being prepared, as luck can only take you so far. My luck ran out on several occasions while writing this book, and I am thankful that I was prepared to deal with the consequences on each occasion. Take this as a warning to plan ahead.

About the hikes and road access:
Ease of hikes: I do not rate hikes by their difficulty. In my experience, the difficulty of a hike is based on so many subjective factors that any rating is completely pointless. Some people find hikes of 5 miles and no elevation gain to be difficult while others can hike as much as 30 miles with 6,000 or more feet of elevation in a single day. Complicating matters further are trail and weather conditions. For example, a hike with little shade and a moderate amount of elevation gain can become a very difficult hike on a hot day. I remember the first time I hiked Elk Lake Creek (Hikes 11, 12 and 28), the trail had not been maintained in many years and there were hundreds of downed trees on the trail, turning a moderate hike into a very difficult and tiring day. Everything is subjective.

If you simply must have difficulty ratings, here is a good guide:
- Easy – less than 7 miles and 1,000 feet of elevation gain
- Moderate – 6 – 10 miles with less than 2,000 feet of elevation gain
- Difficult – 8 or more miles with more than 2,000 feet of elevation gain
- Very Difficult – 12 or more miles with more than 3,000 feet of elevation gain
- Hiking Legend – 15 or more miles with more than 4,000 feet of elevation gain

Maps: Maps in this book were created using CalTopo. All trails are marked with a thick black line, which represents my GPS track of the hike. These are the most accurate locations of each trail. Sometimes the Forest Service marked the trail in the wrong location; you will see a thin dashed line that diverges from my thick black line in these cases. Additional hiking options not part of the main hike are marked by thin dashed lines on each map.

Road Access: Most of the hikes in this book are accessible with a standard 2-wheel drive low-clearance vehicle. Naturally, some roads are better than others. While many trailheads in this book are found on 2-lane paved roads, others are at the far end of gravel forest roads. Some of these roads are rocky and rough (The Skyline Road in the Olallie area and the road to Elk Lake are both legendary for being terrible), while some hug the edge of massive cliffs (like those north of Detroit), forcing some drivers to come face to face with their greatest fears. Be prepared for absolutely anything on the roads. I have made every effort to ensure the accuracy of my driving directions and clearly explain the road conditions where there might be a cause for concern. US and state highways are labeled as US or OR (for example: US 20 and OR 22) while forest roads (which are maintained by the Forest Service), are labeled as FR (for example, FR 46 or FR 4690). As a general rule, federal and state highways are well-maintained, plowed in the winter and well-signed. Forest roads

We found this upside-down sign on an abandoned trail near Breitenbush Pass.

vary, but two-number forest roads (such as FR 46) tend to be paved or good gravel, and are well-maintained. Four-number forest roads vary wildly in both quality and frequency of maintenance. Furthermore, the condition of gravel roads tends to change with each year and in some cases every season. Roads that do not receive regular maintenance and steep, winding roads are the ones most likely to be in rough shape. If you are still not sure about road conditions after reading this book, check with your local ranger station or ask online (see links below)- somebody out there will probably know.

Additional Resources:
These websites will give you a lot of useful additional information as you plan your hikes in the Opal Creek and Mount Jefferson areas.

- **Off the Beaten Trail** (http://www.offthebeatentrailpdx.com) - This is my website and I update it whenever I have time. Here you'll find high-resolution maps, current conditions, photos, the occasional essay and extra hikes that did not make this book. You'll also find information about my other books, both past and future.
- **Oregon Hikers** (http://www.oregonhikers.org) – An online forum and field guide dedicated to hiking, snowshoeing and backpacking throughout Oregon, with a focus on the Portland area (the website was formerly known as Portland Hikers). In the forums you can view trip reports for up-to-date information on hikes all across the region. Stop here before you leave the house for current information and browse the forums for great ideas!
- **Trail Advocates** (http://www.trailadvocate.org) – This group of dedicated volunteers in the Clackamas Ranger District maintains and restores all of the area's many trails. On their website you can find directions, topographic maps and pictures of trails both known and obscure. Their hard work and dedication are much appreciated!

- **Oregon Wildflowers** (http://oregonwildflowers.org) – Similar to Oregon Hikers but with a focus on wildflowers. You can view trip reports and see some of the web-master Greg Lief's excellent wildflower photos. This is an indispensable resource for planning trips to the area's wildflower meadows.
- **Northwest Waterfall Survey** (http://www.waterfallsnorthwest.com/nws/) – This website should be indispensable for those who love waterfalls. Waterfall guru Brian Swan has catalogued every known waterfall in Oregon and Washington and many are featured with full write-ups, great directions and absolutely spectacular photos.
- **Summit Post** (http://www.summitpost.org) – This is perhaps the world's greatest climbing website and is indispensable for information about mountains and the routes climbers use to summit them. The pinnacles and peaks in the Detroit area and around Mount Jefferson are lovingly chronicled here, with directions and descriptions of how to visit and climb some of the more incredible front-country and backcountry destinations.
- **Cascade Ramblings** (http://www.cascaderamblings.com) – This website is devoted to detailing all of the lakes, trails and highlights in Northwest Oregon, with a particular focus on the Mount Jefferson and Opal Creek areas. You can easily spend hours reading about explorations deep into the Mount Jefferson backcountry.

For questions about specific places, current conditions and specific information, here is the contact information of each National Forest Ranger District covered in this book:

- Clackamas Ranger District (Mount Hood National Forest): (503) 630-6861
- Detroit Ranger District (Willamette National Forest): (503) 854-3366
- Sweet Home Ranger District (Willamette National Forest): (541) 367-5168
- Sisters Ranger District (Deschutes National Forest): (541) 549-7700

These four ranger districts also have websites, and each are updated with varying degrees of frequency. The web addresses for each are too long to list here, but a quick internet search will give you all the information you need. The Deschutes National Forest in particular is very good about updating its website with current conditions, and is well worth bookmarking. The Sweet Home and Detroit Ranger Districts also frequently update the current conditions page of the Willamette National Forest website.

Should you not want to set out into the wilderness on your own, consider hiking with an area hiking club! The Chemeketans, based out of Salem, offer frequent trips into the Opal Creek and Mount Jefferson areas. To get involved with the Chemeketans, just visit their website and sign up for a hike. This is also a great way to get to know fellow hikers, many of whom are similarly passionate about the great outdoors. To find the Chemeketans, see: http://www.chemeketans.org/

The Mazamas, based out of Portland, also sometimes lead trips into the Opal Creek and Mount Jefferson areas (full disclosure – I am a hike leader for the Mazamas), and you do not need to be a member to go on a hike with them. I often lead trips to the Opal Creek area in fall and winter and the Mount Jefferson area in the summer. For more information about the Mazamas, see: http://www.mazamas.org

With all that said, let's go hiking!

SECTION 1: TABLE ROCK AND BULL OF THE WOODS

		Distance	EV Gain
1.	Table Rock	7.4	1,500
2.	Rooster Rock	10.8	3,800
3.	Pechuck Lookout and Rooster Rock	7.0	2,500
4.	Upper Molalla Divide	6.1	1,800
5.	Thunder Mountain and Skookum Lake	6.2	2,000
6.	Whetstone Mountain	4.2	1,600
7.	Bagby Hot Springs and Silver King Lake	15.4	2,400
8.	Pansy Lake and Bull of the Woods	7.4	2,900
9.	Bull of the Woods	6.8	1,700
10.	Big Slide Lake	12.2	3,100
11.	Elk Lake Creek	10.4	1,500
12.	Mother Lode Loop	20.6	4,700
13.	Rho Creek and Big Bottom	8.2	2,400
14.	Mount Lowe	6.4	1,400

The Table Rock Wilderness and the northern half of the Bull of the Woods Wilderness is where Mount Jefferson country begins. That is to say, this is where Mount Jefferson becomes the biggest, baddest and closest major peak on the horizon, and where the forest begins to change character, more closely resembling the magical forests in the Opal Creek and Breitenbush areas. The peaks in this area are rugged and the forests similarly magical, full of moss and sparkling waterfalls. But it does not come easy.

The hikes in this area are rugged, often climbing steeply from valley floors up to rocky viewpoints that stretch from the volcanoes of southwest Washington all the way south to the Three Sisters, and sometimes even further south. The area surrounding the Table Rock Wilderness is heavily logged, but the Bull of the Woods Wilderness offers some of the nicest ancient forest left in the entire Oregon Cascades. Even better, this area features one of the most comprehensive trail systems in the Cascades, offering many opportunities for longer hikes, loops and adventure. A good topographic map is a must when visiting this neck of the woods.

One thing to keep in mind when visiting this area is that many of these hikes are extremely remote and require long drives on forest roads of varying quality. Before visiting this area it is a good idea to check your car and tires to be sure everything is in working order. Do not count on your phone or your charms to get you out of a dangerous situation in this area. I recommend bringing a spare tire, a good topographic map and an ax or chainsaw every time you drive up this way. The best strategy is vigilance.

Photo on opposite page: Beargrass at Rooster Rock (Hikes 2 and 3)

1.   TABLE ROCK

Distance: 7.4 miles out and back
Elevation Gain: 1,500 feet
Trailhead elevation: 3,382 feet
Trail high point: 4,890 feet
Season: June – October
Best: June – July
Map: Opal Creek Wilderness (Imus)

Directions:
- From the junction of OR 213 and OR 211 on the western edge of Molalla, drive 2.1 miles through town to a junction with South Mathias Road.
- Veer right on South Mathias Road here.
- Drive this road for 1 mile south to a junction with S Feyrer Park Road, and veer left.
- Continue on this road for 1.6 miles until you cross the Molalla River and meet South Dickey Prairie Road.
- Turn right on Dickey Prairie Road and drive 5.4 miles to a sign on your right marking the Molalla River Recreation area.
- Turn right and cross the Molalla River. Here the road curves to the left immediately and becomes the Molalla River Road.
- Continue on this road for 11 miles to a junction with the Horse Creek Road on your right.
- Continue straight (ignoring the road veering downhill to the right) and drive another 1.7 miles to a junction with the road to Table Rock.
- Turn left onto gravel Table Rock Road and drive 2.5 miles to a junction with a road up towards Table Rock.
- Turn right and drive 4 miles to the end of the road.

Hike: By far the most popular hike in the small Table Rock Wilderness, the trail to the summit of the wilderness area's eponymous peak is surprisingly well-graded and fairly easy. The views from the summit are magnificent and wide-ranging, and there are even a couple of campsites at the summit if you feel like camping overnight (bring water, though). If you time it correctly, you may even come home with a bag full of delicious huckleberries – a delightful treat indeed!

Begin by following the old road, now a wide trail east to where it washed out in 1996. At 0.3 mile, the trail cuts uphill to the right into a lovely forest of lichen-draped hemlocks to avoid the washout that closed the road. After a few tenths of a mile, the trail rejoins the road, which you follow for almost a mile to the old trailhead. Turn right here.

The trail passes a decaying signboard and begins a moderate ascent up the surprisingly gentle north face of Table Rock. After one mile of uphill, the trail switchbacks under the massive, fortress-like rock face and talus slopes below the summit. Here you will likely hear the meep of the pika, a small, round-eared mammal that lives in rockslides. Wear boots on this hike – this stretch is quite rocky as the trail follows cairns through this maze of rockfall. The basalt formations on the huge walls of the mountain are among the most impressive in this part of the Cascades. Once past the rockslide, the trail climbs to meet an unsigned junction with the trail over to Rooster Rock (Hike 2). Turn left here and climb 0.6 mile, skirting along the huge basalt cliffs but never close enough for discomfort, to the wide summit. Here the view is incredible — you can see snowpeaks from Mount Rainier to the Three Sisters, as well as most of the Willamette Valley. What is less impressive, so to speak, is the tremendous number of clearcuts visible below — a testament to the small size of the Table Rock Wilderness as well as the huge amount of logging on BLM land. There are a few campsites if you feel like spending the night but make sure to bring your own water — there is none anywhere close to the summit.

Return the way you came, or head over to Rooster Rock to extend your hike. If you choose this second option, however, be warned that the stretch of trail over to Rooster Rock is far rougher and steeper as it rides the rollercoaster of Table Rock's broad ridge 2 miles to Rooster and Chicken Rocks (see Hike 2 for more information).

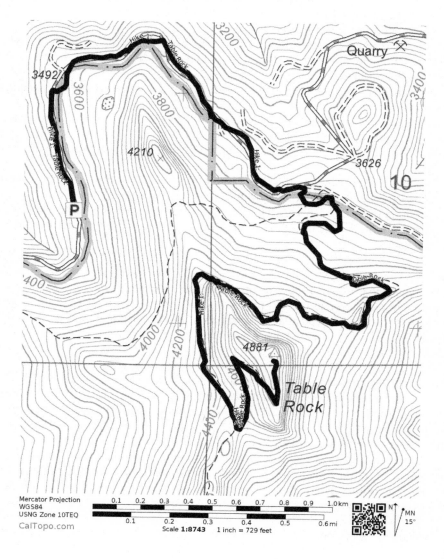

2.   ROOSTER ROCK

Distance: 10.8 miles out and back
Elevation Gain: 3,700 feet
Trailhead elevation: 1,261 feet
Trail high point: 4,559 feet
Season: May- November
Best: June- July
Map: Opal Creek Wilderness (Imus)
Map note: For a detailed, high-resolution map, see my website.

Directions:
- From the junction of OR 213 and OR 211 on the western edge of Molalla, drive 2.1 miles through town to a junction with South Mathias Road.
- Veer right on South Mathias Road here.
- Drive this road for 1 mile south to a junction with S Feyrer Park Road, and veer left.
- Continue on this road for 1.6 miles until you cross the Molalla River and meet South Dickey Prairie Road.
- Turn right on Dickey Prairie Road and drive 5.4 miles to a sign on your right marking the Molalla River Recreation area.
- Turn right and cross the Molalla River. Here the road curves to the left immediately and becomes the Molalla River Road.
- Continue on this road for 11 miles to a junction with the Horse Creek Road on your right.
- Continue straight (ignoring the road veering downhill to the right) and drive another 1.7 miles to a junction with the road to Table Rock.
- Ignore the fork to the left signed for Table Rock, and turn right on Rooster Rock Road.
- Cross the Table Rock Fork of the Molalla River and immediately turn into the Old State Trailhead on the left.

Hike: It's a long way up to Rooster Rock, but when you get there you won't regret making the trek. The pinnacle stands above fields of wildflowers, while you have outstanding views out to Mount Jefferson and the rest of the central Cascades. Even on a hot day, a gentle breeze cools you off while you relax for lunch up on this scenic ridgetop. Though there are other, easier hikes in the Table Rock Wilderness, this one is the closest to Portland, the easiest to find and perhaps the least crowded.

Begin on the High Ridge Trail, a well-maintained path that climbs uphill above the Table Rock Fork of the Molalla River. Bright orange Tiger lilies and pink rhododendrons add color to this lower section of the trail in June and July. Continue uphill on a long series of switchbacks in second-growth forest until the trail opens up in a series of south-facing meadows with spectacular wildflower displays. The flower show here is fascinating, with an unusual mix of flowers that generally tend to grow in far drier climates. Look for little yellow sunflowers, blue-eyed Mary, red paintbrush and rosy plectritis, a pinkish poofball flower that grows in great profusion here. Re-enter the forest and soon reach a crossing of a wide trail that was once a road. Continue straight on the High Ridge Trail.

You will steeply switchback uphill from here until you reach the bottom of a long series of

Mount Jefferson and Rooster Rock from on top of Chicken Rock.

rock outcrops, which you parallel as the trail begins to level out. The High Ridge Trail then follows this ridgecrest through a forest of second-growth lodgepole pine. Along the way, you'll pass a series of gigantic anthills – don't rile the millions within! At a little less than 5 miles from the Old Bridge Trailhead, the trail emerges into the huge summit meadows below Rooster Rock. In June and July, these meadows feature one of the most impressive wildflower displays in this part of the Cascades. Look for masses of yellow sunflowers, red paintbrush, blue and purple larkspur, lupine, fuzzy cat's ears, and in favorable years, huge white stalks of beargrass. The High Cascades spread out to the south, with views out to the peaks of the Bull of the Woods Wilderness and south to the Three Sisters.

Reach a junction with the Saddle Trail and turn left. Head up to the top of the ridge below Rooster Rock, where you reach another junction. Turn left and hike this short trail up to a rocky viewpoint known as Chicken Rock. Here the view is considerably better than the meadow below, with views north to Mounts Hood, Saint Helens, Adams and Rainier and views south to the Three Sisters. A better lunch spot would be hard to find in this area. When you are done, return the way you came or arrange a car shuttle to one of the other trailheads in the area.

EXTENDING YOUR TRIP:
If you have the time and energy, consider extending your trip to check out historic Pechuck Lookout. The views aren't as good as at Rooster Rock but it's mostly level all the way to Pechuck. In winter people have been known to snowshoe to the lookout this way- even in winter, expect company (and mice) at the lookout. For more information, see Hike 3.

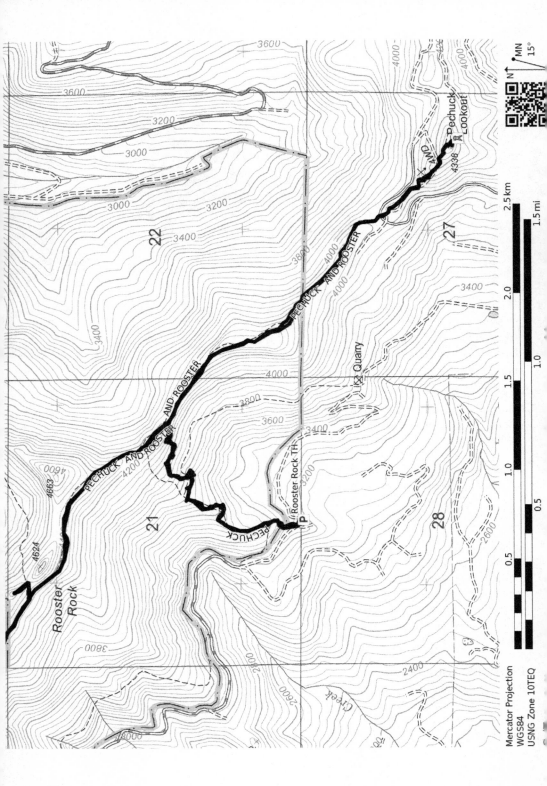

Rooster Rock

Pechuck Lookout

4338

PECHUCK AND ROOSTER

PECHUCK AND ROOSTER

PECHUCK

4624

4663

4399

Rooster Rock TH

Quarry

Creek

4WD

Mercator Projection
WGS84
USNG Zone 10TEQ

N MN 15°

3. PECHUCK LOOKOUT AND ROOSTER ROCK

Distance: 7 miles out and back
Elevation Gain: 2,500 feet
Trailhead elevation: 3,287 feet
Trail high point: 4,559 feet
Season: May- November
Best: June- July
Map: Opal Creek Wilderness (Imus)

Directions:

- From the junction of OR 213 and OR 211 on the western edge of Molalla, drive 2.1 miles through town to a junction with South Mathias Road.
- Veer right on South Mathias Road here.
- Drive this road for 1 mile south to a junction with S Feyrer Park Road, and veer left.
- Continue on this road for 1.6 miles until you cross the Molalla River and meet South Dickey Prairie Road.
- Turn right on Dickey Prairie Road and drive 5.4 miles to a sign on your right marking the Molalla River Recreation area.
- Turn right and cross the Molalla River. Here the road curves to the left immediately and becomes the Molalla River Road.
- Continue on this road for 11 miles to a junction with the Horse Creek Road on your right.
- Continue straight (ignoring the road veering downhill to the right) and drive another 1.7 miles to a junction with the road to Table Rock.
- Keep right and drive another 0.6 mile to a junction with Rooster Rock Road.
- Turn left here onto Rooster Rock Road and drive 2.7 miles to another junction.
- Keep left and drive 3.5 miles to road's end at the Rooster Rock Trailhead.

Hike: Once you've found the elusive trailhead, the hike up to Pechuck Lookout and Rooster Rock is a joy. Though surprisingly popular, this area is not overflowing with the masses of people that flock to the more popular destinations to the south and east. Even better, Pechuck Lookout is a great destination for an easy backpacking trip, and is open on a first-come, first-served basis should you wish to stay there! So what are you waiting for?

Begin on a trail that climbs uphill, at times steeply, for one mile to an unsigned junction with the trail from Rooster Rock (see Hike 2). Though the Table Rock Wilderness remains obscure to most Portlanders, it is definitely not so to those living in the Molalla area, and you will meet a good deal of people up here; on the flip side, crowds bring excellent trail maintenance, and this is a good tradeoff. From the junction, turn right and follow the ridge trail as it undulates up and down the ridge, ultimately losing elevation as you near the lookout.

When you reach an old trailhead at a closed road, continue straight on the trail as it climbs up to the old lookout. Pass a toilet and join an old road that switchbacks up to the lookout. Built in 1932, the Pechuck Lookout was abandoned in the 1960s as the Forest Service decommissioned the vast majority of their lookout structures. This one is different, and its cupola-style stone lookout is on the only remaining tower of its kind in the region. It was lovingly restored by volunteers and reopened in 1995, and has been a popular destination for lovers of lookout towers ever since. If you wish to spend the night, come early, bring water and be willing to deal with the resident mouse population (there are lots).

If you wish to continue your hike, return 1.5 miles of mostly-uphill trail to the junction with the trail from Rooster Rock. Continue straight and keep climbing uphill another 0.8 mile to a trail junction in a meadow just west of Rooster Rock. Turn right here and switchback uphill amidst outstanding flower displays for 0.1 mile to a junction at a saddle between Rooster Rock on your right and a knoll on your left (this knoll is also the destination of Hike 2). Turn left and hike uphill on a spur trail to the summit of so-called Chicken Rock, where the view is eye-popping! Look north to a trio of Washington volcanoes (Saint Helens, Rainier and Adams), with Mount Hood out of sight behind the massif of Table Rock. Mount Jefferson rises immediately to the left of Rooster Rock's volcanic plug, with Battle Ax between Jefferson and Rooster Rock. To the south of Mount Jefferson, the view stretches as far south as Diamond Peak on a clear day, while behind you is the entirety of the Willamette Valley from Portland (those with binoculars can pick out the buildings and bridges of Portland) to Eugene. At the far end of the valley is humped Marys Peak, the highest point in the Coast Range. What a view! Return the way you came.

4. UPPER MOLALLA DIVIDE

	Nasty Rock:	Joyce Lake:	Baty Butte Loop:
Distance:	2.8 miles out & back	0.7 mile loop	2.6 mile loop
Elevation Gain:	600 feet	200 feet	1,000 feet
Trailhead Elevation:	4,169 feet	3,851 feet	3,851 feet
Trail High Point:	4,650 feet	3,996 feet	4,548 feet
Season:	June- November	June- November	June- November
Best:	July- October	July- October	July- October

Directions:
- From the junction of OR 213 and OR 211 on the western edge of Molalla, drive 2.1 miles through town to a junction with South Mathias Road.
- Veer right on South Mathias Road here.
- Drive this road for 1 mile south to a junction with S Feyrer Park Road, and veer left.
- Continue on this road for 1.6 miles until you cross the Molalla River and meet South Dickey Prairie Road.
- Turn right on Dickey Prairie Road and drive 5.4 miles to a sign on your right marking the Molalla River Recreation area.
- Turn right and cross the Molalla River. Here the road curves to the left immediately and becomes the Molalla River Road.
- Continue on this road for 11 miles to a junction with the Horse Creek Road on your right.
- Continue straight (ignoring the road veering downhill to the right) and drive another 1.7 miles to a junction with the road to Table Rock.

- Turn left onto gravel Table Rock Road and drive 2.5 miles to a junction with a road up towards Table Rock.
- Continue straight and begin a long stretch on what is generally good gravel road. There are occasional stretches of road where the BLM has laid down large, chunky gravel that may cause some drivers problems. For the most part, however, the roads are in very good shape and passable for any passenger car.
- You will pass many junctions on the way, most with gated logging roads; stay on the main road for 12.2 miles until you reach an unmarked pullout on your right which serves as the trailhead for Joyce Lake and Baty Butte.
- To find Nasty Rock's extremely remote trailhead, stay on this same road another 3.9 miles to its end at the unmarked trailhead.
- **Note 1**: As this area is heavily logged, roads and junctions can change on a yearly and even monthly basis. I suggest downloading my GPS track of the drive to Nasty Rock and using that to drive to the trailhead.
- **Note 2**: DO NOT attempt to drive these roads on weekdays. They are built for and maintained by logging companies, and you will almost certainly meet scores of logging trucks driving very fast.

Hike: Three short but excellent hikes await those patient enough to navigate the seemingly endless gravel roads in the upper Molalla Divide. Up here, the forests are so remote that many groves have escaped the wrath of the chainsaw (unlike those you passed on the way to these trailheads) and you will have the chance to see the nicest forest still left in the Molalla drainage. Plan on a full day of exploration to get the most out of this area.

Due to its remoteness, it is best to start at Nasty Rock and then work your way back towards the Valley. The Nasty Rock Trail departs from a crude set of rock steps about 100 feet west of the small parking area at the trailhead. While the trail is not easily apparent from the

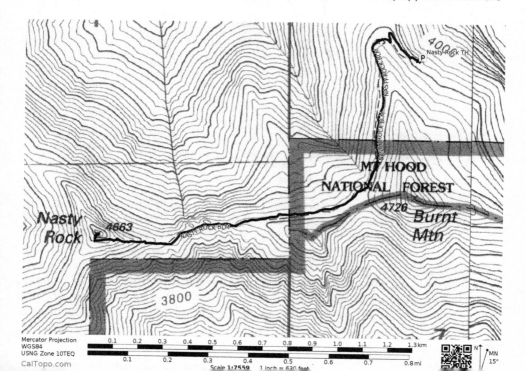

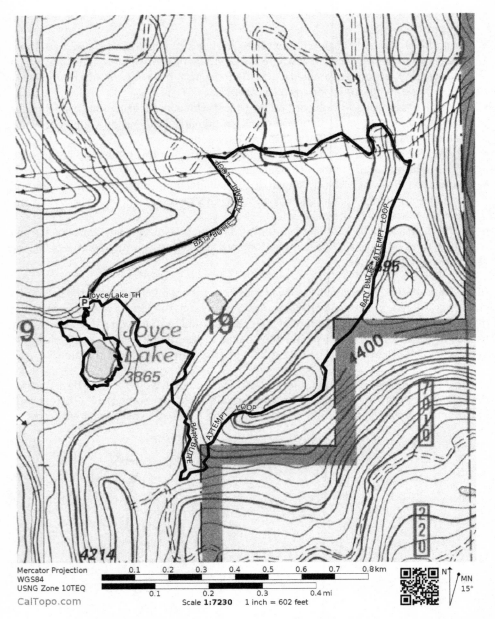

Mercator Projection
WGS84
USNG Zone 10TEQ
CalTopo.com

Scale **1:7230**   1 inch = 602 feet

road, look for a pair of white diamonds on a tree to locate the trail. The trail climbs through the brush and then briefly parallels the road before reaching equilibrium as it follows Nasty Rock's long ridge. After a bit the trail emerges at a scenic cliff, complete with a tree at the cliff edge that invites contemplation, directly above the headwaters of the Molalla River. Views here open up to the south, towards Mount Jefferson and the Three Sisters. The great views continue all the way to Nasty Rock, which you reach at 1.4 miles from the trailhead. The trail meets a junction with a rough climbers trail to a different Nasty Rock one mile further to the west; from this junction, it is quite easy to scramble to the summit of Nasty

Joyce Lake casts fantastic reflections on quiet days.

Rock . The views here are exceptional, stretching south over the Opal Creek Wilderness towards Mount Jefferson and the Three Sisters. Speaking of Opal Creek: despite the long drive to the Nasty Rock Trailhead, you are in fact standing directly above Opal Creek's busy trailhead, less than a mile below you. You can follow the rough climbers trail for more views and miles, or else you can return the way you came.

Joyce Lake is 3.9 miles back the the road you drove in on, and is unsigned. You will likely have no trouble finding the lake, however, as it is by far the most popular destination up this way - expect to see a few cars parked at the trailhead. A wide trail cuts between ancient trees directly to a campsite at the edge of the beautiful green lake, complete with a metal fire grate. From here, the trail leads around the lake, eventually looping back around to the first campsite. This is an excellent place to spend the night, but expect competition.

Although it is also unsigned, the Baty Butte Trail also departs from the Joyce Lake Trailhead. Look for the flagged and obvious trail on your left about thirty feet from the trailhead. This spur trail climbs through a mossy forest of ancient Douglas and noble firs for 3/4 of a mile to a junction with the Baty Butte Trail, up on the ridge above Joyce Lake. The Baty Butte Trail climb steeply before leveling out on the ridge, which serves as the divide separating the Molalla and Clackamas River drainages. At 1.6 mile from Joyce Lake, meet a road where the powerlines cross the ridge. You can walk up a bit here to good views under the powerlines. The Baty Butte Trail continues north along the divide for many miles (also see Hike 5), but the stretch north of the powerlines here becomes very difficult to follow as it cuts through an old clearcut. So instead, follow the powerline access road downhill 0.6 mile to the gravel road and turn left. Walk up the gravel road 0.5 mile back to the Joyce Lake Trailhead and your car.

5. THUNDER MOUNTAIN AND SKOOKUM LAKE

	Thunder Mountain	Skookum Lake	Baty Butte
Distance:	3.2 miles out & back	6.2 miles out & back	10 miles out & back
Elevation Gain:	900 feet	2,000 feet	3,300 feet
TH Elevation:	4,227 feet	4,227 feet	4,227 feet
High Point:	5,164 feet	5,164 feet	5,164 feet
Season:	June- October	June- October	June- October
Best:	June- October	June- October	June- October
Map:	Map on my website.		

Directions:
- From Estacada, drive southeast on OR 224 for approximately 25 miles to the old guard station at Ripplebrook.
- Continue on what is now FR 46 another 3.5 miles to a junction with FR63.
- Turn right and follow this road for 3.0 miles. Just before FR63 meets FR70, turn right onto paved road FR 6320. If you reach a junction with FR70 to Bagby Hot Springs, you've gone too far.
- Stay on FR 6320 for 1.2 miles before forking right yet again on gravel FR6322.
- Stay on FR 6322 for 5.9 miles of mostly good gravel (one short rutted section excepted) and then turn left on FR 4620.
- Travel on this road for 3 miles to the trailhead, which is on a rather nondescript pullout on the right. As of this writing there is a new sign, but if the sign isn't there, the trail departs straight out of the road.

Hike: Most people have never heard of Thunder Mountain or Skookum Lake, and they are among the most remote destinations in the western Cascades. After you visit this area, however, you'll be happy you made the effort. The hike to the summit of Thunder Mountain climbs through a lovely old-growth forest to a good viewpoint at a former lookout site, while the trail to Skookum Lake drops to the lake, hidden in a dark and mysterious forest. With more time and energy, you can set off to the west towards a great viewtop at Baty Butte. If you like adventure, you will love this hike.

The Thunder Mountain trail begins by climbing through an old clearcut where the understory is beginning to take over. Fight through the brush in a straight line for 0.2 mile until the trail repents and enters a sublime forest of large Douglas firs and mountain hemlocks. The next mile of trail is well-maintained and climbs steadily up the side of Thunder Mountain. Reach an excellent viewpoint of Mount Jefferson at 1 mile, and then climb up to two junctions shortly afterwards. Ignore the first (a sketchy trail out to a view of Lost Creek Ridge) and arrive at the second, the junction with the Skookum Lake Trail. Turn right and climb 500 feet to the summit, a former lookout site. The view remains excellent, stretching from Mount Rainier in the north to the Three Sisters in the south. Mount Jefferson is somewhat obscured but visible through the trees. The rumpled green quilt of the Bull of the Woods Wilderness Area stretches to the south, accentuated by Battle Ax's pointy silhouette. While this is an excellent destination for an easy hike, it's almost too easy and too

Snowy forest on the north slope of Thunder Mountain.

short for such a long drive. Instead, continue down to Skookum Lake.

To find Skookum Lake, return to the trail junction and turn right. The trail traverses around the side of Thunder Mountain, descending through forest touched by a recent fire. Begin switchbacking down steeply to a fascinating rock formation at 2.2 miles from the trailhead. Stop for a minute to inspect this strange and bedeviling spot, which resembles an altar in a church; here a hole is being formed in a crack between two large basalt formations. Continue your descent, finally leveling out at an unmarked junction with the Baty Butte Trail in a meadow. This junction is sometimes marked by a yellow paper sign. Turn right.

The Skookum Lake Trail now passes over a trickling creek and then plows through a jungle of rhododendron 0.3 mile to the lake. A landslide has deposited a large amount of downed trees into the lake, adding to the primeval scene. Thunder Mountain's spires cast shadows across the lake. The silence here is almost overwhelming. Follow the trail around the left side of the lake, arriving at a spacious campsite complete with a large picnic table. If this seems strange, remember that this was a drive-up campground before floods destroyed the Fish Creek road network in 1996. Look through the trees below and you'll see the remnants of the campground access road below, now open only to the handful of off-road vehicle enthusiasts who have figured out how to get here. Chances are that you won't encounter anyone or anything up here besides deer or perhaps Sasquatch. When you decide to return, remember to turn left at the junction in the meadow to hike back up Thunder Mountain, then right to descend back to the car. Hikers who wish to hike to Baty Butte

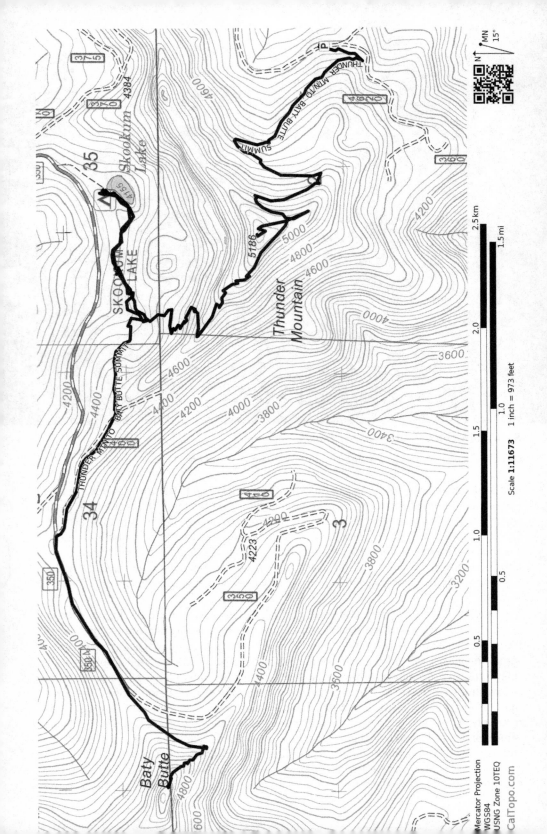

should be prepared to navigate faint trail, follow old roads and bushwhack to the summit of a steep, cliffy peak. A GPS and the knowledge to use it is highly recommended for this leg of your trek.

To continue on towards Baty Butte, return to the trail junction in the meadow and instead of turning left to head back, continue straight. The junction can be hard to spot but look for flagging and head in a generally westerly direction. You will climb gradually on faint trail that is generally easy enough to follow until you hit the remains of FR 350. Continue on this old road for 1 mile until it begins curving around the forested side of Baty Butte. Here look for a trail headed off to the right and begin a gradual climb of 0.4 mile through lichen-draped forest until the trail begins to curve around the side of Baty Butte.

From here, you can continue on the Baty Butte Trail many miles towards Joyce Lake (see Hike 4), but you'll likely be ready to finish your day with a bang. Instead, set off steeply uphill towards the summit of Baty Butte on a faint trail that devolves into a bushwhack. There is generally only one way up, so if you hit cliffs, turn around and look for the faint trail. Towards the top you will need to use your hands and branches to help you reach the summit, but the way is never overly dangerous if you stay on track. Again, if you hit cliffs or are uncomfortable with the exposure, there is no harm in turning around! The views are spectacular on Baty Butte's narrow, rocky summit ridge – look out to Mount Jefferson and south to the Three Sisters, as well as the full sweep of the Central Cascades. This is a view worthy of an arduous climb!

Return the way you came, paying close attention to the junctions on the way back. Follow the Baty Butte Trail east towards the old road; turn left on the old road, following flagging through a few unsure spots, until you reach the trail down to Skookum Lake. If you cannot find the trail, look for a log with the word "TRAIL" cut in huge letters. Hike down to the junction with the Skookum Lake Trail, and turn right to climb back up towards Thunder Mountain. Ignore the side trail to Thunder Mountain and continue straight on the Thunder Mountain Trail downhill to your car.

6. WHETSTONE MOUNTAIN

	Whetstone Mountain	Whetstone - Bagby Junction
Distance:	4.2 miles out & back	8.4 miles out & back
Elevation Gain:	1,600 feet	1,800 feet
Trailhead Elevation:	3,974 feet	3,974 feet
Trail High Point:	4,970 feet	4,570 feet
Season:	June- October	June- October
Best:	June- July	June- November
Map:	Opal Creek Wilderness (Imus)	

Directions:

- From Estacada, drive southeast on OR 224 for approximately 25 miles to the old guard station at Ripplebrook.
- Just past Ripplebrook OR 224 becomes FR 46. Continue straight on FR 46 for 4.2 miles from Ripplebrook to a junction with FR 63, where you turn right, following signs for Bagby Hot Springs.
- Drive this 2-lane paved road for 3.5 miles to a junction with FR 70, signed for Bagby Hot Springs.
- Turn right on FR 70 and drive 6 miles to the crowded Bagby Hot Springs trailhead on your left.
- Continue on FR 70 for 1.3 miles to a junction with FR 7020 on your left.
- Turn left and drive up this road, keeping straight at forks in the road at 1.9, 4.0 and 5.5 miles, respectively.
- At 5.9 miles, reach a junction with FR 7030. Keep left here on FR 7020 and drive 0.7 miles to a junction with FR 028 on your left, just before the end of FR 7020.
- Turn left here and drive 50 yards into the trailhead parking lot.

Hike: From the summit of Whetstone Mountain, you can see out over the entire Bull of the Woods Wilderness and southeast to Mount Jefferson. To get there, you have two choices – an easy hike but a long drive into the heart of Upper Clackamas country, or a long hike with a short drive from Salem. This hike describes the short hike from the northern trailhead (if you want to hike the long version, see Hike 24). If this is not enough hiking for you, try extending your hike east towards the Bagby Trail and Silver King Mountain.

The trail begins in an old clearcut and descends quickly into a magnificent old-growth forest of six-foot thick Douglas firs. Mosquitos are a nuisance in June and July but the profusion of pink rhododendrons along the trail is ample compensation. After 0.8 mile the forest begins to open some, offering views of Mount Hood to the north and passing a few small ponds before climbing to a forested saddle and trail junction with the Gold Creek Trail at 1.2 miles. At this junction you are presented with two options: you can turn right 1.2 miles to the summit of Whetstone Mountain, or left on a scenic hike along a forested ridge top. For hikers seeking the summit and a moderate hike, turn right and switchback though dense forest and more rhododendrons to a trail junction at 2.2 miles from the trailhead. Fork to the right here and switchback uphill another 0.3 mile to the rocky summit of Whetstone Mountain, a former lookout site. The view here stretches from the Willamette Valley to the peaks of the High Cascades. Look for distinctive Battle Ax, with Mount Jefferson looming behind it to the east. Return to the junction the way you came.

If you wish to extend your hike before returning to the trailhead, continue straight (east) from the junction in the saddle with the Whetstone Trail towards Silver King Mountain. The Whetstone Trail rides a rollercoaster of ups and downs through magnificent ancient forest until the trail breaks out into the open with views south to Battle Ax and Mount Jefferson. Reach a trail junction with the Bagby Trail 2.6 miles from the junction with the trail to the summit. To continue on to Silver King Lake, turn left here and descend 0.7 mile to a trail junction with the trail to Silver King Lake. Turn left and hike 0.2 mile to the small, brushy lake tucked beneath the very ridge you just traversed on the Whetstone Trail. For more information on this area, see Hikes 7 and 24.

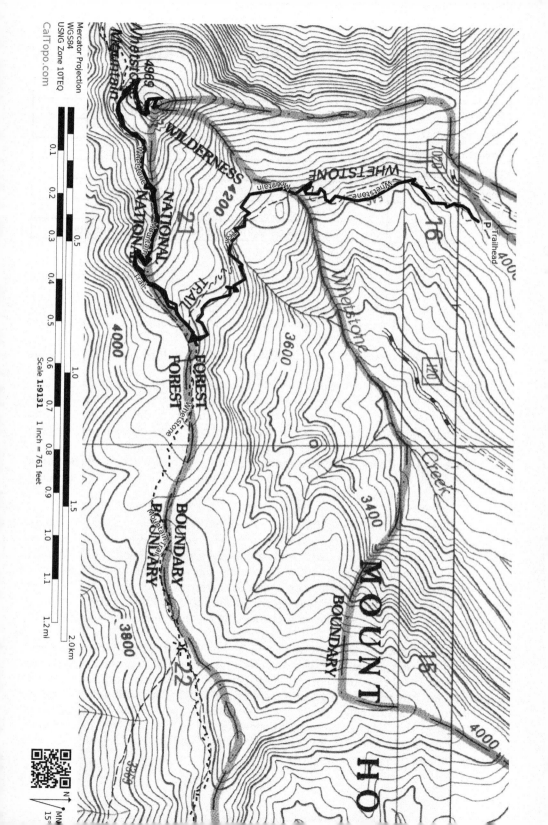

7. BAGBY HOT SPRINGS AND SILVER KING LAKE

	Bagby Hot Springs	Silver King Lake
Distance:	3.2 miles out & back	15.4 miles out & back
Elevation Gain:	200 feet	2,400 feet
Trailhead Elevation:	2,081 feet	2,081 feet
Trail High Point:	2,334 feet	4,157 feet
Season:	all year	June- November
Best:	March- May, October	June- November
Map:	Opal Creek Wilderness (Imus)	**See map on my website.**

Directions:
- From Estacada, drive southeast on OR 224 for approximately 25 miles to the old guard station at Ripplebrook.
- Just past Ripplebrook OR 224 becomes FR 46. Continue straight on FR 46 for 4.2 miles from Ripplebrook to a junction with FR 63, where you turn right, following signs for Bagby Hot Springs.
- Drive this 2-lane paved road for 3.5 miles to a junction with FR 70, signed for Bagby Hot Springs.
- Turn right on FR 70 and drive 6 miles to the hectic, well-signed trailhead on your left.
- **Note 1:** Leave nothing of value at this trailhead – due to its extreme popularity, the Bagby Trailhead has been a frequent target in the past of car clouters, people who break into your car and steal anything of value. There is now somebody watching the trail at all times so your car should be fine – but vigilance is a good idea.
- **Note 2:** A special pass is also required for this trail. You may purchase one either at Ripplebrook or at the trailhead. The extra $5 is intended to help maintain the aging but very popular buildings at the hot springs.

Hike: Hike a beautiful trail through huge old-growth forest less than 2 miles to extremely popular Bagby Hot Springs, where you WILL encounter people. Lots of people. I've been here many times in all sorts of weather and have always seen a minimum of thirty or forty people here. To minimize the number of people you encounter and assure yourself of a more pleasant experience, come here on a week day in the fall or winter. If you come here in the off-season, be sure to check the forecast and call the Clackamas Ranger Station to see if the road is snowed in – getting stuck here in the winter would not be pleasant.

Begin by hiking the wide trail, which very soon crosses the Hot Springs fork of the Collawash River on a large bridge. You will soon enter a majestic forest of ancient Douglas firs, some as many as eight feet thick. The trail is almost level, which no doubt aids in the area's popularity. You may notice an older alignment of the trail on your right. After 1.5 miles, cross another bridge and enter the area of the hot springs. Do not enter the guard station or any other locked buildings. Clothing is optional at the restored bathhouses but liquor and other controlled substances are prohibited. You may need to wait in line for one of the private rooms but the wait is well worth it!

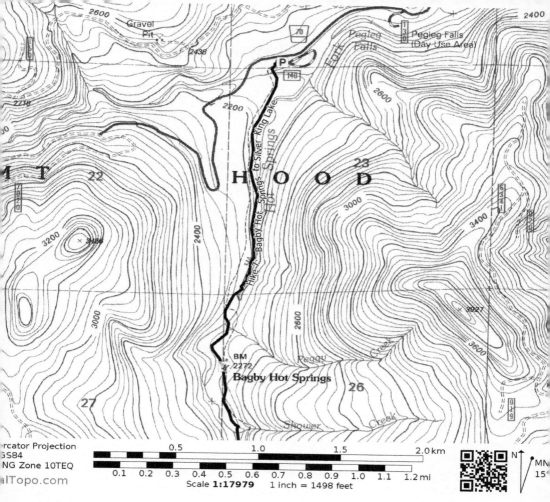

Scale **1:17979**   1 inch = 1498 feet

Beyond the hot springs, you will cross directly under Shower Creek Falls, where some come for a cold refresher after their hot soak. The trail soon becomes a narrower, more rugged wilderness path —with the spotty maintenance you would expect for such a remote trail. You will cross several creeks without the aid of bridges (though none are difficult to cross) and hike through grove after grove of outstanding old-growth forest as you penetrate deeper and deeper into the Bull of the Woods Wilderness. You'll cross the Hot Springs Fork at 5.7 miles from the trailhead. This is a good turnaround spot if you've come here in the winter as the river will likely be running high and you are almost certain to hit snow not long after you cross the river. Beyond the river crossing the trail becomes rougher and plagued by blowdown but is never all that faint.

Eventually, at 6 miles from the hot springs and 7.5 miles from the trailhead, reach the signed junction with the spur to Silver King Lake. Turn right and hike uphill 0.2 mile to the brushy lake, where you will find one good campsite – if you are backpacking and the site is taken you may be out of luck. You can also reach this spot by hiking from Whetstone Mountain (Hike 6). You can use this trail to set up a car shuttle or return the way you came.

8. PANSY LAKE AND BULL OF THE WOODS

Distance: 7.4 mile loop
Elevation Gain: 2,900 feet
Trailhead elevation: 3,609 feet
Trail high point: 5,509 feet
Season: June- October
Best: July
Map: Opal Creek Wilderness (Imus)

Directions:
- From Estacada, drive southeast on OR 224 for approximately 25 miles to the old guard station at Ripplebrook.
- Just past Ripplebrook OR 224 becomes FR 46. Continue straight on FR 46 for 4.2 miles from Ripplebrook to a junction with FR 63, where you turn right, following signs for Bagby Hot Springs.
- Drive this 2-lane paved road for 3.5 miles to a junction with FR 70, signed for Bagby Hot Springs.
- Continue straight on FR 63 for 2.1 miles to a junction with FR 6340.
- Turn right and drive 7.8 gravel miles uphill to the junction of FR 6340 with FR 6341.
- Fork to the right and drive 3.5 miles of rough pavement to the well-signed trailhead. Parking is on the right side of the road while the trail departs from the left side of the road.

Hike: This tour through ancient forest up to the summit of Bull of the Woods is perhaps the most complete day hike in the Bull of the Woods Wilderness. Not only do you get the ancient forest in Pansy Creek's scenic valley and the panoramic views from the summit of Bull of the Woods, you also get two lakes and the option to extend you hike all the way to the rocky heights of Big Slide Mountain. This is one of the most popular hikes in the Bull of the Woods Wilderness, and there is no mystery why.

The trail begins with a gradual climb through ancient forest. As you hike away from the road, you'll have views through the trees of the rugged mountains that surround Pansy Lake and Pansy Basin. The trail climbs at a very gradual rate, and is never steep. After about 0.8 mile, reach a junction with an abandoned trail down into rugged Pansy Basin. Continue straight on the main trail. At 1.2 miles, reach a junction with the Dickey Lake Trail (549). As with all trail junctions in the Bull of the Woods, the junction is marked with only a number. For the time being, continue straight to a profusion of trails that encircle Pansy Lake. The main trail heads left around the lake, but you may want to investigate the lake. There are a number of excellent campsites around the lake, making the lake an outstanding destination for a family-friendly backpacking trip.

To continue the loop, return to the main trail and switchback up 0.8 mile to a saddle, where you meet the Mother Lode Trail (558), which descends down into the burned forest on your right. Keep left and begin climbing, at times steeply, through ancient forest on the south slopes of Bull of the Woods. Occasional views through the trees open up to Mount Jefferson to the southeast. At 1.2 miles from the junction at the saddle, meet the Welcome Lakes Trail (554) at another saddle. Turn sharply to the left and hike 0.5 mile through dense

Pansy Lake in early morning.

forest until the trail opens up into alpine splendor just below the summit of the mountain. The trail switchbacks steeply up to the open summit, with an abandoned lookout tower and panoramic views stretching from Mount Rainier to the Three Sisters. In July, the flower display here is outstanding, with red paintbrush and white cat's ears dominating. What a fantastic spot! Sadly, you cannot enter the lookout tower, as it is locked and closed to public visits.

When you decide it's time to leave, follow the trail that heads north from the summit (550) as it descends a scenic ridgecrest one mile to a junction with the Dickey Lake Trail (549) on your left. Turn here and begin descending through scenic forest with an incredible amount of rhododendrons. You will reach shallow Dickey Lake in about a mile, and soon after that, you'll meet the Pansy Lake Trail. Turn right here and hike 1 mile back to the trailhead and your car.

EXTENDING YOUR TRIP:
Big Slide Mountain: This is the easiest way to get to Big Slide Mountain's scenic summit. Here you'll find views north to Mount Hood and down to turquoise Lake Lenore, whose surroundings were absolutely incinerated in the 2011 Mother Lode Fire. The trail continues down to the lake, which is understandably a much less inviting spot than it once was. To find the summit, retrace your steps to the junction with the Welcome Lakes Trail 0.5 mile south of Bull of the Wood's summit. Here, turn right and hike 0.2 mile along the ridgecrest to a junction with the Schreiner Peak Trail (555). Turn left and drop steeply to a junction with the Dickey Creek Trail (553) in another 0.6 mile. Keep straight, pass a junction with the West Lake Way Trail (556) at a pond just 0.1 mile later, and keep straight yet again on the Schreiner Peak Trail (555). 1 more mile of hiking along the ridgecrest brings you to the rocky summit of Big Slide Mountain. The views are very similar to those on Bull of the Woods, but with a better perspective of just how much the 2010 and 2011 fires changed the landscape in the wilderness. The fires came very near the summit of Big Slide Mountain, and you can look down into the ghostly forests below. A faint trail drops steeply 0.3 mile to Lake Lenore, but most hikers will prefer to stay on the summit before returning the way they came.

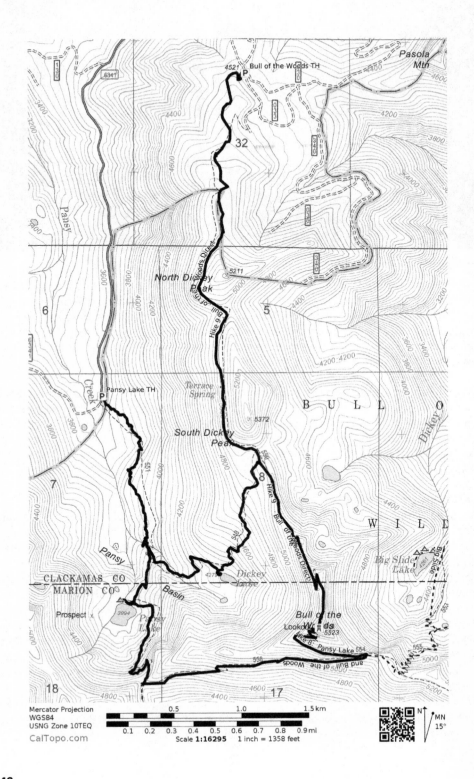

Bull of the Woods TH

4521

Pasola Mtn

32

North Dickey Peak

5211

Hike 9 - Bull of the Woods Direct

6

5

Pansy

Creek

Pansy Lake TH

Terrace Spring

5372

South Dickey Peak

B U L L   O

Dickey

7

551

Hike 9 - Bull of the Woods Direct

8

W I L D

Pansy

Big Slide Lake

CLACKAMAS CO

MARION CO

Basin

4276

Dickey Lake

Prospect x

3994

Pansy Lake

Bull of the Woods Lookout

5523

Hike 8 - Pansy Lake

554

and Bull of the Woods

18

17

Mercator Projection
WGS84
USNG Zone 10TEQ
CalTopo.com

0.5   1.0   1.5 km

0.1 0.2 0.3 0.4 0.5 0.6 0.7 0.8 0.9 mi

Scale 1:16295   1 inch = 1358 feet

N
MN
15°

9. BULL OF THE WOODS

Distance: 6.8 miles out and back
Elevation Gain: 1,700 feet
Trailhead elevation: 4,513 feet
Trail high point: 5,509 feet
Season: July- October
Best: July
Map: Opal Creek Wilderness (Imus)

Directions:
- From Estacada, drive southeast on OR 224 for approximately 25 miles to the old guard station at Ripplebrook.
- Just past Ripplebrook OR 224 becomes FR 46. Continue straight on FR 46 for 4.2 miles from Ripplebrook to a junction with FR 63, where you turn right, following signs for Bagby Hot Springs.
- Drive this 2-lane paved road for 3.5 miles to a junction with FR 70, signed for Bagby Hot Springs.
- Continue straight on FR 63 for 2.1 miles to a junction with FR 6340.
- Turn right and drive 7.8 gravel miles uphill to the junction of FR 6340 with FR 6341.
- Keep left and continue on FR 6340 another 1.5 narrow gravel miles to the trailhead at road's end.

Hike: With a panoramic view stretching from Mount Rainier to the Three Sisters and almost all points in between, the 5533' summit of Bull of the Woods is one of the more popular destinations in its namesake wilderness area. Many people make it a side trip on a backpack through this rugged, spectacular wilderness, while others hike up on a loop from Pansy Lake. Unlike the rugged loop from Pansy Lake (Hike 8), the Bull of the Woods Trail provides a gentle approach to the summit of Bull of the Woods, making this option attractive to hikers in search of an easy or moderate hike.

The trail begins in a recovering clearcut spangled with thriving wildflowers. Look for impressive displays of lupine and penstemon here in July. Soon leave the meadows and enter an impressive old forest dominated by mountain hemlock. At 0.6 mile from the trailhead, curve around a meadow with a small tarn; while this is a lovely scene, the meadow is very fragile. Tread with care! The trail climbs deeper and deeper into the forest and at a gentle clip as you work your way around first North and then South Dickey Peaks.

At 2.1 miles from the trailhead reach a junction with the Dickey Lake Trail (549), which darts downhill to your right (see Hike 8). Instead, continue straight, hiking along the divide towards the summit of Bull of the Woods. As you near the summit, views begin opening to the left (east) of Mount Hood and Mount Jefferson, with a new clearing at the edge of the ridge seemingly every few hundred yards or so. At 3.0 miles from the trailhead leave the forest for good and climb steeply 0.2 mile to the open summit and its lookout tower. The view here is stunning! The entirety of the Bull of the Woods Wilderness is at your feet, and the volcanoes of Oregon and Washington stretch out into the far distance. The lookout itself is locked and closed to the public. The wide summit invites exploration and picnics! When you can pull yourself away from this place, return the way you came.

10. BIG SLIDE LAKE

Distance: 12.1 miles out and back
Elevation Gain: 3,100 feet
Trailhead elevation: 2,892 feet
Trail high point: 4,359 feet
Season: June- November
Best: July- October
Map: Opal Creek Wilderness (Imus)

Directions:
* From Estacada, drive southeast on OR 224 for approximately 25 miles to the old guard station at Ripplebrook.
* Just past Ripplebrook OR 224 becomes FR 46. Continue straight on FR 46 for 4.2 miles from Ripplebrook to a junction with FR 63, where you turn right, following signs for Bagby Hot Springs.
* Drive this 2-lane paved road for 3.5 miles to a junction with FR 70, signed for Bagby Hot Springs.
* Continue straight on FR 63 for 2.1 miles to a junction with FR 6340.
* Turn right on this gravel road and drive 0.6 mile to a junction, where you keep straight.
* Continue on FR 6340 another 2.1 miles to a junction with FR 140 with a sigh for the Dickey Creek Trail. Turn left here.
* Drive this narrow, rocky road for 1 mile to a t-junction. The trailhead is on the right, but the best parking is on the left. There is also room for a couple of cars on the shoulder FR 140 about twenty yards before the junction.

Hike: The long trek from the Dickey Creek Trailhead to Big Slide Lake is yet another fantastic hike in the Bull of the Woods Wilderness, one that can stand up to any other hike in this extremely underrated preserve. Of course, there are drawbacks: the hike is long, begins on a decommissioned road and then plummets 500 feet on a rough, extremely steep track to the bottom of Dickey Creek's canyon. Don't fret – this just keeps the casual hiker away!

Begin by hiking on the remains of FR 140, now a decommissioned road, for about 0.5 mile until the trail meets a small creek crossing. Contour around the remains of a bridge to an easier crossing, and almost immediately begin descending on a rough trail into Dickey Creek's deep canyon. Trail crews have installed stairs in some places to help control erosion but it makes the descent no less steep. A little over a mile into the hike, finally arrive at the canyon floor, where you are greeted by some huge trees and a thick carpet of moss on a trail that feels even more remote than it actually is.

The next couple miles are a joy, as you hike through a glorious grove of ancient forest, pass through a swamp, and curve around a lily pad-covered pond that always seems to be full of ducks and other wildlife. This part of the trail supports an incredible population of Rough-skinned newts, so keep an eye out to avoid crushing these beautiful amphibians. Soon you join Dickey Creek, and at about 3.5 miles from the trailhead, reach a junction next to the creek. Ignore a user trail that continues straight up the canyon and instead turn left to cross the creek. The crossing is easy later in the year when you can rock-hop to keep your feet dry, but in the spring you will probably have to find a log. The simplest and surest way to

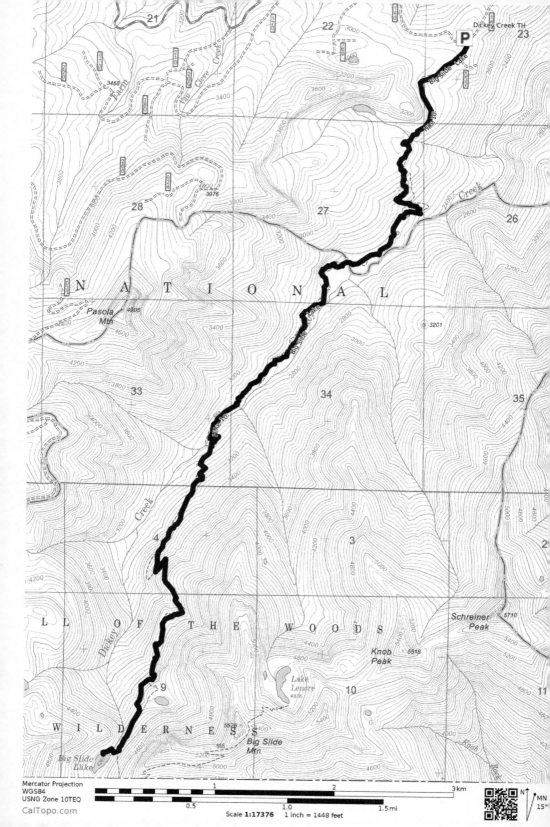

cross at this time is to wade, but that can be cold and potentially dangerous if the creek is running high. If you are unsure of the crossing, there is no shame in turning around!

Once across the creek, the trail switchbacks up the walls of the canyon at a steady grade, leveling out after a little over a mile from the crossing. From here, traverse a series of rock slopes far above Dickey Creek until you reach an unmarked junction with the spur to Big Slide Lake at 5.8 miles from the trailhead. Turn right and descend steeply to the lake. Follow this trail across Dickey Creek to a series of excellent campsites beside the lake. At this distance, you can see why many would prefer to spend the night here rather than immediately turn around and make the long trek back. And indeed, there is much to do here! You can go for a swim, seek out secret lakes off trail, and follow trails up to either Bull of the Woods (Hike 9) or Big Slide Mountain. Given your proximity to several other area trails, you can also use Big Slide Lake as a base camp to explore even further into the Bull of the Woods Wilderness. Unless you've established a car shuttle, however, when it comes time to turn around you should return the way you came.

11. ELK LAKE CREEK

Distance: 10.4 miles out and back
Elevation Gain: 1,500 feet (there are lots of small ups and downs)
Trailhead elevation: 2,476 feet
Trail high point: 2,867 feet
Season: June- October
Best: June- October
Map: Opal Creek Wilderness (Imus)

Directions:
- From Estacada, drive southeast on OR 224 for approximately 25 miles to the old guard station at Ripplebrook.
- Just past Ripplebrook OR 224 becomes FR 46 at a junction with FR 57. Stay on the main road (ignore signs for Timothy Lake) and continue straight on FR 46 for 4.2 miles from Ripplebrook to a junction with FR 63, where you turn right, following signs for Bagby Hot Springs.
- Drive this 2-lane paved road for 3.5 miles to a junction with FR 70, signed for Bagby Hot Springs.
- Continue straight on FR 63 for 5.3 miles, crossing the Collawash River and transitioning to gravel in the process, to a junction with FR 6350 signed for Graham Pass.
- Fork to the right and begin a long stretch of road where you alternate pavement and gravel. You need to watch out for the gravel stretches, which often have large potholes where the pavement ends. Drive 3.7 miles of this "pavement" until you reach a junction with FR 6370.
- Fork to the right on what is now FR 6380 and continue another 2.3 miles of gravel to a fork in the road at a bridge over the East Fork Collawash River.
- Turn right to cross the bridge and fork to the left on rough gravel for 0.5 mile to the trailhead parking lot.

Emerald Pool is a good place to sit and contemplate.

Hike: Elk Lake Creek features some of the giant old growth and emerald green pools that made nearby Opal Creek famous, but with far fewer people. A trail parallels the creek for almost ten miles, providing hikers with many opportunities for hikes of all levels of difficulty. For a moderate hike, trek 3.3 miles to Emerald Pool, a deep hole in Elk Lake Creek set in a narrow, wildly scenic gorge. A more difficult hike is Battle Creek Flats, a series of outstanding campsites at the confluence of Elk Lake Creek and Battle Creek, 5.2 miles from the trailhead. Whatever you choose, this hike is certain to become one of your favorites.

Before we get to the hike, please note that every experience in this area is wildly different – trail maintenance is infrequent, the creek may be difficult to cross when running high and the area shows some damage from a 2010 fire. Be on the lookout for downed trees and be willing to turn around if Elk Lake Creek is running high.

The trail begins in an old clearcut and quickly enters the fire zone as it traverses a steep slope above the creek. The first views of Elk Lake Creek are attained shortly afterwards with a view down towards a waterfall and the first of many deep green pools below. At 0.6 miles in the trail crosses Pine Cone Creek amidst blowdown from the fires. This is the first of six creek fords and by far the easiest. From here the trail enters the Wilderness area. Once into the protected forests of the Wilderness, the fire damage lessens and the scenery gets better with each step. At 2.0 miles into the hike cross Knob Rock Creek and Welcome Creek in quick succession, a task that is difficult without getting wet no matter the season. Take a minute to inspect the waterfall on Welcome Creek; there are other tiers above the one near the trail! A short 0.2 mile later you'll reach a junction with the Welcome Lakes Trail (554). Continue straight and soon after you'll reach the first ford of Elk Lake Creek.

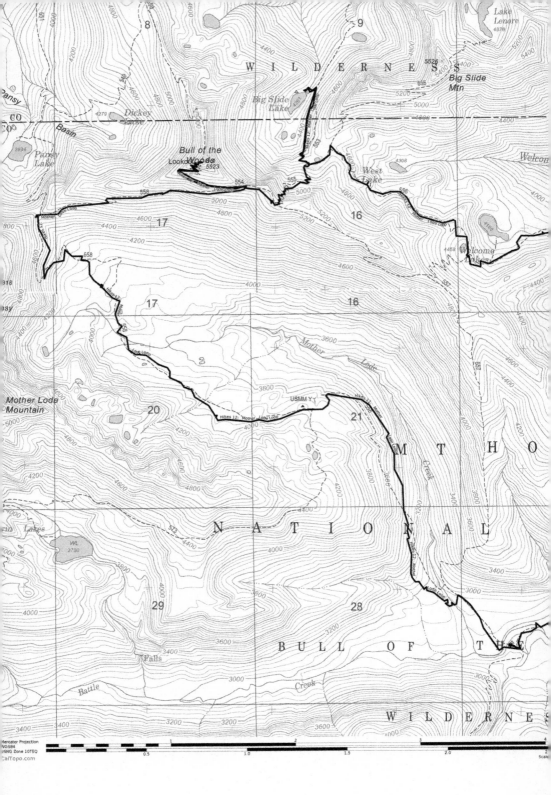

If the creek is running high don't feel ashamed to turn back – indeed, were it not for the creek crossings this hike would be open most of the year. What is remarkable is the incredible clarity of Elk Lake Creek; while the creek may appear to be only inches deep you'll be surprised to discover that the creek is knee to waist deep, depending on the season. A hiking stick or trekking poles are helpful as the rocks on the creek bottom can be slippery. From here you'll climb into a jungle of huckleberry and rhododendron in deep old-growth forest. At 3.3 miles from the trailhead the trail passes above Emerald Pool, a remarkably deep gorge with water so clear you'll likely see fish swimming by if you stop. There is a rocky bench above the pool that makes an excellent lunch or snack spot. You might even decide nothing will top this and wish to turn around. If you're continuing, you have another ford of Elk Lake Creek waiting for you less than half a mile up the trail.

For a longer hike, continue past the second ford about 1.9 miles to the site of the old Battle Creek Shelter. After re-crossing the creek, the Elk Lake Trail begins to climb a bit to avoid the wide channel of the creek. Here sporadic trail maintenance necessitates looking for flagging and blazes on occasion. After skirting a talus slope the trail descends down into another jungle at the confluence of Elk Lake Creek and Battle Creek. Ford Battle Creek and just a hundred yards later, at 5.2 miles from the trailhead you'll reach the large open camping area at the site of the old Battle Creek shelter, which collapsed in 1988 under the weight of heavy winter snow. Excellent campsites abound on this scenic of peninsula in deep old growth. Here you'll also find the junction with the Mother Lode Trail (558) near the largest and best of the area's campsites. Return the way you came or arrange a car shuttle to the upper trailhead, if possible. The trail continues another 4 miles upstream to the west end of Elk Lake, where you will find a number of excellent campsites. This section of the Elk Lake Creek Trail is described in Hike 28.

12. MOTHER LODE LOOP

Distance: 20.6 mile loop
Elevation Gain: 4,700 feet
Trailhead elevation: 2,476 feet
Trail high point: 5,509 feet
Season: June- October
Best: July
Map: Opal Creek Wilderness (Imus). Also see map on previous page.

Directions:
* See directions for Elk Lake Creek (Hike 11).

Hike: This two or three-day loop from Elk Lake Creek to the summit of Bull of the Woods back through the idyllic valley of Mother Lode Creek is the supreme tour of the Bull of the Woods Wilderness. There are many excellent side trips and with many other trails in this area, there is the opportunity to turn this 20.6 mile loop into a much longer, even more satisfying affair.

Begin by hiking along beautiful Elk Lake Creek. You will pass above a waterfall and slowly hike downhill as you near creek level. Pass Pine Cone Creek and enter the Bull of the Woods Wilderness Area at 0.8 mile. At 2.1 miles from the trailhead, cross first Knob Rock and then Welcome Creeks in short succession; at Welcome Creek, look upstream to see a series of graceful waterfalls in Welcome Creek's narrow canyon. At 2.3 miles, you will arrive at a junction with the Welcome Lakes Trail (this is trail 554 – as most trail signs in this area are designated only by a number, I will give the number for each trail) and the start of your loop. As this loop is easier to navigate in a counter-clockwise direction, I suggest turning right here.

The Welcome Lakes Trail climbs gradually above Welcome Creek's narrow canyon, never once approaching the creek. Rhododendrons overhang the trail in many places, and indeed the Welcome Lakes Trail is quite brushy. The trail is easy to follow and very pleasant for the first 1.5 miles above Elk Lake Creek but once you enter forest burned in the 2010 Mother Lode Fire the trail becomes plagued with blowdown. Trail maintenance crews rarely make it up here so expect to climb over some trees. Reach Lower Welcome Lake at 4.5 miles from the trailhead and enter a proliferation of brush. If you lose the trail, follow flags around the side of the lake until you reach a junction with the spur trail down to the lower lake. Despite the name, the Welcome Lakes are a most unwelcoming place these days and camping at either lake is not recommended. Snags from the fire threaten anybody who stays the night and there are few good places to camp. Instead, hike uphill for a brushy quarter-mile and and reach a poorly-signed junction with the West Lake Way Trail (556) at 4.8 miles from the trailhead. While either trail will get you to Bull of the Woods, the West Lake Way Trail is in slightly better shape than the Welcome Lakes Trail and is a more direct approach to Big Slide Lake, your destination for the first night of your trip. So turn right here.

Despite its name, the West Lake Way Trail never approaches West Lake. Instead, the trail passes tiny Upper Welcome Lake and climbs out of the Welcome Lakes basin. Look behind you at the crest to an excellent view of Mount Jefferson – the first in a series of excellent views you will have on this loop. The trail curls around the side of a ridge, offering views down to the upper canyon of Welcome Creek and West Lake, inaccessible from here. At 1.1 miles from Upper Welcome Lake, reach a junction with the Schreiner Peak Trail (555). Turn left here. You'll soon pass a small pond that may be dry later in the season. Less than 0.2 mile from the West Lake Way junction, reach another junction, this time with the Dickey Creek Trail (553). Turn right and drop down 0.5 mile to beautiful Big Slide Lake. There is an unmarked junction on your left that leads to the lake. The best campsites are near the outlet and on the west side of the lake.

On the second day of your backpack, hike back out of Big Slide Lake and return to the junction with the Schreiner Peak Trail. Turn right here and climb up a series of well-graded switchbacks a little under a half-mile to a trail junction – in fact a reunion with the Welcome Lakes Trail. To climb to the view-packed summit of Bull of the Woods, turn right. In just 0.2 mile you will meet yet another trail junction, this time with the Mother Lode Trail (557). Keep right and climb 0.5 mile to the 5533' summit of Bull of the Woods and its lookout tower. The view is as good as you were hoping it would be, stretching from Mount Rainier in the north all the way south to the Three Sisters and virtually everything in between. In July, a carpet of wildflowers blankets the summit. The lookout tower is falling into disrepair, and is locked and closed to the public. Once you finish your visit, return to the junction with the Mother Lode Trail and turn left.

The Mother Lode Trail descends gradually for 1.1 mile to a junction with the Pansy Lake Trail. Keep left here to stay on the Mother Lode Trail and drop into forest burned during the 2010 fire. Despite its name, the Mother Lode Fire did not burn much of the area on the trail. After a short stretch through fire damage, enter ancient forest as the trail drops into the upper canyon of Mother Lode Creek. The creek is often dry later in the season. You will continue downhill another 2.5 miles to a junction with the Twin Lakes Trail. You will continue straight as the trail begins to descend precipitously. You will eventually level out into Mother Lode Creek's narrow canyon. Near the creek crossing the trail is a little faint, so look for flagging to help guide you. The trail crosses Mother Lode Creek, climbs uphill and then crosses Battle Creek – for this last ford you will likely get wet, as the creek is usually too deep to cross on rocks. Beyond Battle Creek the trail passes several excellent campsites before meeting the Elk Lake Creek Trail, 4.7 miles from the Pansy Lake junction on the side of Bull of the Woods. There are many excellent campsites in this area, and I recommend camping here.

From the junction of the Mother Lode and Elk Lake Creek Trails, turn left (north) and you will very soon meet Battle Creek. As was the case when you crossed Battle Creek on the Mother Lode Trail, you will likely need to take off your shoes and wade. Continue down the trail as it follows a small creek bed and climbs up to a rockslide to avoid a washout in the creek before you reach a ford of Elk Lake Creek at about 1.5 miles from Battle Creek. Take off your shoes and wade, and on the far side the trail climbs into the forest on the east bank. Reach Emerald Pool after another 0.8 miles, and then reach another ford of Elk Lake Creek, this one the deepest of all, at 2.8 miles from Battle Creek. Cross the creek and reunite with the Welcome Lakes Trail to close the loop. Continue another 2.2 miles to the trailhead and the end of your trip.

13. RHO CREEK AND BIG BOTTOM

Distance: 8.2 miles out and back
Elevation Gain: 2,400 feet
Trailhead elevation: 2,624 feet
Trail high point: 4,529 feet
Season: May- November
Best: June
Map: Neither trail is on current maps- see page 62 or my website for a map of this hike.

Directions:
- From Estacada, drive southeast on OR 224 for approximately 25 miles to the old guard station at Ripplebrook.
- Just past Ripplebrook OR 224 becomes FR 46 at a junction with FR 57. Stay on the main road (ignore signs for Timothy Lake) and continue straight on FR 46 for 4.2 miles from Ripplebrook to a junction with FR 63.
- Keep straight here, and drive another 12.3 miles south on FR 46.
- At a junction with FR 4670, turn right and drive 0.3 miles to a bridge over the Clackamas River and then a fork.
- Keep left on paved FR 4670 and drive 1.1 miles to a junction with FR 4671.

Lonely and wild, Rho Creek tumbles through a narrow canyon deep in Clackamas country.

- Fork to the left and drive exactly 1 mile of pavement to the trailhead on your right.
- There is room for approximately 2 cars to park on the side of the road. Otherwise, continue another 0.2 mile to the road's crossing of Rho Creek, where there are a few more spaces to park.

Hike: This lovely and little-known hike traces a cascading stream through a mossy and magical forest just south of Big Bottom. The trail is at times very faint but it is well-marked, and generally easy to follow. Best of all, because this is a trail that is very much off the beaten trail, the chances are that you will have it all to yourself. Because of this, I do not recommend hiking it alone – this place is very, very remote – but also very, very beautiful.

First of all, a word of thanks should go to the fine folks at Trail Advocates (http://www. trailadvocate.org) who helped reopen the trail and now maintain it. We all owe them a huge debt of gratitude for resurrecting such a beautiful trail! While officially still abandoned, the trail is reasonably easy to follow for the most part, with only a few faint sections. If you are unsure of your ability to follow trails like this, either download my GPS track and map or turn around when you feel uncomfortable.

Begin at a signpost on the side of FR 4671. The trail climbs swiftly above the road and angles to the south, towards Rho Creek's narrow canyon. The trail soon descends slightly to meet the creek, passing over a verdant carpet of moss. At about 0.7 mile from the trailhead, the Rho Creek Trail crosses Tumble Creek on a large fallen log (if you can't see the crossing, look around – the trail bends to the left and crosses Tumble Creek on a log about ten feet above creek level), then bends uphill to follow Rho Creek. For a nice and easy hike, I recommend turning around at the crossing as it doesn't get better than this.

From the crossing, the trail climbs uphill above Rho Creek and eventually enters a recovering clearcut. Here, the trail becomes faint and will test the navigational abilities of most hikers. Just keep straight and keep your eyes on the trail ahead – there is nowhere else for the trail to go but straight (the creek is downhill while uphill would lead you further into the old clearcut). Eventually, the trail becomes easier to follow for a little while, but becomes faint again when it reaches a boggy spot along Rho Creek just a little ways up the trail. Here, you curve to the left, cross the creek and climb a short ways to Fadeaway Spring on your left. A natural pool about three feet deep at the edge of a clearcut, this is a really neat spot! From here, the trail switchbacks up to a crossing of FR 4672 at 2.9 miles from the trailhead. Look for flagging to help you find the trail on the way down, as the Rho Creek Trail is not obvious heading back the opposite direction.

Across the road, the trail becomes very obvious as it has received recent maintenance. You will hike steeply uphill until the trail reaches the edge of Rhododendron Meadow, now mostly grown-in (there is a meadow, but finding it requires bushwhacking). From here, blowdown becomes an issue and the trail becomes somewhat faint. Pass a signpost marking a junction, but without destinations – no junction indeed – and continue to a faint junction just after a final crossing of Rho Creek. Left leads to the ruins of an old guard station, but you should turn right. The trail climbs up to a campsite just off FR 4670 known as "Bear Camp" at 4.1 miles from the trailhead. Just across FR 4670, the Rho Ridge Trail heads south towards Graham Pass and north towards Mount Lowe (Hike 14). The summit of Mount Lowe is 2.6 miles and 800 feet of elevation gain to your right- so if you choose to continue, your overall hike will be 13.4 miles out and back with approximately 3,000 feet of elevation gain. Either arrange a car shuttle or return the way you came.

Less experienced hikers should probably turn around at Fadeaway Spring, as the trail from this point, though flagged, is occasionally fainter than most hikers would prefer. There is a lot to explore up here, and combining this hike with Mount Lowe would make for a rewarding and challenging day hike; do not stray off-trail in this area, however, as massive amounts of downed trees and thick rhododendrons make off-trail travel a nightmare.

Big Bottom:
If you are in the area and have extra time and a willingness to explore, you should consider checking out Big Bottom's tremendous grove of ancient trees. To find Big Bottom, drive back to the junction of FR 4671 and FR 4670 and continue north on FR 4670 for 1 mile to the junction with FR 4651 on the west bank of the Clackamas. Continue straight, now on FR 4651, for 1 mile to a pullout on your right at a junction with what was once FR 4651-120. The trail is the decommissioned road, cutting right through the heart of a recent clearcut.

One of western Oregon's newest wilderness areas, Big Bottom features some of the Cascades' finest old growth timber – and serves as a lesson of the perils of logging virgin forest. Begin by hiking down decommissioned road FR4651-120. This old logging road descends gently amid land that seems to have been cut 30-40 years ago – a juxtaposition that will seem jarring as you leave the grove on the way out. At one point Big Bottom was a proposed timber sale but years of citizen activism eventually resulted in its inclusion in the Lewis & Clark Wilderness Act of 2009. Soon reach open fields of daisies that are slowly erasing this old road. After approximately a mile of alternating daisy fields and newer-growth forest, follow the old road past and over a few downed trees into the heart of Big Bottom.

When the road curves into deep forest, the old growth becomes increasingly impressive. Six to eight-foot thick Douglas Firs reign supreme over a lush understory complete with many massive downed giants. The old road becomes an avenue of giants, a sort of Fifth Avenue with treescrapers on each side of the road. After about 1.8 miles the trail disintegrates near the edge of a marshy creek. You can continue on the remains of the road but it's best to stop at the creek with old-growth giants around you on all sides. This makes an excellent pit stop before turning back.

The fun of Big Bottom is exploring off the road. Off-trail travel reveals mossy meadows, enormous cedars and fantastic displays of color in the fall. Remember this though: off-trail travel is inherently tiring, and climbing over huge downed trees takes a toll. Furthermore, while it is very difficult to get truly lost in Big Bottom (being that it is located between a gravel road and the Clackamas River), it is very easy to get disoriented, as the woods here have a uniformly beautiful quality that makes routefinding difficult. It is **very easy** to get turned around here. Allow lots of time to find your way out if you decide to head off-trail.

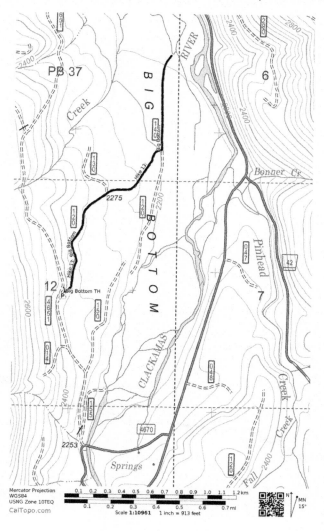

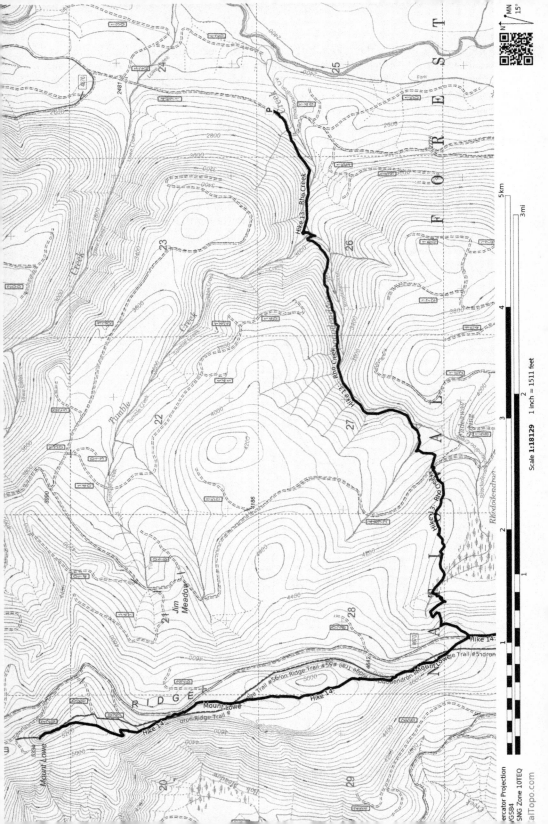

14.   MOUNT LOWE

Distance: 6.4 miles out and back
Elevation Gain: 1,400 feet
Trailhead elevation: 4,328 feet
Trail high point: 5,321 feet
Season: June- October
Best: July
Map: Green Trails #525 (Breitenbush)

Directions:
- From Estacada, drive southeast on OR 224 for approximately 25 miles to the old guard station at Ripplebrook.
- Just past Ripplebrook OR 224 becomes FR 46 at a junction with FR 57. Stay on the main road (ignore signs for Timothy Lake) and continue straight on FR 46 for 4.2 miles from Ripplebrook to a junction with FR 63, where you turn right, following signs for Bagby Hot Springs.
- Drive 3.5 miles of pavement to a junction with FR 70, where you keep straight (ignore signs for Bagby Hot Springs).
- Continue 5.1 miles on this road (it changes to gravel in 2.3 miles) to a junction with FR 6350 on your left.
- Following a sign for Graham Pass, turn left onto paved FR 6350 and drive 5.6 miles of alternating gravel and pavement to a junction with FR 6355.
- Fork to the left to stay on FR 6350 and continue 1 mile to Graham Pass.
- Turn right into a large unsigned parking lot. This is the trailhead.
- Note: There are two other ways to get here, both of which are fairly easy. The first involves driving FR 4670 from its junction on FR 46 for 14.3 miles to Graham Pass. The other involves driving FR 6350 from the Hawk Mountain Trailhead (Hike 30) another 7.3 miles to Graham Pass. Either is a good way to get to Graham Pass, but the shortest route from Portland is the Collawash River approach described above.

Hike: Near the far northern end of Rho Ridge, Mount Lowe offers an outstanding view of Mount Jefferson and the upper Clackamas River canyon. This moderate to easy hike is an ideal trip for a lazier day in July, when beargrass blankets the ridge in favorable years and the views are at their best. Because the hike is completely surrounded by roads, car shuttles are easy to arrange to any number of hikes in the area, among them Burnt Granite, Hawk Mountain and Rho Creek. You can also make a shuttle to Mount Lowe's northern trailhead, just 1.5 miles north of the summit.

The trail departs from Graham Pass and heads north, paralleling FR 4670. Look for the trail on the right side of FR 4670. The trail parallels the road for 0.5 mile before rejoining the road. Hike along the road for 0.1 mile and then look for the trail heading off to the left, immediately opposite a side road that leads to Bear Camp and the Rho Creek Trail. Once the trail leaves FR 4670 for the second time, it climbs a bit to distance itself from the road, and then drops into a cool forest carpeted with beargrass. The forest here is quite beautiful, and is a cool reprieve on hot days when many of the open areas near here swelter in the summer heat.

Mount Hood and Mount Rainier from the slopes of Mount Lowe.

At 2.5 miles, the trail skirts the road for a second time, providing yet another opportunity for shuttles and loops. Pass through a huge meadow where the views begin to open up to the south. Mount Jefferson looks surprisingly close here, and views soon open up to points even further south – Three-Fingered Jack, the Three Sisters and Mount Washington all line up here like one large massif – impressive indeed! To the north, the summit of Mount Lowe is directly ahead of you, so keep going.

The trail climbs uphill through a large meadow, and then enters a cool forest below a series of rocky openings. You will want to wander off trail a bit here, as a little exploration will deliver you to a fantastic viewpoint of Mounts Hood, Adams and Rainier towering above a long rockslide – a potential lunch spot and one of the highlights of the hike. Back on the trail, a short spur trail on your left leads to the summit of Mount Lowe at 3.2 miles. A former lookout site, the summit is dotted with ruins of the erstwhile lookout (which was dismantled in the 1960s). Watch where you sit, as there is broken glass everywhere (and likewise, the remains of the lookout are federally protected, so leave it where it is). One interesting feature of the summit is the three windbreaker-style shelters, which offer places for hikers to sit. The view has grown in some since the lookout was dismantled, and is no longer panoramic – though impressive views remain of Mount Hood and points north, Mount Jefferson is mostly blocked by trees from most vantage points. Perhaps the most impressive view is to the west, where you have an almost aerial, map-like view of the canyon of the Collawash River and the charred peaks of the Bull of the Woods Wilderness. Either arrange a shuttle or return the way you came.

The Rho Ridge Trail continues south from Graham Pass towards Hawk Mountain. For more information, see Hike 30.

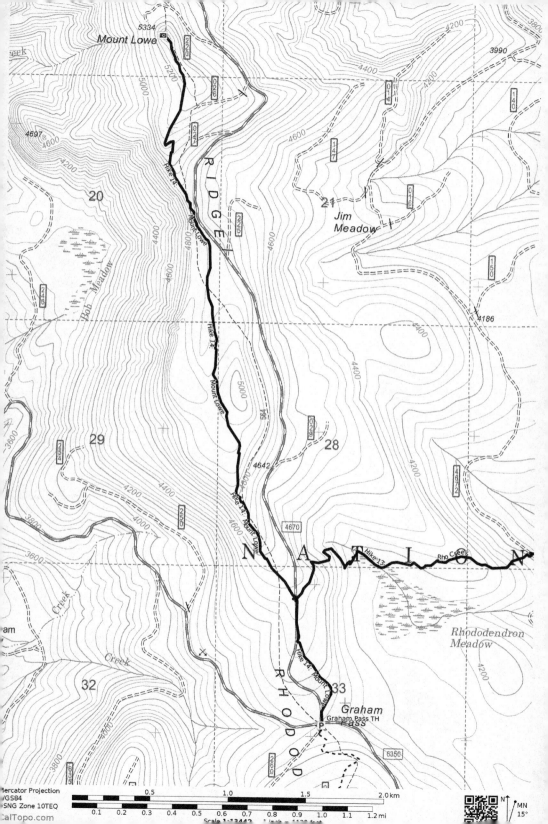

SECTION 2: OPAL CREEK AND BATTLE AX

		Distance	EV Gain
15.	Natural Arch and Rocky Top	2.5	1,200
16.	Sardine Mountain	14.4	4,600
17.	Dome Rock	10.0	3,600
18.	Tumble Lake	5.3	2,000
19.	Elkhorn Ridge	5.0	1,400
20.	Little North Santiam River	9.0	1,800
21.	Henline Falls	2.0	400
22.	Henline Mountain	7.6	3,000
23.	Opal Creek	10.8	1,500
24.	Whetstone Mountain Loop	16.2	4,000
25.	Phantom Bridge and Opal Lake	6.4	2,300
26.	French Creek Ridge	5.6	1,100
27.	Battle Ax	6.0	2,300
28.	Battle Creek and Emerald Pool	12.2	1,600
29.	Gold Butte	3.2	800
30.	Hawk Mountain and Round Lake	5.4	1,200

The Opal Creek and Bull of the Woods Wilderness Areas form the largest contiguous expanse of ancient forest left in Oregon. Unsurprisingly, the highlight of virtually every hike in this area is the forest, and fans of the area compare groves of old-growth here only against the nearby competition. Not to be outdone, the creeks and rivers in the area are often an electric shade of green, a reflection of the green rock underneath the flowing water. These two attributes reach their zenith in the Little North Santiam River Trail (Hike 20), Opal Creek (Hike 23) and the Elk Lake Creek Trail (Hikes 11 and 28), three of the finest low-elevation forest hikes in the state of Oregon.

Hikes in this area frequently follow a creek past waterfalls or a ridge top to a viewpoint or rock formation, but very few do both – and those that do are often quite difficult. The low-elevation hikes in this area are open all winter, and you'll find yourself coming back to this area again and again. There is, after all, only one Opal Creek. The long battle to save the forests and ridgetops from logging left scars, both in the communities here but also in the land itself. Hundreds of miles of logging roads snake across the Opal Creek area, and in many places it is possible to determine the Wilderness boundaries just by looking at the terrain. Regardless of your opinions about logging, it is a jarring contrast.

The challenge of visiting this area lies mainly in the road access. While many of the hikes in this area are accessible year-round, many of the roads in this area are narrow, steep and subject to the frequent washouts and rockslides. A constant vigilance is required - these roads are a reflection of the rugged nature of this area.

15.   NATURAL ARCH AND ROCKY TOP

	Natural Arch	Rocky Top
Distance:	1 mile out & back	1.5 miles out & back
Elevation Gain:	500 feet	700 feet
Trailhead Elevation:	3,866 feet	4,323 feet
Trail High Point:	3,866 feet	5,014 feet
Season:	June- October	June- October
Best:	June- October	June- October
Map:	See my website.	See my website.

Directions:
- From Salem, drive approximately 34 miles to Mill City on OR 22.
- From Mill City, continue on OR 22 for 6.6 miles to Niagara Heights Road (FR 2211), which is on the left next to a small water wheel.
- Drive exactly 6 miles on this twisting, gravel road, always keeping to the main road and following signs that read "Natural Arch", to the Natural Arch Trailhead on the left side of the road.
- The Rocky Top Trailhead is another 1.9 miles of occasionally rocky gravel road further to the north.
- The Rocky Top Trailhead is at a turnaround on the left at a pass. Look for the trail at a small post on the left.

Hike: Two short but excellent hikes, Natural Arch and Rocky Top are an ideal pair for a lazy day out in the mountains. There's enough intrigue to make it worth the drive, enough elevation gain to get your blood going and enough scenery to satisfy even the weary hiker. The only downside is that these hikes aren't long enough, and the drive is occasionally irritating.

Begin at the poorly-signed but very obvious Natural Arch Trailhead. The trail dives downhill at a steady but steep grade, losing 700 feet in only a half-mile to the arch. The arch remains out of sight until you are upon it, and once you see it you will want to spend time exploring the area. A series of caves around the arch provide unique views, but the real star is the arch – at fifty feet tall, it is large enough to drive a bus through it! The arch was uncovered after the Sardine Mountain Fire burned this area thoroughly in 1951, and has remained relatively obscure up to the present. Once you are ready to turn around, motor it back up the trail to the trailhead and drive (or walk) 1.9 miles to the Rocky Top Trailhead.

The Rocky Top Trail climbs from its trailhead above Arrowhead Pass at a steady and relatively gradual grade. You will gain 700 feet in just 0.7 mile, but the trail is so well-graded you'll barely notice. The trail passes underneath a rock pinnacle and wraps around the northern side of Rocky Top, where you'll have views north to Elkhorn Ridge and the peaks of the Bull of the Woods Wilderness. Reach the summit at 0.7 mile, where views open up to a full panorama that stretches from Mount Rainier to the Three Sisters. Mount Jefferson is the star attraction, but it is fun to pick out all of the lesser summits nearby, as well as look back the valley to the west – among them Sardine Mountain, Battle Ax, Table Rock and so many

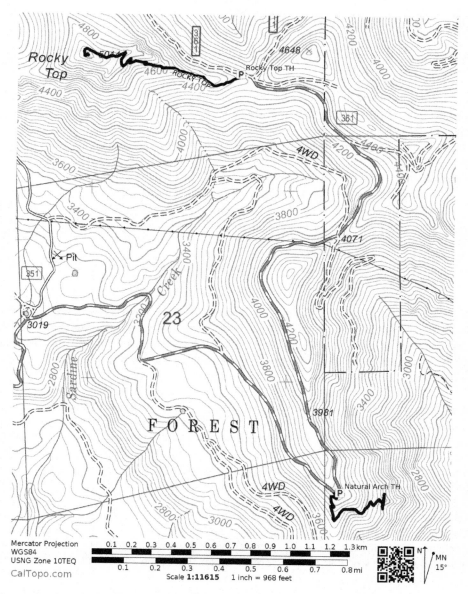

others. The flat-topped peak immediately in front of Three-Fingered Jack is Coffin Mountain (Hike 32), while the Three Pyramids (Hike 37) appear immediately in front of the Three Sisters like miniature doppelgangers. Mary's Peak's humped summit looms on the western horizon, behind the green swath of the Willamette Valley. As you might expect, Rocky Top was the site of a lookout tower (the tower here was destroyed in 1964 amongst a spate of tower removals in the area). All that remains of the tower is some broken glass, a few nails and a few of the support rods – and the view, of course. With a view as great as this, you'll want to stay long enough to see how many summits you can identify, and long enough to justify the short hike. Return the way you came.

16. SARDINE MOUNTAIN

Distance: 14.4 miles out and back (if starting at the lowest trailhead)
Elevation Gain: 4,600 feet
Trailhead elevation: 1,257 feet
Trail high point: 4,924 feet
Season: all year (bring snowshoes in winter)
Best: January- April
Map: See my website for a high-resolution map of this area.

Directions:
- From Salem, drive east approximately 39 miles on OR 22 to Big Cliff Dam.
- Drive past Big Cliff Dam exactly 0.4 mile to an unsigned road on your left, at a clearing.
- Turn left here, and soon you will see a sign that reads: "Drive at your own risk".
- Drive as far up this narrow, rocky road as far as you feel comfortable, and park on the left side of the road at one of the several pullouts.
- High clearance vehicles can make it as far as 3 – 4 miles up the road, but low-clearance vehicles will want to park no further than 1 mile up the road.

Hike: Sardine Mountain is a huge elevation gain hike that is great at any time of year, but never more so than on clear days in winter, when the mountains are draped in snow, the area deserted and the views seemingly endless. In summer you can drive to the upper trailhead, making this hike an attractive shuttle destination. It is a much better hike in the winter, however.

Begin somewhere on the Sardine Road. I started the hike just after the bridge over Sardine Creek, but you can continue driving up the road a ways if you so wish. The road follows cascading, boulder-strewn Sardine Creek up its narrow canyon, offering many views of scenic rapids and small waterfalls along the way. Short bushwhacks into the canyon reveal hidden waterfalls and scenic gorges. At about 1 mile from the Sardine Creek bridge, the road switchbacks away to the right and begins the long climb towards Sardine Mountain. After just a few tenths of a mile, reach a junction. It's worth exploring this road 0.5 mile to an unbridged crossing of one of the forks of Sardine Creek, just below an unfathomably huge log jam and tumbling waterfall (continuing beyond this point will eventually take you to Rocky Top). This side trip adds an extra mile to your day's hike (included in the total distance above) but is well worth it; furthermore, in winter the way is reliably snow-free up to this point, making for an easy hike that is a lot of fun in the winter.

From the road junction, the Sardine Creek Road gets down to business and begins climbing at a grade that is difficult to imagine for a road. You will have occasional views up to your day's goal, the rocky summit of Sardine Mountain. You will pass another junction at about 3 miles from the trailhead, where you keep right. Lose a bit of elevation before you begin climbing at a furious grade on a road that is now little more than a jeep trail. After a long uphill climb and many switchbacks, reach Knutson Saddle at 5.3 miles, where at last the road levels out. If you came here in the summer you will almost certainly see cars in this area, as the saddle is not far beyond the upper trailhead for Tumble Lake (Hike 18 – if you wish to drive to this upper trailhead, follow the directions for Hike 18 and continue another few hundred yards to a junction; fork left and drive a little over a half-mile to the saddle).

Mount Jefferson looms over Dome Rock and Tumble Lake's basin from Sardine Mountain.

Coming in the winter, however, will bring you almost total solitude and great views on clear days!

From the saddle, you can find views of Mount Jefferson by heading straight for a few hundred yards around a bend until the mountain comes into view, framed by Dome Rock and the pinnacles of Tumble Lake's narrow basin. There is a better view worth seeking, however. From Knutson Saddle, look for a path heading into the woods right at the saddle. It is not easy to see, so look for a path curving around a large burnt stump. In the winter, just head uphill through the trees! From here, this rough user trail winds through the woods for a bit before emerging below the rocky summit of Sardine Mountain. The views here on a clear day are fantastic! Look down to Tumble Lake, nestled in a small basin overhanging Detroit Lake; look out to Mount Jefferson, and down to Three-Fingered Jack, looming over flat-topped Coffin Mountain; and look south to the Three Sisters, which slowly come into view above Water Tower Mountain. The higher up Sardine Mountain you go, the harder the scrambling becomes, and many will be content to stop at the false summit, where the views are great. Climb up the rocky peak as far as you feel comfortable; in the winter an ice ax is a very good idea, as is the judgement to know when you should turn around. At the summit, views open up to the north towards Mount Hood and Washington's volcanoes, as well as all of the neighboring peaks.

Return the way you came, or arrange a shuttle to the summit; similarly, it is easy to arrange a shuttle via the Dome Rock and Tumble Trails (Hikes 17 and 18); to find the Tumble Trail, continue another 7.3 miles up OR 22 from the Sardine Road turnoff to Tumble Lake's trailhead. Shuttling this hike will likely be impossible in winter as snow blocks the upper reaches of the Tumble Trail until May; keep that in mind when planning a visit to the area.

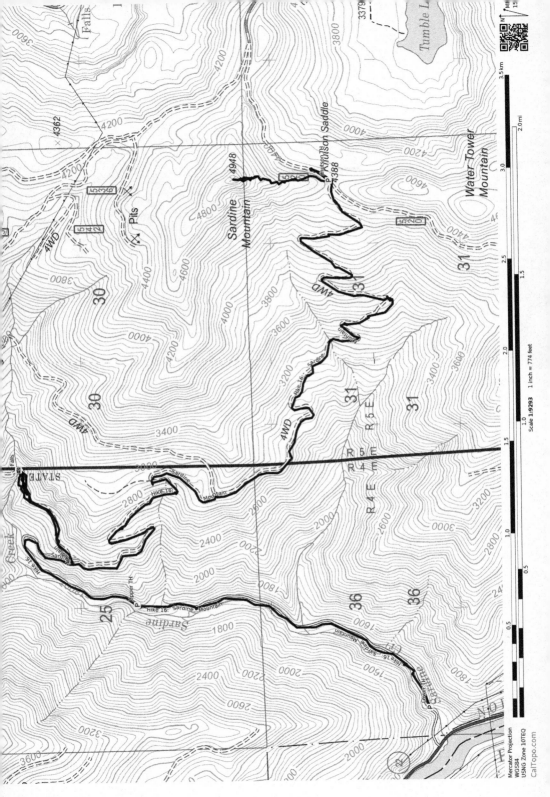

17. DOME ROCK

Distance: 10 miles out and back
Elevation Gain: 3,600 feet
Trailhead elevation: 1,590 feet
Trail high point: 4,793 feet
Season: June- November
Best: June- July
Map: See my website for a high-resolution map of this area.

Directions:
* From Salem, drive east on OR 22 for 41.2 miles to the dam over Detroit Lake.
* Continue straight on the highway for 5 miles to the Tumble Trailhead, on the left side of the highway, just after the road crosses Tumble Creek.
* The trailhead is approximately 1 mile before the Detroit Ranger Station. If you reach this point, you have driven too far.

Hike: The trailhead for this excellent hike is conveniently located at Detroit Lake, ensuring it is open all year. Whether you come in the summer for the flowers or in the winter for a long but rewarding snowshoe, the summit of Dome Rock provides an outstanding destination. On a clear day, you can see from Mount Hood to the Three Sisters and almost every point in between. The stout (and those able to establish a car shuttle) can continue down to Tumble Lake (Hike 18) for a full day of hiking.

The trail begins on an old roadbed that follows cascading Tumble Creek for 0.4 mile to a trail junction on your right. Turn right here and begin switchbacking steeply up through second-growth forest. Openings in the forest provide occasional views down to Detroit Lake and out to Mount Jefferson but for the most part you remain in the forest for several miles. In June thousands of pink rhododendrons crowd the trail, while stalks of white beargrass are profuse along the trail in favorable years.

At about 3.5 miles from the trailhead, leave the forest and enter an old clearcut known as Margie Dunham. Cross an old road, and then enter the most scenic stretch of the trail, where you alternate forest and views as the trail snakes around the crest of the ridge below Dome Rock. At 4.5 miles from the highway, meet a junction with the spur trail to the summit of Dome Rock. Turn right and switchback up to the summit of Dome Rock. Just below the summit, views open up down to Tumble Lake, glistening in the basin below. Pass a rock affectionately known as Toilet Rock (you'll understand why when you see it) and gain the summit, with its true panoramic view. Hikers who frequent the area will have fun picking out all of the minor summits in the area in addition to the snow-capped volcanoes. On a clear day, humped Marys Peak is visible far to the west, across the expanse of the Willamette Valley. Look for thumb-shaped Table Rock, sticking out from above the west end of the Bull of the Woods Wilderness. Battle Ax is the imposing summit just to the right of Mount Hood. Mount Jefferson rises above the long expanse of the North Santiam River. As I said – be sure to visit on a clear day!

Return the way you came, or continue down to Tumble Lake if you have the time and energy, or a car shuttle waiting for you at the remote upper trailhead.

18.   TUMBLE LAKE

Distance: 5.3 miles out and back
Elevation Gain: 2,000 feet
Trailhead elevation: 4,329 feet
Trail high point: 4,793 feet
Season: June- October
Best: June- July
Map: See my website for a high-resolution map of this area.

Directions:
* From Salem, drive OR 22 east for 49 miles to a bridge immediately before you enter the town of Detroit. Do not cross the Breitenbush River and do not drive into Detroit.
* Directly before the bridge, turn left on French Creek Road [FR 2223] and follow this one-lane paved road 4 miles to a fork junction with FR 2207.
* Turn left and continue on FR 2223, now gravel, for exactly 3.9 very cliffy miles.
* The trailhead is unmarked on the left side of the road but is fairly obvious if you are paying attention. There is limited room for parking on the right near a cliff edge – if this is too much exposure for you, continue to a road junction about a quarter-mile further up the road.
* Beware that FR 2223 has steep drop-offs that will unnerve many drivers.

Hike: Set in a dark bowl above Detroit Lake and guarded jealously by a fascinating collection of rock pinnacles and spires, Tumble Lake is a setting fit for a Tolkien novel. It is a most worthwhile destination, but be prepared to work to get there. The hike in to the lake requires a steep descent through rough, brushy terrain – elevation you have to gain on your way back out. There are a number of excellent campsites around the lake. Know this – Tumble Lake is a fascinating place, one that you will want to visit over and over again.

The hike begins with a short uphill as you climb above FR 2223. Quickly gain a ridge and follow this ridgeline for 0.5 miles to a junction with the Tumble Lake Trail. The choice is yours as to when you want to go to Dome Rock (or if you want to go there) but it's probably easier to go before you hike down to Tumble Lake. To visit Dome Rock, continue past the Tumble Lake Trail for 0.4 mile to the spur trail to Dome Rock. Turn left and hike another 0.4 mile to the summit of Dome Rock, with its view of Mount Jefferson and Detroit Lake. You may decide that nothing is going to top this vista, but look down – doesn't Tumble Lake look inviting? You're here, after all – you should go for it. But know that the way out is a massive pain. Tumble Lake is worth the effort. Of course, if you came here all the way from the Tumble Trailhead on OR 22, you may not feel that way.

To hike to Tumble Lake, hike back down from the summit of Dome Rock and turn right. Follow the ridge crest for 0.4 miles to a junction with the trail down to Tumble Lake. Turn left and begin descending steeply through mixed forest. After switchbacking down for about 0.7 mile, the trail reaches a steep, rocky gully. This is the trail! Continue working your way downhill through this section, following the faint tread. Once you are down into the basin that holds Tumble Lake the trail begins to level out. Follow the trail through a brushy meadow as you work your way towards the lake. As you approach the lake, look out for shaggy-barked Alaska Cedars (which are quite rare this far south) and copious amounts of

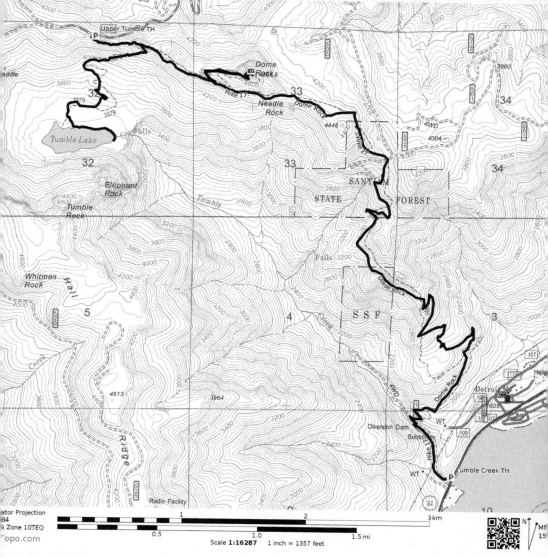

huckleberries, which ripen in August and September.

At 1.7 miles from your car (or 3.1 if you went to Dome Rock first), reach the lake and a number of attractive campsites. Look across the lake up to Needle Rock, Elephant Rock and other such rock pillars that loom above Tumble Lake. There is a nice beach on a series of rocky bluffs that is perfect for swimming at the south end of the lake. Continue following the user trail around the lake until you reach a logjam over placid Tumble Creek. Cross the creek and arrive at the rocky bluffs over the lake. This makes a suitable turnaround spot.

You might notice that Tumble Falls is only a few hundred yards downstream of the lake. While it is possible to follow user trails to an overlook of the falls, the view is disappointing and the terrain extremely steep. Thickets of rhododendron block travel on the west side of Tumble Creek, making for rough travel. Unless you simply have to see the top of the falls, it is best to just stay at Tumble Lake. Return the way you came.

19.   ELKHORN RIDGE

Distance: 5 miles out and back
Elevation Gain: 1,400 feet
Trailhead elevation: 3,827 feet
Trail high point: 4,740 feet
Season: June- November
Best: June- July
Map: Opal Creek Wilderness (Imus)

Directions:
- From Salem, drive OR 22 east for 23 miles to the second flashing light in Mehama.
- At a sign for the Little North Fork Recreation Area (and directly across from the North Fork Crossing restaurant), turn left.
- Follow the paved two-lane road up the Little North Fork for 14.5 miles to a junction with Elkhorn Drive SE in the small community of Elkhorn.
- Turn right and drive across the bridge over the river.
- Drive 6 miles of steep, twisting gravel road to a junction with the road to Elkhorn Lake.
- Keep right and drive another 1.5 miles to a road junction on your left. Though unsigned, this is the trailhead. There are a few spots to park on the side of FR 201, opposite the side road to your left.
- The trail departs steeply uphill from between the two roads.

Hike: The Elkhorn Ridge Trail is seldom maintained and is much worse for it. Were it not for such sporadic maintenance, this would be a fantastic and highly rewarding hike; as of now, it is all of those things but it also cannot be recommended for anybody other than those hikers who love bashing through brush and following faint trails.

The trail begins climbing steeply up Elkhorn Ridge, and wastes no time marching directly to the top of the ridge. After a half-mile or so, the trail levels out somewhat but this is where the blowdown begins in earnest. Thankfully, the trail is easy to follow. Once you are on the ridgetop, look for openings to your left; a quick jaunt off-trail leads to an outstanding clifftop viewpoint that stretches from Battle Ax and Mount Jefferson south to the Three Sisters. Watch your step here, as it's a long, long way down.

The trail follows the crest of the ridge up and down for another 2 miles, and for the most part is easy to follow. While the trail suffers from a lot of blowdown, the tread is good, the trail well-blazed and very easy to follow. When the trail descends off the ridge via a series of switchbacks at 2.5 miles, however, things fall apart. This is the end of the recommended hike.

Beyond this point, the trail becomes a series of frustrations. Slide alder and rhododendron crowd the trail, often obscuring it completely; the trail zigzags through a series of thickets and rockslides, sometimes changing direction in unexpected ways; and in some places, blowdown makes it very difficult to stay on the trail despite frequent and copious flagging. If you are in any way uncomfortable, you should turn around – even navigating with a GPS is difficult here.

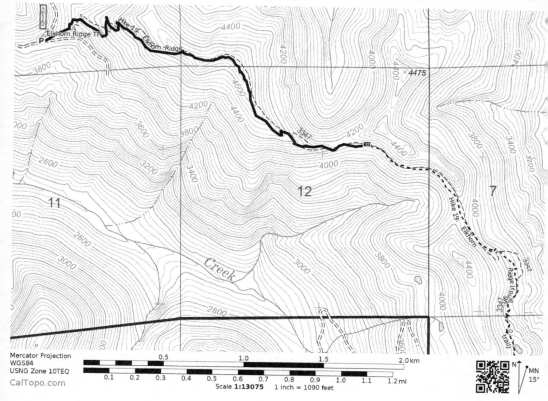

Mercator Projection
WGS84
USNG Zone 10TEQ
CalTopo.com

Scale **1:13075**   1 Inch = 1090 feet

At 3 miles, reach first a pond and then a small lake amidst old-growth hemlock, Douglas fir and Alaska cedar. From here, the trail climbs back up to a ridgetop, reaching the junction with the spur to Phantom Bridge at a downed log 4.4 miles from the trailhead. Turn left and walk fifty yards to the natural rock arch, hidden at the end of the ridge (see photo below). Return the way you came or organize a shuttle with the rest of the French Creek Ridge Trail, as noted in Hike 25.

Elkhorn Lake: Either before or after your hike, be sure to check out beautiful Elkhorn Lake. To find the lake, turn left at the unmarked junction 6 miles from the Little North Fork Road and drive down a few hundred yards to a small parking lot near the lake. A short trail leads to the lake, which is set in a classic old-growth forest and features several excellent campsites. The lake also supports an unusually large population of salamanders. Unfortunately the campsites near the lake are frequently trashed by less considerate outdoor lovers, and you may want to bring some garbage bags to help clean up. In spite of these issues this is a very beautiful place, and one worthy of visiting again and again.

20.   LITTLE NORTH SANTIAM RIVER

Distance: 9 miles out and back
Elevation Gain: 1,800 feet
Trailhead elevation: 1,294 feet
Trail high point: 1,791 feet
Season: all year
Best: all year, but especially October- April
Map: Opal Creek Wilderness (Imus)

Directions:
- From Salem, drive OR 22 east for 23 miles to the second flashing light in Mehama.
- At a sign for the Little North Fork Recreation Area (and directly across from the North Fork Crossing restaurant), turn left.
- Follow the paved two-lane road up the Little North Fork for 14.5 miles to a junction with Elkhorn Drive SE in the small community of Elkhorn.
- Turn right and drive across the bridge over the river.
- Drive 0.5 mile to the trailhead, a parking lot on your right with a signboard.

Hike: The Little North Santiam River Trail gets no respect. It has the same emerald pools, roaring waterfalls, magnificent old-growth as Opal Creek, just three miles upstream, with just a fraction of the crowds. Few people come here except on summer weekends, and the area's low elevation makes this a year-round hike destination. In many respects, this hike is even better on a rainy winter day.

The trail begins at the edge of the small community of Elkhorn. You will skirt through a re-covering forest with houses in sight for the first 0.2 mile before crossing a small side stream and descending into glorious woods beside the even more glorious Little North Santiam. Everything is green, moist and radiant! At 0.6 mile follow a short side trail to a bench beside a roaring cascade in the river. This is a great place to relax but don't turn back yet as the best is yet to come! The next mile is a joy as you wind through deep forest just above the Little North Santiam, crossing roaring side creeks on scenic wooden bridges beneath towering Douglas firs. Notice how the river seems to be an electric shade of green; this is not the water but the green rock below magnified by the incredible clarity of the water. This feature is common throughout the Little North Santiam drainage and is found on all of the creeks upstream.

Soon the canyon begins to contract and the trail climbs to avoid a very narrow gorge. Along the way up, listen for the roar of Triple Falls on Henline Creek, tumbling directly into the river just across the gorge. The falls is visible but tree branches make it difficult to get an unobstructed view of the falls. Once past the falls, the trail continues its climb up the canyon wall, topping out at a rocky bluff high above the river with a view across to Henline Mountain's cliffs. Note the madrone tree on this bluff, a rarity in the Cascades. This makes a nice spot to stop and catch your breath and if it's clear, the views of the Little North Santiam canyon will be outstanding. The trail stays high above the river for a bit before dropping swiftly back to river level at 3.0 miles.

At 3.3 miles, you can look across the river to Three Pools, a popular day-use site. Here the

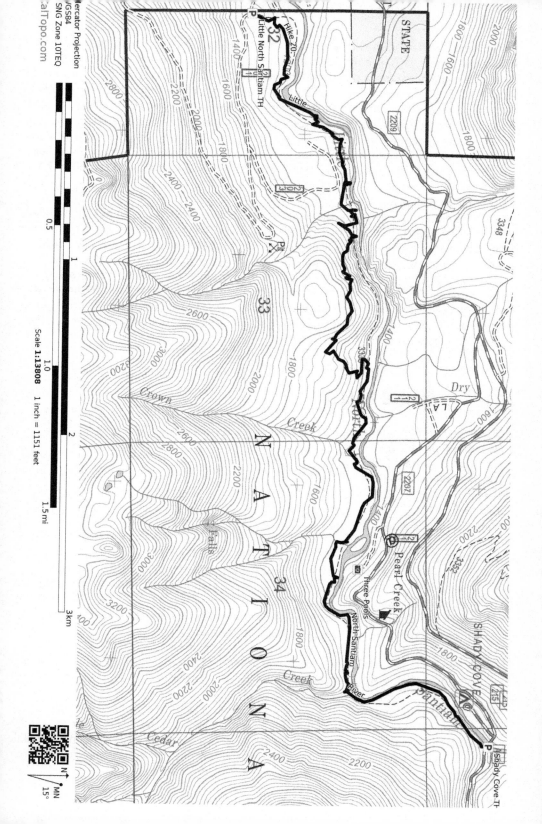

Little North Santiam roars through a series of narrow rock channels, creating three deep, swimmable pools. A single rock pillar stands sentinel above the scene. Downstream the river flows gently through a placid stretch of water that is almost too green to be believed. Three Pools is extremely popular on summer weekends...and is almost deserted in other seasons. Sadly, you cannot cross the river here (consider stopping by after the hike) so continue hiking upstream. Along the way you'll cross Little Cedar Creek on a new bridge before reaching the upper trailhead, at a scenic wooden road bridge over the Little North Santiam River 4.5 miles from your car. Across the river is lovely Shady Cove Campground. You could shuttle this hike but then, you won't have the pleasure of hiking it again, now will you?

Other hiking options:
Cedar Creek: I'm going to tell you a secret: in the winter when snow blocks the upper reaches of FR 2207, this road walk is a pleasant and occasionally gorgeous alternative to the Little North Santiam River Trail or a peaceful and scenic addition to your day's adventure. Follow the gravel forest road south from Shady Cove Campground for 1.8 miles as it winds through old-growth Douglas firs above roaring Cedar Creek to Sullivan Creek Falls. User paths lead to impressive and seldom-visited waterfalls on Cedar Creek in the vicinity of Sullivan Creek Falls. Following these cascades, the road continues 1.1 mile further to a bridge over Cedar Creek. Make this your turnaround spot, as FR 2207 begins a climb up the ridge, leaving the creek for good.

21. HENLINE FALLS

Distance: 2 miles out and back
Elevation Gain: 400 feet
Trailhead elevation: 1,559 feet
Trail high point: 1,900 feet
Season: all year
Best: March- May
Map: Opal Creek Wilderness (Imus)

Directions:
- From Salem, drive OR 22 east for 23 miles to the second flashing light in Mehama.
- At a sign for the Little North Fork Recreation Area (and directly across from the North Fork Crossing restaurant), turn left.
- Follow the paved two-lane road up the Little North Fork for 15 miles to the end of pavement at the entrance to the Willamette National Forest.
- Continue another 1.5 miles of gravel road to a junction with FR 2207.
- Continue straight and drive just 0.1 mile to the signed Henline Falls Trailhead on your left. There is room for 3 – 4 cars at the trailhead.

Hike: Located only a few miles from Opal Creek, Henline Falls has long been a popular hiking destination. Once the site of the Ogle Mountain mine, the trail to the falls is easy and beautiful. Hikers with more energy can explore the viewless and steep Ogle Mountain Trail, adding extra miles onto the day's hike. Note that some of this trail was damaged in a fire in 2015; expect a few downed trees and blackened scenery for several years.

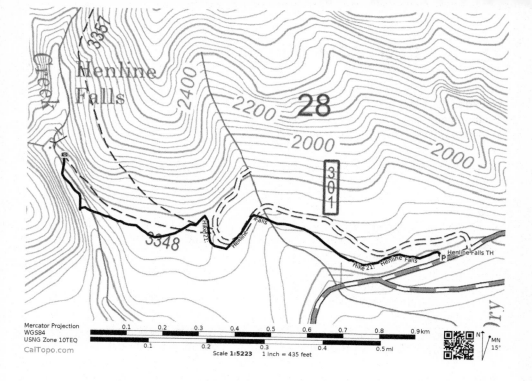

Begin with the easy hike to Henline Falls. This short trail follows an old roadbed 0.5 mile to a trail junction. Turn left to continue on the Henline Falls Trail (right climbs steeply through the forest on the Ogle Mountain Trail). You will cut through a replanted forest of tall, thin trees another 0.4 mile to the falls, a 126-foot plunge into a narrow canyon. Remnants of a mining tramway can be found directly in front of the falls. If you come here in the winter you will almost certainly be soaked by the spray the waterfall puts off. It is possible to scramble up the rocks to the immediate right of the falls to a mine shaft, now closed to public access. Though less than 2 miles round trip, you could easily spend two hours here – between the photographic opportunities, the mine shaft and mining relics, there is a great deal to see. When you are done, return the way you came or spend an hour exploring the Ogle Mountain Trail (to do so, turn left at the trail junction halfway back to your car).

Ogle Mountain:

To hike the Ogle Mountain Trail, return to the junction 0.5 mile from Henline Falls and turn left. Despite its name, the trail goes nowhere near Ogle Mountain or its famed mine. Instead, the rough and rocky trail climbs steeply above Henline Creek's canyon to a bench above the cascading creek. Some adventurous hikers use the trail to access the numerous off-trail waterfalls on Henline Creek, but the trail goes nowhere near these falls - instead, it continues climbing until it ends at the National Forest boundary about a mile from the Henline Falls junction.

The trail is rough and rocky, and is very infrequently hiked. In truth, it isn't really worth your time unless you have a lot of energy and time to kill. It doesn't really go anywhere, has no views to speak of and is at times very narrow. There are a few spots where the trail passes above Henline Creek's narrow gorge that will intimidate hikers with a fear of heights. Regardless, some will love this trail for those qualities. Return the way you came.

22. HENLINE MOUNTAIN

Distance: 7.6 miles out and back
Elevation Gain: 3,000 feet
Trailhead elevation: 1,879 feet
Trail high point: 4,620 feet
Season: May- November
Best: May- June
Map: Opal Creek Wilderness (Imus)

Directions:
- From Salem, drive OR 22 east for 23 miles to the second flashing light in Mehama.
- At a sign for the Little North Fork Recreation Area (and directly across from the North Fork Crossing restaurant), turn left.
- Follow the paved two-lane road up the Little North Fork for 15 miles to the end of pavement at the entrance to the Willamette National Forest.
- Continue another 1.5 miles of gravel road to a junction with FR 2207.
- Following signs for Opal Creek, keep straight (left) on FR2209 and continue 1 mile to the poorly-signed trailhead on your left. There is room on the right side of the road for 3 – 4 cars. Look for the trail cutting out of the slope uphill to your left.

Hike: Henline Mountain dominates the canyon of the Little North Santiam River. Driving west from Opal Creek, its crags impress even the most unimpressed hikers. It seems a herculean feat to get up to the summit of Henline, and yet the trail to its summit is surprisingly moderate. Don't get me wrong – you are going to gain 3,000 feet in just 3.8 miles, but that seems incongruous with how impressive Henline Mountain is relative to its surroundings.

Begin by hiking uphill from FR 2209. The trail wastes no time beginning its climb. During your ascent, watch out for poison oak, rare elsewhere in this area but common on the lower reaches of this trail. On the way up you will pass by nearby cliffs but the trail never approaches them, instead staying in the forest for most of the first 2 miles. After this the trail begins to open up, alternating forest with meadows of beargrass and manzanita where views begin to open up of the Little North Santiam River's long canyon. Switchback around a series of talus slopes with views out to nearby Nasty Rock and then pass by a series of cliffs to a junction at about 3 miles from the trailhead. Turn right and walk 50 yards to an open viewpoint, the site of Henline Mountain's long-gone lookout. All that remains are the views, which are outstanding! Follow the Little North Santiam's canyon to hatchet-shaped Battle Ax and out to Mount Jefferson. Most hikers will want to turn around here but dedicated hikers will enjoy the rougher trip up to the true summit of Henline Mountain.

Walk back to the junction near the lookout site and turn right. From here to the true summit the trail is maintained by volunteers and while still easy to follow, is rougher and steeper. Climb and descend on a rollercoaster ride of ups and downs until you reach the true summit at 3.8 miles from the trailhead. The views are more limited than at the lookout site but do extend north to Mount Hood as well as much of the Bull of the Woods Wilderness. The trail ends at the true summit in a tangled grove of second-growth forest. Return the way you came.

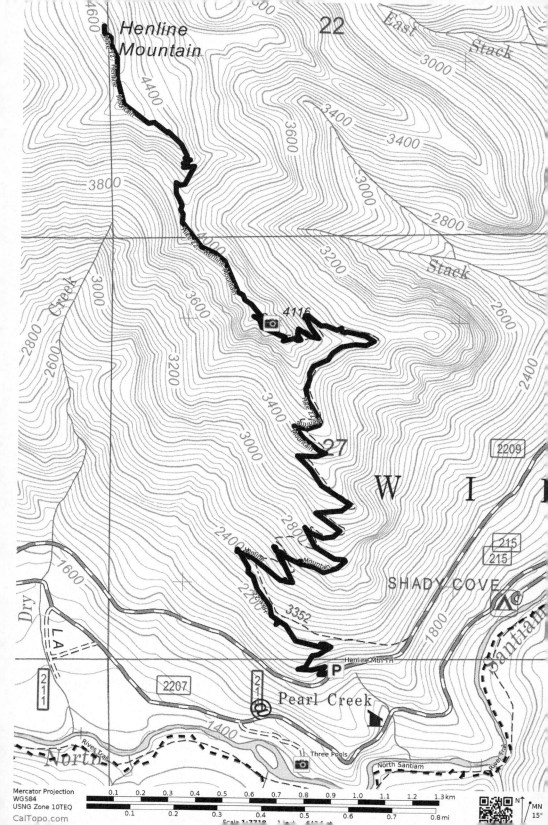

23. OPAL CREEK

Distance: 10.8 miles out and back (semi-loop)
Elevation Gain: 1,500 feet (expect lots of minor ups and downs)
Trailhead elevation: 1,952 feet
Trail high point: 2,372 feet
Season: all year except in winter storms
Best: April- May, October
Map: Opal Creek Wilderness (Imus)
Map note: See my website for a high-resolution map of this hike.

Directions:
- From Salem, drive OR 22 east for 23 miles to the second flashing light in Mehama.
- At a sign for the Little North Fork Recreation Area (and directly across from the North Fork Crossing restaurant), turn left.
- Follow the paved two-lane road up the Little North Fork for 15 miles to the end of pavement at the entrance to the Willamette National Forest.
- Continue another 1.5 miles of gravel road to a junction with FR 2207.
- Following signs for Opal Creek, keep straight (left) on FR2209 and continue 4.2 miles to the trailhead at a large metal gate on the road. There is room for several dozen cars to park – and yet the trailhead will be full on many nice weekends.
- A Northwest Forest Pass is required to park at the trailhead. There is a feebox located at the signboard just before the gate.

Hike: With its ancient forests and emerald pools, Opal Creek is justifiably famous. In the 1980s, this was the site of one of Oregon's fiercest battles over the fate of the area's magnificent groves of old-growth timber. Many years of citizen activism saved the grove, and today you can enjoy one of Oregon's special places in peace and quiet. Though the hike is extremely popular, the area holds people well and feels solitary even when there are dozens of cars at the trailhead.

The trail to Jawbone Flats is actually a road, one that only the handful of employees of the Opal Creek Ancient Forest Center residents are permitted to drive. Pass the gate and set off on a slight downhill course. After 0.4 miles cross Gold Creek on a high and rustic bridge. Look down to your left at the waterfall on Gold Creek and the emerald-green pool below; it is the first of many such pools you will see on this hike. Continue to a junction with the Whetstone Mountain Trail and keep straight. The road skirts a cliff on a series of half-bridges at 1.2 miles and enters gorgeous cathedral forest of Douglas firs. This is one of the most photogenic groves of ancient forest you will ever see; mosses drape down off the understory while giants frame the old road on each side. At 2.1 miles pass the remnants of Mertin Mill and take a short side trail down to Sawmill Falls (also known as Cascadia de los Niños), a 20-foot plunge on the Little North Santiam River. Be careful around the rocks as they can be slippery and the pools are deep on each side of the rock.

After returning to the main trail, ignore the Kopetski Trail junction 0.2 mile later (this is your return route) and continue down the old road another 1.2 miles to the rustic village of Jawbone Flats. Built on the site of the Santiam Indians' winter retreat, Jawbone Flats is a former mining town that has been converted into a non-profit educational retreat. You can

Opal Pool from creek level. This is a popular swimming hole in the summer.

rent restored cabins and bunkhouses and munch on delicious vegetarian cuisine at reasonable rates should you decide against roughing it on an overnight into the area. Be sure to reserve your room well in advance!

If you aren't staying the night in Jawbone Flats, head straight through town and turn right, crossing Battle Ax Creek and following signs for Opal Pool. Please stay on the main road and respect the privacy of the residents and guests. After leaving town, the road becomes narrow and rocky and you come to a junction with the trail down to Opal Pool. If you are ready to turn around, turn right here for a loop back to the trailhead; otherwise continue 100 yards further up the road and turn right on the Kopetski Trail.

The Kopetski Trail switchbacks into the ancient forest above Opal Creek. Continuing upstream alongside magnificent Opal Creek, you will pass more giant trees while the creek tumbles over ledges into deep green pools, each more beautiful than the last. It is almost impossible to avoid stopping over and over again to take pictures. The Opal Creek trail winds uphill a bit and then descends quickly into Cedar Flats at 5.2 miles from the trailhead. A collection of thousand year-old cedars that lord over a campground beside Opal Creek, Cedar Flats is where most hikers and backpackers turn around – and this is where you should turn around. Though the trail does continue beyond the flats, it becomes rough, faint and difficult to follow as it navigates through ancient forest. It does not really go anywhere; don't bother unless you love climbing around on huge fallen trees, clawing through rhododendrons and searching for elusive waterfalls hidden down in Opal Creek's canyon. I have tried this many times; it is a lot of fun but the terrain is absolutely unforgiving and the scenery not any better than what you've already seen.

On your return you can and should make a loop by turning left at the sign for Opal Pool just before you enter Jawbone Flats. You will descend a switchback to a bridge over Opal Pool, where you can follow user trails to the base of Opal Pool. Hiking downstream, you'll pass through spectacular old-growth forest and stellar vistas of the Little North Santiam River to your right. At 1.5 miles from Opal Pool, the trail forks right to cross the bridge over the river. Across the river, turn left on the road to return to your car.

24.   WHETSTONE MOUNTAIN LOOP

Distance: 16.2 mile loop
Elevation Gain: 4,000 feet
Trailhead elevation: 1,952 feet
Trail high point: 4,970 feet
Season: June- October
Best: June- October
Map: Opal Creek Wilderness (Imus)
Map: See my website for a high-resolution map of this hike.

Directions:
•   See directions for Opal Creek (Hike 23).

Hike: The Opal Creek Wilderness is one of Oregon's most special places. Crystalline waters flow over numerous waterfalls into emerald green pools that seem impossibly deep. Massive and ancient Douglas firs and cedars seem as tall as the rocky peaks that loom above. One visit to this area will hook you for life. Amazingly, the area in and around the Little North Santiam River and Opal Creek came perilously close to being logged numerous times in the 1980s; it took a large citizen campaign and many compromises to secure the preservation of this special, special place. To truly take in all that the Opal Creek Wilderness has to offer, hike high and low on this full tour of the Opal Creek Wilderness. While the loop described below is a worthy trip for a long dayhike, perhaps the best way to see this area is on a longer multi-day trek that also visits Battle Ax and Battle Ax Creek in addition to Whetstone Mountain.

Pass the gate and set off on a slight downhill course on the closed road. After 0.4 miles you will cross Gold Creek on a high and rustic bridge. Continue 0.2 mile to a well-signed junction with the Whetstone Mountain Trail. Here turn left and begin climbing above Gold Creek on what is actually an old mining road. After approximately 1 mile, the trail switchbacks to the right and begins a gradual climb out of Gold Creek's canyon on a long series of switchbacks. In June this section of trail explodes with pink rhododendrons. The grade stiffens as you begin to furiously climb a series of switchbacks before the trail levels out some in a dense old-growth forest. The going now becomes much easier, as you approach the summit of Whetstone Mountain.

At 5 miles from the trailhead, reach an unsigned junction with a short spur to the summit of Whetstone Mountain's former lookout site. Turn left and switchback up to the summit, where you will be treated with a view that stretches from Mount Rainier to the Three Sisters. Mount Jefferson rises above hatchet-shaped Battle Ax (Hike 24). The valleys of Opal

Battle Ax Creek upstream of the Gold Creek Trail.

and Battle Ax Creeks stretch out beneath you. Even though you have hiked just 5.3 miles, you may be tempted to stop for lunch here. If you're here for the dayhike, it is better to continue, as you still have almost 10 miles to go.

Following the summit, descend down into old-growth subalpine woods for 1 mile to a junction with the Whetstone Mountain Trail. Didn't you just hike to Whetstone Mountain? Yes, you did; this trail arrives from the north (see Hike 6) and is a much shorter approach to the summit. Continue straight through magnificent old-growth forest another 0.8 miles to a signed junction with the Gold Creek Trail on your right, which is, in fact, a continuation of the very trail you've been hiking. As is the case with most trails in this area, the sign reads only the trail's number. To return to Opal Creek and your car, turn right on the Gold Creek Trail (3369).

The Gold Creek Trail drops to the bottom of Battle Ax Creek's canyon via a series of well-graded switchbacks. Despite its remoteness and obscurity, the trail is shockingly well-maintained and has an excellent tread. Just 2.1 miles from the trail junction at the ridge top (and 1,600 of elevation lower), you reach a bridgeless crossing of Battle Ax Creek. If you've come here in June or July the creek might be raging from snowmelt further upstream but later on it is easy to cross dry-footed on rocks laid across the creek. Once across the creek, you will switchback up to a junction with the Battle Ax Creek Trail. Turn right and hike the road just under 2.7 miles to a junction with the trail down to Opal Pool. Here you are faced with a choice: it's 4.1 miles back to your car if you detour via the Kopetski Trail, and 3.5 miles if you just continue down the road. I recommend turning left, crossing Opal Creek and hiking the Kopetski Trail until you cross the Little North Santiam River just upstream of Merten Mill. At a junction with the Jawbone Flats road, turn left and hike 2.3 miles back to the trailhead.

EXTENDING YOUR TRIP:
If your goal is a longer trip, you can make a 3-day loop out of the Whetstone, Bagby and Battle Ax Creek Trails. This is an enticing but difficult trip, and one I never completed. I will describe it for you as it was described to me. The total loop is about 25 miles with nearly 5,000 feet of elevation gain. Expect to encounter faint and brushy trails, long stretches without water and poor campsites throughout.

From the junction of the Whetstone and Gold Creek Trails on Whetstone Ridge, continue straight 2.2 miles to a junction with the Bagby Trail. Turn right and hike south on the Bagby Trail, which here can be very brushy and overgrown. After 1 mile, you come to a junction with the Twin Lakes Trail (573). Continue straight another 1.5 miles to a junction with the Battle Ax Mountain Trail. Turn right here and climb over the summit of Battle Ax before dropping down to Beachie Saddle at 2.7 miles from the previous junction. Turn right on the Battle Ax Creek Trail to continue the loop.

The Battle Ax Creek Trail (3339) descends into its namesake canyon on the remains of a road that once connected Elk Lake to Jawbone Flats. The way is a bit rough, overgrown and has few scenic highlights. You'll cross several creeks and hike through a peaceful forest for 4.4 miles to a junction with the Gold Creek Trail (3369) on your right.

From the junction, the trail follows the creek at a safe distance for 2.5 miles, passing several old mines. Keep left at both forks on this trail / road. Eventually you will descend to a trail junction on your left signed for Opal Pool. From here you are on familiar ground: left follows the river on the Kopetski Trail while straight leads you to Jawbone Flats. Either way takes you back to the trailhead.

25. PHANTOM BRIDGE AND OPAL LAKE

	Phantom Bridge	Opal Lake
Distance:	4.8 miles out & back	1.6 miles out & back
Elevation Gain:	1,900 feet	400 feet
Trailhead Elevation:	4,086 feet	3,708 feet
Trail High Point:	4,598 feet	3,708 feet
Season:	June- October	June- October
Best:	June- October	June- October
Map:	Opal Creek Wilderness (Imus)	Opal Creek Wilderness (Imus)

Directions:
- From Salem, drive OR 22 east for 48 miles to the town of Detroit.
- Immediately before you cross the Breitenbush River, turn left on the French Creek Road (FR 2223). Do not continue into Detroit!
- Drive north on this paved road for 4 miles to a fork in the road, a junction with FR 2207.

Opal Lake on a rainy, misty day. The trail drops down from the other side of the lake.

- Fork to the right onto FR 2207 and drive 3.6 miles of narrow and occasionally cliffy gravel road to a pass. Turn right here into a small parking lot, which is for both the trail to Phantom Bridge and the French Creek Ridge Trail (Hike 26).
- Opal Lake's unmarked trailhead is another 2.1 miles down this road to the north.
- **Warning**: The last two miles of FR 2207 hug a huge cliff and can be frightening for people with a fear of heights. Exercise caution.
- **Note**: You can also drive to this spot by driving to the upper trailhead for the Little North Santiam River Trail (Hike 20) at Shady Cove Campground and continuing on FR 2207 for 10.2 more miles to the French Creek / Phantom Bridge Trailhead. This drive is much longer, is maintained less frequently, and is just as cliffy as the preferred option.

Hike: Though short, the trails to Phantom Bridge and Opal Lake are steep, infrequently maintained and absolutely gorgeous. The up-and-down trail to Phantom Bridge's natural rock arch leads over a rugged, highly scenic ridge while the steep trail down to Opal Lake is a miserable 15 minutes that leads to one of the prettiest lakes in this part of the Cascades. If you've got the energy, the patience and the intestinal fortitude to drive the scary gravel road to the trailhead, this makes for an ideal day in the mountains.

Begin by hiking uphill on a narrow, brushy trail towards Phantom Bridge. The trail begins an up and down traverse along the ridge, mostly in the forest. Though the trail is brushy, it is never difficult to follow. Keep an eye for some blowdown. The trail winds around Dog Tooth Rock, climbs up to a knoll, and then drops to a junction at shallow, brush-lined Cedar Lake at 1.3 miles. The trail heading downhill to your right leads to FR 2207 and then Opal Lake; instead, keep straight here and begin climbing anew on trail that is plagued with blowdown. Soon you will reach the ridgetop, where views stretch from Mount Hood to the

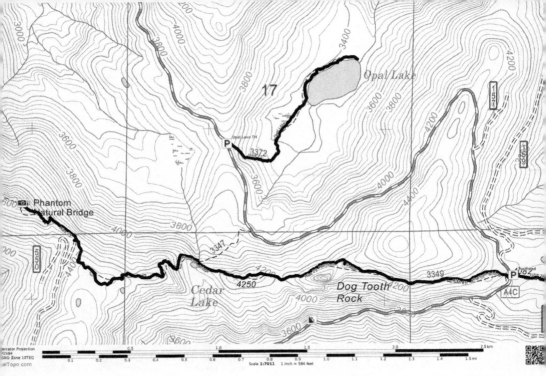

Three Sisters. Cairns help lead the way across the ridge, as the trail up here is faint. Soon you will drop again, and the trail seems to end at an old trailhead at the end of FR 2233. Don't bother trying to drive here- one wrong turn and you'll regret you ever tried! On the far end of this parking lot, look for the trail heading straight uphill, following the ridge. Climb uphill another 0.3 mile to Phantom Bridge's unmarked spur trail, located at a cairn where a large log has fallen across the trail. Turn right here and walk fifty yards to the arch. Getting a good photo is very difficult, as most angles only reveal bad photos. Some people do walk out onto the arch, but I cannot recommend this to anybody. Please don't try this!

To hike to Opal Lake, you have two choices: you can return to the French Creek Ridge trailhead and drive 1.7 miles to the Opal Lake Trailhead, or you can hike there from the junction near Cedar Lake and then return to your car by walking FR 2207. Either is a good option. To hike down from Cedar Lake, return to the junction and drop down a narrow but generally well-maintained trail 0.5 mile to an unmarked trailhead on FR 2207. Turn left here and walk 0.3 mile to the Opal Lake Trailhead, marked by a signboard. To drive to this spot, drive down FR 2207 another 2.1 miles from the French Creek Ridge Trailhead to the Opal Lake Trailhead on the road.

The Opal Lake Trail drops down steeply, mostly in a rocky gully, into Opal Lake's basin. Once you reach the bottom of the valley, the trail pushes through a brushy, mushy swamp until you reach the lakeshore at 0.5 mile from the trailhead. The lake is absolutely gorgeous, set in a deep bowl of ancient forest. A trail leads around the north side of the lake to its outlet – the swampy origins of the famed Opal Creek. There are a few excellent campsites on this side of the lake should you wish to backpack. When you are done, return to the Opal Lake Trailhead and your vehicle, or if you came down here from Phantom Bridge, turn left and walk the road 2.1 miles to the French Creek Ridge Trailhead.

26. FRENCH CREEK RIDGE

Distance: 5.6 miles out and back
Elevation Gain: 1,100 feet
Trailhead elevation: 4.086 feet
Trail high point: 4,979 feet
Season: June- October
Best: June- July
Map: See my website for a high-resolution map of this hike.

Directions:
* See directions for Phantom Bridge (Hike 25).

Hike: A continuation of the Elkhorn Ridge and Phantom Bridge Trails, the French Creek Ridge Trail is just like its two predecessors to the west: it climbs up and down on a scenic ridge amidst old-growth forest, features fantastic views, and suffers from a chronic lack of trail maintenance. Most should plan on a moderate hike to a series of rock formations on the ridge; adventurous hikers can continue on a much fainter, rougher trail to the summit of Mount Beachie.

The trail begins at the signboard on the east side of the trailhead. You'll be hiking on an old roadbed at first, one that is overgrown with rhododendron and huckleberry. The trail seems overly brushy at first, but improves once you enter ancient forest at the base of rugged Marten Buttes. You'll emerge at the foot of the rocky butte and its talus slopes at about 1 mile from the trailhead. Downhill in the canyon below is famed Opal Creek, with the peaks of the Bull of the Woods Wilderness on the horizon. Over the next 1.8 miles, you'll have excellent views as the trail skirts the ridgetop. In general, this stretch of trail is in pretty good shape.

At 2.5 miles from the trailhead, the trail passes under a series of rock castles and shortly thereafter, descends to a saddle where you meet the Beachie Trail. The French Creek Trail actually turns right here, descending around Byars Peak to a very remote and hard-to-find trailhead in the cliffs above Detroit. The recommended hike ends at this trail junction, as both trails are seldom maintained and occasionally difficult to follow.

Should you wish to continue, turn left on the Beachie Trail and descend steeply for 0.3 mile until the trail levels out on the wide saddle between Boulder Peak and Mount Beachie. This stretch of trail is extremely brushy and sometimes difficult to follow. Continue another 0.3 mile to an open spot on the ridge- a quick scramble up the talus slope here reveals fantas- tic views and an excellent place to eat lunch. This viewpoint is so good there's basically no point in continuing. If you choose to do so, the French Creek Ridge Trail (now known as the Beachie Trail) continues a little under a mile to near the summit of Mount Beachie; before the trail begins to descend, you can turn right and bushwhack to the summit of Mount Beachie, just above Elk Lake. From here, the Beachie Trail curves around the far side of Mount Beachie and descends 2.5 rough and brushy miles to an old, abandoned trailhead at Beachie Saddle. Here, you can connect to the hikes to Whetstone Mountain (Hike 24) and Battle Ax (Hike 27), while Elk Lake is about 1 mile downhill from here.

27.   BATTLE AX

Distance: 6 mile loop
Elevation Gain: 2,300 feet elevation gain
Trailhead elevation: 4,022 feet
Trail high point: 5,559 feet
Season: July- October
Best: July- October
Map: Opal Creek Wilderness (Imus)

Directions:
- From Salem, drive OR 22 for 49 miles to Detroit.
- Immediately after crossing the Breitenbush River, turn left at a sign for Breitenbush and Elk Lake on FR 46.
- Drive 4.5 miles to a poorly-signed junction with FR 4696.
- Turn left here and drive this paved road 0.8 mile to a junction with FR 4697.
- Turn left again, pass a sign stating that this road is not maintained for passenger cars and begin climbing. The first two miles of this road are good gravel but soon the road becomes rough and rocky.
- After 4.5 miles, turn left at a junction marked only by a green post to continue on FR 4697.
- Drive 1.4 rough, rocky miles to a bridge over Elk Lake Creek at the east end of Elk Lake.
- Continue another 0.6 mile of terrible road to a sign for Elk Lake's campground. There are several wide spots here where you can park. Do not drive any further up the road, as it deteriorates past this point until it is soon impassable.
- Be very aware of your car's ability to handle FR 4697 – a vehicle with low clearance and good tires can handle these roads if you drive very, very slowly. Vehicles with higher clearance will manage just fine.

Hike: No matter where you are in this part of the Cascades, Battle Ax's rugged, sharp profile seems to be on the horizon. As you would expect, the view at the summit is impressive, encompassing pretty much everything from Mount Rainier to Diamond Peak. With such a great view and only a moderate hike to the summit, you would also expect this hike to be popular, and it is; but beware: the drive to the Battle Ax trailhead is a massive pain in the butt. Of course, getting there is half the fun, and once you're there, you won't want to leave anytime soon. It's a good thing there's a campground right at the trailhead!

Begin your hike at a parking spot near the campground spur. You'll walk up the road for 0.3 mile to the Bagby Trailhead on your right. This is the start of your loop. Continue walking up the road as it rapidly deteriorates into a narrow, brushy trail. At 1 mile from the campground, reach Battle Ax's former trailhead at Beachie Saddle. The saddle is in fact a 4-way trail junction: on your left is the seldom-used Beachie Trail (see Hike 26), while the equally quiet Battle Ax Creek Trail (actually an old mining road) continues downhill ahead of you, reaching Jawbone Flats after 6.5 rough miles (see Hike 24). For Battle Ax, turn right on the Battle Ax Trail.

As you ascend, views open up at every step. Look down to deep blue Elk Lake and out to Mount Jefferson. Paintbrush and beargrass line the way up. You will pass some strange,

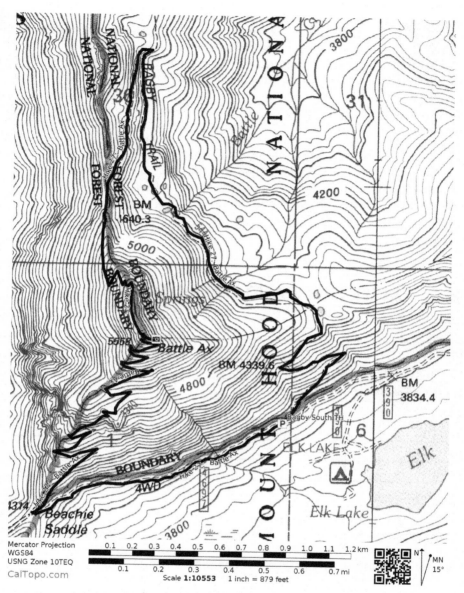

Mercator Projection
WGS84
USNG Zone 10TEQ
CalTopo.com

Scale **1:10553**   1 inch = 879 feet

fluted rock formations that are fascinating to investigate. After 1.5 miles of gradual climbing, you will reach the 5,558 foot summit of Battle Ax. The view is fantastic. Look north to Mount Hood and the entirety of the Bull of the Woods Wilderness, scarred in 2010 and 2011 fires. East is hulking Mount Jefferson, and to the south, views stretch to the south all the way to Diamond Peak. The concrete blocks at the summit are the remnants of an erstwhile lookout building; three separate lookouts stood on the summit here, the last of which was removed in the late 1960s.

Before you continue on your loop, take a minute to hike down the southeast side of Battle Ax to a breathtaking viewpoint almost directly above Elk Lake – you are close enough to hear people conversing in the campground from this vantage point! Then hike back up to the summit and look behind and to the left of the summit block for the continuation of the trail. The next mile begins following the ridgeline of Battle Ax, offering more spectacular views, but eventually begins to steeply switchback down the back side of the mountain. When you reach a junction with the Bagby Trail (544), turn right.

From here the way is easy going as the trail traverses around a couple of talus slopes and passes a few small ponds. After a mile or so, reach a series of springs that flow through a massive rockslide where wild rose and other brush crowds the trail. Springs here will necessitate rock hopping for much of the hiking season. For this reason, long pants and good boots are a good idea! Following this section, the trail is once again easy. Reach a viewpoint out to Elk Lake and Mount Jefferson before switchbacking down to the Bagby Trailhead on FR 4697. Turn left to hike 0.3 mile to your car.

28. BATTLE CREEK AND EMERALD POOL

	Battle Creek	Emerald Pool
Distance:	8.2 miles out & back	12.2 miles out & back
Elevation Gain:	1,200 feet	1,600 feet
Trailhead Elevation:	3,789 feet	3,789 feet
Trail High Point:	3,890 feet	3,890 feet
Season:	June- October	June- October
Best:	June- October	June- October
Map:	See map on my website.	See map on my website.

Directions:
- From Salem, drive OR 22 for 49 miles to Detroit.
- Immediately after crossing the Breitenbush River, turn left at a sign for Breitenbush and Elk Lake on FR 46.
- Drive 4.5 miles to a poorly-signed junction with FR 4696.
- Turn left here and drive this paved road 0.8 mile to a junction with FR 4697.
- Turn left again, pass a sign stating that this road is not maintained for passenger cars and begin climbing. The first two miles of this road are good gravel but soon the road becomes rough and rocky.
- After 4.5 miles, turn left at a junction marked only by a green post to continue on FR 4697.
- Drive 1.4 rough, rocky miles to a bridge over Elk Lake Creek at the east end of Elk Lake.
- The trailhead is at a signboard just after the road crosses the creek.
- Be very aware of your car's ability to handle FR 4697 – a vehicle with low clearance and good tires can handle these roads if you drive very, very slowly. Vehicles with higher clearance will manage just fine.

Elk Lake and Battle Ax in morning light.

Hike: This is a hike in reverse, starting at Elk Lake and dropping down to the former site of the Battle Creek shelter in the dark green heart of the Bull of the Woods Wilderness. Energetic hikers can continue downstream another 2 miles (enduring two major creek crossings on the way) to Emerald Pool, an unforgettable abyss of deep green water on Elk Lake Creek. The lower segment of this hike is described in Hikes 11 and 12.

Begin at Elk Lake. On the east end of the lake, look for the Elk Lake Creek Trail, departing from a signboard. The trail sets off into a stupendous forest of massive Douglas firs, some of them as large as eight feet thick. The first mile of the trail is a feast of the senses, as the trail cuts a path through this magnificent woods. You will of course need to lose some elevation, but for the first three miles or so the path is relatively level as it follows Elk Lake Creek at a distance. The creek is out of sight to the east as it tumbles through a gorge of hidden waterfalls few have ever seen.

The serious descent begins at about mile 3, but even then it's never steep. The trail switchbacks down into Elk Lake Creek's deep canyon, reaching the creek at 4 miles from the trailhead. Just a few short steps later, meet the Mother Lode Trail (see Hike 12) at the site of the old Battle Creek Shelter, which collapsed under the weight of winter snow in 1988. There is an excellent campsite here where the shelter once stood, and exploration of the flats here will reveal many more excellent campsites. This is an excellent place to turn around if you are up for a moderate hike. If you have more energy, the best is yet to come as you continue downstream along Elk Lake Creek.

The good stuff comes with a price, and you'll find your first payment waiting for you just 0.1 mile from the Mother Lode junction: an unbridged crossing of Battle Creek. The crossing is easy enough most of the time, and late in the year you may be able to escape with dry feet. The best strategy is to remove your boots and wade. On the far side, the trail begins a climb up and over a narrow spot in the canyon. This stretch of trail is often brushy. At 1.6 miles from the Mother Lode junction, you'll find your next payment: a crossing of Elk Lake Creek proper. As with the crossing of Battle Creek, the best strategy is to remove your boots and wade. On the far side, the next 0.4 mile is wildly scenic as the trail hugs a mossy bench above the creek. At 2 miles from the Mother Lode junction (and 6.1 miles from the trailhead), reach Emerald Pool. The pool is a deep hole in the creek, so deep that swimming here is actually pretty intimidating. The fish who live here have no such problem, and you will almost certainly see some of the trout who call this place home. This is a special place.

Return the way you came, remembering that you still have two creek crossings on your return. Continuing downstream, it's 3.3 miles to the remote northern trailhead. A car shuttle is possible but extremely time-consuming; see hike 11 for more details.

EXTENDING YOUR TRIP:
Twin Lakes Loop: You can make a number of loops here. Perhaps the easiest is to hike down to Battle Creek shelter site, where you meet the Mother Lode Trail, as described above. Here you turn left and hike 2.6 miles uphill to a junction with the Twin Lakes Trail. The Twin Lakes Trail climbs uphill and then drops, reaching Upper Twin Lake at 3.3 miles from the Mother Lode Trail- and 10.1 miles from the Elk Lake Creek Trailhead. Though Upper Twin Lake is at about the same elevation as Elk Lake, you have to gain approximately 3,000 feet of elevation, much of it on steep trail, to get to Twin Lakes. Plan on spending the night here. Day 2 is easier. Hike up the Twin Lakes Trail a little over 2 miles to a junction with the Bagby Trail. Turn left here and hike the Bagby Trail a total of 3.6 miles to its southern trailhead, just above Elk Lake Campground. Walk down the road 0.9 mile to the Elk Lake Trailhead and your vehicle. This loop is tough: at 16.6 miles, its constant ups and downs give the loop a whopping total of nearly 5,000 feet of elevation gain.

29.   GOLD BUTTE LOOKOUT

Distance: 3.2 miles out and back
Elevation Gain: 800 feet
Trailhead elevation: 3,800 feet
Trail high point: 4,609 feet
Season: May- November
Best: May- November
Map: Opal Creek Wilderness (Imus)

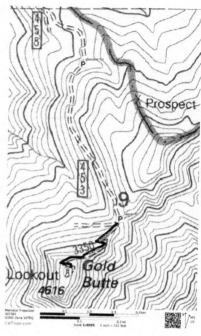

Directions:

* From Salem, drive east on OR 22 for 49 miles to Detroit.
* Immediately after crossing the Breitenbush River, turn left at a sign for Breitenbush and Elk Lake on FR 46.
* Drive 4.5 miles to a poorly-signed junction with FR 4696.
* Turn left here and drive this paved road 0.8 mile to a junction with FR 4697.
* Turn left again, pass a sign stating that this road is not maintained for passenger cars and begin climbing. The first two miles of this road are good gravel but soon the road becomes extremely rough and rocky, with huge potholes and embedded boulders.
* After 4.5 miles, reach a junction marked only by a green post.
* Left leads to Elk Lake, but you should turn right for Gold Butte.
* Unless you are staying at the lookout tower, you should park at the first gate.
* If you are staying at the lookout, drive through the first gate and park at the second.

Hike: The short hike to Gold Butte's lookout building is among the most rewarding in this area. Furthermore, if you've had the sense to reserve the lookout tower, you can spend the night in this special place. The only catch is the poor road access- but it's worth the hassle.

Unless you are spending the night, park at the first gate. Walk the road for 0.5 mile to the Gold Butte Trailhead, where there is a second green gate. Continue walking up the road another 0.8 mile to the old trailhead, where there is a small parking area. Here you trade road for trail, as a sign points the way to Gold Butte. You will follow this trail as it switchbacks uphill for 0.3 mile to the lookout.

The view at the lookout is magnificent! Mount Jefferson looms over the long canyon of the Breitenbush River, and the peaks of the Central Cascades stretch out in a long line to the south. Mount Hood peeks out from over Elk Lake Creek's canyon to the north, and Battle Ax rises over the Elk Lake Valley to the west. If you aren't staying the night, please give whoever has reserved the lookout their privacy. It goes without saying then that the way to visit this special place is to reserve the lookout and stay the night. To do so, visit http://www.recreation.gov and make a reservation. The lookout is very tough to book- you need to make a reservation as much as 6 months in advance and be willing to stay on a week day. It is absolutely worth it! Return the way you came.

30. HAWK MOUNTAIN AND ROUND LAKE

	Hawk Mountain	Round Lake
Distance:	4.2 miles out & back	1.2 miles out & back
Elevation Gain:	1,000 feet	200 feet
Trailhead Elevation:	4,559 feet	3,559 feet
Trail High Point:	5,270 feet	3,736 feet
Season:	June- October	June- October
Best:	July	June- October
Map:	Green Trails #525 (Breitenbush)	Green Trails #525 (Breitenbush)

Directions:
- From Salem, drive OR 22 east approximately 49 miles to Detroit.
- Turn left at a sign for Breitenbush, Elk Lake and Olallie Lake onto FR 46.
- Drive 16.6 miles on FR 46 to a pass where you enter the Mount Hood National Forest.
- Continue another 0.6 mile to a junction with FR 6350, angling sharply away on your left.
- If you are coming from Portland, this junction is exactly 28.1 miles from the Ripplebrook Guard Station on US 224. Keep a very close eye for FR 6350 on your right, which is very difficult to see if coming from the north.
- Fork to the left on the wide gravel road and drive 4.7 miles to a four-way junction with FR 6355.
- Turn left on this road for 0.3 mile to another junction with FR 150.
- The trailhead is on your right at this junction but the best parking is down the side road to the left.

Hike: Hidden on a ridge top near Breitenbush Pass, Hawk Mountain features an outstanding view of Mount Jefferson to the south. A cabin remains where a lookout once stood, offering a fascinating look at the history of the area and a place to stay should you wish to spend the night. Wildflowers scent the mountaintop while butterflies light at your feet. In an area with many nice hikes, this is one of the nicest.

Begin by hiking through a meadow that is slowly becoming forested. After only 100 yards look for a large clump of beautiful white-pink Cascade lilies in July; these showy flowers have a delightful perfume when fresh. The trail winds through this meadow for almost a half-mile, treating the hiker with more wildflowers and outstanding views of Mount Jefferson. Here the trail is faint as beargrass is beginning to obscure the tread, but the way is never difficult. Switchback away from Mount Jefferson and climb slightly, entering forest 0.8 mile from the trailhead. Here descend into a lovely old-growth forest of mountain hemlock and silver fir and then begin climbing slightly again to make up what you just lost. After nearly a mile of slight climbing, reach a junction with the spur to the summit of Hawk Mountain at the edge of Round Meadow, a long, narrow meadow that serves as the headwaters to Round Lake two miles to the west. Turn right.

On the spur, climb steadily through deep forest for 0.4 mile to the wide-open summit of

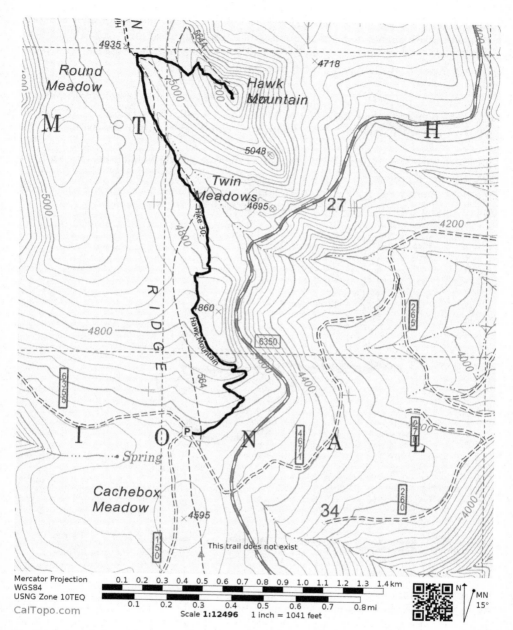

Round Meadow

Hawk Mountain

4718

4935

4671

5000

5048

Twin Meadows

4695

27

Hike 30:

4800

4800

Hawk Mountain

860

564

6350

6400

4400

4200

M T RIDGE I O N A L 34

P

Spring

Cachebox Meadow

4595

This trail does not exist

4000

Mercator Projection
WGS84
USNG Zone 10TEQ
CalTopo.com

0.1 0.2 0.3 0.4 0.5 0.6 0.7 0.8 0.9 1.0 1.1 1.2 1.3 1.4 km
0.1   0.2   0.3   0.4   0.5   0.6   0.7   0.8 mi
Scale **1:12496**   1 inch = 1041 feet

N↑
MN
15°

Hawk Mountain, where you are greeted by its rustic lookout cabin. The lookout tower that stood here was removed in 1967 but the recently-restored cabin remains. The staffers of the lookout stayed here and you may also stay in it if you wish to do so. As it is first-come, first-served, plan ahead and bring backpacking gear in case the cabin is occupied. In July the summit meadow is speckled with yellow arnica, red paintbrush, blue lupine and larkspur and white cat's ears. The view of Mount Jefferson to the southeast is even better than the flower display. This is a spectacular site! Return the way you came or arrange a car shuttle at the Graham Pass trailhead 5 miles to the north (see Other Hiking Options).

Round Lake: If you are in the area and wish to do a little more hiking, consider checking out Round Lake's abandoned campground. While this suggestion may evoke thoughts of the *Friday the 13th* movie series, this is a nice place that sees very little use since the more direct approach to the lake washed out many years ago.

To find the lake, follow FR 150 for 0.8 mile from the Hawk Mountain (Rho Ridge) Trailhead. Fork to the right (downhill) on FR 220 for 2 miles to a T junction with FR 6370. Turn right on FR 6370 and drive 3.5 miles to the signed trailhead on the right side of the road.

The trail departs from a signboard and climbs to the lake. As you would expect for a former campground, there are several excellent campsites here. After the trail crosses an inlet creek it becomes very rough; you can continue around the lake on a rough and very brushy trail to make a 1.2 mile loop but it is much easier to return the way you came.

Other Hiking Options:

Hawk Mountain via Graham Pass: You may also hike to the summit of Hawk Mountain by way of the Rho Ridge Trail from Graham Pass (see Hike 14 for directions). This approach is more than twice as long, has very few views and wanders through recovering clearcuts where the tread is frequently obscured by rhododendron and huckleberry. Though the tread is sometimes faint, yellow diamond-shaped signs that read "ULT 564" are posted on trees along the route to mark your way. You'll also cross several decommissioned logging roads along the way, where in favorable years there are excellent displays of beargrass. You will reach the aforementioned junction with the Hawk Mountain spur trail at 4.8 miles from the trailhead, just after passing Round Meadow. Turn left here and hike uphill 0.4 mile to Hawk Mountain's summit. This approach is 10.4 miles with 1,400 feet of elevation gain.

SECTION 3: THE OLD CASCADES

		Distance	EV Gain
31.	Stahlman Point and Blowout Arm	4.4	1,600
32.	Coffin Mountain	2.8	1,000
33.	Bachelor Mountain	3.8	1,100
34.	Bachelor Mountain via Bugaboo Ridge	7.6	2,100
35.	Daly, Parish and Riggs Lakes	3.6	600
36.	Scar Mountain and the Old Cascades Crest	11.6	4,100
37.	Three Pyramids	4.6	1,900
38.	Middle Santiam River via South Pyramid Creek	15.0	2,300
39.	Cascadia State Park	1.5	500
40.	Rooster Rock and the Menagerie Wilderness	6.8	2,400
41.	Santiam Wagon Road	6.0	600
42.	House Rock	1.2	300
43.	Gordon Meadows	7.8	2,200
44.	Iron Mountain	6.6	2,100
45.	West Browder Ridge	11.4	2,200
46.	Echo Basin and Hackleman Grove	3.4	900
47.	Crescent Mountain	9.6	2,500
48.	East Browder Ridge and Heart Lake	8.6	2,100
49.	Clear Lake	5.0	200
50.	Sahalie and Koosah Falls	2.8	400

The Old Cascades are aptly-named: this range of mountains to the west of the Cascade's great volcanoes predate their more explosive cousins by many millions of years. These Cascades are of volcanic origin as well, and the soil is highly fertile. As a result, you will find some of the finest wildflower meadows in the region.

The valleys of the Old Cascades also harbor some of the finest stands of ancient forest left in Oregon, but also some of the state's most ghastly clearcuts. You'll see both traveling through the area. Take the time to appreciate this highly complex blend of rock pinnacles and rounded peaks, of tall trees and vast clearcuts, and of wildflower meadows and quiet canyons. The beauty of this area is how all of these blend together seamlessly. Even all of the clearcuts help illustrate the struggled many faced saving the special places in this area.

Of the six regions in this book, this one is by far the least well-known to area hikers. It is my arbitrary distinction, but to me the Old Cascades encompasses the high peaks between Detroit Lake and US 20 north to south, and from the foothills to OR 22 west to east. While some hikes such are crowded and well-loved, many other hikes are isolated and solitary, and it is in these places that you may find a peace and quiet that fills mind, body and soul.

31. STAHLMAN POINT AND BLOWOUT ARM

Distance: 4.4 miles out and back
Elevation Gain: 1,600 feet
Trailhead elevation: 1,825 feet
Trail high point: 2,953 feet
Season: March- November
Best: March- November
Map: Green Trails #556 (Detroit)

Directions:
- From Salem, drive OR 22 east approximately 49 miles to Detroit.
- Continue on OR 22 past Detroit for 2.9 miles to a turnoff on your right for Blowout Road (FR 10).
- Turn right and drive this 2-lane paved road for 3.7 miles to the unmarked Stahlman Point Trailhead on your left.

Hike: Tucked away in the forest south of Detroit Lake, this short trek is a great early-season hike that rises to a commanding view of the North Santiam River canyon and all the way to Mount Jefferson. I was initially skeptical when I started the hike, and I was pleasantly surprised – this is a really nice hike that has a lot to offer in a short package.

The hike begins in regrowing forest on the south side of Detroit Lake and begins with a sharp ascent through second-growth forest on a trail that follows a creek. While never steep, the climbing does not relent until you are close to the summit. On your way up, views begin to open up of Detroit Lake below. Below is Piety Island, whose humped top seems surprisingly close from this vantage point.

After one mile, you round a bend, where you are greeted with a fantastic surprise, as the trail enters a patch of ancient forest in a steep gully. Hike under a number of huge trees that have fallen over the trail and continue climbing. Pass by a spring and round another bend, where the trail levels out in an open forest populated by immense amounts of rhododendrons. Round another bend on your left and begin ascending towards the summit block. The trail reaches a cliff end at the summit block. Turn right and scramble up some twenty feet to the summit, a former lookout site. You will find the bases of a few concrete pillars but little else to remind you of the structure that once stood here.

Though the lookout was dismantled in 1966, the view remains. Mount Jefferson rises over the North Santiam canyon, surprisingly close. Stretching out below you is spacious Detroit Lake, the playground of the central Willamette Valley. In summer, see how many boats you can pick out on the lake below! Keen eyes can spot huge Tumble Falls on the opposite side of the canyon, while Tumble Rock, Elephant Rock and others rise above Tumble Lake's pocket basin (see Hike 18). While noise from Oregon 22 intrudes on your solitude, the view makes up for it. Return the way you came.

Blowout Arm:
This is such a strange hike – descend a wide trail 0.2 mile to a huge suspension bridge over Blowout Arm, on the backside of Detroit Lake. It seems to be a huge party spot in

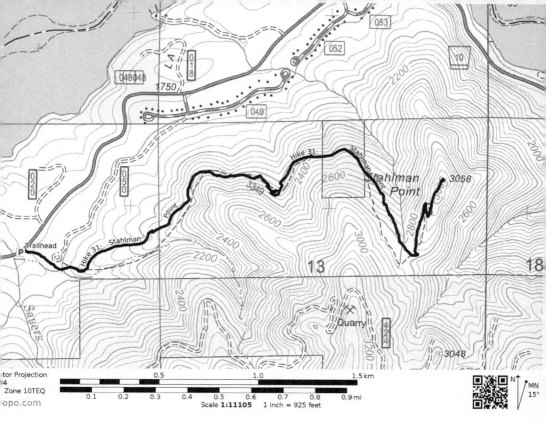

the summer, but when I came here in October it was deserted. The star of the hike is the suspension bridge, one of the nicest such bridges in the state of Oregon – and it happens to be over an isolated part of Detroit Lake. Strange indeed.

To find the Blowout Arm Trailhead, continue another 3 miles on FR 10 past the Stahlman Point Trailhead to a fork in the road. Fork to the right and drive 0.7 mile of narrow, potholed gravel to a turnoff on your right at a "No Camping" sign. Turn right here into the unsigned trailhead.

There is not much to tell you about the hike. You begin in a nice forest and descend to a junction with an old road or trail of some sort. Turn right here to locate the continuation of the trail. After just a few minutes, reach the massive bridge. It's a fascinating place, one worthy of a lengthy stop. Below you, the turquoise waters of Detroit Lake snake around the long cove of Blowout Arm. Past the bridge, the trail climbs 0.2 mile towards its death in a dark, spooky forest. Don't bother continuing past the bridge. On your way back, the trail looks a little different; remember to turn right on the old road, and then locate the continuation of the trail on your left shortly after.

32. COFFIN MOUNTAIN

Distance: 2.8 miles out and back
Elevation Gain: 1,000 feet
Trailhead elevation: 4,713 feet
Trail high point: 5,733 feet
Season: July- October
Best: July
Map: Green Trails #556 (Detroit)

Directions:
- From Salem, drive OR 22 east approximately 49 miles to Detroit.
- Continue past Detroit on OR 22 for 19 miles to a junction with the Straight Creek Road (FR 11) on your right.
- Turn right and drive this winding but paved road for 1.4 miles to a junction with FR 1168. Ignore this junction and continue on paved FR 11.
- Continue another 2.6 miles to another junction with FR 1168, veering sharply off to the right.
- Turn right and drive this gravel road 1.4 miles to a fork with FR 368.
- Keep left on FR 1168 and continue another 2.4 winding miles to a junction with FR 450.
- Turn left and drive 50 yards to the signed trailhead.

Hike: This is a wonderful hike up to the cliffy, flat-topped summit of Coffin Mountain that is short enough to do in just a few hours but exciting enough to make a day destination. The trail climbs up an open slope that is absolutely filled with wildflowers to a lookout tower with a panoramic view of the Cascade Range – it doesn't get better than this!

Begin by charging uphill on a rocky trail, once a jeep road. Soon you will leave the forest and emerge on a steep, open slope that is carpeted with beargrass. The views out to

the Cascades are stupendous, with Mount Jefferson dominating the view to the east while views to the south stretch out to the Three Sisters and all the way south to Diamond Peak.

Continue climbing on a winding trail up through the beargrass until you reach the summit plateau at 1.3 mile. Above you to the left is a radio tower on one end of the plateau. Continue on towards the lookout tower ahead of you, which you reach at 1.5 miles. The tower is staffed in the summer by an individual whose job it is to spot fires – do not enter the lookout unless you are invited to do so. The view, as you might imagine, is stupendous. In addition to the peaks to your east and south, Mount Hood and Mount Adams rise to the north. Below you to the immediate north is Detroit Lake. When you are done at the summit, return the way you came. For a bit of variety on the way back, follow a user trail near the

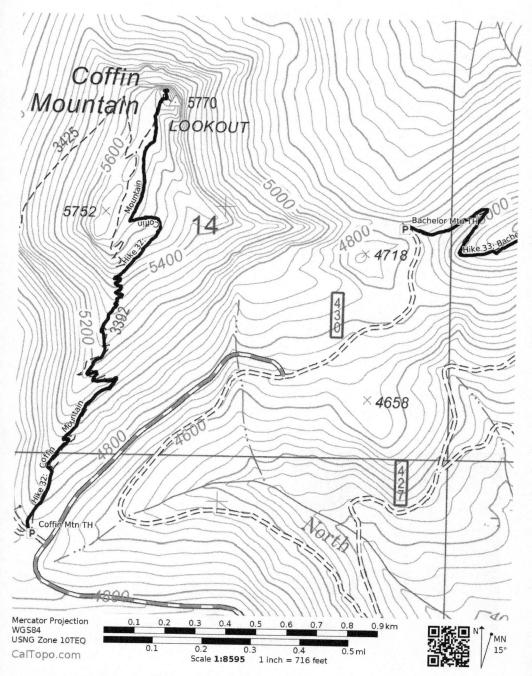

Mercator Projection
WGS84
USNG Zone 10TEQ
CalTopo.com

0.1 0.2 0.3 0.4 0.5 0.6 0.7 0.8 0.9km
0.1   0.2   0.3   0.4   0.5mi
Scale **1:8595**   1 inch = 716 feet

N↑ MN 15°

summit off towards the radio tower on the other end of Coffin Mountain's summit to the end of the ridge. The flowers on this end of the summit are outstanding, with lots of paintbrush, phlox and many other flowers. You can follow user trails back down to the main trail and back to the trailhead.

33. BACHELOR MOUNTAIN

Distance: 3.8 miles out and back
Elevation Gain: 1,100 feet
Trailhead elevation: 4,832 feet
Trail high point: 5,946 feet
Season: July- October
Best: July- October
Map: Green Trails #556 (Detroit)

Directions:
- From Salem, drive OR 22 east approximately 49 miles to Detroit.
- Continue past Detroit on OR 22 for 19 miles to a junction with the Straight Creek Road (FR 11) on your right.
- Turn right and drive this winding but paved road for 1.4 miles to a junction with FR 1168. Ignore this junction and continue on paved FR 11.
- Continue another 2.6 miles to another junction with FR 1168, veering sharply off to the right.
- Turn right and drive this gravel road 1.4 miles to a fork with FR 368.
- Keep left and continue another 2.4 winding miles to a junction with FR 450.
- Turn left and drive 50 yards to the signed trailhead on your right.
- From the junction of FR 1168 and FR 450 (50 yards from the Coffin Mountain trailhead), continue another 0.7 mile on FR 1168 to a junction with FR 1168-430, angling away to the left.
- Turn left here and drive 0.5 mile of narrow, rocky gravel to road's end at the Bachelor Mountain trailhead on your right. Above you is an exceptional view of Coffin Mountain to your left (see photo below).

Hike: Just one mile east of Coffin Mountain, the trail up Bachelor Mountain is longer, more forested and in many ways very different from its neighbor to the west. Like Coffin Mountain, the trail up Bachelor Mountain passes through spectacular wildflower meadows with outstanding views out to the high Cascades off to the south and east.

The trail begins by climbing uphill through an impressive forest on the northwest side of Bachelor Mountain. You will soon emerge onto an open, wildflower-spangled ridge. The sheer quantity and variety of wildflowers here boggles the mind – on my trip here I counted over thirty different varieties, and with some time you could easily identify twice that number. The most common species you will find on this hike are red, trumpet-shaped scarlet gilia (also known as skyrocket), large, fragrant Cascade lilies, yellow arnica and white beargrass.

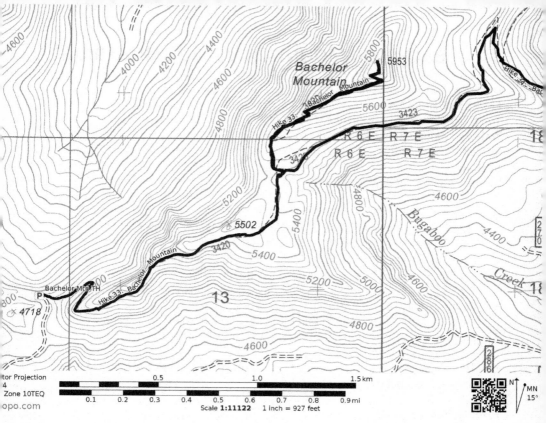

tor Projection
4
Zone 10TEQ
opo.com

Scale **1:11122**   1 inch = 927 feet

Look ahead to the many false summits of Bachelor Mountain – there are many, so keep moving straight ahead. Leave the ridgecrest and arrive at a basin with phenomenal views ahead to Mount Jefferson, just ten miles to the east. You are hiking through the Buck Mountain burn, which torched this area in the 1970s. Soon you will leave the burn area and enter a classic alpine forest, which in July of some years is completely carpeted with white beargrass blooms. At 1.3 miles from the trailhead, arrive at a junction with the Bruno Meadows Trail. Turn left on the Bachelor Mountain Trail and begin climbing up through forest and then open meadows for 0.7 mile to the summit of Bachelor Mountain. Though Coffin Mountain has a lookout tower and has for many years, you may be surprised to discover that Bachelor Mountain had a lookout tower as well. All that remains of the tower, which was built in 1934 and destroyed in 1967, is some glass and metal rods. The view remains outstanding, though, with a panorama north to Mount Adams and all the way south to at least the Three Sisters. Mount Jefferson dominates the skyline to the east. When you are finished, return the way you came.

Other things to do:

Along the way to or from the Coffin Mountain and Bachelor Mountain trailheads, be sure to stop near the trailhead at a stupendous viewpoint of the Cascades right off the road. The view is perhaps as impressive as anything on either the Coffin Mountain or Bachelor Mountain Trails, but with no effort required. Like I needed to tell you to stop – you'll know the viewpoint when you reach it!

34. BACHELOR MOUNTAIN VIA BUGABOO RIDGE

Distance: 7.6 miles out and back
Elevation Gain: 2,100 feet
Trailhead elevation: 4,160 feet
Trail high point: 5,946 feet
Season: June- October
Best: July
Map: Green Trails #556 (Detroit)

Directions:
- From Salem, drive OR 22 east approximately 49 miles to Detroit.
- From Detroit, drive south 16 miles to Marion Forks.
- Continue past Marion Forks another 1.5 miles to a junction with FR 2234 on your right. There isn't really a sign so you'll have to watch closely.
- Turn right here and immediately cross the North Santiam River on a concrete bridge.
- Continue uphill about 2.5 miles to a confusing junction with several side roads on your left at a curve. There are two side roads here, one of which has a gate.
- Stay on the main road (FR 2234) here and drive another 0.5 mile to a junction with another side road on your left.
- The trailhead is 100 yards down this road on your right but the best place to park is right at the junction.

Hike: Little-known and seldom-traveled, the Bugaboo Ridge Trail is for the adventurous. This is not to say that it's extremely difficult, or hard to follow, or anything like that —it's just that the Bugaboo Ridge Trail feels wild in a way that the shorter, more popular Bachelor

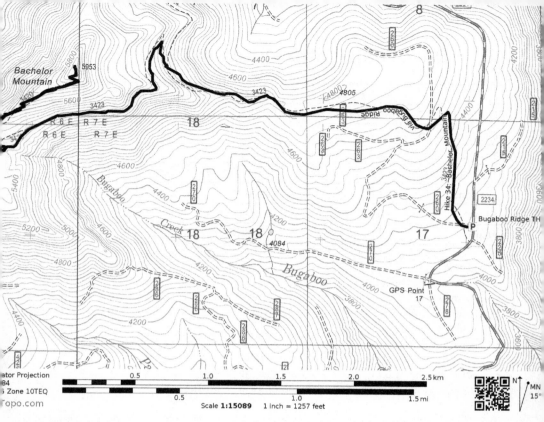

ator Projection
84
Zone 10TEQ
Topo.com

Scale **1:15089**   1 inch = 1257 feet

Mountain Trail does not. You are unlikely to meet anybody on this trail until you near the summit, and the views and wildflower meadows are superior to that of the more well-known approach to Bachelor Mountain. But you have to earn it, as the way is steep and brushy.

Begin your hike in a lush old-growth forest as the trail climbs gradually at first. You will soon leave the forest, instead trading woods for an open, bushy ridge that is a remnant of the 1970 Buck Mountain fire. After a little under a mile, the trail crosses a gravel road and then returns to the forest as the climbing continues. Soon the trail becomes brushy as you enter a meadow that is completely overgrown, as bracken fern and several species of wildflowers overhang the trail. It is here that you will meet the Bruno Meadows Trail, yet another approach to Bachelor Mountain. Keep straight here and climb out of this meadow into a series of exceptional flower gardens as the trail skirts through an open forest. Here you have excellent views out to Mount Jefferson, looming across the canyon to the east.

The best part comes next, as the Bugaboo Ridge Trail curves around an open ridge end, amidst hanging gardens and absolutely spectacular views that stretch all the way south to the Three Sisters and points further south. Beyond this point, brush encroaches on the trail but this section is mercifully short. Just a little bit later, you'll meet the well-maintained Bachelor Mountain Trail, at which point you turn right and hike 0.7 mile to the summit. The views here are incredible, but especially great is the view to Mount Jefferson, just seven miles to the east. Return the way you came or arrange a shuttle with the other Bachelor Mountain Trail, described in Hike 33.

35. DALY, PARISH AND RIGGS LAKES

	Daly Lake:	Parish Lake:	Riggs Lake:
Distance:	1.4 mile loop	1.2 miles out & back	1 mile out & back
Elevation Gain:	200 feet	200 feet	200 feet
Trailhead Elevation:	3,651 feet	3,534 feet	3,306 feet
Trail High Point:	3,755 feet	3,534 feet	3,495 feet
Season:	June- November	June- November	June- November
Best:	July- October	July- October	July- October
Map:	Green Trails 556	Green Trails 556	Green Trails 556

Directions:
- From Salem, drive OR 22 east approximately 49 miles to Detroit.
- From Detroit, drive approximately 24 miles south on OR 22 to a junction with Parish Lake Road (FR 2266) on your right. There will be a sign that reads "Old Cascades Crest Trails".
- Drive this road for 3.1 paved miles to a junction with FR 2047 on your left.
- Here the road changes to gravel. Keep straight.
- Drive another 1.6 miles to a junction with FR 450. Turn right.
- Drive 0.5 mile to the signed trailhead on your right. There is room for 7 – 8 cars.

Hike: Three lakes set in classic old-growth forest, all of them lovely and worth visiting, and all of them short hikes; if you are in the area, why not visit all three? Each is quite different from the others, and you'll find things to love about all three.

Daly Lake: Begin with Daly Lake, the largest and most-visited of the three. The paved, all-access trail to the lake descends through a forest of impressive and ancient Douglas firs to the lake, where you will find a picnic table at the beginning of a loop around the lake. Turn right to begin the loop. The trail stays well-maintained for another 0.1 mile, where it becomes brushy and faint almost immediately. Before long you'll find yourself crossing a muddy outlet stream on a rotting beaver dam. Remember, I never said it would be easy!

Past the outlet stream, the trail repents, becoming easier to follow as it winds around huckleberry bushes amongst huge trees. On the far side of the lake, you will pass a number of campsites before you reach the conclusion of the loop at the picnic table. When you reach the end of the loop, turn right to hike the 0.2 mile of paved trail back to the trailhead.

Parish Lake: To find Parish Lake, drive back 0.5 mile on FR 450 to Parish Lake Road (FR 2266) and turn right. Drive 0.5 mile on FR 2266 (or 5.2 miles from OR 22) and park in the signed trailhead on your left.

The trail begins by dropping at a steady but well-graded pace through a lovely forest. If you come here in July you may find your progress retarded by the masses of blue huckleberries that grow along the trail! Just 0.6 mile from the trailhead, reach the lake, with its excellent campsites and views south to North Pyramid. The lake is a quiet place – listen for the hum

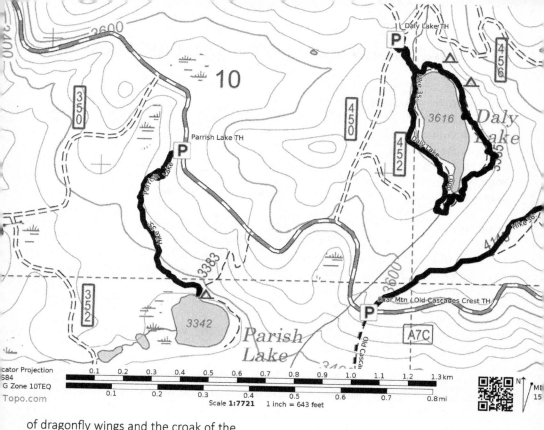

of dragonfly wings and the croak of the frog, both of which are common here. Whether you come for a few minutes or a few days, return the way you came.

Riggs Lake: To find Riggs Lake, continue west on FR 2266 past the Parish Lake Trailhead for another 1.2 miles (or 6.4 miles from OR 22) to the Riggs Lake Trailhead on your right.

The trail to Riggs Lake is short on highlights but is worth hiking if you're already in the area. Hike uphill for 0.4 mile to the lake, set in a bowl surrounded by rocky bluffs and rhododendrons. There aren't any campsites and there is scarcely a place to even sit down, so save this one for last. With some luck you may be able to locate the rough, abandoned trail up to Don Lake in the basin north of Riggs Lake. Return the way you came.

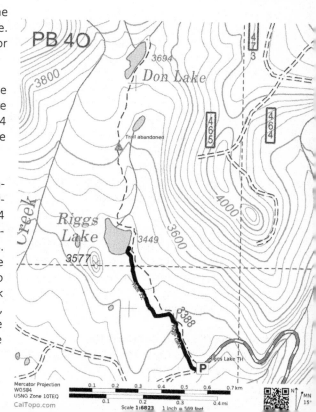

36. SCAR MOUNTAIN AND THE OLD CASCADES CREST

Distance: 11.6 miles out and back
Elevation Gain: 4,100 feet
Trailhead elevation: 3,533 feet
Trail high point: 4,908 feet
Season: June- October
Best: June- July
Map: Green Trails #556 (Detroit)
Map note: For a detailed map of the Old Cascades Crest Trail, see my website.

Directions:
* From Salem, drive OR 22 east approximately 49 miles to Detroit.
* From Detroit, drive approximately 24 miles south on OR 22 to a junction with Parish Lake Road (FR 2266) on your right. There will be a sign that reads "Old Cascades Crest Trails".
* Drive this road for 3.1 paved miles to a junction with FR 2047 on your left.
* Here the road changes to gravel. Keep straight.
* Drive about 1.2 miles to the North Pyramids Trailhead, where the Old Cascades Crest Trail crosses FR 2266. Park here.

Hike: Scar Mountain's imposing white cliffs are visible on the horizon everywhere in the Old Cascades, looking as forboding as any in the region. And yet, the Scar Mountain Trail leads hikers right to the edge of the mountain's summit cliffs. It doesn't come easy; the way rides the ups and downs of the long ridge enough to give hikers seasickness. By the end of the hike, you will accumulate over 4,100 feet of elevation gain. But the views, the solitude and the ancient forest are enough to satisfy most hikers. Backpackers looking for a serious challenge can tackle the Old Cascades Crest Trail, which continues beyond the summit of Scar Mountain. Bring water as there is absolutely none on the hike.

Begin at the North Pyramids Trailhead. The trail climbs steadily through the forest above Daly Lake as you make your way up towards Trappers Butte. The trail mostly climbs over the first three miles on its way to the summit of Trappers Butte. You will stay in the forest for the most part but there are occasional views northeast to Mount Jefferson. Beyond Trappers Butte, the trail begins a seesaw up and down the ridge towards Scar Mountain. In the next 2.8 miles, you will lose and gain more than 1,000 feet- and because you are doing this trail as an out and back, this is elevation you have to gain both ways.

At 5.8 miles from the trailhead, the trail finally reaches the summit of Scar Mountain. The true summit is atop a rocky pinnacle unreachable to all but the most foolhardy (seriously, don't try this without climbing gear). The views are excellent here, stretching from Mount Hood south towards the Three Sisters. You can scramble off the trail a short ways to Scar Mountain's cliffs but do watch your step- a fall would absolutely be fatal. Return the way you came, unless you are planning on hiking the Old Cascades Crest Trail.

About the Old Cascades Crest Trail:
The Old Cascades Crest Trail would be an excellent loop trip but for two things: there is absolutely no water for a stretch of more than 16 miles and there are few if any developed

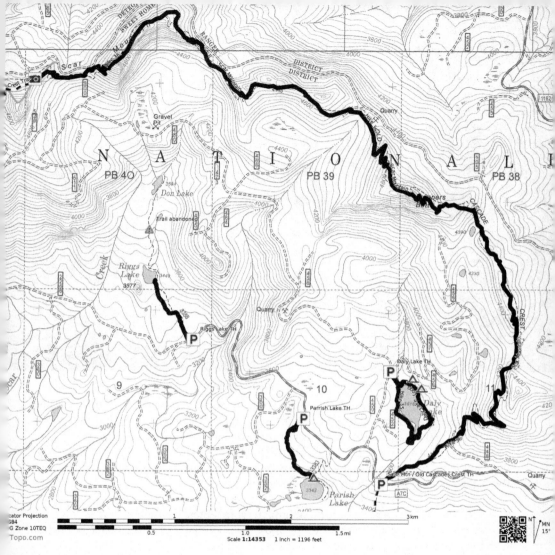

campsites over the waterless crest of the area. Extremely fit backpackers will be able to navigate these issues, but almost anybody else will find the experience exhausting.

Beyond the summit of Scar Mountain, the Scar Mountain Trail continues 4.2 miles of ups and downs, climbing about 1,000 feet and losing more than 1,600 feet to a junction with the Gordan Peak Trail. Along the way, you'll climb over a lot of downed trees, pass through some old clearcuts and hike through several nice groves of ancient forest. When you reach the Gordan Peak Trail on your left, you are faced with a choice.

If you continue straight, you'll follow the Swamp Peak Trail until it meets the Knob Rock Trail. But there's no water this way either; instead, you should turn left on the Gordan Peak Trail. From here, you'll pass a poor campsite almost immediately, climb a little and then descend on a brushy trail through ancient forest for 3.7 miles to a junction with the Chimney Peak Trail. From here, you can turn right and hike a little over a mile to excellent camps at Donaca Lake.

The Old Cascades Crest Trail near the Donaca Lake junction.

To continue the Old Cascades Crest Loop, turn left on the Chimney Peak Trail and hike downhill through gorgeous ancient forest for 2.5 miles to the crossing of wide Pyramid Creek, your first reliable water. For most of the year the creek is too deep to rock hop, so you'll need to take off your boots and wade. On the far side of Pyramid Creek, there is an excellent campsite set amongst a collection of huge Douglas firs. If you are keeping score, this is the first good campsite in more than 16 miles from the trailhead.

The next 2.1 miles are a gorgeous romp through more fantastic ancient forest as you enter the Middle Santiam Wilderness. The ups and downs continue until you reach a junction with the trail over to Shedd Camp (see Hike 38). If you have the time, you should absolutely take the time to go see the Middle Santiam River and Shedd Camp Shelter. For this detour, turn right; otherwise, turn left to continue your loop. From this junction, turn left on the South Pyramid Creek Trail. You will begin climbing out of the Middle Santiam River canyon. In 2 miles, the trail seems to end at FR 2047 but a sign tells you to turn right for 800 feet. Walk down FR 2047 and locate the continuation of the trail. From here you'll climb 1,700 feet over the next 3.4 miles to a trailhead on FR 572. Keep left and continue 1.5 miles of ups and downs to the Three Pyramids Trailhead.

You're in the home stretch now. Climb 2 miles to Middle Pyramid's summit spur trail and then continue downhill approximately 4 miles to the North Pyramids Trailhead. Overall, this loop is about 31 miles with so much elevation gain I won't even list it here. As stated above, I can only recommend this backpack to the fittest of fit backpackers. There is so little water that you'll need to carry at least 4 liters for each day, and downed trees discourage trail running. The best plan is to plan for two very long days, and camp at either Donaca Lake or Pyramid Creek. With proper planning, enough water and lots of energy, this is a great trip.

37.　THREE PYRAMIDS

Distance: 4.6 miles out and back
Elevation Gain: 1,900 feet
Trailhead elevation: 3,888 feet
Trail high point: 5,551 feet
Season: July- October
Best: July
Map: Green Trails #588 (Echo Mtn) and Green Trails #556 (Detroit)

Directions:

- From Salem, drive OR 22 east approximately 49 miles to Detroit.
- Continue another 26.7 miles to a junction with Lava Lake Meadow Road on the right .
- Turn right and drive 1.9 miles to a junction with FR 560, just after a bridge.
- Turn right on FR 560 and drive 3.5 miles, ignoring all side roads, to road's end at the Pyramids TH.

Hike: It seems like the Three Pyramids are on the horizon everywhere in this book, but in truth it's because they are so recognizable. A short, steep and lovely trail leads up to an excellent viewpoint at the top of the Middle Pyramid. Plan for a sunny, clear day when you do this hike, as the view is exceptional.

Begin at the Pyramids Trailhead and almost immediately arrive at a junction. Turn right and begin climbing following a trickling fork of Park Creek. Pass by a small waterfall and then cross the creek near its source in Pyramid Cirque. A short uphill will bring you to a great view of the cirque, a rarity in this part of the Cascades. Take a moment to check out the cirque, where a fork of Park Creek emerges from the Middle Pyramid's cliffs.

Back on the trail, keep climbing at a steady clip out of the cirque until the trail bends around Middle Pyramid's wide north flank. At 2 miles, reach a junction with the spur trail to the summit of Middle Pyramid. Turn left here and continue the uphill, switchbacking up to a saddle between Middle Pyramid's two summits. Turn right and climb over some rocks to find the continuation of the spur trail. In a few short minutes, reach the summit of Middle Pyramid where the view is outstanding (see photo below). A lookout stood on the summit here from 1934 to 1967, and a few remnants of the lookout remain. Watch where you step - the dropoff to the east is huge. Return the way you came.

The Old Cascades Crest Trail: This hike is part of the Old Cascades Crest Trail, a 31 mile loop through the heart of this area. For more information see Hike 36.

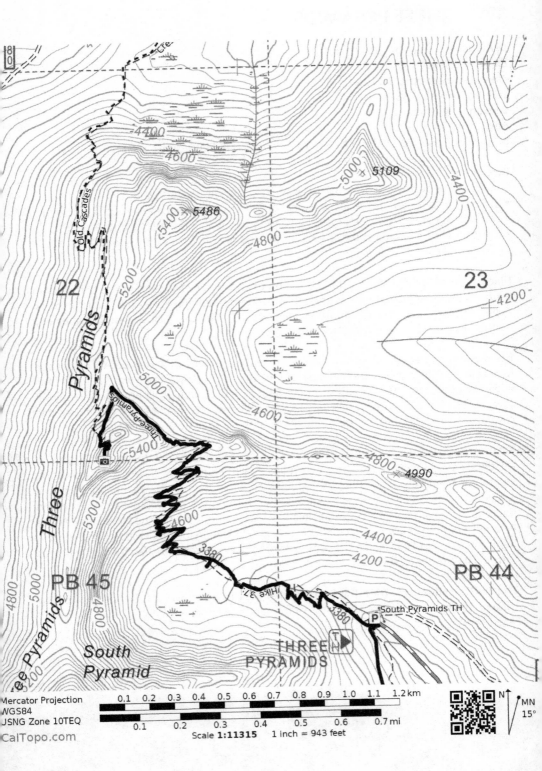

Scale 1:11315   1 inch = 943 feet

38. MIDDLE SANTIAM RIVER VIA SOUTH PYRAMID CREEK

Distance: 15 miles out and back
Elevation Gain: 2,300 feet (most of it on the way back)
Trailhead elevation: 3,922 feet
Trail high point: 4,343 feet
Season: June- October
Best: June- October
Map: Opal Creek Wilderness (Imus)
Map note: For a detailed map of this hike and the Old Cascades Crest Trail, see my website.

Directions:
- See directions for Three Pyramids (Hike 37).

Hike: The long trek into the canyon of the Middle Santiam River is one of contrasting choices. You can drive to three other trailheads than the one I am describing here, shortening the long downhill trek into this remote canyon. But there's that word: remote. The choice presented here opts for a longer hike in lieu of a longer drive. And with reason: navigating the confusing, seemingly endless gravel logging roads in this area is enough to make most people opt for the longer hike.

Begin at the Pyramids Trailhead. Just 100 feet into the hike, meet a junction: right leads to Three Pyramids (Hike 37) but you want to turn left. The South Pyramid Creek Trail climbs around the side of the South Pyramid amid ancient forest and then drops to the first of the three alternate trailheads on FR 572 at 1.5 miles. Across the road to your left is the Crescent Mountain Trail, which leads to the summit of Crescent Mountain (Hike 47) in approximately 4 miles. As it is, this trailhead is the easiest of the three alternate trailheads to find: if you wish to start here and cut 1.5 miles each way off your overall hike distance, turn left off FR 560 at 3 miles (or 0.5 mile before the Pyramids Trailhead) onto FR 572 and drive 1.25 miles to the signed trailhead on your right.

Beyond this trailhead, the South Pyramid Creek Trail keeps to the right side of the road, climbs a bit and then drops into South Pyramid Creek's narrow canyon. This stretch of trail is absolutely beautiful, with many large trees and looks down at the cascading creek. Eventually you will leave the deep forest behind and enter a recovering clearcut, which is your hint that you are nearing another road. At 4.7 miles from the Pyramids Trailhead, the South Pyramid Creek Trail seems to end at FR 2047. A sign reads "Trail Continues 800 FT.->". Turn right here and walk down the road about 800 feet until you see the South Pyramid Creek Trail on your left, just before the turnoff for a remote horse campground. This is the second of three alternate trailheads; this one is still easy to find, but requires far more driving on remote gravel roads. You can drive here from near Daly Lake (Hike 35) but 1.6 miles from the turnoff to Daly Lake (3.1 miles from OR 22), turn left on FR 2047 and drive 7.3 miles to the trailhead, just after the horse camp. You can also drive to this spot from US 20 to the south, but you are faced with 13.2 miles of circuitous gravel road on FR 2047 to get to this spot from the south.

Back on the South Pyramid Creek Trail, you will continue to descend another 2.2 miles to a junction with the Chimney Peak Trail on your right. Continue straight another 0.3 mile to

Shelter Falls on the Middle Santiam River. The only way to reach the pool is by hiking to the Shedd Camp Shelter first and then descending to the river on social trails.

a crossing of the wide and rocky Middle Santiam River. You'll need to take off your shoes and wade across the wide river as it is far too deep to cross on rocks for most of the year. Don't be tempted to cross above the waterfall - one false step and you'll have problems. Once across the river, follow the trail up to Shedd Camp Shelter, set deep in mossy, ancient forest. A trail leads down to the river and a view of the waterfall, known as Shelter Falls. A deep green pool below the falls invites a long stay and a quick swim. This is an almost ideal place to spend the night, and after such a long hike, you'll likely want to.

The third and final alternate trailhead is a little over a half-mile uphill from Shedd Camp Shelter. With such a short trail, you might expect more people at the shelter but consider this: to find this third trailhead, you have to navigate more than 13 miles of gravel road through the depressing, clearcut slopes of the Soda Fork's long canyon. Some won't mind but most will. The directions are too complicated to list here; consult the Sweet Home Ranger Station for more information. So in a sense, it actually is easier to hike the long way to the shelter.

Return the way you came but save some energy- it's almost all uphill on the way back. You can of course arrange a car shuttle with one of the other trailheads, but the most convenient trailheads are the ones you passed on the hike, and the least convenient is the Middle Santiam Trailhead near Shedd Camp- which of course would be a long car shuttle indeed.

The Old Cascades Crest Trail: The Pyramids Trail is part of the Old Cascades Crest Trail, a 31 mile loop that links the Three Pyramids and Scar Mountain with the Middle Santiam River. See Hike 36 for more details.

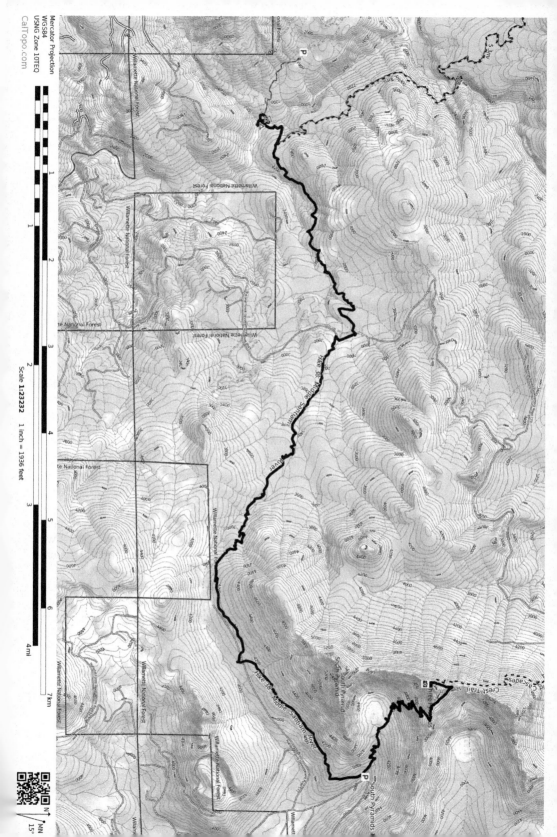

39. CASCADIA STATE PARK

Distance: 1.5 miles out and back
Elevation Gain: 500 feet
Trailhead elevation: 851 feet
Trail high point: 1,226 feet
Season: all year
Best: April- June
Map: None needed.

Directions:
- Drive east of Sweet Home on US 20 for 10 miles.
- Turn left at a sign for Cascadia State Park.
- Drive over the South Santiam River and turn right into a day-use parking lot next to a bathroom and picnic area.

Hike: Only a short walk but far nicer and more interesting than you might imagine, this lovely jaunt up to Lower Soda Falls is worth an hour of your time if you are in the area – especially during Oregon's seemingly endless winter. A fair warning is in order – the trail is muddy, and will be especially so in the winter.

Begin from the parking lot by walking on the paved road right from the bathrooms towards a bridge over Soda Creek. Just after the creek, look for a trail sign on your left. Turn onto this trail and begin hiking up a narrow, verdant canyon that is seemingly overhung with salmonberry bushes. Along the way you will cross Soda Creek twice on bridges as you climb up the canyon.

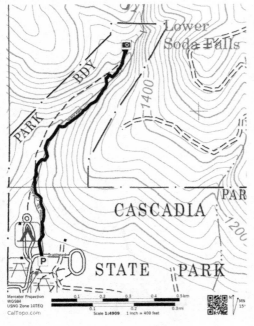

As you near the falls, you will enter a surprisingly nice forest of a few ancient Douglas firs as the canyon contracts. Reach the falls at 0.7 mile, where you are presented with a choice – left to a huge boulder with a nice view of the falls, or right to the base of the falls? You've barely broken a sweat, so why not do both? The falls tumbles in three drops totaling 134 feet, though it is quite difficult to see the top tier of the falls. Take some time to get the best photo compositions – there are many, and the falls is quite photogenic.

When you are finished taking photos and relaxing, return the way you came.

Other Hiking Options:
Cascadia Cave: Also located at Cascadia State Park is Cascadia Cave. A trail leads from the campground to the cave, actually

Lower Soda Falls in Cascadia State Park.

a huge overhanging rock, where you will see petroglyphs that date back centuries. Because of the cultural significance of this spot, and because it is located on private property outside of Cascadia State Park, the only way to see the cave is to take a private tour offered through the Sweet Home Ranger District. See http://www.recreation.gov for more information and to sign up.

40. ROOSTER ROCK AND THE MENAGERIE WILDERNESS

Distance: 6.8 miles out and back
Elevation Gain: 2,400 feet
Trailhead elevation: 1,242 feet
Trail high point: 3,568 feet
Season: April- November
Best: April- May
Map: Menagerie Wilderness and Middle Santiam Wilderness (USFS)

Directions:
- Drive east of the Quartzville Road junction at the eastern edge of Sweet Home on US 20 for 15.6 miles to the poorly-marked Trout Creek Trailhead. The trailhead is located on your left not far past milepost 49.
- The trailhead is just after Trout Creek Campground on the right side of the highway.

Hike: The hike up to Rooster Rock in the Menagerie Wilderness is short on highlights. It's a shame that the builders of this trail did not see fit to extend the trail to anywhere more interesting; for that, you have to take matters into your own hands. This may be the least interesting hike in the Old Cascades; and in spite of that, it is a useful trail for its easy access, and is good for a spring conditioner. Just make sure to continue further into the Menagerie for the good stuff.

First of all, about the Menagerie: The Menagerie Wilderness is a collection of fascinating rock pinnacles with colorful, animal-themed names, among them Turkey Monster, Rabbit Ears, and of course, Rooster Rock. The trick is to find the way to see all of them, and that isn't easy. Get started on the Trout Creek Trail. The trail charges uphill at an almost constant grade- never too steep, but rarely level. The forest has clearly been logged before, and has a fairly uniform quality. Keep an eye out for poison oak on both sides of the trail all the way to the summit; though a rarity elsewhere in this book, it's everywhere here. A few madrone trees spice things up as you ascend- look for the peeling bark of this beautiful tree, which is far more common further south.

At 2.9 miles, reach a junction with the shorter, steeper Rooster Rock Trail. Continue straight as the trail steepens considerably, making its final ascent towards Rooster Rock. Reach the rock just before the end of the trail. The trail passes the rock, offering chances for climbers equipped to handle the route to the top of Rooster Rock. Unless you are climbing, switch-back to the left and reach the former lookout site at a ridge end at 3.4 miles. The view is underwhelming, to put it lightly: the only thing you can see is the ridge on the far side of Keith Creek's canyon.

To see and truly understand the Menagerie, you need to follow a rough climbers trail out to Panorama Point. Walk back 100 steps from the summit to a junction with the climbers trail. The climber's trail leads deeper into the wilderness, into the domain of the adventure climber. What you find depends on what you are looking for- and I'll leave the adventure up to you.

Walton Ranch: Before you leave the area, be sure to check out the short trail to Walton Ranch. It departs from the Trout Creek Trailhead and proceeds to cross Trout Creek immediately on a nice bridge. You will climb a bit to an overlook directly above the highway of a prairie across the river. Each winter, a herd of elk winters at this prairie and if you visit from November to April, you may just see them. Even when the elk aren't there, this is a worthy detour just for the crossing of Trout Creek alone- after all, the Trout Creek Trail never once approaches Trout Creek.

Rooster Rock via the Rooster Rock Trailhead: You can also reach the summit of Rooster Rock via the shorter, more direct Rooster Rock Trail. This trail gains 1,300 feet in about 1.5 miles, so it's far steeper than the Trout Creek Trail. The advantage to this approach is that it is more direct, and some will appreciate its brevity. To find the Rooster Rock Trailhead, continue east beyond the Trout Creek Trailhead on US 20 another 2.7 miles to the signed trailhead on the left. There is a small trailhead loop and room for plenty of cars.

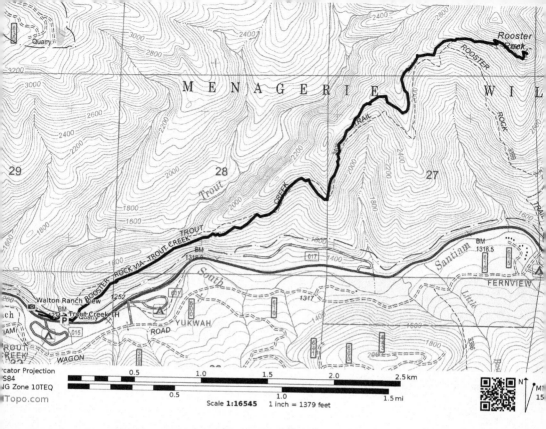

41.   SANTIAM WAGON ROAD

Distance: 6 miles out and back
Elevation Gain: 600 feet
Trailhead elevation: 1,418 feet
Trail high point: 1,914 feet
Season: all year
Best: October- November
Map: For a high-resolution map of this area, see my website.

Directions:
*   Drive east of the Quartzville Road junction at the eastern edge of Sweet Home on US 20 for 19.3 miles to the Santiam Wagon Road Trailhead.
*   The trailhead is located on your right between mileposts 52 and 53.
*   The trailhead is just after the Mountain House restaurant (now a private residence).

Hike: The Santiam Wagon Road once stretched from Oregon's eastern border to the Willamette Valley, connecting travelers and settlers to the Valley's fertile farmlands. Some sections of the wagon road still exist, and one such segment is found in the canyon of the South Santiam River. Best of all, this section is at such a low elevation that it is open all winter, offering winter-weary hikers a chance to stretch their legs all year long. The best time of all to come here is in the fall, when the trail is carpeted with huge fallen maple leaves,

adding much color to an already beautiful scene.

Begin at the poorly-marked trailhead, where a wooden pedestrian bridge leads hikers over the South Santiam River. There is a signboard across the river as well as a trail sign. The wagon road is more of a trail for most of this hike. Brush occasionally overhangs the trail but for the most part the path is wide and very well-maintained. Signposts mark each mile you hike beyond the trailhead. None of the side creeks have bridges, but most of them are easy to cross with dry feet. At 1.2 miles, you'll meet Elk Creek, the one that may get your feet wet. It is obvious that the creek has washed out the trail before - you may need to scramble down to the creek.

As you near House Rock (see Hike 42), you will enter a grove of very large Douglas firs near the trail. Meet the trail down to House Rock at 2.1 miles; the sign points the opposite direction (away from the road), an indication that most people who come here are from House Rock's car campground. Just a short while later, you'll pass the trail down to House Rock Falls. Take a moment to hike down to this beautiful falls, set in a narrow, bouldery canyon. It is very difficult to get a good photo of the falls, as it is hard to see in its entirety even at river level.

House Rock Falls is a good place to turn around. The wagon road continues another 0.7 mile to a gate at FR 2044. Return the way you came.

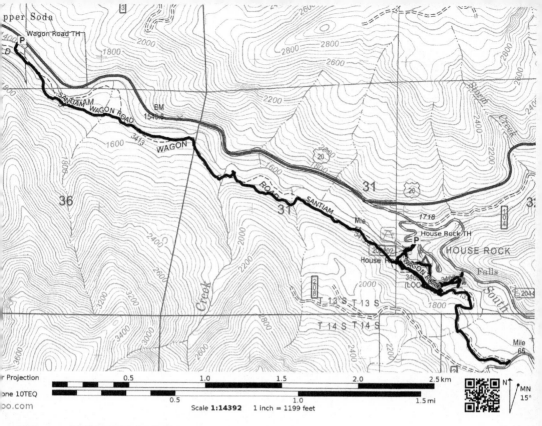

r Projection
one 10TEQ
po.com

Scale **1:14392**   1 inch = 1199 feet

42.   HOUSE ROCK

Distance: 1.2 mile loop
Elevation Gain: 300 feet
Trailhead elevation: 1,608 feet
Trail high point: 1,796 feet
Season: all year
Best: all year
Map: See map for Hike 41.

Directions:
- From Sweet Home, drive 26 miles on US 20 up the South Santiam River to a junction with Latiwi Creek Road (FR 2044), signed for House Rock Campground.
- Turn right here, and drive 200 yards downhill to a junction.
- Turn right and drive downhill 0.3 mile to a parking area on your right, just before a bridge. The trail leaves from a spot about 100 feet back up the road before the sign-board.

Hike: Though short, the loop over to House Rock Falls and back on the Santiam Wagon Road packs in a lot of intrigue in just 1.2 miles. You have a waterfall, a huge boulder that served as an emergency shelter for pioneers, ancient forest and a historic wagon road. It makes for a perfect leg stretcher if you are camped at lovely House Rock Campground, or if you just happen to be in the area.

Begin at the signboard and follow a trail to a boulder near the South Santiam River. Though it seems like the trail should turn right, you will look for a set of stairs chiseled into the boulder that lead to a new wooden bridge over the South Santiam River. Cross the bridge and turn left, hiking upriver. Arrive at a junction with a connector trail over to the Santiam Wagon Road. Ignore this junction for now and continue hiking upriver. After just a few steps, arrive at House Rock, a boulder so massive that pioneer families once took refuge underneath it during a storm. Continue past the boulder for 0.3 mile to another junction with a spur trail up to the Santiam Wagon Road. Ignore this junction too, veering to the left and downhill towards the river. Soon you will arrive at an obstructed viewpoint above the falls, a 20-foot chute on the South Santiam River. It is quite fun to climb around on the rocks but it is very difficult to get a clear view of the falls.

After the falls, return back to your last trail junction and turn left. Switchback up through ancient forest and quickly arrive at a junction with the Santiam Wagon Road. Turn right here. Walk down this road, which was constructed in the 1860s as a route across the Cascades for white settlers. When US 20 was constructed in 1920s, the road soon fell into disuse and was abandoned in 1930. Though it is no longer drivable, it is certainly worthy of hiking. Reach another junction, potentially unsigned, in 0.3 mile. Turn right and drop quickly back to the House Rock Trail right before the bridge over the South Santiam River. Turn left to cross the river, and then turn right on the opposite side of the river to return to the trailhead.

43.   GORDON MEADOWS

Distance: 7.8 miles one-way
Elevation Gain: 2,200 feet
Trailhead elevation: 2,936 feet (Falls Creek TH); 3,956 feet (Gordon Lakes TH)
Trail high point: 4,301 feet
Season: June - October
Best: June- July
Map: See my website for a high-resolution map of the Gordon Meadows area.

Directions to the Falls Creek Trailhead:
- From the junction of US 20 and Quartzville Road east of Sweet Home, drive approximately 13 miles on US 20 up the South Santiam River to a junction with FR 2032, signed for Longbow Organizational Camp.
- Turn right here and drive 1.6 miles to a junction with Longbow Camp.
- Keep on FR 2032 for another 1.6 miles to a confusing 4-way junction.
- Turn a slight left on the left main fork to stay on FR 2032 and drive 1.7 miles to milepost 5 on FR 2032.
- The trailhead is in a small clearing up a short access road on the left.

Directions to the Gordon Lakes Trailhead:
- From Sweet Home, drive 26 miles on US 20 up the South Santiam River to a junction with Latiwi Creek Road (FR 2044), signed for House Rock Campground.

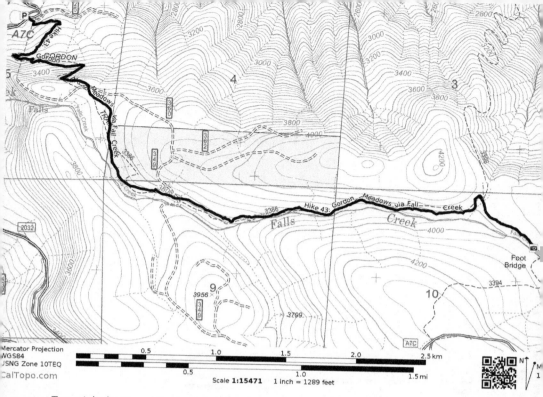

Mercator Projection
WGS84
USNG Zone 10TEQ
CalTopo.com

Scale **1:15471**   1 inch = 1289 feet

- Turn right here and ignore any signs for House Rock Campground.
- Continue downhill to a bridge and then begin climbing on a sometimes-rocky road for 5.2 miles. Ignore any side roads along the way.
- At a hiker-symbol sign, turn right on FR 2044-230 (which may just be signed 230).
- Drive 2.7 miles to the trailhead at road's end.

Hike: Two different trailheads but two very similar trails lead to spacious and peaceful Gordon Meadows, set at the crest of the Old Cascades. While both are worthwhile hikes on their own, the best way to see the area is to establish a car shuttle and do this hike one way, either uphill or downhill. If that isn't possible, two separate dayhikes or one long trip will suffice. This is an ideal hike for a cloudy, foggy day in June or July.

Begin at the Falls Creek Trailhead. The Falls Creek Trail bends around a ridge and begins a long but very gradual climb through a gorgeous, electric-green forest. The Falls Creek Trail climbs around an old clearcut until it tops out in a mossy forest a little over a mile into the hike. Before long you will cross a gravel road and level out in a dark, mossy forest where scattered huge Douglas firs blot out the sun even on bright days. Descend a little bit to another crossing of the same road, near Falls Creek. The trail parallels Falls Creek for the next 1.6 miles, most of which are essentially level. At 3.6 miles, meet an old trail on your left. Keep right and continue one-third of a mile to a junction with the Gordon Meadows Administrative Trail at the edge of huge Gordon Meadows. There is no direct trail to the meadow, but there are several opportunities for exploration. When you have a chance, peel off to your right through the trees and hike out to the meadow's edge. Look for lots of yellow buttercups, blue camas and white marsh marigolds. Try not to crush any of the fragile meadow vegetation!

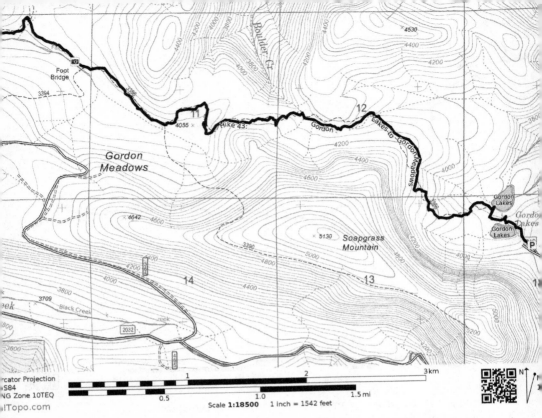

Scale **1:18500**   1 inch = 1542 feet

If you are hiking beyond Gordon Meadows, the trail wraps around the huge meadows and heads back into the forest. The trail begins a long stretch in deep forest as it traverses around Soapgrass Mountain's cliffs. There are occasional uphill and downhill stretches, but for the most part the trail remains more or less level. After 3.4 miles of very pleasant trail, meet a junction with the spur trail down to Lower Gordon Lake. Left leads to the lower lake, while right heads around a small knoll to the upper lake. There are several excellent campsites at both lake, but expect to see a few campers- you are quite close to the upper trailhead. Once you pass the upper lake, it is a short quarter of a mile to the upper trailhead far above the canyon of the South Santiam River.

44.   IRON MOUNTAIN LOOP

Distance: 6.6 mile loop
Elevation Gain: 2,100 feet
Trailhead elevation: 4,234 feet
Trail high point: 5,382 feet
Season: June- October
Best: July
Map: Green Trails #588 (Echo Mtn)

Directions:
- From Sweet Home drive east on US 20 for 35 miles to Tombstone Pass.
- Turn right into a large lot with a bathroom.
- If you are coming from the east, the trailhead is 11.1 miles west of the split with OR 22.

Hike: The Iron Mountain Loop is the most popular hike in the Old Cascades, and with good reason. The flower displays rival any in the entire Cascade Range, the views are outstanding and the hike easy enough for anybody in reasonable hiking shape. For the best experience, come in late June or early July, check online to see how the flowers are doing, and show up early. If you can come on a weekday, all the better.

Begin at Tombstone Pass and hike downhill slightly through the forest paralleling US 20. At about a half-mile from the trailhead, you will cross US 20. Look both ways and carefully cross the highway. From here, the trail climbs gradually up through the forest until you reach Cone Peak's meadows at a little over 2 miles. In flower season, the next mile of trail is among the finest in the Cascades: acres of wildflowers carpet the meadows, while Iron Mountain looms across the valley to the west. Look for countless blue and purple larkspur, red paintbrush, yellow Oregon Sunshine, a small daisy-like flower. Photographers will want to spend a long time here.

Beyond Cone Peak's meadows, the trail dips into the forest a bit as it traverses around Iron Mountain's forested north face. At 3.6 miles, meet the Iron Mountain Spur Trail on your left. Turn left here and hike 0.7 mile of uphill to the summit, where you will find a huge observation deck with benches. The view is exceptional, stretching from Mount Adams to Diamond Peak and pretty much everything in between. US 20 stretches out like a river

Walking over Cone Peak toward Iron Mountain's cliffs.

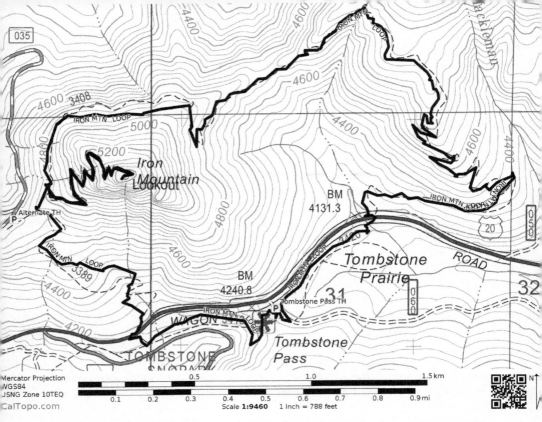

Scale **1:9460**   1 Inch = 788 feet

below you as it heads east towards Central Oregon. A lookout tower stood on the summit until 2008 and an observation deck now stands in its place. You will likely need to share the summit with many other admirers, but that's fine- everybody here is as happy to be there are you are.

Return to the junction and turn left to continue your loop. In just a bit, you'll pass a junction with the Iron Mountain trail on your right. Most of the people who hike to the summit of Iron Mountain do so from this trailhead, but they miss out on Cone Peak's flower meadows. Continue downhill until you reach another crossing of US 20. Carefully cross the highway and descend into the forest below Tombstone Pass. You have to regain a bit of elevation over the next 0.6 mile, but once you top out, you're back at the trailhead.

Other hiking options:
Iron Mountain the short way: Many people who hike to the summit of Iron Mountain do so from this shorter trailhead. Going this way avoids Cone Peak's wildflower meadows but delivers you to the top of Iron Mountain in less than a mile. To find this alternate trailhead, drive up US 20 towards Santiam Pass a total of 29 miles from the Quartzville Junction at the edge of Sweet Home. At a junction with FR 035 on your left, turn left and drive 2.6 miles to the end of this road at the large Iron Mountain Trailhead.

45. WEST BROWDER RIDGE

	Browder Ridge	Heart Lake
Distance:	11.4 miles out and back	13 miles out and back
Elevation Gain:	2,200 feet	3,200 feet
Trailhead Elevation:	4,085 feet	4,085 feet
Trail High Point:	5,672 feet	5,672 feet
Season:	June- October	June- October
Best:	June- July	July- October
Map:	Green Trails #588 (Echo Mtn)	Green Trails #588 (Echo Mtn)

Directions:

- From the junction of US 20 and Quartzville Road east of Sweet Home, drive approximately 30 miles on US 20 up the South Santiam River to a junction with FR 15.
- If you are coming from the east, this junction is on your left 11.7 miles after the OR 22 / US 20 split.
- Turn right here onto FR 15 and drive 2.5 paved miles to the trailhead, a small parking lot with a "P" sign on the right. The trailhead is located at the junction of FR 15 and FR 080.
- The trail departs from the left side of the road at a signboard.

Hike: The western approach to Browder Ridge's wildflower meadows is all but forgotten. While you can expect brush and blowdown on occasion, the access is easier than the more popular eastern approach to Browder Ridge and the scenery just as good. The only difference is that the trail is in worse shape, and marginally more difficult. This hike is so great I doubt you'll care all that much.

Begin at the Browder Ridge Trailhead on FR 15. The trail begins with a mostly-level stretch through a cool forest. At a little under a mile from the trailhead, reach a seemingly endless meadow of bracken ferns, stretching all the way to the top of the ridge. Getting to the top looks daunting, but the trail switchbacks all the way to the top without ever feeling steep. Occasional forays into the forest keep hikers from overheating. When you reach the top at about 2 miles from the trailhead, you are almost done with your elevation gain for a good long while.

The next 2.5 miles are pure pleasure. Sure, you'll have to deal with occasional stretches of faint and brushy trail, but there is so much to see! The trail follows Browder Ridge just below its crest, passing through meadow after meadow with views south to the Three Sisters. The wildflower displays here in June and July are among the best in the Cascades: look for lots of blue and purple larkspur, red paintbrush, yellow Oregon sunshine, pink owl's clover, blue and purple lupine and so many more. At 3 miles or so from the trailhead, the trail enters a small piece of fire-damaged forest and becomes vague- cut straight through the forest to locate the trail on the far side. Stay straight and you cannot get lost. Over the next 1.5 miles the trail becomes quite brushy and narrow in some spots, but remains very beautiful.

Mount Washington and the Three Sisters from Browder Ridge.

At 4.5 miles, the Browder Ridge Trail meets the Gate Creek Trail coming from the east (see Hike 48). Turn left here and start up the Heart Lake Trail. You will begin climbing again through the forest for about 0.5 mile until the trail emerges under Browder Ridge's summit cliffs. The views, flowers and cliffs make for a sublime setting. At 0.9 mile from the trail junction, the Heart Lake Trail reaches a saddle. The trail continues downhill to Heart Lake (a noble adventure), but first you should turn left on a faint social trail that departs from the saddle. The trail leads you left (right goes to Heart Lake), first through the trees and then steeply up to the summit of Browder Ridge. Watch your step in a few places as the ridge is narrow here. You don't need to hike all the way to the true summit of the ridge for the fantastic views, but you do need to hike above treeline. At the top you'll see far to the south, with the Three Sisters appearing surprisingly close. To the north and west, Mount Jefferson rises above the true summit of Browder Ridge while Mount Hood looms on the far horizon. Bachelor Mountain (Hikes 33 and 34) and Coffin Mountain (Hike 32) are immediately to the left of Mount Hood. Most hikers will want to turn around here.

To visit Heart Lake, continue downhill on the narrow, rough and steep Heart Lake Trail. You'll lose nearly 700 feet in just 0.7 mile on the way to the scenic lake- a steep price to pay after the long hike to Browder Ridge from the west. For more information about the detour down to Heart Lake, see Hike 48. Return the way you came.

Oh, and one more special message to go: this would be an easy car shuttle if you have the means to set one up. For directions to the eastern Browder Ridge Trailhead (known as the Gate Creek Trailhead) and more information on the trail down to Heart Lake, see Hike 48.

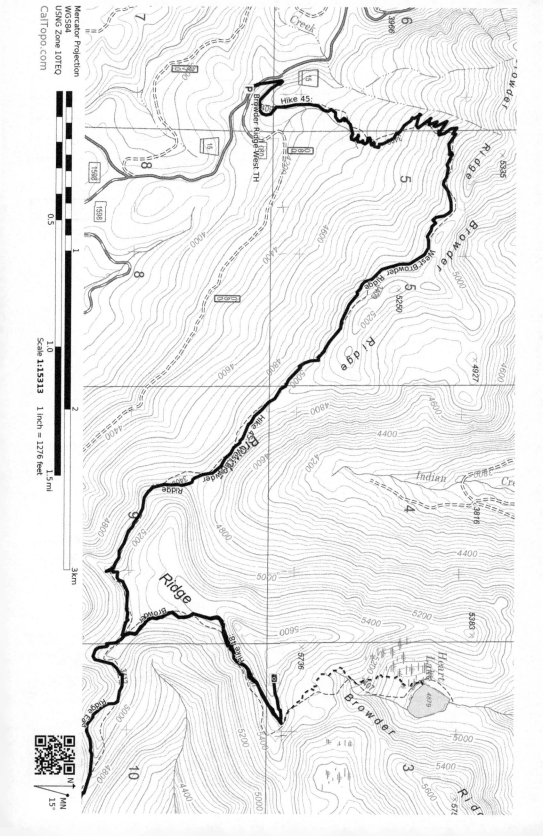

46. ECHO BASIN AND HACKLEMAN GROVE

	Echo Basin	Hackleman Grove
Distance:	2.2 mile loop	1.2 mile loop
Elevation Gain:	700 feet	200 feet
Trailhead Elevation:	4,188 feet	3,525 feet
Trail High Point:	4,814 feet	3,566 feet
Season:	June- October	May- October
Best:	June- July	May- October
Map:	Green Trails #588 (Echo Mtn)	Green Trails #588 (Echo Mtn)

Directions to Hackleman Grove:
- From the junction of US 20 and Quartzville Road east of Sweet Home, drive 33.3 miles on US 20 to a junction with FR 055.
- If you are coming from the east, this junction is 8.4 miles west of Santiam Junction.

Directions to Echo Basin:
- From the junction of US 20 and Quartzville Road east of Sweet Home, drive 33.5 miles on US 20 to a junction with FR 055.
- This junction is 0.2 mile east of Hackleman Grove.
- If you are coming from the east, this junction is 8.2 miles west of Santiam Junction.
- Turn left up FR 055 and drive 2 gravel miles to the Echo Basin trailhead near road's end.

Hike: Here are two short but excellent hikes high up in the Old Cascades; both are so short you'll still have time to do something else, but both are perfect for one of those days where you only have a few hours to play up in the mountains. For Echo Basin, plan on a visit in June or July to experience the basin's wildflower meadows at their peak.

Begin with Echo Basin. The sign at the trailhead reads "Echo Mtn. Old Growth Trail" and the name is not a misnomer. You will start by hiking quickly uphill in second-growth forest but soon you will enter a magnificent grove of Alaska cedars, here at the southern boundary of their range. At 0.6 miles, and after 500 feet of elevation gain, meet a trail junction at the edge of Echo Basin's meadows. Either direction is fine, but as usual, I recommend going counterclockwise. Turn right and pass under a grove of huge Alaska cedars. While their size pales in comparison to some Western red cedars you may have seen, the Alaska cedar does

not grow huge like its bottomland cousins, and as such, these are among the largest specimens of Alaska cedar you will ever see. The trees in this grove are hundreds of years old. As you enter the basin, you will see notice the obvious: this is a wetland meadow, and it is very boggy. Boots are highly recommended here. In season, you will see lots of shooting stars, columbine, lousewort, cinquefoil and larkspur. Boardwalks have been constructed in some places to keep

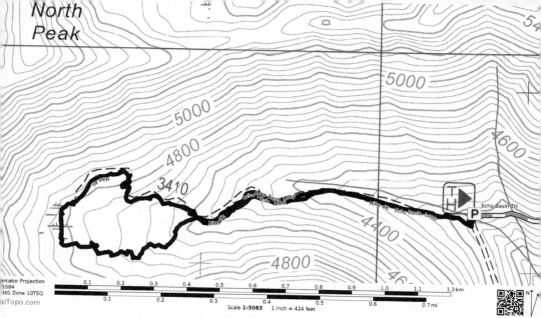

your feet dry (and, of course, to keep you from trampling the fragile vegetation). Eventually the trail leaves the basin as it ducks back into the forest below Echo Mountain's cliffs. At 1.6 miles, the loop ends and all that's left is a quick 0.6 mile descent to the trailhead.

Drive over to Hackleman Grove's trailhead, on US 20. The paved trail descends quickly and gradually to a junction. Hikers should turn left. The trail drops through lovely forest to the banks of Hackleman Creek. The trail follows the creek for a bit, finally reaching a junction. Left leads to the paved trail again, but right leads to the nicest of the grove's towering Douglas firs. Both options here make loops back to the trailhead, but you came here for the

trees. Turn right and walk into heart of the grove. Your neck may hurt from gazing up towards the tops of these very tall trees. Even though the hike is a little over a mile, you may want to spend an hour here just taking in the forest! Eventually, all good things must come to an end; when you reach the end of the loop, turn right and return to the trailhead.

If you still have lots of time and energy, consider pairing these two hikes with either Iron Mountain (Hike 44) or Clear Lake (Hike 49), both of which are moderate hikes and easy drives from Hackleman Grove's roadside trailhead. Hackleman Grove is a worthwhile stop after any hike in this area if you have an extra thirty minutes.

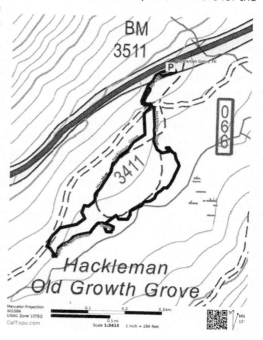

47. CRESCENT MOUNTAIN

Distance: 9.6 miles out and back
Elevation Gain: 2,500 feet
Trailhead elevation: 3,724 feet
Trail high point: 5,740 feet
Season: June- October
Best: July
Map: Green Trails #588 (Echo Mtn)

Directions:
- From the junction of US 20 and Quartzville Road east of Sweet Home, drive 37.7 miles east on US 20 to a junction with Lava Lake Road, FR 2067.
- This junction is about 0.5 mile west of the junction of US 20 and OR 126 and about 3.5 miles east of the junction of OR 22 and US 20. If you are driving here from Salem or Bend, drive to Santiam Junction and turn right for 3.5 miles to the junction with Lava Lake Road (FR 2067).
- Turn left (or right if driving west on US 20) and drive 0.9 mile north on this paved road.
- Turn left at a hiker sign on to FR 580.
- Drive 0.7 mile to a large parking lot at road's end.

Hike: This excellent hike is ideal in any season but no more so than in late June and early July, when its sunny slopes are carpeted with one of the more spectacular wildflower displays in the Cascades. Every few years the display of beargrass on this hike is absolutely mind-boggling – try and time this hike for one of those years if possible.

The trail begins with a gentle descent along placid Maude Creek. The forest here is beautiful, with huge hemlock trees and a variety of woodland flowers. Look for yellow violets, pink bleeding hearts and early in the season, lots of trillium. The trail crosses Maude Creek on a bridge at about 1.1 miles and begins a well-graded but steady uphill through a dark forest. Note the copious amounts of yellow lichen on the sides of the trees here – the height of the lichen on the trees indicates the depth of the winter snowpack, showing that this area is typically covered with six to eight feet of snow in the winter.

At about 2.5 miles into your hike, the trail exits the forest and enters the hanging meadows for which this area is famous. Look for lots of larkspur, bleeding hearts, paintbrush and wallflowers. Equally impressive are the views; Three-Fingered Jack seems close enough to touch as it looms just across the valley to the east. The trail switchbacks up the hanging meadows for almost a mile until it re-enters the forest, at which point you are nearing the summit. At 4.6 miles from the trailhead, reach a junction with the unmarked but very obvious spur to the summit of Crescent Mountain. Turn right and climb 0.1 mile to the summit. The remains of the erstwhile lookout tower, abandoned to the elements in the 1950s, dot the summit. As you would expect, the view is outstanding, stretching from Mount Hood to the Three Sisters in an excellent 180 degree panorama. Look down to remote Crescent Lake, situated at the base of Crescent Mountain's cliffs.

Return the way you came, or arrange a shuttle to the northern trailhead for Crescent Mountain at the beginning of the Old Cascades Loop. Please note that I did not hike this northern section of trail and it is purported to be rough in spots. If you visit and have something to add, please send me a note!

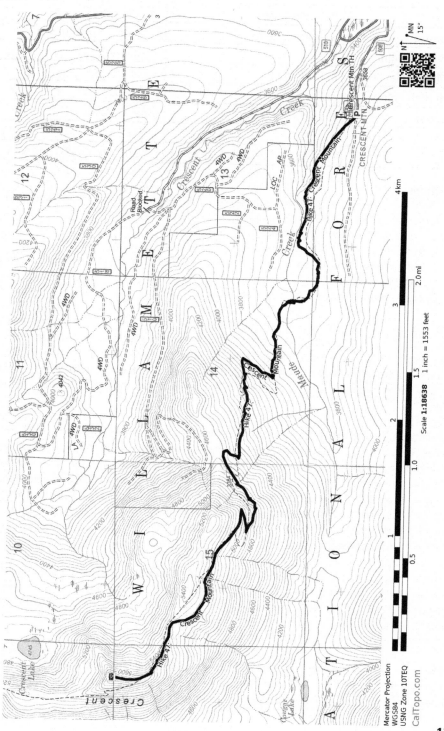

Mercator Projection
WGS84
USNG Zone 10TEQ
CalTopo.com

Scale 1:18638   1 inch = 1553 feet

48. EAST BROWDER RIDGE AND HEART LAKE

	Browder Ridge	Heart Lake
Distance:	8.6 miles out and back	10.2 miles out and back
Elevation Gain:	2,100 feet	2,900 feet
Trailhead Elevation:	3,721 feet	3,721 feet
Trail High Point:	5,672 feet	5,672 feet
Season:	June- October	June- October
Best:	June- July	July- October
Map:	Green Trails #588 (Echo Mtn)	Green Trails #588 (Echo Mtn)

Directions:
- From Sweet Home, drive approximately 41 miles east on US 20 to a junction with Hackleman Creek Road, FR 2672. This junction is only 1 mile west of OR 126.
- Drive south 0.7 mile to a fork and keep left.
- Turn right on FR 2672 and drive another 1 mile to a sign for the Gate Creek Trail.
- Turn right again, this time on FR 1598, and drive 2.8 miles to the trailhead on the right side of the road.
- There is room for several cars on the left side of the road, opposite the trailhead.

Hike: The hike up to Browder Ridge takes you up onto a ridge with fantastic views and outstanding flower displays. You have to earn it, though. Though there is an excellent viewpoint only 1.4 miles from the trailhead, the best flowers and views are reached only by hiking up onto Browder Ridge's flower-spangled meadows. The truly adventurous can hike all the way down to deep Heart Lake, tucked in a forested bowl on the north side of Browder Ridge.

Begin from the Gate Creek Trailhead. Like so many trails in the Cascades, the trail leaves its namesake and begins a steep climb up the slope above Gate Creek. After 0.8 mile, the trail levels out briefly to traverse a beautifully mixed forest of Douglas fir, hemlock and lodgepole pine. Soon you will resume your ascent, but there are rewards – before long, the trail emerges into steep hanging meadows, meadows that feature excellent flower displays in June and July. The trail rounds a ridge end at 1.4 miles with excellent views out to the High Cascades from Mount Jefferson to the Three Sisters. This makes an excellent turnaround spot for hikers looking for a short trek.

Those interested in a longer hike to the summit of Browder Ridge should continue. From here the trail climbs to the top of the forested ridge, where it loses and gains elevation with the terrain. At 3.3 miles from the trailhead, reach an unmarked fork. You could continue straight, continuing to follow the grassy ridge. To hike to the summit of Browder Ridge, however, turn right on the possibly unsigned Heart Lake Trail.

From here, the trail plows through the forest for almost a mile, passing under the huge rock ramparts of Browder Ridge's summit before reaching a saddle, where you will find an unsigned trail junction. Left leads you steeply up to the summit of Browder Ridge, while right

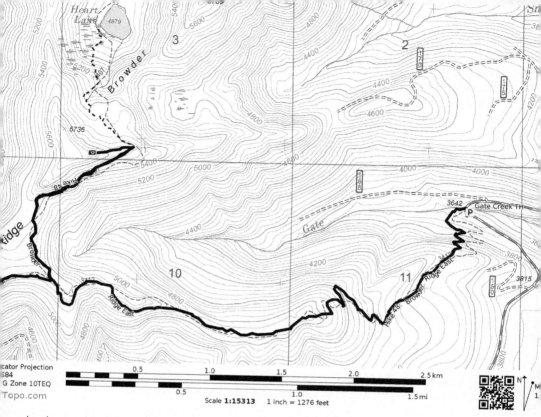

Scale **1:15313**   1 inch = 1276 feet

leads you downhill on to Heart Lake. With enough time and energy, you should do both. The views from the summit are outstanding, stretching from Mount Hood to the Three Sisters. Most will want to turn around here, at the viewpoint.

Now, about Heart Lake: this beautiful lake, set in ancient forest and tucked inside Browder Ridge's cliffs, is an excellent side trip or backpacking destination. But it is not for the faint of heart! The trail is occasionally faint and excessively steep. It's worth it, though, if you have the energy to climb back out of Heart Lake's basin. Begin at the saddle below Browder Ridge's summit. The trail drops into a small basin and levels off temporarily. Look for flagging to help guide you through the fainter spots of the trail. At 0.4 mile from the saddle, you've only dropped about 150 feet of elevation; over the last 0.4 mile to Heart Lake, the trail loses 600 feet. It is even steeper than it looks on paper. Thankfully, the trail is reasonably easy to follow but it's hell on the knees, and it will be hell on your lungs going back up. Reach the lake at 0.7 mile from the saddle (and 6.4 miles from the western Browder Ridge Trailhead) and rejoice! You've discovered one of the prettier "secret" places in the Cascades. The area around the lake is marshy and you'd be well advised to stay away from the fringes of the lake if you want to keep your feet dry. On the northern (far) end of the lake, there is one excellent campsite with a view back towards Browder Ridge's cliffs. This would be a great place to spend the night if you don't mind hauling a pack down here (and back out). Return the way you came.

Return the way you came, or arrange an easy car shuttle to the western Browder Ridge Trailhead (see Hike 45).

49. CLEAR LAKE

Distance: 5 mile loop
Elevation Gain: 200 feet
Trailhead elevation: 3,033 feet
Trail high point: 3,093 feet
Season: all year (bring snowshoes in winter)
Best: April- October
Map: For a high-resolution map of Clear Lake and the McKenzie River, see my website.

Directions from Sweet Home:
- From the junction of US 20 and Quartzville Road east of Sweet Home, drive 38.4 miles east on US 20 to a junction with OR 126 on your right.
- Turn right and drive 3.7 miles south on OR 126 to the turnoff on your left for Clear Lake.
- Drive down the access road to a parking lot next to Clear Lake's store.

Directions from Salem:
- Drive OR 22 for approximately 80 miles to its end at Santiam Junction, where OR22 meets US 20.
- Turn right on US 20 and drive 3.2 miles to a junction with OR 126 on your left.
- Turn left and drive 3.7 miles south on OR 126 to the turnoff on your left for Clear Lake.
- Drive down the access road to a parking lot next to Clear Lake's store.

Directions from Sisters:
- Drive US 20 from Sisters, crossing over Santiam Pass, a total of 25.7 miles to Santiam Junction.
- Continue straight on US 20 another 3.2 miles to a junction with OR 126 on your left.
- Turn left and drive 3.7 miles south on OR 126 to the turnoff on your left for Clear Lake.
- Drive down the access road to a parking lot next to Clear Lake's store.

Hike: Clear Lake is a fascinating and beautiful place. The lake was created by lava flows over 3,000 years ago that blocked the headwaters of the McKenzie River, creating a deep blue lake that drowned the forests along the bank of the river. On this easy loop around the lake, you will cross the McKenzie River at its source, hike through several outstanding groves of ancient forest, traverse across the lava flows that created the lake, find surprisingly decent views of Mount Washington and the Three Sisters and pass innumerable vistas of Clear Lake's magical waters. What could be better?

Begin at the Clear Lake Resort's visitor parking lot, or the day-use lot just south of the resort (this is preferable). Follow the main trail south from the parking lot (fisherman trails braid closer to the lake, but the main trail is wide and well-marked). You will pass several excellent views of the lake, backed by the spire of Mount Washington. At 1.2 miles from the trailhead, you will cross the headwaters of the McKenzie River on a wooden bridge and soon reach a junction with the McKenzie River Trail. Right leads to Sahalie and Koosah Falls (Hike 50) but for this loop, keep left.

The trail traverses around the bays on the south side of the lake, where views open to the

Gene kayaking Clear Lake with the Three Sisters in the background.

lake's waters. The water color is a luminous shade of turquoise in its shallow waters and a deep, deep blue in the deeper waters — and you'll find yourself snapping photos by the dozen to capture both. In fact, the best time for photography here is in the fall, when the reds and yellows of the vine maple along the lake add contrast to the blues and greens you see all around you. The trail passes beneath Coldwater Cove's campground, conveniently located between tongues of the lava flow. Benches along the lake provide excellent lunch stops.

At a little under 4 miles from the trailhead, reach the incredible turquoise waters of Great Spring, tucked away from the lake and surrounded by massive Douglas fir trees. Hike around the spring and soon you find yourself at the northern end of the lake. It seems your hike should be almost over, right? First, you have to traverse around both Fish Creek's long canyon and the swamps of Ikenick Creek, time-consuming endeavors. In between the two creeks is one of the highlights of the hike, a view across the long turquoise expanse of Clear Lake to the Three Sisters, which seem surprisingly close. Once you make it around the swamps, it is a short and easy trek back to the resort parking lot.

EXTENDING YOUR TRIP:

You can connect this hike to the loop around Sahalie and Koosah Falls (Hike 50) by hiking a connector trail 0.7 mile, crossing OR 126 in the process (look both ways and cross only when the coast is clear!) to a bridge over the McKenzie River, where the loop begins. This figure-eight loop ends up being a shade under 10 miles with a little under 1,000 of elevation gain. With a full day and enough space on your camera, you'll probably want to do both hikes!

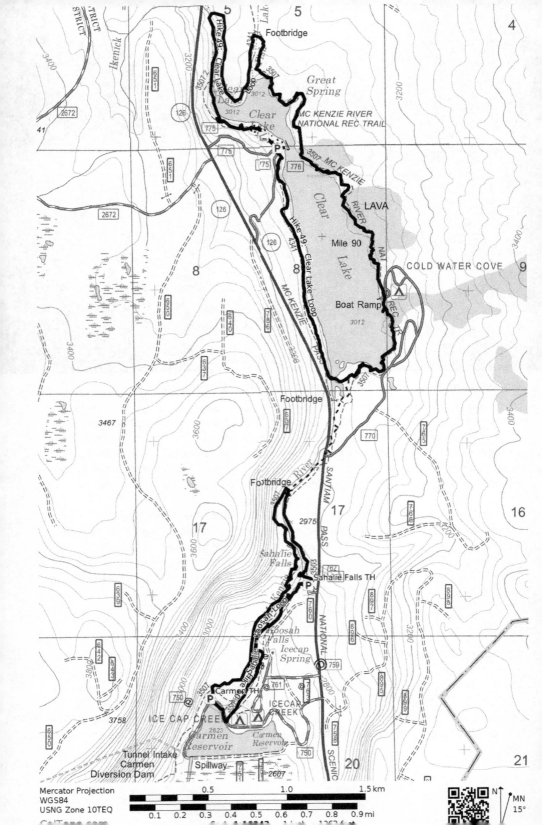

Mercator Projection
WGS84
USNG Zone 10TEQ

0.5   1.0   1.5 km

0.1 0.2 0.3 0.4 0.5 0.6 0.7 0.8 0.9 mi

N
MN
15°

50.   SAHALIE AND KOOSAH FALLS

Distance: 2.8 mile loop
Elevation Gain: 400 feet
Trailhead elevation: 2,630 feet
Trail high point: 3,011 feet
Season: all year (avoid icy periods in winter)
Best: April- June, October
Map: For a high-resolution map of Clear Lake and the McKenzie River, see my website.

Directions from Sweet Home:
* From the junction of US 20 and Quartzville Road east of Sweet Home, drive 38.4 miles east on US 20 to a junction with OR 126 on your right.
* Turn right and drive 5.7 miles south on OR 126 to a turnoff on your right for Carmen Reservoir.
* Turn right, drive down the road to a bridge over the reservoir, then park on the far side by a bathroom.
* You will pass trailheads along the way at both Sahalie and Koosah Falls; you can also begin your hike at both of these trailheads.

Directions from Salem:
* Drive OR 22 for 80 miles to the OR 22 / US 20 merger at Santiam Junction.
* Turn right on US 20 and drive 3.2 miles to a junction with OR 126 on your left.
* Turn left and drive 5.7 miles south on OR 126 to a turnoff on your right for Carmen Reservoir.
* Turn right, drive down the road to a bridge over the reservoir, then park on the far side by a bathroom.
* You will pass trailheads along the way at both Sahalie and Koosah Falls; you can also begin your hike at both of these trailheads.

Directions from Sisters:
* Drive US 20 from Sisters over Santiam Pass for a total of 25.7 miles to Santiam Junction.
* Continue straight on US 20 another 3.2 miles to a junction with OR 126 on your left.
* Turn left and drive 5.7 miles south on OR 126 to a turnoff on your right for Carmen Reservoir.
* Turn right, drive down the road to a bridge over the reservoir, then park on the far side by a bathroom.
* You will pass trailheads along the way at both Sahalie and Koosah Falls; you can also begin your hike at both of these trailheads.

Hike: In a state overflowing with beautiful rivers, the McKenzie River is among the most beautiful. Just one mile from its source, the river tumbles over two magnificent waterfalls and rages through narrow slots. The water is a luminous shade of electric blue. This short loop passes these features from both sides of the river, and is an ideal hike for out-of-town guests.

There are several trailheads in this area, but I like to start the hike from the Carmen Reservoir. This way you can start from the lowest point, which is always welcome. Just across the bridge over the McKenzie River at the reservoir, look for a hiker symbol sign on the east (right) bank of the river. The trail climbs upstream, passing numerous vistas of the electric river as it rages through its narrow canyon. Pass 82 foot Koosah Falls at about 0.5 mile. You will pass many viewpoints of the falls; my favorite is the first, which has a short spur trail to a viewpoint looking upriver at the falls. If you time your visit for midday on a sunny day, there will likely be a rainbow across the falls (just as with Sahalie Falls upriver).

Continue hiking upstream another 0.5 mile to 63-foot Sahalie Falls, which is just as spectacular as Koosah. There are numerous places to stop for photos, and you'll find yourself stopping at each viewpoint available. I stop at every single one of them even though I've been here many times. The spray can be intense when the river is flowing high (which it frequently is). From the top of Sahalie Falls, continue upriver on a much quieter trail another 0.4 mile to a junction. Straight will take you to Clear Lake (Hike 49) in 0.7 mile, but unless you parked up there, you need to turn left.

Cross the McKenzie River on a rickety wooden bridge and begin to parallel the river downstream. Even though you are at most 200 feet from the popular trail on the east side of the river, this trail feels very different. It is more rugged, climbs up and down and offers different views of river and falls. You will likely meet mountain bikers headed downriver as well, so keep an eye out. The views of both Sahalie and Koosah Falls are not as impressive from this side of the river, but rugged and faint spur trails offer views to those daring enough to seek them out. Beyond Koosah Falls, the trail switchbacks away from the river a bit and descends into a verdant forest before ending on the west side of Carmen Reservoir at a small trailhead, complete with bathroom. If you are parked here, this is the end of your hike. If you parked at Sahalie or Koosah Falls, walk the road across the river and turn left at the hiker symbol to continue upstream, towards your car.

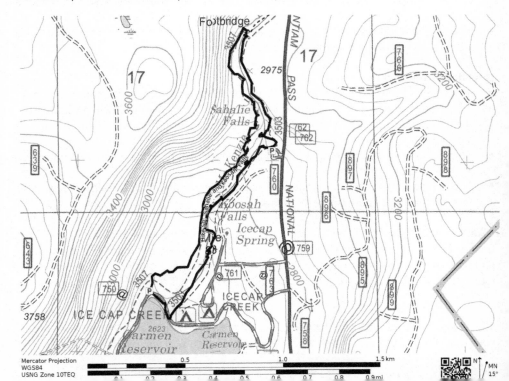

Sahalie Falls thunders down a ledge of basalt into a mossy grotto. Photographing both Sahalie and Koosah Falls presents a set of challenges and dilemmas. On one hand, it is a much easier waterfall to photograph on misty, cloudy days when both river and moss take on surreal shades of blue and green; on the other hand, you should absolutely plan on visiting on a sunny day to see the rainbows created by the incredible amount of spray at the base of the waterfall (Koosah Falls also has rainbows on sunny days). Better yet, visit often to see the many moods of these two beautiful waterfalls.

SECTION 4: OLALLIE SCENIC AREA

		Distance	EV Gain
51.	Sisi Butte	5.8	1,400
52.	Russ and Jude Lakes	2.5	400
53.	Lodgepole Loop	11.1	1,200
54.	Olallie Butte	7.4	2,600
55.	Fish Lake	6.0	900
56.	Olallie and Monon Lakes	6.7	200
57.	Double Peaks and Timber Lake	7.0	1,300
58.	Olallie-Ruddy Hill Loop	10.3	1,300
59.	Red Lake and Potato Butte	7.3	1,700
60.	Breitenbush Cascades	0.3	150
61.	Ruddy Hill-Gibson Lake Loop	5.0	900
62.	Pyramid Butte	3.3	900
63.	Park Ridge and Jefferson Park	6.8	1,400

The Olallie Scenic Area is unique, a large and mostly flat area that straddles both sides of the Cascades. Hundreds of lakes dot this scenic plateau, allowing outdoor lovers countless opportunities for exploration. The trails are mostly level and well-maintained, allowing for many easy hikes. There are also several exceedingly steep spur trails leading to outstanding viewpoints, and each and every one of these are different enough that all are worth hiking.

Olallie Lake is a long drive from Portland and an equally long drive from Salem. The best plan of action to visit is to drive into the area and set up camp for a few days - or better yet, plan a stay at the rustic Olallie Lake Resort. Many of the hikes are accessible just by hiking the Pacific Crest Trail north or south through the area. Getting to Olallie Lake can be a challenge; while the Skyline Road receives annual maintenance up to Olallie Lake, winters are cruel up here and the road is frequently rutted and rocky. The Skyline Road gets progressively worse as you drive south towards Monon and Horseshoe Lakes; by the time you reach Breitenbush Lake it's a full-scale nightmare. Driving this southern stretch of the Skyline Road from Monon Lake to FR 46 requires high clearance and lots of patience.

The best time to visit this area is in August and September, when the mosquitos are gone, as are the crowds, and the huckleberries are profuse. Later in the fall, after the berries are gone, huckleberry leaves burn red in a fantastic display of color that spreads across the area from high to low. Winters here are long and cruel, so plan ahead to visit this area- its remoteness ensures that it is all but inaccessible from November to June.

Finally, please note that many of the hikes in this region pass through sections of the Warm Springs Reservation. The Warm Springs can close a trail at any point for any reason they like. If you are on a trail and see that it is closed, please respect the wishes of the Warm Springs and turn around.

51. SISI BUTTE

Distance: 5.8 miles out and back
Elevation Gain: 1,400 feet
Trailhead elevation: 4,237 feet
Trail high point: 5,613 feet
Season: June- October
Best: September- October
Map: Green Trails #525 (Breitenbush)

Directions:
- From Estacada, drive southeast on OR 224 approximately 25 miles to the Ripplebrook Guard Station.
- A short distance after Ripplebrook, OR 224 becomes FR 46 at a junction with FR 57. Continue straight (right) on FR 46.
- Drive another 22.3 miles on FR 46 to a junction with the Olallie Lake Road (FR 4690) – you will notice that "Olallie" is painted on the road with an arrow to mark the direction.
- Turn left here onto FR 4690 and drive 6.1 miles of narrow pavement and another 1.9 miles of rocky gravel to a junction with the Skyline Road, FR 4220.
- Turn left here and drive 1.8 miles of rocky dirt road and then 0.5 paved miles to the unsigned junction with Sisi Butte's access road on your left.
- Park on the side of the road but do not block the gated access road.

Hike: This isn't a hike in a traditional sense; there's no trailhead, no trail and no sign of your destination until you reach it. But this is a fun hike just the same! You will hike up a steep, rough and hot jeep road to Sisi Butte's lookout tower, where the view is everything

you would expect from a lookout tower. The best time to come here is in the fall, when the weather isn't as toasty and the lookout tower is deserted, allowing hikers the chance to hike up to an observation deck without disturbing the occupant of the fire tower.

Begin at the unsigned trailhead, marked only be a rusting green gate. Walk up the road through the woods on a road so bad it will make you thankful you don't have to drive it. Soon, the forest begins to thin, offering excellent views to the south of Mount Jefferson, rising above Olallie country. At 2.5 miles from the trailhead, reach a junction with a rough road angling off to the right towards Sisi Butte's other summit (which, as it so happens, is one foot higher than the summit with the lookout tower). Keep left here and walk up the road 0.4 mile to the lookout, which towers over a collection of buildings on the south summit of Sisi Butte.

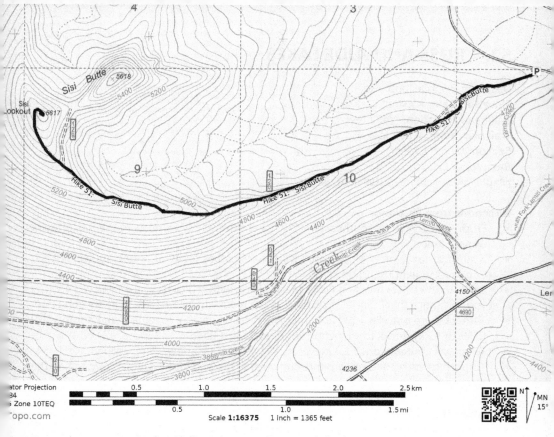

ator Projection
34
Zone 10TEQ
opo.com

Scale **1:16375**   1 Inch = 1365 feet

Everywhere you go in the Olallie Lake area, Sisi Butte's lookout tower seems to be on the horizon, including long stretches of the drive to the trailhead. As you would expect for such an isolated peak rising high above its surroundings, the view is fantastic. But here's the catch: you can't see anything from the summit. You have to climb up the lookout tower until the views unfold beneath you. The first incarnation of the lookout was built originally in 1940, and then dismantled in 1996. The present lookout, an eight-sided cab atop a 50' pole tower, was constructed in 1997. The tower is staffed in the summer, and it is entirely at the discretion of the staffer to let you come up for a visit. Once the staffer leaves, the top deck is locked but you are free to climb up to the deck below, where the view is every bit as good.

It is possible to bushwhack over to the other summit but it's a lot more work for a similar view. Unless you just have to see the other summit, return the way you came.

52.   RUSS AND JUDE LAKES

Distance: 2.5 mile loop
Elevation Gain: 400 feet
Trailhead elevation: 4,487 feet
Trail high point: 4,693 feet
Season: June- October
Best: June- October
Map: Green Trails #525 (Breitenbush)

Directions from Portland:
- From Estacada, drive southeast on OR 224 approximately 25 miles to the Ripplebrook Guard Station.
- A short distance after Ripplebrook, OR 224 becomes FR 46 at a junction with FR 57. Continue straight (right) on FR 46.
- Drive another 22.3 miles on FR 46 to a junction with the Olallie Lake Road (FR 4690) – you will notice that "Olallie" is painted on the road with an arrow to mark the direction.
- Turn left here onto FR 4690 and drive 6.1 miles of narrow pavement and another 1.9 miles of rocky gravel to a junction with the Skyline Road, FR 4220.
- Turn right here and drive 1.4 gravel miles to Olallie Meadows Campground.
- Turn left to enter the campground, and drive to the end of the campground to find the trailhead.

Directions from Salem:
- From Salem, drive OR 22 east approximately 49 miles to Detroit.
- Turn left at a sign for Breitenbush, Elk Lake and Olallie Lake onto FR 46.
- Drive 16.6 miles on FR 46 to a pass where you enter the Mount Hood National Forest.
- Continue another 6.6 miles (for a total of 23.2 miles from Detroit) to a junction with FR 4690 on your right, signed for Olallie Lake.
- Turn right onto FR 4690 and drive 6.1 miles of narrow pavement and another 1.9 miles of rocky gravel to a junction with the Skyline Road, FR 4220.
- Turn right here and drive 1.4 gravel miles to Olallie Meadows Campground.
- Turn left to enter the campground, and drive to the end of the campground to find the trailhead.

Hike: This short hike to a pair of scenic lakes is ideal for a quick stroll if you are camping in the area, but backpackers are sure to be disappointed; as the lakes are located on the Warm Springs Reservation, any camping is completely off-limits, and fishing is not legal without a Warm Springs Tribal Fishing Permit. That being said, this is a beautiful area that is well worth a visit, and you will likely have the place to yourself in September and October when the weather turns colder.

Begin by following the Lodgepole Trail south from Olallie Meadows. You will soon arrive at a junction with the Russ Lake Trail. Keep right here and continue to another trail junction after just 0.25 mile. Turn left here, away from the Lodgepole Trail and hike this unmarked but obvious trail for approximately 100 yards to a junction with the Pacific Crest Trail. Turn left on the PCT and enter the Warm Springs Reservation. You will turn north here and hike 0.35 mile north to a junction with the Russ Lake Trail. Turn right here. The Russ Lake Trail

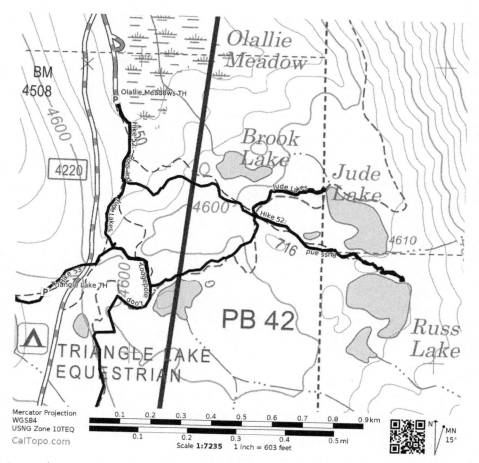

Mercator Projection
WGS84
USNG Zone 10TEQ
CalTopo.com

Scale **1:7235**   1 Inch = 603 feet

cuts a path straight through the forest, passing just south of Jude Lake (visible through the trees) to Russ Lake, where you will find several excellent campsites at trail's end. Stay for a while, but do not camp unless you are a member of the Warm Springs. Fishing is permitted with a Warm Springs Tribal Fishing permit.

Return to the PCT and turn right here for about 0.25 mile north to Jude Lake. When you reach a wide footbridge over Jude Lake's outlet creek, take a moment to bask in the beauty of the lake. This spot is particularly scenic later in the day, when the blue of the lake and sky accentuates the browns and greens of the forest. From here, the PCT begins its long trek into the Warm Springs Reservation, but you have no reason to continue; instead, turn around and return to the Russ Lake Trail junction. This time, turn right and descend on this occasionally rocky trail to the first junction with the Lodgepole Trail, where you turn right to return to your car.

EXTENDING YOUR TRIP:

You can combine this hike with the Lodgepole Loop (Hike 53) to create a 13.2 mile loop. The loop is relatively easy despite its length. See Hike 53 for more details.

53. LODGEPOLE LOOP

Distance: 11.1 mile loop
Elevation Gain: 1,200 feet
Trailhead elevation: 4,581 feet
Trail high point: 5,367 feet
Season: July- October
Best: September
Map: Green Trails #525 (Breitenbush)

Directions from Portland:

- From Estacada, drive southeast on OR 224 approximately 25 miles to the Ripplebrook Guard Station.
- A short distance after Ripplebrook, OR 224 becomes FR 46 at a junction with FR 57. Continue straight (right) on FR 46.
- Drive another 22.3 miles on FR 46 to a junction with the Olallie Lake Road (FR 4690) – you will notice that "Olallie" is painted on the road with an arrow to mark the direction.
- Turn left here onto FR 4690 and drive 6.1 miles of narrow pavement and another 1.9 miles of rocky gravel to a junction with the Skyline Road, FR 4220.
- Turn right here and drive 2 gravel miles to Triangle Lake Horse Camp.
- Turn right and drive into the obvious trailhead in the campground.

Directions from Salem:

- From Salem, drive OR 22 east approximately 49 miles to Detroit.
- Turn left at a sign for Breitenbush, Elk Lake and Olallie Lake onto FR 46.
- Drive 16.6 miles on FR 46 to a pass where you enter the Mount Hood National Forest.
- Continue another 6.6 miles (for a total of 23.2 miles from Detroit) to a junction with FR 4690 on your right, signed for Olallie Lake.
- Turn right onto FR 4690 and drive 6.1 miles of narrow pavement and another 1.9 miles of rocky gravel to a junction with the Skyline Road, FR 4220.
- Turn right here and drive 2 gravel miles to Triangle Lake Horse Camp.
- Turn right and drive into the obvious trailhead in the campground.

Hike: This long loop encompasses much of the Olallie Scenic Area, touching on many of the more scenic spots in the entire basin. In spite of this, it feels less remote than a long hike should as many of these places happen to be close to a road. It is a good hike in nice weather but equally nice in the foggy, misty weather of either June or October, when the forest in this area takes on a mystical quality.

Begin at Triangle Lake's horse campground. While you can hike this loop in either direction (and of course, you can also start at Olallie Lake), it is more rewarding to hike this loop counterclockwise, beginning at Triangle Lake and heading southwest on the Lodgepole Trail towards the Lower Lake area. Hiking in this direction, you save the nicest areas for the middle part of the hike and the long and less interesting stretch on the Pacific Crest Trail for the end of your day.

Begin at shallow Triangle Lake, which often dries up by the end of the summer. The Lodgepole Trail curves around the lake and turns south, beginning a long and slow (and gradual)

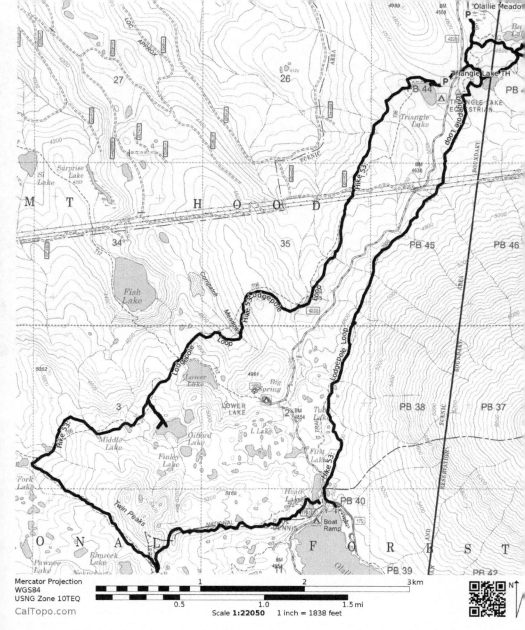

Mercator Projection
WGS84
USNG Zone 10TEQ
CalTopo.com

Scale **1:22050**   1 inch = 1838 feet

1   2   3km

0.5   1.0   1.5 mi

ascent into the Olallie basin. Pass through lovely Cornpatch Meadows at 3 miles from the trailhead and shortly afterwards reach a junction with the Fish Lake Trail. Left here leads to Lower Lake (which is worth checking out if you have a few extra minutes) while right leads downhill to Fish Lake (see Hike 55). You should instead continue straight, hiking uphill on the Lodgepole Trail. In a little under 0.4 mile, arrive at an unsigned junction with the Gifford Lake Trail and the first destination of your loop. While the junction is not marked, it is quite obvious; look for a fresh blaze on a tree in front of you and an obvious trail headed off into the woods on your left. Turn left here and hike 0.2 mile to a campsite at the lake, which is absolutely gorgeous: set in a bowl surrounded by cliffs, the lake is a magnificent shade of

Gorgeous Gifford Lake is no longer a secret - come early for a good campsite!

turquoise and blue. If you are backpacking you may need to look around for sites as the lake is quite popular – despite the lack of an official trail to the lake, it seems to be a great number of people's "secret spot". It isn't a secret anymore. There are other lakes in this small basin that may provide you more privacy if you are willing to hike off trail.

Beyond Gifford Lake, the Lodgepole Trail climbs and then descends for 1 mile to a junction with the Red Lake Trail at Fork Lake. For a quick detour, you can turn right here and hike 0.2 mile to Sheep Lake (see Hike 59). Otherwise, turn left and begin an irritating stretch of trail. The Red Lake Trail seems to have been forged out of a neverending series of creek beds, and for the 0.7 mile or so you'll be climbing up a trail so rocky you'll be cursing everyone involved with building and maintaining the trail. This stretch is mercifully short, and you'll meet the Pacific Crest Trail at one mile from the last junction (about 6.2 miles from the start of your hike). Turn left here and begin perhaps the nicest stretch of this hike, as you follow the Pacific Crest Trail gradually downhill towards Olallie Lake. After a few tenths of a mile, the PCT rounds a bend and views open up to the south. Look for a rocky promontory here with an excellent view south to Mount Jefferson – an excellent spot for a picnic! Continue another mile east on the PCT until you reach a junction only a few yards from the Olallie Lake's PCT trailhead parking lot. While the PCT turns left here, consider crossing the Skyline Road for a stop at the Olallie Lake Resort, only a few minutes away. When open, you can purchase snacks and beverages to help liven up your hike. Even better, the view of Mount Jefferson across Olallie Lake from the porch of the resort is iconic. To find the PCT from the resort, return to the Skyline Road and walk north, away from Olallie Lake, until you see the PCT cutting away from the road on your right.

This final stretch of the hike, on the well-maintained and relatively level PCT, is pretty boring. The trail cuts through the dry forest north of Olallie Lake for a little over 3 miles to an unsigned junction on your left. Along the way, ignore the first unsigned junction you reach – this is the trail to Olallie Butte (Hike 54); likewise, if you reach Jude Lake (Hike 52), you've gone too far. At the unsigned junction a little over 3 miles from Olallie Lake, turn left and hike a short trail that leads to the Lodgepole Trail. Turn left, cross the Skyline Road and arrive at Triangle Lake's horse campground and the trailhead.

54. OLALLIE BUTTE

Distance: 7.4 miles out and back
Elevation Gain: 2,600 feet
Trailhead elevation: 4,648 feet
Trail high point: 7,207 feet
Season: July- October
Best: July- October
Map: See map on the next page- this trail is often left off trail maps of the area.

Directions from Portland:
- From Estacada, drive southeast on OR 224 approximately 25 miles to the Ripplebrook Guard Station.
- A short distance after Ripplebrook, OR 224 becomes FR 46 at a junction with FR 57. Continue straight (right) on FR 46.
- Drive another 22.3 miles on FR 46 to a junction with the Olallie Lake Road (FR 4690) – you will notice that "Olallie" is painted on the road with an arrow to mark the direction.
- Turn left here onto FR 4690 and drive 6.1 miles of narrow pavement and another 1.9 miles of rocky gravel to a junction with the Skyline Road, FR 4220.
- Turn right here and drive 2.6 gravel miles to a clearing under some high-tension wires.
- Park on either side of the road here. The trailhead is on the left side of the road, at a paper sign.

Directions from Salem:
- From Salem, drive OR 22 east approximately 49 miles to Detroit.
- Turn left at a sign for Breitenbush, Elk Lake and Olallie Lake onto FR 46.
- Drive 16.6 miles on FR 46 to a pass where you enter the Mount Hood National Forest.
- Continue another 6.6 miles (for a total of 23.2 miles from Detroit) to a junction with FR 4690 on your right, signed for Olallie Lake.
- Turn right onto FR 4690 and drive 6.1 miles of narrow pavement and another 1.9 miles of rocky gravel to a junction with the Skyline Road, FR 4220.
- Turn right here and drive 2.6 gravel miles to a clearing under some high-tension wires.
- Park on either side of the road here. The trailhead is on the left side of the road, at a paper sign.

Hike: The view from the summit of Olallie Butte, the highest point between Mount Hood and Mount Jefferson, is among the best in the state – on a clear day you can see the entirety of northwest Oregon, with the star attraction being a face-to-face view of Mount Jefferson. The trail to the summit is a breeze despite its large elevation gain, and is never

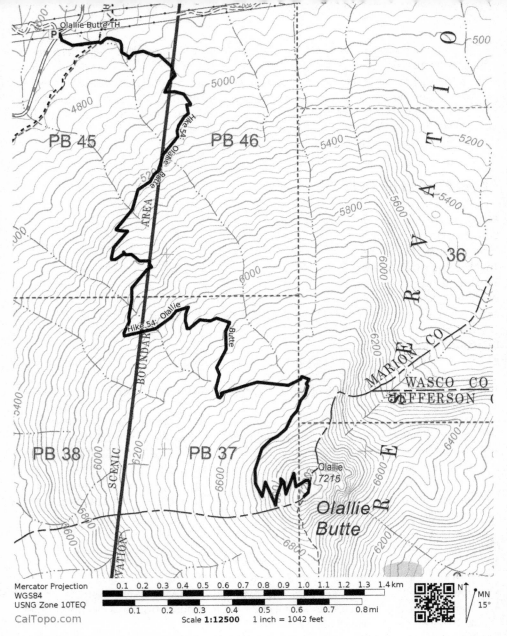

Mercator Projection
WGS84
USNG Zone 10TEQ

CalTopo.com

Scale **1:12500**   1 inch = 1042 feet

steep at any point as it switchbacks gradually up through ancient forest on its way to the summit crater. There is, however a monumental catch: at 1.5 miles the trail enters the Warm Springs Reservation, and it is unclear whether or not you are allowed to continue.

Indeed, a sign at the trailhead reads "Warm Springs Reservation Ahead – Hike at Your Own Risk!" The trail is well-maintained as it climbs up the gradual slopes of Olallie Butte. After a short distance, cross the Pacific Crest Trail at an unsigned junction and continue hiking uphill. You will have occasional glimpses north to Mount Hood, but otherwise the trail stays in the forest almost the entire way to the summit.

The view seems to stretch forever from the huge, open summit of Olallie Butte.

Enter the reservation at 1.5 miles. As mentioned, it is not clear whether this trail is open to non-tribal members. In general, the Warm Springs do not allow access to their land anywhere other than a handful of lakes. That being said, the Warm Springs are usually very clear about not allowing access to places – if they do not want non-tribal members to go somewhere, they will put up yellow "No Trespassing" signs. I did not see any such sign and thus continued my hike; if you see a no-trespassing sign, turn around at the boundary and go somewhere else.

From the reservation boundary, the trail continues its gradual uphill. The forest here is beautiful and the trail mostly very well-maintained. At about 3 miles from the trailhead, at an elevation of about 6,500 feet of elevation, the trail begins to break out of the forest and the views become increasingly fantastic. Reach the summit at 3.7 miles and rejoice – the view is simply incredible! Mount Jefferson towers above the fire-scarred and lake-dotted Olallie plateau. To the left of Mount Jefferson are the Three Sisters and Broken Top. To the east is central Oregon, stretching out as far as the eyes can see. To the north is Mount Hood and Washington's volcanoes. To the west lies the rumpled quilt of the Old Cascades, from Table Rock to Iron Mountain. This is, without a doubt, the most wide-reaching view found in this book.

Take some time to explore the summit. On the northern end of the summit is the collapsed remains of Olallie Butte's lookout tower, abandoned in 1967. The summit is huge and offers a number of different perspectives, not just of the mountains but also the butte itself. Please remember though – you are on Warm Springs land. Do not start a fire, do not camp, and do not venture far off-trail. This trail can be closed at any time, for any reason the Warm Springs see fit. Return the way you came.

55. FISH LAKE

Distance: 6 miles out and back
Elevation Gain: 900 feet
Trailhead elevation: 4,829 feet
Trail high point: 4,873 feet
Season: June- October
Best: June- October
Map: Green Trails #525 (Breitenbush)

Directions from Portland:

- From Estacada, drive southeast on OR 224 approximately 25 miles to the Ripplebrook Guard Station.
- A short distance after Ripplebrook, OR 224 becomes FR 46 at a junction with FR 57. Continue straight (right) on FR 46.
- Drive another 22.3 miles on FR 46 to a junction with the Olallie Lake Road (FR 4690) – you will notice that "Olallie" is painted on the road with an arrow to mark the direction.
- Turn left here onto FR 4690 and drive 6.1 miles of narrow pavement and another 1.9 miles of rocky gravel to a junction with the Skyline Road, FR 4220.
- Turn right here and drive 4.2 gravel miles to Lower Lake Campground on your right.
- Turn into the campground and drive to the trailhead parking area at the far end of the campground.

Directions from Salem:

- From Salem, drive OR 22 east approximately 49 miles to Detroit.
- Turn left at a sign for Breitenbush, Elk Lake and Olallie Lake onto FR 46.
- Drive 16.6 miles on FR 46 to a pass where you enter the Mount Hood National Forest.
- Continue another 6.6 miles (for a total of 23.2 miles from Detroit) to a junction with FR 4690 on your right, signed for Olallie Lake.
- Turn right onto FR 4690 and drive 6.1 miles of narrow pavement and another 1.9 miles of rocky gravel to a junction with the Skyline Road, FR 4220.
- Turn right here and drive 4.2 gravel miles to Lower Lake Campground on your right.
- Turn into the campground and drive to the trailhead parking area at the far end of the campground.

Hike: This is a hike with two trailheads that allows you to hike it in either direction – but in all honesty, it's actually easier and perhaps more scenic to start at the upper trailhead, at Lower Lake's car campground. Fish Lake is among the most impressive backcountry lakes in this book, but also one of the most abused – despite not being on a road, the last time I was there I saw somebody who had driven his jeep up the trail to the lake. A floating dock out on the lake sometimes sees barbecues, and the area around the lake shows signs of abuse. As you might imagine, this is an excellent short backpack – just expect that there will be plenty of others at the lake.

Begin at Lower Lake's campground. A signboard departs from a small trailhead parking lot at the west end of the campground loop. The trail cuts straight through the forest, quickly reaching beautiful Lower Lake. Although it may appear shallow from the shore, Lower Lake is actually the deepest lake in the entire Olallie basin with a depth of 73 feet. The lake, like

Scale **1:18249** 1 inch = 1521 feet

many others in this area, has a beautiful color that varies depending on the weather (turquoise in sunny weather, cobalt on cloudy days). Keep going around the lake, passing a few excellent campsites, until you reach a 4-way trail junction just beyond the lake. Left leads towards Gifford Lake while right heads north towards Olallie Meadows. Keep straight and

Looking down to Fish Lake, with Sisi Butte in the background.

begin descending slightly. At 0.9 mile, the trail reaches a cliff directly above huge and deep Fish Lake. Sisi Butte (Hike 51) looms over the northern part of the Olallie basin, with Mount Hood peeking over a ridge to the right of Sisi Butte. Watch your step here!

From the overlook, the trail descends at a moderate pace to the lake. Along the way, you will trade the dry forests of the Olallie basin for the lush forest of ancient Douglas fir more characteristic of the upper Clackamas River canyon. Reach the shore of Fish Lake at about 1.5 miles from the trailhead. The lake is absolutely gorgeous! If you come here early in the season, you may be lucky enough to see a waterfall that flows directly into the lake during snowmelt. As mentioned previously, there are plenty of excellent campsites around the shores of the lake. But remember: this is a favored spot of a certain element of society that has figured out how to drive to the lake, so do not expect privacy nor peace and quiet.

Beyond the lake, the trail crosses BP's powerline access road (which is how people generally drive to the lake) and then descends gradually to long, narrow and shallow Surprise Lake. A short spur trail leads to the lake, which is quite brushy and not easy to explore. If you continue downhill, you will arrive at Si Lake just 0.2 mile before the northern terminus of the trail. Beyond Si Lake you can continue to the more remote lower trailhead, just a few hundred yards beyond Si Lake. Don't bother trying to drive to this trailhead- the road washed out at Squirrel Creek years ago and has not yet been repaired. If you want to give it the old college try, the turnoff is just 3.5 miles up FR 4690 from the junction with FR 46 (it's the first road on your right). Once on this road follow signs to the Fish Lake Trailhead.

56. OLALLIE AND MONON LAKES

Distance: 6.7 mile loop
Elevation Gain: 200 feet
Trailhead elevation: 4,956 feet
Trail high point: 5,011 feet
Season: July- October
Best: September
Map: Green Trails #525 (Breitenbush)

Directions from Portland:

- From Estacada, drive southeast on OR 224 approximately 25 miles to the Ripplebrook Guard Station.
- A short distance after Ripplebrook, OR 224 becomes FR 46 at a junction with FR 57. Continue straight (right) on FR 46.
- Drive another 22.3 miles on FR 46 to a junction with the Olallie Lake Road (FR 4690) – you will notice that "Olallie" is painted on the road with an arrow to mark the direction.
- Turn left here onto FR 4690 and drive 6.1 miles of narrow pavement and another 1.9 miles of rocky gravel to a junction with the Skyline Road, FR 4220.
- Turn right here and drive 5.1 gravel miles to the Olallie Lake Resort.
- Drive past the resort entrance and 100 feet later, turn right into the signed parking area for the Pacific Crest Trail.

Directions from Salem:

- From Salem, drive OR 22 east approximately 49 miles to Detroit.
- Turn left at a sign for Breitenbush, Elk Lake and Olallie Lake onto FR 46.
- Drive 16.6 miles on FR 46 to a pass where you enter the Mount Hood National Forest.
- Continue another 6.6 miles (for a total of 23.2 miles from Detroit) to a junction with FR 4690 on your right, signed for Olallie Lake.
- Turn right onto FR 4690 and drive 6.1 miles of narrow pavement and another 1.9 miles of rocky gravel to a junction with the Skyline Road, FR 4220.
- Turn right here and drive 5.1 gravel miles to the Olallie Lake Resort.
- Drive past the resort entrance and 100 feet later, turn right into the signed parking area for the Pacific Crest Trail.

Hike: Olallie and Monon Lakes are separated only by a narrow band of rock, so it makes sense to hike around the both of them in one day. Although there are loop trails around both lakes, allowing for two different hikes, each lake is different in character and neither loop is all that long, making a full day circuit ideal. Please note that swimming is banned in Olallie Lake, as the lake serves as the drinking water source for the resort. If you want to go for a swim, Monon Lake is the place to be.

Begin your hike at the Olallie Lake Resort. Follow the road through first the resort and then Paul Dennis Campground. When you reach the end of the campground, look for a trail setting off to the east between sites 14 and 16. It may be a bit vague at first (and is unsigned) but soon becomes obvious. You will hike just above the lakeshore through a forest of spindly lodgepole pine. Along the way, excellent views of Mount Jefferson open up through the trees. At 0.9 mile, pass an unsigned junction with the trail to Long, Dark and Island Lakes.

This trail heads east into the Warm Springs Reservation (in fact, you are in the reservation at this junction) and is not recommended unless you have a Tribal Fishing Permit and actually plan on fishing (otherwise, don't bother). Instead, keep right to continue following the Olallie Lake shoreline. After another 0.5 mile, reach another fork, this time with the Monollie Trail. This short trail connects Olallie and Monon Lakes. If you want to hike around Olalli Lake only keep straight here, but if you prefer the larger loop, turn left and hike the short distance to Monon Lake. This short trail passes tiny Nep-Te-Pa and Mangriff Lakes, reaching another fork above Monon Lake just 0.1 mile later (or 1.5 miles from the trailhead).

Turn left on the Monon Lake Trail. You will traverse around Monon Lake's bays as you hike through forest burned in a 2001 fire. The top half of Mount Jefferson rises above the far end of the lake but the view is not as impressive as that of Olallie Lake. Shallower than Olallie Lake, Monon Lake also has better reflections on calm days and is a delightfully deep shade of blue on sunny days. As you traverse around Monon Lake, you will come to the realization that it is much larger than you thought when you first saw it. The many bays and inlets in the lake make this a much longer hike than you thought it would be (it isn't long, but it's longer than it looks on a map). Eventually you leave the burn behind and begin walking on a series of boardwalks designed to keep your feet dry. Monon Lake actually grows in size during snowmelt, so this part of the lakeshore is quite soupy. Huckleberries grow in tremendous quantities here, providing hikers with a tasty treat in August and September! At 3.1 miles from the trailhead (and 1.3 from the Monollie Trail), reach the end of the Monon Lake Trail at a campsite on the Skyline Road. Turn right.

You will follow the Skyline Road for 0.3 mile until you reach the northern trailhead for Monon Lake. Turn right here and hike 0.9 mile along the north shore of Monon Lake to the junction with the Monollie Trail. Turn left here and hike the 0.2 mile back to Olallie

Lake, where you will turn left again. Follow the trail around Olallie Lake. The views here up to Olallie Butte are particularly impressive. Just a short distance later, reach Peninsula Campground, where the Olallie Lake Trail seems to disappear. Follow user trails (or the campground loop road) until you find the continuation of the trail, which departs from near the group site at the northwestern end of the campground. Continue another 0.3 mile on this wide trail until it dead ends at the Skyline Road, near site 10 at Camp Ten Campground. Turn right and walk the Skyline Road for about a mile to the PCT Trailhead and your car on the left.

EXTENDING YOUR TRIP:
Hikers with a lot more energy and time can undertake a longer loop that passes Cigar and Upper Lakes on its way to Ruddy Hill's summit viewpoint, returning via Horseshoe, Monon and Olallie Lakes. See Hike 58 for more details.

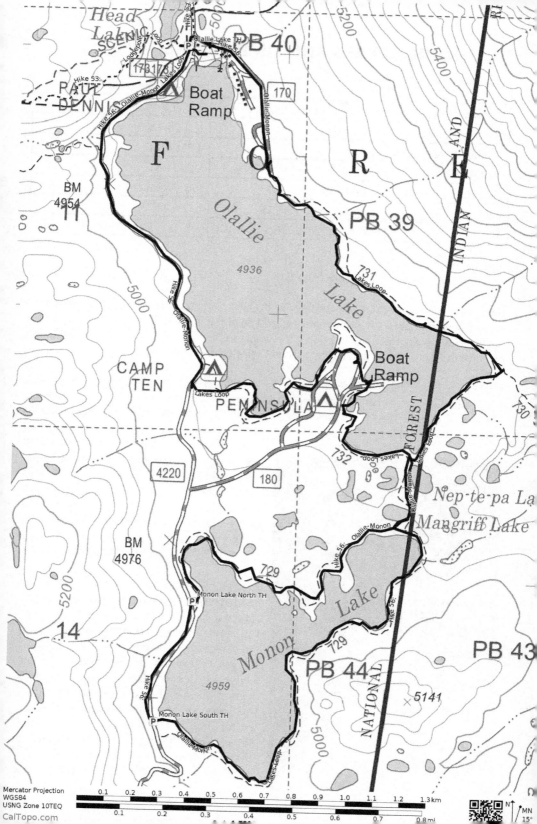

57.   DOUBLE PEAKS AND TIMBER LAKE

	Double Peaks	Timber Lake Loop
Distance:	5.6 miles out and back	7 mile loop
Elevation Gain:	1,100 feet	1,300 feet
Trailhead Elevation:	4,956 feet	4,956 feet
Trail High Point:	5,946 feet	5,946 feet
Season:	June- October	July- October
Best:	July- October	July- October
Map:	Green Trails #525 (Breitenbush)	Green Trails #525 (Breitenbush)

Directions:
- See directions for Olallie Lake (Hike 57).

Hike: This is an excellent tour of the interior of Olallie Country. There is much to see: an excellent viewpoint atop a rocky summit, several beautiful lakes and some of the area's best huckleberry fields. I recommend doing the whole loop, but if you just want the view, you can hike to Double Peaks and back from the Olallie Lake Resort.

Begin at the Pacific Crest Trail's inconspicuous trailhead. As you might expect, the trail is well-graded and well-maintained. The trail curls around a series of rocky bluffs as it climbs above Olallie Lake. The PCT passes a series of bluffs with excellent views south to Mount Jefferson. At 1.5 miles, you meet the Red Lake Trail at a 4-way junction. Left takes you

very quickly to Top Lake and the conclusion of your loop, but doing so skips Double Peaks. You should instead continue straight towards Double Peaks. You will reach Cigar Lake in a little under a half-mile. At the lake, look for a junction with the spur trail to Double Peaks, marked by a sign on the ground that reads "TR. NO 735" (see picture to the left).

The Double Peaks Trail is at times poorly-defined as it skirts around the south side of Cigar Lake but becomes very easy to follow once you leave the lake. What follows is perhaps the steepest half-mile of trail in this book, as you gain 600 feet in very short order. The last few switchbacks come at a grade of nearly 45 degrees - or about as close to straight up as you'll ever find on a trail. Once you've reached the top, you'll meet a junction. For the best views, turn left and immediately reach a splendid view of Mount Jefferson, rising above the whole of Olallie Country. Plan on a

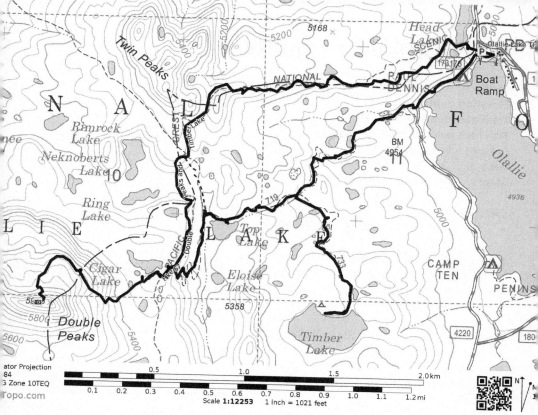

picnic here, above the lake country. When you finish, return to Cigar Lake; you can return the way you came but for the loop, retrace your steps to a junction with the unmarked trail down to Top Lake a few hundred yards back the PCT.

Though unsigned, the trail down to Top Lake is obvious as it drops off to the right. The trail switchbacks down through huckleberry bushes, reaching Top Lake after a little under a half-mile. There is an excellent view out to Olallie Butte. Follow the trail to the north end of the lake, where you meet the Red Lake Trail. Turn right here.

The Red Lake Trail cuts a level path through the forest for a half-mile to a well-marked junction with the spur trail to Timber Lake. Though your loop is almost done, take the time to detour to Timber Lake, one of the nicest backcountry spots in Olallie country. The Timber Lake Trail heads south through open woods and huckleberry fields to its eponymous lake, where you will find a number of convenient campsites. You can follow user trails to the right to a bluff over the lake with an excellent view of not just the lake, but the top half of Mount Jefferson. A social trail on the lake's left bank once extended to View Lake, 0.6 mile to the south; this trail has since been lost in blowdown in the aftermath of the 2010 View Lake Fire. When finished, return to the Red Lake Trail and turn right.

The Red Lake Trail climbs ever so slightly and then descends towards Olallie Lake, meeting its end at the Skyline Road at a little over 0.6 mile from the Timber Lake junction. Turn left and walk 0.4 mile north on the Skyline Road to the PCT trailhead.

58. OLALLIE-RUDDY HILL LOOP

Distance: 10.3 mile loop
Elevation Gain: 1,300 feet
Trailhead elevation: 4,949 feet
Trail high point: 5,928 feet
Season: July- October
Best: July- October
Map: Green Trails #525 (Breitenbush)

Directions:
* See directions for Olallie Lake (Hike 56).

Hike: There are many different ways to reach the summit of Ruddy Hill but perhaps the best and most satisfying is to start at Olallie Lake and hike there on the Pacific Crest Trail. This approach also has the easiest road access, making this approach all the more appealing. This is, without a doubt, the most complete tour of Olallie country.

Begin at the PCT Trailhead. The trail climbs uphill around a series of bluffs, passing a stunning viewpoint of Mount Jefferson at just under a mile. At 1.5 miles, reach a junction with the Red Lake Trail. Keep straight on the PCT, and soon you reach Cigar Lake, where you meet the spur trail to Double Peaks (see Hike 57). Keep straight on the PCT another 0.4 mile to Upper Lake, where you will find a variety of excellent campsites tucked away in the forest under the south face of Double Peaks. At 2.4 miles this is a good place to stop if you are looking for an easy hike, but you won't regret continuing to the summit of Ruddy Hill.

The PCT now begins a long, slow climb towards Ruddy Hill. Not far past Ruddy Hill, you will hike through a long, narrow meadow with an excellent view south to Mount Jefferson. After the meadow the trail switchbacks up to a rocky viewpoint of the Olallie basin just above View Lake. An old sign, no doubt leftover from the Skyline Trail days, points to the viewpoint. This spot is now known as the Many Lakes Viewpoint. The long, slow climb ends at a junction with the Ruddy Hill Trail at 4.4 miles from the trailhead. To visit the area's best viewpoint, turn right here.

The Ruddy Hill Trail wastes no time, climbing 400 feet in 0.36 mile to the summit. The view of Mount Jefferson is stupendous. The remains of a wooden phone box lean against a tree- though the box dates to the 1920s or 1930s, Ruddy Hill was not a lookout site and so the purpose of the phone box remains un-

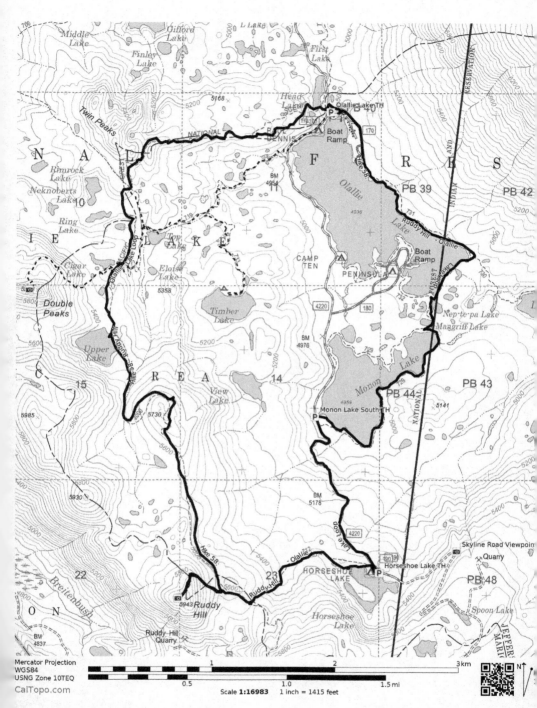

known. For an even better view, walk to your right out of the trees to the edge of the summit. Here you will understand why this mountain is called Ruddy Hill: it is a gigantic pile of red cinders. To the south and below you is the best view of southern Olallie country:

Mount Jefferson towers over Park Ridge, Pyramid Butte and Dynah-Mo Peak, while the dark canyon of the North Fork of the Breitenbush leads the eye towards the rugged peaks of the Bull of the Woods Wilderness on the far horizon. Keen eyes can follow the long curve of the Skyline Road below, and the lake at the foot of Ruddy Hill is seldom-visited Spinning Lake. The summit is large enough to accommodate several tents if you wish to spend the night but bring water - there's none anywhere around here.

Return to the PCT and turn right to continue the loop. Just about 200 steps later, arrive at a junction with the Horseshoe Saddle Trail on your left. Turn left. The Horseshoe Saddle Trail, also known as the Rondy Trail (after US Forest Service employee Howard Rondthaler, known as Rondy, who worked most of his adult life in this area), descends softly into Horseshoe Lake's basin. At 0.9 mile, the trail ends at site 5 in Horseshoe Lake's car campground. Take a moment to check out this beautiful alpine lake before continuing your hike.

From the campground, turn left and hike downhill 1.1 mile on the rough and tumble Skyline Road. Now, about the Skyline Road: this historic route was built in the 1920s in hopes of creating a scenic driving route that would connect Mount Hood to the southern Cascades. Rough terrain stopped construction just north of Mount Jefferson, and over time, the route was either paved over (much of the route near Mount Hood is now paved) or left to the elements. This is the original road, and walking downhill, you may be inclined to think it hasn't gotten any maintenance since the 1920s. In many places, the road is worn down to bedrock. As a result, there is little traffic on the road aside from the occasional jeep or truck, and it makes for a pleasant walk. At 1.1 mile from Horseshoe Lake, reach the southern end of Monon Lake and a trailhead on your right for the Monon Lake Trail. Turn right to resume hiking on trail.

The Monon Lake Trail follows the southern edge of the large lake, offering excellent views north to Olallie Butte. Puncheon bridges offer passage across marshy stretches of the trail. At 1.3 miles from the Skyline Road, reach an unsigned junction with the Monollie Trail at a cairn. This short trail connects hikers to Olallie Lake, but is easy to miss. Take a moment to look one last time across Monon Lake; the top half of Mount Jefferson rises above the lake here. If you plan on swimming, this is perhaps the place to do it as swimming is not allowed in Olallie Lake. Turn right and hike the short trail to Olallie Lake, passing two other small lakes on the way. At Olallie Lake, turn right and hike 1.5 miles along the lake shore to the Olallie Lake Resort. The view of Mount Jefferson from this stretch of trail is good enough to put on a postcard, and when you reach the resort you may in fact have a chance to purchase a postcard with such a view. The resort also sells soft drinks, ice cream and beer- so refreshing on a hot summer day! To find your car, walk out the resort's short access road and turn left on the Skyline Road. A quick few steps brings you to the PCT Trailhead on your right.

Photo on opposite page: The iconic view of Mount Jefferson from Olallie Lake.

59. RED LAKE AND POTATO BUTTE

Distance: 7.3 miles out and back
Elevation Gain: 1,700 feet
Trailhead elevation: 3,631 feet
Trail high point: 5,302 feet
Season: June- October
Best: August- September
Map: Green Trails #525 (Breitenbush)

Directions from Portland:
- From Estacada, drive southeast on OR 224 approximately 25 miles to the Ripplebrook Guard Station.
- A short distance after Ripplebrook, OR 224 becomes FR 46 at a junction with FR 57. Continue straight (right) on FR 46.
- Drive another 22.3 miles on FR 46 to a junction with the Olallie Lake Road (FR 4690) — you will notice that "Olallie" is painted on the road with an arrow to mark the direction.
- Continue straight on FR 46 for exactly 4.9 miles to a poorly-signed junction with FR 380 on your left.
- Fork to the left here and drive this rocky, narrow road 0.9 mile to the trailhead, marked by a sign on your left.

Directions from Salem:
- From Salem, drive OR 22 east approximately 49 miles to Detroit.
- Turn left at a sign for Breitenbush, Elk Lake and Olallie Lake onto FR 46.
- Drive 16.6 miles on FR 46 to a pass where you enter the Mount Hood National Forest.
- Continue another 1.7 miles (for a total of 18.3 miles from Detroit) to a junction with FR 380 on your right, marked by battered sign for the Red Lake Trail.
- Turn right here and drive this rocky, narrow road 0.9 mile to the trailhead, marked by a sign on your left.

Hike: Want to hike into the Olallie Lake basin without making the sometimes tedious drive to Olallie Lake? This moderate hike to Red Lake and on up to Potato Butte lets you sample many of the area's charms without testing either you or your vehicle. Be sure to avoid this hike during mosquito season, typically late June and early July, when the invertebrates are the area's apex predator.

Begin at the obscure Red Lake Trailhead, on the east (left) side of rocky FR 380. The Red Lake Trail cuts through a screen of young trees and enters ancient forest, where it begins to climb steeply. The tread is occasionally obscure here but is easy enough to follow. After just 0.4 mile reach what seems to be trail's end at a gravel spur road. Turn left here and walk 50 feet to a junction with another road. Turn right here and walk 90 steps (approx. 350 feet) to a cairn on your left, where the Red Lake Trail continues. The trail passes under a set of powerlines and begins to climb at a fairly steep pace for another mile until you cross Red Lake's cascading outlet creek and reach the edge of the Olallie Lake plateau. Here the trail levels out and soon after, reaches Red Lake. At a cairn, turn right and follow a short user trail down to the shallow lake, where there are several nice campsites. Views stretch out to the tip of Mount Jefferson. This makes for a nice rest stop but is not scenic enough to be

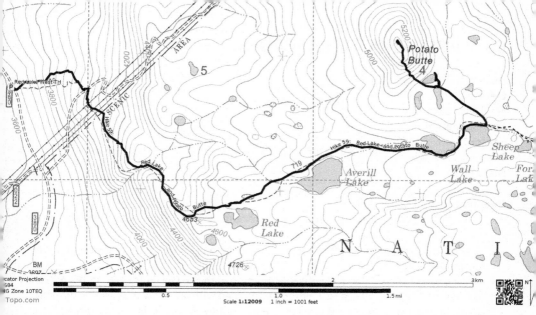

a final destination; plan on continuing up and into the Olallie Plateau to larger and more scenic lakes.

Return to the main trail and turn right. Now level, the trail continues another 0.3 mile to larger Averill Lake, where once again there are several very nice campsites. Continue on the Red Lake Trail, which becomes very rocky; when snow is melting in this area expect water to run down the trail. At 2.7 miles reach beautiful Wall Lake to your left, backed by Potato Butte. Continue on mostly level trail to Sheep Lake on your right. When you first reach the lake, look for a great view of Olallie Butte ahead. Then continue to the far end of Sheep Lake, where you reach a trail junction that may or may not be signed. To hike the steep trail up to the summit of Potato Butte, turn left here.

The spur trail up Potato Butte begins deceptively level. Traverse through huckleberry fields for 0.3 mile to a large meadow that may be a pond early and late in the season. While it looks like the trail turns right, you should instead continue straight along the edge of the meadow (the trail that turns right ends at a pond). Past the meadow, the trail launches uphill so steeply you'll very soon be gasping for breath. Puff up to the mile-high summit of Potato Butte at 3.7 miles, where the view is limited to Mount Hood through the trees to the north and Olallie Butte to the east. For a truly great view, retrace your steps down the Potato Butte Trail a few hundred yards to a junction with a spur trail on your left. Turn left here and walk out to some boulders. Climb on top of these boulders for an outstanding view south to Mount Jefferson, just to the right of Twin Peaks. Soak in the view and then return the way you came. When you reach the spur road 0.4 mile from the trailhead, remember to turn right on the first spur road, walk 90 steps (approx. 350 feet) to another road, turn left and walk 50 steps to the unsigned continuation of the trail on your right. Then follow the Red Lake Trail 0.4 mile downhill to its end at the trailhead and your vehicle.

60. BREITENBUSH CASCADES

Distance: 0.3 miles out and back
Elevation Gain: 150 feet
Trailhead elevation: 4,663 feet
Trail high point: 4,663 feet
Season: June- October
Best: June- October
Map: None needed.

Directions from Portland:

- From Estacada, drive southeast on OR 224 approximately 25 miles to the Ripplebrook Guard Station.
- A short distance after Ripplebrook, OR 224 becomes FR 46 at a junction with FR 57. Continue straight (right) on FR 46.
- Drive another 22.3 miles on FR 46 to a junction with the Olallie Lake Road (FR 4690) – you will notice that "Olallie" is painted on the road with an arrow to mark the direction.
- Continue past this junction 6.6 miles to a junction with the Skyline Road (FR 4220) on your left at Breitenbush Pass.
- Turn left here and drive 1 mile of gravel road to a large gate.
- Continue past the gate, where the road abruptly worsens into a rocky, narrow and severely rutted track that will test the patience of any passenger car driver to his or her breaking point.
- Drive another 2.5 excruciatingly slow miles to the unsigned but obvious trailhead on your right.
- If you cross the North Fork of the North Fork Breitenbush River, you've gone too far.

Directions from Salem:

- From Salem, drive OR 22 east approximately 49 miles to Detroit.
- Turn left at a sign for Breitenbush, Elk Lake and Olallie Lake onto FR 46.
- Drive 16.6 miles on FR 46 to a pass where you enter the Mount Hood National Forest.
- Turn right here on the Skyline Road (FR 4220) and drive 1 mile of gravel road to a large gate.
- Continue past the gate, where the road abruptly worsens into a rocky, narrow and severely rutted track that will test the patience of any passenger car driver to his or her breaking point.
- Drive another 2.5 excruciatingly slow miles to the unsigned but obvious trailhead on your right.
- If you cross the North Fork of the North Fork Breitenbush River, you've gone too far.

Hike: I'm going to tell you a secret: Breitenbush Cascades is one of Oregon's tallest and best waterfalls. You probably haven't heard of it, but standing next to this behemoth proves its greatness- you can stand at the precipice and look down and the many cascades below. There's only one catch – it is virtually impossible to see the whole thing from any vantage point, so you'll just have to use your imagination (or satellite imagery). Whether or not you believe me, this is a fantastic little hike that is worth a visit on your way to Breitenbush Lake, Ruddy Hill, Pyramid Butte or Park Ridge (Hikes 61, 62 and 63).

The first tier of Breitenbush Cascades, one of Oregon's great waterfalls.

After navigating the Skyline Road, the Breitenbush Cascades will be a welcome relief. Descend three quick switchbacks, each passing the brink of a tier of the waterfall. On your way down look through the trees to a glimpse of Mount Jefferson, just six miles to the south. The first switchback is located at the very brink of the falls. At the second turn left for fifteen feet to a spot face-to-face with the highest tier of the falls, a twenty-foot veil of water. While this spot is nice, the next tier is even better.

You will switchback first to the right and back left towards the base of the second tier. When you reach the falls, use your hands and feet to carefully step over a large boulder at the edge of the narrow promontory inside the base of the second tier. Set in a mossy boulder garden, you'll find yourself snapping pictures by the dozen. Be careful, however! The mossy rocks can be slippery and it is prudent to stay away from the lip of this tier of the falls as much as you possibly can. This is a very precarious spot and it must be respected.

DO NOT attempt to continue downstream. Breitenbush Cascades drops approximately 1,200 feet over many tiers on its way to meet the South Fork of the North Fork Breitenbush River. The terrain here is extremely rocky, rough, steep, cliffy and treacherous. Once upon a time I tried to bushwhack down the side of the falls and nearly paid for the effort with my life. After getting cliffed out on a loose shale slope just above a cliff edge, I decided it was perhaps best to let Breitenbush Cascades remain the mystery it deserves to be. Do believe me when I say that this is an adventure best left to the birds. From the end of the trail, the best plan is to return the way you came.

61. RUDDY HILL AND GIBSON LAKE

Distance: 5 mile loop
Elevation Gain: 900 feet
Trailhead elevation: 5,506 feet
Trail high point: 5,936 feet
Season: July- October
Best: August- September
Map: Green Trails #525 (Breitenbush)

Directions from Portland:
* From Estacada, drive southeast on OR 224 approximately 25 miles to the Ripplebrook Guard Station.
* A short distance after Ripplebrook, OR 224 becomes FR 46 at a junction with FR 57. Continue straight (right) on FR 46.
* Drive another 22.3 miles on FR 46 to a junction with the Olallie Lake Road (FR 4690) – you will notice that "Olallie" is painted on the road with an arrow to mark the direction.
* Continue past this junction 6.6 miles to a junction with the Skyline Road (FR 4220) on your left at Breitenbush Pass.
* Turn left here and drive 1 mile of gravel road to a large gate.
* Continue past the gate, where the road abruptly worsens into a rocky, narrow and severely rutted track that will test the patience of any passenger car driver to his or her breaking point.
* Drive another 5.8 excruciatingly slow miles to the signed trailhead on your right, at a large parking lot made of bright red cinders.

Directions from Salem:
* From Salem, drive OR 22 east approximately 49 miles to Detroit.
* Turn left at a sign for Breitenbush, Elk Lake and Olallie Lake onto FR 46.
* Drive 16.6 miles on FR 46 to a pass where you enter the Mount Hood National Forest.
* Turn right here on the Skyline Road (FR 4220) and drive 1 mile of gravel road to a large gate.
* Continue past the gate, where the road abruptly worsens into a rocky, narrow and severely rutted track that will test the patience of any passenger car driver to his or her breaking point.
* Drive another 5.8 excruciatingly slow miles to the signed trailhead on your right, at a large parking lot made of bright red cinders.

Note: Whatever you do, **DO NOT** try to drive here from Olallie Lake in anything smaller than a high-clearance truck. Passenger cars can make it okay to Monon Lake, but the 1.1 miles from Monon Lake to Horseshoe Lake are extremely rough in some spots, and quite steep. A Subaru can make it to Horseshoe Lake with some patience. The 2.5 miles of the Skyline Road from Horseshoe Lake to the PCT Trailhead at Breitenbush Lake are the worst stretch of road I have ever seen. No matter how bad the Skyline Road is west of Breitenbush Lake, driving up from Horseshoe Lake is infinitely worse. Don't say I didn't warn you.

Hike: The rugged backcountry north of Mount Jefferson is one of the most spectacular places in Oregon. Though the scenery culminates with the incomparable Jefferson Park

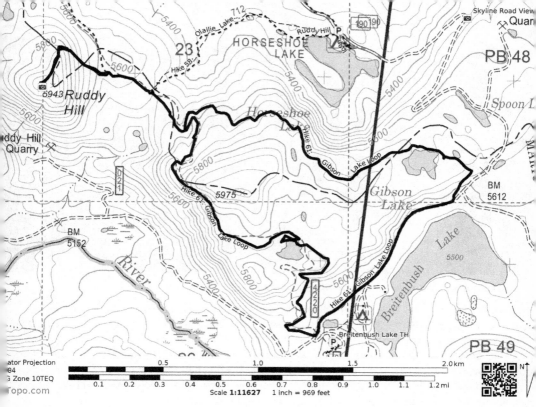

Scale **1:11627** 1 inch = 969 feet

(Hikes 63, 70, 73 and 74), there are other destinations in the area that are nearly as spectacular and almost completely unknown, and two of the best are Gibson Lake and Ruddy Hill. You will climb up a lonely part of the Pacific Crest Trail to a jaw-dropping view of Mount Jefferson from Ruddy Hill's red cinder porch before returning via a seldom-used trail that passes an aquamarine pool with a view of Mount Jefferson. Sound like fun? It should, despite the terrible access road. Ruddy Hill can also be accessed from Horseshoe Lake (Hike 58) but this route is longer and has more sights to see along the way.

From the parking lot, the PCT heads north, uphill and away from the Skyline Road. The trail ascends through forest burned in the 2010 Pyramid Butte Fire. Reach the top of the ridge 0.5 mile from the trailhead and begin a slow descent into the Olallie plateau. Just 0.1 mile later reach an unnamed lake to your left; walk around this pretty pool for a view of Mount Jefferson and some excellent campsites. Back on the trail, continue alternating minor ups and downs and pass another small, unnamed lake to your left. Eventually you leave the forest to skirt the edge of a massive talus slope (the very same one you passed on the drive in) where the views are massive. Look forward to your destination, blood red Ruddy Hill; look down to the canyon of the North Fork of the Breitenbush River; look back behind you to a smashing view of Mount Jefferson. Take in the view, because you will only get it once (unless you forego the loop)!

Shortly after this view, re-enter the forest and soon after come to three trail junctions in short succession. Ignore the first two to Gibson Lake and Horseshoe Lake respectively and arrive at the third, to Ruddy Hill, at 2.2 miles from the trailhead. Turn left and climb this

177

Hiking the PCT north from Breitenbush Lake towards Ruddy Hill.

absurdly steep spur trail for 0.4 mile to the summit of Ruddy Hill, so named for the blood red pumice that marks its west face. The remains of a wooden phone box from the 1920s are leaning against a tree on the summit. The view of Mount Jefferson is breathtaking. Hike around the trees to your right 50 yards to an even better view – Jefferson to your left, elusive Spinning Lake and the North Fork Breitenbush canyon below you and all the way out to the Bull of the Woods to your right. You could easily kill a couple hours exploring the summit; this is a superb place for a picnic! When finished, return to the PCT and hike 0.3 mile south to the junction with the Gibson Lake Trail on your left. Remember – this is the second junction on your left (the first leads down to Horseshoe Lake).

Turn left, pass some good views north to Olallie Butte and hike 1.8 brushy miles to Gibson Lake. Before you reach the lake you will enter the Warm Springs Reservation. Here, as anywhere else on the reservation, remember that fishing, camping and huckleberry picking are not permitted. The azure lake with its glimpse out to the top half of Mount Jefferson is captivating. After passing the lake, quickly descend to the Skyline Road. To return to the PCT Trailhead, walk back 0.6 mile around Breitenbush Lake to the trailhead. Access to the lakeshore is now prohibited (I took the photo on the right before the closure) so stay on the road and obey the tribe's "No Trespassing" signs when posted. The trailhead is just past the far end of the lake, where the red pumice road leads you to your vehicle.

62. PYRAMID BUTTE

Distance: 3.3 mile loop
Elevation Gain: 900 feet
Trailhead elevation: 5,506 feet
Trail high point: 6,081 feet
Season: July- October
Best: August- September
Map: Mount Jefferson Wilderness (Geo-Graphics)

Directions:
- See directions for Ruddy Hill and Gibson Lake (Hike 61).

Hike: From almost every angle, Pyramid Butte's sharp volcanic plug appears imposing- and yet, there is an easy trail to the summit. This is a short hike with a big payoff! Although the route to the summit was scarred by the Pyramid Butte Fire in 2010, this is still a lovely hike and one worth your time if you happen to be in the area.

Begin at the Breitenbush Lake Trailhead. You'll follow the Pacific Crest Trail south through the heather and pine as it slowly gains elevation on its way towards Park Ridge (Hike 63). The PCT quickly enters the burn near the boundary with the Mount Jefferson Wilderness, crosses a rockslide with a view out towards Pyramid Butte and reaches the Pyramid Butte Trail at about 0.55 mile. There may be a sign, or there may not be- if there is no sign, look

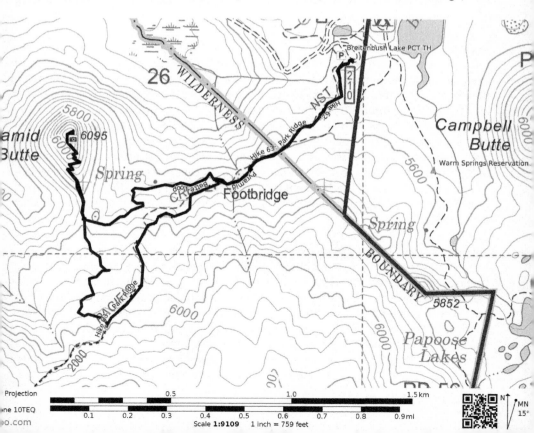

Looking north from Pyramid Butte to Ruddy Hill, Olallie Butte and Mount Hood.

for an obvious trail headed downhill into the burn zone on your right, towards the direction of Pyramid Butte.

Once on the Pyramid Butte Trail, you'll have a few minor ups and downs as it traverses through the rocky, burned meadows below Pyramid Butte. After a half-mile, you will reach the spur trail to the summit of Pyramid Butte. Look here for a weathered sign leftover from the Skyline Trail - this old sign miraculously survived the fire, and hopefully it will last a long time into the future! Turn right on the spur up Pyramid Butte, and quickly climb several switchbacks to Pyramid Butte's summit at about 1.4 miles from the trailhead. Hidden elsewhere on this hike, Mount Jefferson pokes its glaciated head over Park Ridge's rocky crest. Perhaps more impressive is the view behind you, which stretches over the entirety of the Olallie Scenic Area towards Mount Hood. Keen eyes can spot vehicles struggling to navigate the rocky arc of the Skyline Road as it winds around Ruddy Hill's blood-red south face. The lookout tower that once stood here was removed during the purge of lookouts in the 1960s.

Return to the junction at the weathered sign, where you are faced with a choice: it would be more direct to return to Breitenbush Lake the way you came, but I recommend instead turning right to continue on your loop. This trail sees only occasional maintenance but is easy to follow as it meanders through a procession of gorgeous meadows, now out of the burn. Looking behind you provides many excellent views of Pyramid Butte's sharp face, which will cause many hikers to wonder just how you got up there so easily. At 2.2 miles you'll finally reach the PCT, where you are faced with another choice: while right leads towards Park Ridge's rocky crest and tremendous viewpoint (Hike 63), this recommended loop leads you left. It is 1.1 easy miles on the PCT to the trailhead and your vehicle.

63.   PARK RIDGE AND JEFFERSON PARK

	Park Ridge	Russell Lake
Distance:	6.8 miles out and back	10.8 miles out and back
Elevation Gain:	1,400 feet	2,500 feet
Trailhead Elevation:	5,506 feet	5,506 feet
Trail High Point:	6,886 feet	6,886 feet
Season:	July- October	July- October
Best:	August	August
Map:	Mount Jefferson Wilderness	(Geo-Graphics)

Directions:
- See directions for Ruddy Hill and Gibson Lake (Hike 62).

Hike: After driving into the trailhead on the Skyline Road, you could be forgiven for wondering if this hike is worth the trouble it took getting there. It most definitely is. The view from the summit of Park Ridge is impossibly great: Mount Jefferson reigns supreme over the parklands and lakes of Jefferson Park. A more scenic destination is difficult to imagine. Once you've seen Jefferson Park from above, it is almost impossible to resist the temptation to continue on down to Jefferson Park, where Mount Jefferson fills the sky above an alpine wonderland of gorgeous lakes and meadows filled with wildflowers. Unlike many places, even the hyperbole cannot prepare you for Jefferson Park.

Pick up the PCT at a signboard at the trailhead. Hike a hundred yards to a junction where you meet up with the main trail. Turn left and hike through alpine forest with small meadows as you ascend gently out of the basin that holds Breitenbush Lake. Pass by a couple of talus slopes where pikas meep as you pass and enter forest burned in the Pyramid Butte Fire in 2010. Look out to your right to rocky Pyramid Butte (Hike 62), badly scorched in the fire bearing its name. Once you leave the fire zone behind you will begin a moderate ascent through unburned forest until you reach a crest at about 6,100 feet. Descend for a bit before beginning another moderate climb; soon the trail levels out and passes through a series of rocky meadows that are covered in snow until late in July most years. The tip of Mount Jefferson peeks out behind Park Ridge, reminding you of your destination ahead.

At approximately 2.5 miles from the trailhead, leave the forest behind and enter a moonscape of rockslides, snow patches and scattered ponds fed only by snowmelt. The trail braids here in many places as it passes by ponds and through scattered clumps of weather-beaten trees. Follow cairns across this stark, rocky basin until you reach Park Ridge's snowy, boulder-strewn headwall. Soon you will arrive at a permanent snowfield; follow footsteps here up to the summit of Park Ridge, where the view will knock your socks off. Mount Jefferson towers over the meadows and lakes that make up Jefferson Park. A more amazing view is hard to imagine.

Many hikers will want to make this their final destination. Though wildly beautiful, Jefferson Park is 2 miles and 1,000 feet of elevation below the summit of Park Ridge, miles and

This weathered sign from many years ago greets hikers headed north from Park Ridge. Note that the sign references the Skyline Trail, the precursor to the Pacific Crest Trail.

elevation you will need to regain on the way back to your car. If you choose not to hike down to Jefferson Park but have a bit more energy and a willingness to explore more of the rugged landscape up on Park Ridge, you have several options. Exploring either east or west along the ridge crest is highly recommended; every step east or west opens up new views to Mount Jefferson and hidden basins on both sides of the crest. Remember that the boundary with the Warm Springs Reservation is less than a mile east of the Park Ridge viewpoint, and continuing east from there is prohibited. If you are continuing to Jefferson Park, it's 1.9 glorious miles downhill through hidden basins and meadows to a junction with the South Breitenbush Trail just west of Russell Lake. From here, the possibilities are seemingly endless. Return the way you came. For more information about Jefferson Park and points south see Hikes 70, 73 and 74.

Backpacking in Jefferson Park:
Jefferson Park is among the most crowded backcountry destinations in Oregon. If you wish to camp, plan ahead and check to see if a proposed permit system (similar to the one found at Pamelia Lake) has been implemented. In any case, be sure to camp in designated campsites (marked by a post) or at least 250 feet away from any body of water on bare non-vegetated surface.

If you visit in July or August, mosquitos are a major nuisance. This is also peak flower season, and the park is extremely crowded. September brings cool weather and less crowds and best of all, the mosquitos are gone. October brings cold nights and frequent snow showers. The vast huckleberry fields here turn a vivid shade of red, you are more likely to spot wildlife and the solitude is tremendous. You can't beat it if you don't mind the cold.

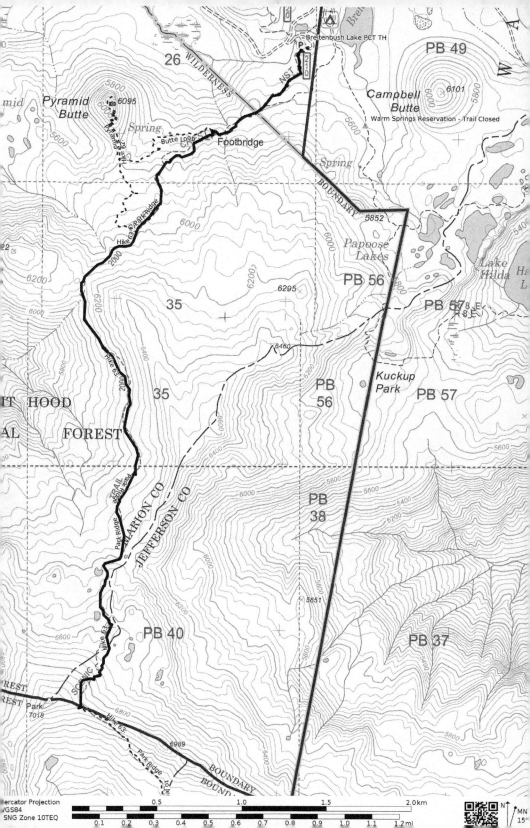

PB 49

Campbell
Butte
6101

Warm Springs Reservation - Trail Closed

26

WILDERNESS

NST

210

Breitenbush Lake PCT TH

P

Pyramid
Butte
6095

Spring

Butte Loop

Footbridge

Spring

BOUNDARY

5852

Papoose
Lakes

PB 56

PB 57
R8E

Lake
Hilda

Hike 63

Park Ridge

35

6295

PB
56

Kuckup
Park

PB 57

6460

IT HOOD

AL FOREST

Hike 63

35

PB
38

5851

MARION CO

JEFFERSON CO

Park Ridge

Hike 63

PB 40

PB 37

REST

REST Park
7018

Hike 63

6989

Park Ridge

BOUNDARY

BOUNDARY

SECTION 5: MOUNT JEFFERSON WEST

		Distance	EV Gain
64.	Humbug Flats	2.2	300
65.	Secrets of the Breitenbush Canyon	2.5	700
66.	Breitenbush Hot Springs Loop	8.6	2,200
67.	South Breitenbush River Trail	6.7	1,100
68.	Crown and Claggett Lakes	3.8	600
69.	Bear Point	7.8	3,000
70.	Jefferson Park via South Breitenbush	12.4	3,500
71.	Triangulation Peak and the Outerson Hoodoos	4.6	900
72.	Wild Cheat Meadow and Triangulation Peak	12.4	2,500
73.	Jefferson Park via Whitewater Trail	13.0	2,300
74.	Jefferson Park via Woodpecker Ridge	11.2	1,500
75.	Pamelia Lake and Grizzly Peak	10.4	2,700
76.	Hunts Cove Loop	19.8	4,000
77.	Bingham Ridge	8.8	1,400
78.	Independence Rock	2.3	500
79.	Marion Lake	6.4	1,000
80.	South Cinder Peak and the Heart of the Jeff Loop	34.0	7,200
81.	Temple Lake and Marion Mountain	10.2	1,400
82.	Pika and Fir Lakes	1.8	400
83.	Duffy Lake, Santiam Lake and the Eight Lakes Basin	10.8	1,200
84.	Maxwell Butte	9.2	2,500
85.	Berley Lakes and Santiam Lake	11.6	900
86.	Grand Mount Jefferson Wilderness Loop	68.0	17,000

Now we've arrived at the big snowy mountain at long last. Hikes 64- 67 follow forks of the beautiful Breitenbush River while Hikes 68- 78 and 80- 86 are found in the Mount Jefferson Wilderness. The hikes are as varied as the terrain; while some follow rushing rivers in dark canyons, others start high and climb higher. Most of these hikes pass lakes on the way, and some pass many lakes. This section also contains some of the best wildflower meadows and viewpoints in the wilderness as well. In short, this area has everything!

While some of these hikes are seldom-traveled, many others are extremely popular. The Triangulation, Whitewater, Pamelia, Marion Lake and Duffy Lake Trails are among the most crowded and popular in the Mount Jefferson Wilderness Area - but also among the most beautiful. Thankfully, there are other beautiful, less crowded trails to explore. It may be hard to believe, but every single one of these trails is beautiful and well worth hiking. If you have the time, the gear and the energy, the best way to visit the area is to do one of the two extended backpacks featured in this section (Hikes 80 and 86).

64.   HUMBUG FLATS TRAIL

Distance: 2.2 miles out and back
Elevation Gain: 300 feet
Trailhead elevation: 1,898 feet
Trail high point: 1,898 feet
Season: all year
Best: all year
Map: None needed.

Directions:
- From Salem, drive OR 22 east for 49.2 miles to Detroit.
- Turn left at a sign for Breitenbush, Elk Lake and Olallie Lake onto FR 46.
- Drive 4.5 miles to Humbug Campground, on your right.
- The trail departs from between campsites 8 and 9.

Hike: This short trail follows the Breitenbush River downstream. The trail is easy to follow, gains almost no elevation and passes by some excellent ancient cedars and Douglas firs. Along the way, you'll have a few very nice views of the Breitenbush River, rushing downstream towards Detroit Lake. The trail is too short to be a real destination day hike, but is a nice leg stretcher if you happen to be in the area.

The trail begins between sites 8 and 9, where there is a sign nailed to a large cedar tree. Pass by a couple of campsites and then begin paralleling the Breitenbush River on a trail that is almost completely level. The trail passes by some large trees, some of them as much as five feet thick. After 0.8 mile, dip into a small gully and cross a boggy stream, then climb back out of the gully. This is your elevation gain for this hike! Soon after you hike out of the gully, reach a trail junction. Although the trail continues straight, you should turn left and follow a well-defined user trail down to a fantastic campsite along the Breitenbush River, a worthy goal for this short excursion. The main trail continues past this junction another 0.1 mile to a long, boggy stretch of trail that ends when the trail meets FR 46. Return the way you came.

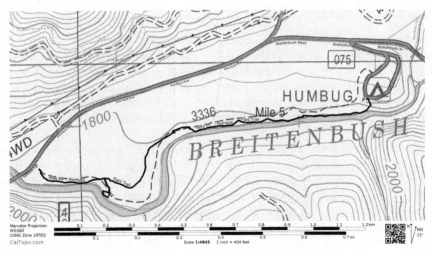

65. SECRETS OF THE BREITENBUSH CANYON

	Lower Breitenbush Hot Springs	Leone Lake
Distance:	1.2 miles out and back	1.3 miles out and back
Elevation Gain:	200 feet	500 feet
Trailhead Elevation:	2,336 feet	3,491 feet
Trail High Point:	2,386 feet	3,788 feet
Season:	all year	May- November
Best:	all year	May- November
Map:	None needed.	See my website.

Directions:
- From Salem, drive OR 22 east for 49.2 miles to Detroit.
- Turn left at a sign for Breitenbush, Elk Lake and Olallie Lake onto FR 46.
- Drive 9 miles to a sign for Breitenbush Hot Springs.
- Turn right on FR 2231 here.
- Immediately after crossing the Breitenbush River, keep left at a sign for Breitenbush Hot Springs.
- Turn right here and drive 0.6 miles to the second fork in the road. Left takes you to Lower Breitenbush Hot Springs while right takes you to Leone Lake.
- For Lower Breitenbush Hot Springs, keep left at this junction and drive another 0.3 mile to the unmarked parking lot that is the trailhead for the hot springs.
- To find Leone Lake, fork to the right at the last junction on to FR 2231 and drive 1.7 miles to a junction with FR 850.
- Keep right and drive another 1 mile to a junction with FR 847 on your left.
- Fork to the left here and drive 0.8 steep, winding and occasionally rough miles to a blank signboard on your right. This is the trailhead. The road is very steep – if you don't want to drive it, just part at the junction of FR 2231 and FR 847 and walk up the road to the trailhead.

Hike: The Breitenbush Canyon holds many secrets: hidden groves of ancient forest, breathtaking viewpoints, secluded waterfalls and much more. Two such secret places, Lower Breitenbush Hot Springs and Leone Lake, aren't much of a secret to those who know the area. Therein lies the problem: secrecy isn't helping either place, and both are routinely trashed by visitors. Many will blanch at the thought of seeing these in a hiking guide, fearing even more problems at both destinations. These fears are not without warrant. My hope is that exposing both will bring more visitors and bring both out of the darkness, where they can be better monitored and protected. Both are outstanding destinations located not far from well-maintained roads, and both are worthy of much better than they receive. Either or both make for a nice short hike if you only have a couple hours to spend in the woods.

Begin by hiking down to the Lower Breitenbush Hot Springs. A wide and well-defined trail departs from the far left side of the unmarked parking area and follows the road for a hundred yards or so before curving downhill to the right. After a quick descent, the trail arrives at the Breitenbush River and turns right to follow the river. Another few hundred steps

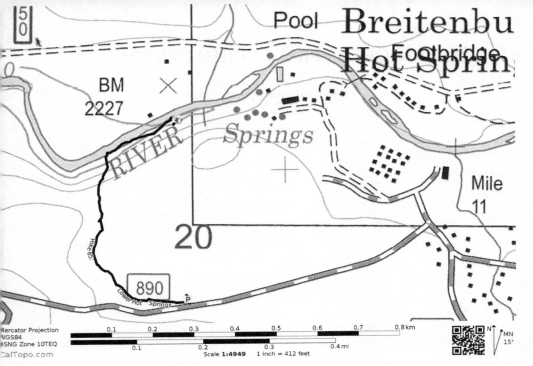

brings you to the abandoned hot springs on the river. A little under a mile downstream from the more well-known Breitenbush Hot Springs resort, this was the site of a different resort. At one time the resort featured cabins, a store and a bridge that led over the river to the springs; in fact, the size of the resort rivaled that of its twin just upstream. Today, the concrete walls and blue-tile tubs are all that remains. In the 1970s a series of floods ravaged both resorts. The resort upstream was eventually restored, and evolved into the nationally famous retreat it is today. The Lower Hot Springs never recovered, and closed in 1979. It was then left to the elements. What remains now has an extremely creepy vibe more reminiscent of a post-apocalyptic novel. When visiting the place it's obvious a lot people know about it; it is not uncommon to find large volumes of trash and broken beer bottles. All is not lost, however; as of this writing the Forest Service is planning on cleaning up and restoring the hot springs, with the hope of creating a public hot springs similar to Bagby Hot Springs (see Hike 7). It will take several years to bring this dream to fruition. In the meantime, if you want to visit, bring a trashbag and whatever else you might need to do your part in helping the restoration of this spot. Once at the Lower Hot Springs, please **DO NOT** hike upstream into the Breitenbush Resort!

When you are finished visiting the lower hot springs, take the time to visit lovely Leone Lake, a few miles uphill. Hidden in a small basin above the Breitenbush River, the lake is not signed, not publicized and unknown to most. The trailhead is unmarked. The lake suffers from the abuse often bestowed upon little-known lakes close to a road (Hike 19, Elkhorn Lake, also suffers a similar fate). Yet, in spite of all this, Leone Lake is an excellent destination for a short hike if you are in the Breitenbush area.

From the signboard described in the directions on the previous page, follow a muddy side road for 100 feet to a campsite, where the trail departs. You will begin climbing at a steep grade, as the trail gains almost 300 feet in just 0.4 mile. Along the way, you'll trade an old

The remains of the tubs at Lower Breitenbush Hot Springs.

clearcut forest for a pocket of verdant ancient forest as you enter Leone Lake's small basin. At 0.5 mile, the trail begins to drop precipitously to the lake, signaling your arrival at the lake. Once there, you will discover a pair of excellent campsites on the lakeshore. As at the hot springs, trash and broken beer bottles are commonplace here. You may want to bring a trashbag and spend a few minutes helping clean up the place. Return the way you came.

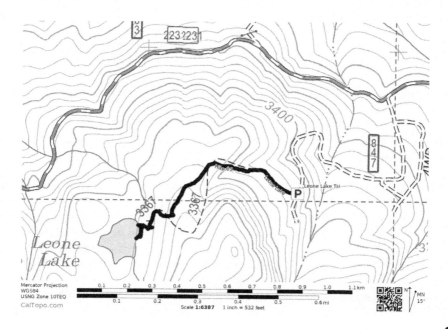

66. BREITENBUSH HOT SPRINGS LOOP

Distance: 8.6 mile loop
Elevation Gain: 2,300 feet
Trailhead elevation: 2,309 feet
Trail high point: 4,458 feet
Season: June- October
Best: June- October
Map: Green Trails #525 (Breitenbush)
Map note: You should also try to obtain a free map at Breitenbush Hot Springs of the trail network near the resort - it is tremendously helpful in navigating the area.

Directions:
- From Salem, drive OR 22 east approximately 50 miles to Detroit.
- Turn left at a sign for Breitenbush, Elk Lake and Olallie Lake onto FR 46.
- Drive almost exactly 11 miles to an unsigned junction with FR 050 at a very sharp right.
- Turn right and drive 0.2 mile to a pullout with a few parking spots on your left.
- The trailhead is just down the road, before the gate into the Breitenbush Hot Springs resort.
- You can also begin the hike at the Hot Springs Parking Lot.

Hike: This lovely loop traverses the mossy forests and steep ridges south of Breitenbush Hot Springs, allowing hikers many options for short and long loops. With enough energy and a tolerance for steep trails, you can even ascend out of the forest and up onto a ridge-top for a splendid (albeit slightly obscured and very exposed) view of Mount Jefferson's glaciated northwest face.

From the South Breitenbush Trailhead, drop down into an impressive forest of ancient cedars to a series of bridges over the braided North Fork of the Breitenbush River. Cross over the bridges and climb slightly into the mossy, almost electric green forest above the South Breitenbush River. After 1.5 miles, reach a junction with the Emerald Forest Trail. While the South Breitenbush Trail continues straight, you should turn right here.

The Emerald Forest Trail drops a couple of switchbacks to a bridge over the South Breitenbush River. From here, climb up through ancient forest for 1 mile to a junction with the Devil's Ridge Trail. For an easier loop, fork to the right on the Spotted Owl Trail for 0.5 mile and continue straight on the Spotted Owl Trail, following signs to Breitenbush Hot Springs. For a rugged side trip to a pair of good viewpoints, however, turn left at this junction.

The Devil's Ridge Trail climbs 0.3 mile to a junction with the Cliff Trail. Turn left here, and soon you will be climbing on a trail that is at times absurdly steep. While well-maintained, the Devil's Ridge Trail does not waste time with switchbacks, maliciously gaining 700 feet in just 0.5 mile. When the trail rounds a bend after some of the steepest trail you will ever hike, take a moment to catch your breath at an excellent viewpoint of the Breitenbush River Canyon. While this view (named Devil's Viewpoint on some maps) is nice, you were probably hoping you could see Mount Jefferson, just 8 miles to the southeast. If this is the case, and if you have enough energy for some more climbing, continue another mile to the summit of Devil's Peak, where at last you will see Mount Jefferson. Much of the summit is

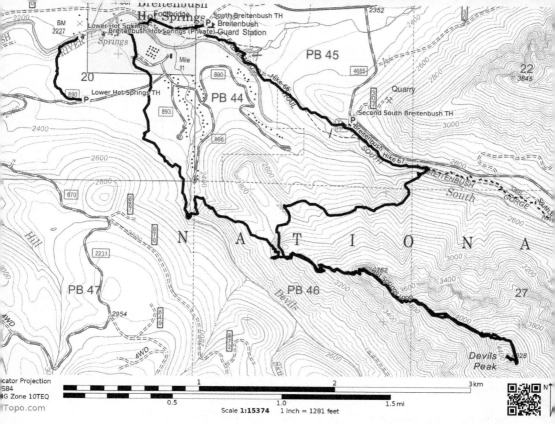

Scale **1:15374**   1 inch = 1281 feet

grown in with trees, and the best views take time and patience. A trail once continued all the way to Triangulation Peak (Hikes 71 and 72) but is now overgrown and very difficult to follow. There are some flat rocks on the summit that invite a picnic but exercise extreme caution – they are dangerously exposed and a stumble here would likely be fatal.

On your return from Devil's Peak, drop precipitously down 1.7 miles to the junction with the Cliff Trail and keep straight, where you drop another 0.5 mile to a reunion with the Spotted Owl Trail. Keep left, following signs for Breitenbush Hot Springs. Here the trail levels out, finally allowing you the opportunity to give your knees a break. Cross Devil's Creek on a footbridge and follow the trail through dark, ancient forest a little over a mile to the Breitenbush Hot Springs resort, where the trail ends at the visitor's parking lot. To return to your car, follow the road through the resort to the lodge. To the right of the lodge, look for a signboard that reads "Gorge Trail". Turn right and follow a wide trail to a huge, wooden bridge over the Breitenbush River. As you cross the river, look up – ahead of you is Devil's Peak. It is always rewarding to see your final destination and realize you made it all the way up there! Continue over the bridge and follow a narrow lane past the private part of the resort to a gate in the road. Beyond the gate is the trailhead, and just beyond that, your car.

Note: If you wish to stay at the resort, you will need to make reservations well ahead of time. It is well worth it to stay at the resort. For more information, call (503) 854-3320 or see http://www.breitenbush.com. Hikers not staying at the resort are allowed to use the trails on Breitenbush property, but be courteous and do not venture into the resort itself.

67. SOUTH BREITENBUSH RIVER TRAIL

	Lower Section	Middle Section	The Whole Trail
Distance:	3.6 miles one way	3.1 miles one way	6.7 miles one way
Elevation Gain:	700 feet	400 feet	1,100 feet
TH Elevation:	2,309 feet	2,767 feet	2,309 feet
High Point:	2,864 feet	3,055 feet	3,055 feet
Season:	March- November	March- November	March- November
Best:	March- November	March- November	March- November
Map:	See my website.	See my website.	See my website.

Directions:
- See directions for Breitenbush Hot Springs Loop (Hike 66).

Hike: The South Breitenbush Trail follows its namesake for 12.9 miles from Breitenbush Hot Springs all the way to Jefferson Park. While some segments are nicer than others, the lower half of the trail is open for most of the year and is a fantastic hike at any time. There are many options here: you can hike just the lower 3.6 miles to Roaring Creek, the middle section from Roaring Creek to the South Breitenbush Trailhead (3.1 miles), or even all 12.9 miles from the hot springs to Jefferson Park. The lower 6.7 miles are ideal for a car shuttle.

Breitenbush Hot Springs to Roaring Creek: The lower segment of the South Breitenbush Trail is far more crowded than the middle segment, but is wildly scenic and accessible most of the year. From the South Breitenbush Trailhead, drop down into an impressive forest of ancient cedars to a series of bridges over the braided North Fork of the Breitenbush River. Cross over the bridges and climb slightly into the mossy, almost electric green forest above the South Breitenbush River. You will reach a junction at 1.1 miles (the trail to your left leads you to a trailhead on FR 4685 in just 300 feet). Continue straight, and just 0.4 mile later, reach a junction with the Emerald Forest Trail.

Continue straight here as the trail follows the lush forest above the South Breitenbush River. Soon you will enter a forest that was pulverized during a 1990 windstorm, during which some trees as much as 8 feet thick were blown down. At 3 miles, you will pass an unsigned turnoff on your right for South Breitenbush Gorge. Blowdown has made the gorge difficult to find; look for two downed trees together on the right side of the trail. Keen eyes may spot the old sign somewhere in this area. Walk down the logs to a flat spot above the gorge, and then limbo under more downed trees to an overlook of the gorge. It is difficult to get a good photo of South Breitenbush Gorge, but at least you can see it: here the river squeezes into a narrow gorge about ten feet wide and forty feet deep.

From the gorge, return to the main trail and continue following an extremely scenic segment of the South Breitenbush Trail as it parallels the river another 0.5 mile to a footbridge over gorgeous, mossy, cascading Roaring Creek. This is one of the most peaceful and beautiful places in the Mount Jefferson area, and it makes for a great rest stop. Return the way you came, arrange a shuttle, or continue hiking upstream on the South Breitenbush Trail.

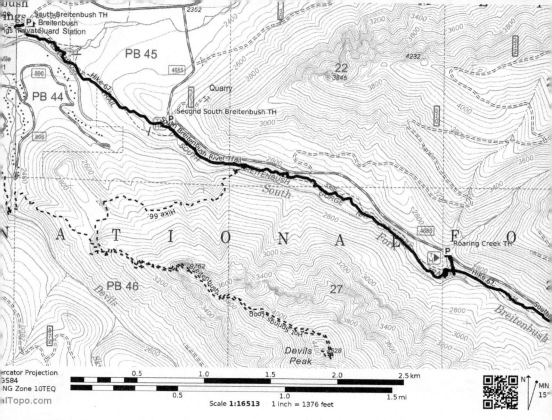

ercator Projection
GS84
NG Zone 10TEQ
alTopo.com

Scale 1:16513   1 inch = 1376 feet

Roaring Creek to Upper TH: Though many maps do not even show this section of trail, the old section of the South Breitenbush Trail from Roaring Creek to the Jefferson Park trailhead is still in good shape, providing for a nice early-season walk in the woods. While there are not any big highlights like South Breitenbush Gorge downstream, the forest is gorgeous, the trail easy and the crowds non-existent. In fact, you might not see anybody on this stretch of trail. That alone should entice you to come hike here!

Descend down the Roaring Creek Trail about 500 feet to a junction with the South Breitenbush Trail and turn left. The trail mostly stays above and away from the river but is always nearby. Meander through mossy forest that is almost uniformly superb; this is to say that it is always beautiful but rarely looks any different. Almost the entire hike looks exactly the same – a narrow but well-defined trail cutting through a radiant carpet of moss between Douglas fir and Mountain hemlock trees. Along the way you will cross a number of side creeks, most of them small enough to step across even in the winter. Occasionally you will notice round rubber wire insulators on trees ten to fifteen feet above the trail; these are remnants of the cables that ran all the way up to Bear Point, where a lookout stood until 1967.

At about 2 miles from the trailhead, you will reach a road where the trail seems to end. Turn left and walk about twenty feet up the road, where you will find the trail cutting diagonally away to your left. Before you continue on the trail, however, it is worth detouring down the road about 300 feet to a bridge over the South Breitenbush River, which has until this point been out of sight of the trail. The river cuts through a forested canyon while the road

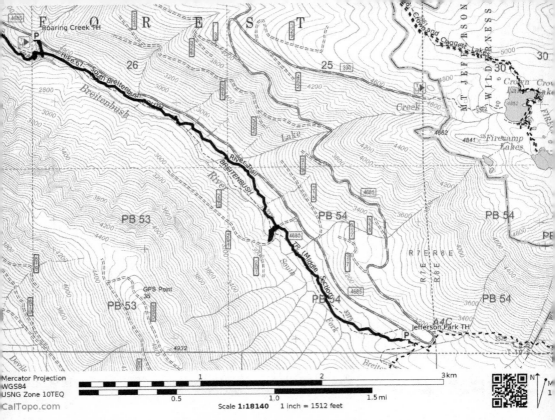

climbs past the river into a recovering clearcut. After inspecting the river, return to the trail, located on your right just after the trail you hiked in on your left.

The South Breitenbush Trail continues, becoming a bit rougher as it leaves the deeper forest downstream and enters a forest of alder and smaller Mountain hemlock. Detour briefly by the river, and then hike away from it as you near the upper trailhead. Keen eyes will glimpse the top of Mount Jefferson peeking over the trees in a few spots. Reach the upper trailhead at 3.1 miles from Roaring Creek, a large field that also serves as the trailhead for Bear Point (Hike 69) and Jefferson Park (Hike 70). Return the way you came, or begin one of the other trails leaving the other side of this grassy parking lot.

EXTENDING YOUR TRIP:
Jefferson Park, the old way: Before the construction of FR 4685, hikers and forest rangers once hiked from Breitenbush Hot Springs to Jefferson Park using the South Breitenbush Trail. Though you will not need to do this now, it is definitely the best way to experience the long and beautiful canyon of the South Breitenbush River. Though the trails are occasionally rough, the way is never steep and you will experience the tranquility of the forest and meadows and indeed, pass through a perfect slice of the Cascades from low to high. Hiking the entire trail (and it is just one trail, albeit with two slightly different names) isn't for everybody, but it just might be for you.

Photo on opposite page: Roaring Creek from the South Breitenbush Trail

68. CROWN AND CLAGGETT LAKES

Distance: 3.8 miles out and back
Elevation Gain: 600 feet
Trailhead elevation: 4,640 feet
Trail high point: 4,986 feet
Season: June- October
Best: June- October
Map: Mount Jefferson Wilderness (Geo-Graphics)

Directions from Salem:
- From Salem, drive OR 22 east for 49.2 miles to Detroit.
- Turn left at a sign for Breitenbush, Elk Lake and Olallie Lake onto FR 46.
- Drive 11.6 miles to a junction with FR 4685 on your right. Turn right.
- This road begins as pavement, crosses the North Fork Breitenbush River and immediately transitions to gravel.
- Drive 7.5 miles to a junction with FR 330.
- Keep left and continue 1.1 miles to the trailhead at a road's end, a rocky turnaround.

Alternate directions from Portland (via Estacada):
- From Portland, drive OR 224 approximately 18 miles to Estacada.
- Continue on OR 224 for 24.7 miles to the Ripplebrook Guard Station.
- Just past Ripplebrook the road becomes FR 46, which is not maintained in the winter.
- Continue on paved, two-lane FR 46 for 28.7 miles to a pass, where you enter the Willamette National Forest.
- Continue downhill on FR 46 another 5 miles to a junction with FR 4685, which will be on your left.
- This road begins as pavement, crosses the North Fork Breitenbush River and immediately transitions to gravel.
- Drive 7.5 miles to a junction with FR 330.
- Keep left and continue 1.1 miles to the trailhead at a road's end, a rocky turnaround.

Hike: Though not as spectacular as some of the other destinations in the northwest corner of the Mount Jefferson Wilderness, Crown Lake is worth a visit if you only have a few hours or if you desire a short, family-friendly backpacking trip. There is a spectacular view of Mount Jefferson from an open knoll not far from Crown Lake, and with some patience, you can find beautiful Claggett and Sheep Lakes in the vicinity.

Begin by hiking uphill on a steep, rocky trail amidst an old clearcut, which has given way to fields of beargrass and huckleberries. You will soon enter a classic alpine forest of hemlock and Douglas fir as the trail begins to level out. At about 0.8 mile, the trail curves to the left away from an opening in the trees. Leave the trail here momentarily and walk out into the opening for a majestic view of Mount Jefferson. Three-Fingered Jack peeks out from behind, with the ridges of the west slope of the Mount Jefferson Wilderness spreading out like a rumpled quilt. This place is awesome! After a few minutes of gawking, return to the trail and begin a gentle descent to shallow Crown Lake, where you will find a number of excellent campsites. While nice, the lake does not compare to some of the nicer lakes in the Mount Jefferson area. Sure, the top half of the big volcano peeks out over Bear Point's

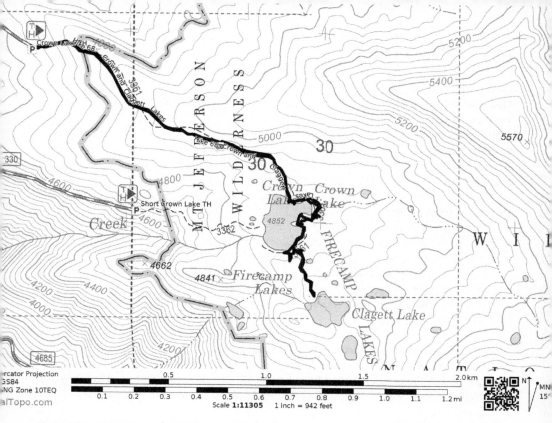

rcator Projection
3S84
NG Zone 10TEQ
alTopo.com

ridge to the south, but the lake is somewhat overused and is a frequent site of parties in the summer. If you've come for the night, consider moving on to secluded Claggett Lake, where there are a few excellent campsites and a better view of Mount Jefferson.

To find Claggett Lake, hike around Crown Lake on user trails (the official trail ends as it reaches Crown Lake) to the left of the lake until you reach the south end of the lake. You will reach a vague junction on the south end of the lake. Turn left on a trail marked by orange and pink spray paint and flagging and climb over a rocky knoll until Claggett Lake comes into sight. The view of Mount Jefferson is much-improved and there are a number of nice campsites. To find Sheep Lake, follow user trails further south to the small lake. Return the way you came.

Other hiking options:

You can also get to Crown Lake by hiking the Crown Lake Trail, which departs from the end of FR 330. Leave the road and hike steeply uphill, arriving at Crown Lake in about 0.3 mile. This approach misses the excellent viewpoint of Mount Jefferson that is found on the Roaring Creek Trail, and is generally known as the party approach to the lake. On summer weekends, groups have been known to haul up as many urban implements to the lake as they can – that is, stereos, coolers and many other things more generally associated with a weekend at Detroit Lake State Park. It is for this reason that I recommend either continuing to Claggett Lake (which has less people and better views of Mount Jefferson) or just coming to this area in September, when the weather is crisp, the huckleberries are ripe and the people mostly gone.

69. BEAR POINT

Distance: 7.8 miles out and back
Elevation Gain: 3,000 feet
Trailhead elevation: 3,029 feet
Trail high point: 6,034 feet
Season: July- October
Best: July- October
Map: Mount Jefferson Wilderness (Geo-Graphics)

Directions from Salem:
- From Salem, drive OR 22 east for 49.2 miles to Detroit.
- Turn left at a sign for Breitenbush, Elk Lake and Olallie Lake onto FR 46.
- Drive 11.6 miles to a junction with FR 4685 on your right. Turn right.
- This road begins as pavement, crosses the North Fork Breitenbush River and immediately transitions to gravel.
- Drive 4.6 miles to a large parking lot on your right, located in a large open flat. There is room for many cars.

Alternate directions from Portland (via Estacada):
- From Estacada, drive approximately 25 miles to the Ripplebrook Guard Station.
- Just past Ripplebrook the road becomes FR 46, which is not maintained in the winter.
- Continue on paved, two-lane FR 46 for 28.7 miles to a pass, where you enter the Willamette National Forest.
- Continue downhill on FR 46 another 5 miles to a junction with FR 4685, which will be on your left.
- This road begins as pavement, crosses the North Fork of the Breitenbush River and immediately transitions to gravel.
- Drive 4.6 miles to a large parking lot on your right, located in a large open flat. There is room for many cars.
- Coming this way is a little longer than the Salem approach but far more scenic.

Hike: While there is no shortage of great views in the rugged backcountry north of Mount Jefferson, few can compare with the panorama from Bear Point's former lookout site. Despite its proximity to the famed Jefferson Park, Bear Point remains virtually unknown. What's more, the hike is 5 miles shorter than the trek to Jefferson Park, it is rarely steep despite climbing 3,000 feet, and melts out on average 2 – 3 weeks before Jefferson Park. So what are you waiting for?

The trail begins in a clearing and tunnels through a forest of alder near the South Breitenbush River, meeting with an old alignment of the trail after a quarter mile. From here the trail turns right and begins a long, slow climb out of the canyon through attractive second-growth forest that blazes yellow and orange in the fall. Though never steep, the climb is continual for the first two miles of the hike. As you ascend out of the wide canyon of the South Breitenbush River, the trail begins to change character, becoming drier and more alpine. You cross several small creeks before passing the ruins of an old seedling shed at 1.5 miles. Continue climbing on rocky tread until you level out somewhat. At 2.2 miles from the trailhead, you will abruptly meet the Bear Point Trail at a signpost buried in a large cairn.

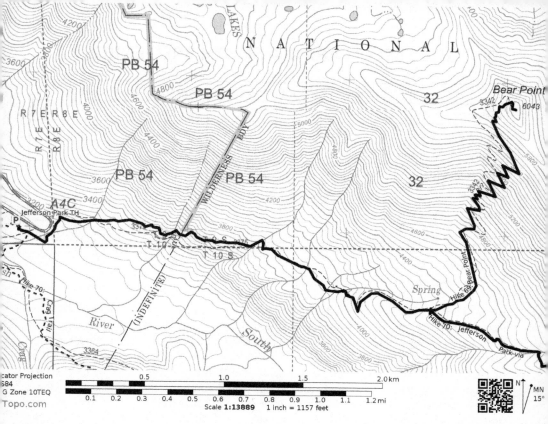

To hike up to Bear Point, turn left and hike aside a trickling creek on brushy trail until you leave the forest. You then begin climbing at a moderate grade up the ridge via a long series of switchbacks. The views become grander and grander, as Mount Jefferson dominates the skyline at the end of each switchback. The trail is rocky and narrow but the route is obvious. Because the trail is open and rocky, an early start on hot days is imperative.

After 1.8 miles and nearly 1,700 feet of elevation gain from the junction, the trail crests the ridge, turns right and leads to the summit of Bear Point. Pick your adjective: The view is stupendous, awe-inspiring, breathtaking, jaw-dropping and so much more. Three miles to the south is snowclad Mount Jefferson, with the Three Sisters and Three Fingered Jack immediately to the right. Below you is secluded, deep and very blue Bear Lake, flanked by elusive Dynah-Mo Peak with Park Ridge behind. Olallie Butte rises over the red cinders of Ruddy Hill and the rugged, fire-scarred canyon of the North Fork of the Breitenbush River to the northeast; keen eyes can spot Breitenbush Cascades (Hike 60) tumbling out of the Olallie Plateau near Ruddy Hill. Below you on your right is the deep canyon of the South Fork of the Breitenbush. Behind you is Mount Hood and points further north. With a view like this, you can imagine why there was a fire lookout here! The remains of the lookout (which was disposed by burning in 1968) dot the summit. Before you sit down for lunch, look around for bits of glass and metal – the only remainders of the erstwhile lookout. The individuals who worked here had the greatest job in the world!

Return the way you came or explore some more around the area- after all, paradise is at your feet. It is up to you to choose your own adventure.

70.   JEFFERSON PARK VIA SOUTH BREITENBUSH

	Jefferson Park out and back:	Crag Trail / Jeff Park Loop
Distance:	12.4 miles out and back	15.2 mile loop
Elevation Gain:	3,500 feet	3,900 feet
Trailhead Elevation:	3,029 feet	3,029 feet
Trail High Point:	5,966 feet	5,966 feet
Season:	July - October	July- October
Best:	July- October	July- October
Map:	Green Trails #557 (Mt.Jeff)	Green Trails #557 (Mt. Jeff)

Directions:
- See directions for Bear Point (Hike 69).

Hike: Jefferson Park is renowned for its flowers, its meadows, its lakes and its close-up views of Mount Jefferson's beautiful northwest flank. This hanging valley has long been known for its incredible scenic beauty and as a result, it has long been the most crowded place in the entire wilderness. There are four different approaches to this holiest of holy places (also see Hikes 63, 73 and 74), but the South Breitenbush Trail may be the best of them all. The trail is rocky and steep in places but compensates with excellent views, surprising meadows and the solitude many assume is not possible in such a noteworthy area. Energetic, adventurous hikers can create a loop by hiking up the abandoned Crag Trail, turning left on a lesser-used stretch of the Triangulation Trail until it connects with the Whitewater Trail, and then returning on the South Breitenbush Trail.

Begin at the South Breitenbush Trailhead and almost immediately reach a junction with the Crag Trail and the beginning of an adventure-filled loop. Most hikers will want to keep straight and continue hiking up the South Breitenbush Trail. This trail climbs at a steady and occasionally steep pace through the forest for 2.1 miles to a junction with the Bear Point Trail. Keep straight here and begin a long stretch of hiking uphill on what is at times a very rocky trail. Mount Jefferson tantalizes above the trees for much of the way but remains mostly out of sight as the trail remains in the forest. The going gets nice at about 3.5 miles into the hike, when you are at last treated to a sublime stretch of trail. Over the next 1.5 miles, you will pass several meadows, a pond with a reflection of the top half of Mount Jefferson and several fantastic views of the snowy volcano. At 4.8 miles, the trail curves around to the right of a forested knoll at an elevation of almost 6,000 feet. For hikers seeking a shorter day, scramble up a short way to the top of this knoll for an outstanding view of Mount Jefferson. Behind you is the South Breitenbush River's long canyon, and behind that, the jumbled peaks of the Bull of the Woods Wilderness.

Back on the trail, curve around the knoll and begin a short and steep descent into Jefferson Park. The last mile of the South Breitenbush Trail is an absolute delight as the trail follows the South Breitenbush River, now little more than a creek, into Jefferson Park. Along the way you will pass kaleidoscopic wildflower meadows and many incredible views of Mount Jefferson. At 6.2 miles, the South Breitenbush Trail meets the Pacific Crest Trail just 100

Entering Jefferson Park on the South Breitenbush Trail.

yards from Russell Lake. Once into Jefferson Park, exploration is a must. Return the way you came.

If you chose to hike up the Crag Trail instead, there are some things you need to know. First of all, the Crag Trail is officially unmaintained. This means that the Forest Service has abandoned it, and you should expect the trail to be very brushy and at times faint. Going this way also adds 3.2 miles to your trip, some of it very steep and unrelenting. This is exactly what makes this trail appealing to some of you out there. Finally: do not hike this trail in the opposite direction- if you want to hike the Crag Trail, hike it uphill and then return via the South Breitenbush Trail. This way you can turn around if you lose the trail at its start.

The Crag Trail begins with a short, meandering stretch through the forest bottomlands before reaching a crossing of the South Breitenbush River on a huge downed log. Find your way on to the log and cross the river. On the other side, the trail becomes faint. Floods have washed out a few small sections of the original tread; follow flagging through this short section until you reach a crossing of Crag Creek, after which the trail becomes clear. This section of the Crag Trail is difficult to negotiate going the other way, and you may have problems finding the right log across the river. As the river is frequently very difficult to cross, this is a real problem. As I said, you should hike the Crag Trail uphill.

Once across Crag Creek, the trail begins a steep climb uphill out of the South Breitenbush River's huge canyon. Some stretches of this climb are very brushy, but the trail is well-flagged and difficult to lose. Other stretches are in excellent shape, and it becomes apparent that this trail has friends. For the most part, the tread is still in fantastic shape as well. At 2.4 miles, the trail tops out on Triangulation Peak's long eastern ridge, some 1,800 feet

The Crag Trail crosses the South Breitenbush River on this huge downed log. This is the only good way across the river, and is much easier to find when starting on the Crag Trail.

above the South Breitenbush Trailhead. The last half-mile of trail is in some places very brushy, as huckleberry and laurel are fast overtaking the tread. Follow flagging straight ahead until you meet the Triangulation Trail at 2.9 miles. Turn left here.

The Triangulation Trail is still brushy but is in much better shape than the Crag Trail. You will hike 1.7 miles of slight ups and downs to a junction with the crowded Whitewater Trail at 4.6 miles from the South Breitenbush Trailhead. Turn left on the Whitewater Trail (see Hike 73) and hike 2.7 miles along a ridge to a junction with the Pacific Crest Trail. Keep left here and hike into Jefferson Park. After 1.7 incredibly beautiful miles, you will reach a junction with the South Breitenbush Trail near Russell Lake. Turn left here and hike 6.2 miles back to the South Breitenbush Trailhead.

Backpacking in Jefferson Park:

Jefferson Park is among the most crowded backcountry destinations in Oregon. If you wish to camp, plan ahead and check to see if a proposed permit system (similar to the one found at Pamelia Lake) has been implemented. In any case, be sure to camp in designated campsites (marked by a post) or at least 250 feet away from any body of water on bare, non-vegetated surface.

If you visit in July or August, mosquitos are a major nuisance. This is also peak flower season, and the park is extremely crowded. September brings cool weather and less crowds, and best of all, the mosquitos are gone. October brings cold nights and frequent snow showers. The vast huckleberry fields here turn a vivid shade of red, you are more likely to spot wildlife and the solitude is tremendous. You can't beat it if you don't mind the cold.

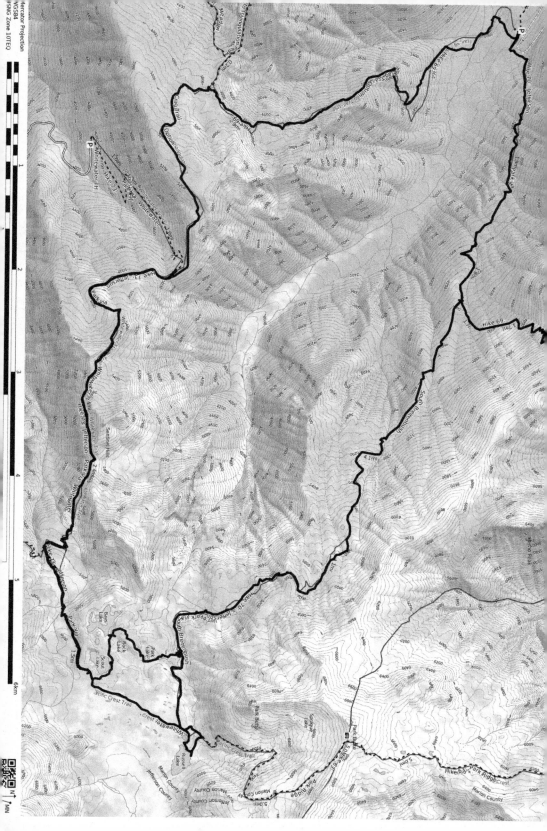

71. TRIANGULATION PEAK

Distance: 4.6 miles out and back
Elevation Gain: 900 feet
Trailhead elevation: 4,772 feet
Trail high point: 5,424 feet
Season: July- October
Best: July- October
Map: Green Trails #557 (Mt. Jefferson)

Directions:
- From Salem, drive OR 22 east for 49 miles to Detroit.
- Continue south on OR 22 for 6 miles to a junction with McCoy Creek Road (FR 2233) on the left.
- Turn left and drive 4 miles of pavement and another 3.7 miles of potholed gravel road to a 4-way junction at McCoy Shelter.
- Turn right and drive 1.3 miles of narrow, rocky, rutted and exposed gravel road to another unsigned junction.
- Turn right here and drive twenty yards to the trailhead at a signboard.

Hike: Triangulation Peak offers perhaps the best view of Mount Jefferson's steep west face. There are two ways to get to this fantastic vista: this is the easy way, but the drive is nastier than the long approach to Triangulation Peak (see Hike 72). It's hard to get more bang for your buck though; this easy hike will be pleasing to everyone once you actually get to the trailhead.

Begin at the signboard and hike slightly downhill on the wide Triangulation Trail. The trail parallels a logging road for a short distance before it enters deep forest at the western edge of the Mount Jefferson Wilderness. The first 1.5 miles of this trail are remarkably level and mostly very pleasant. At 1.5 miles, you reach a junction with the Triangulation Peak Trail, which angles uphill on your right. Turn right here and begin climbing at a moderate grade as the trail angles around Spire Rock. At 2.2 miles, or 0.7 mile from the junction, the trail reaches the rocky summit of Triangulation Peak. The view seems to stretch forever here, from the Washington volcanoes to the Three Sisters, but the real star is the view of Mount Jefferson, just 7 miles to the east. If you come here in July, you'll also be greeted by scores of huge white Cascade lilies and in some years, stalks of beargrass. The lookout that once stood here was dismantled in 1967 but you'll see some broken glass and a few other artifacts of this forgotten age.

On your way back, adventurous hikers can check out Boca Cave. This huge cavern hangs on the eastern face of Triangulation Peak's cliffs and offers a framed view of Mount Jefferson. To find the cave, walk back down the trail to the summit to a saddle and look for a user trail on your right. The well-tread path leads to a steep hill, where the trail drops through the forest and curls around the left side of the mountain's summit cliffs to the cave entrance. This is an incredible spot but also a very fragile one. Do not camp in the cave, do not build fires, and do not do anything to disturb the cave in any way. There's a reason that there's no sign leading to the cave. Return the way you came.

Before you leave the area, make sure you stop and see the Outerson Hoodoos while you are here. This collection of fantastical rock formations is found just off FR 635, only a half-mile from the Triangulation Peak Trailhead. From the trailhead, return to FR 635 and walk or drive up the road heading east. The hoodoos are on the right side of the road where it curls around the south face of Outerson Mountain. Look out to Triangulation Peak and Mount Jefferson - this is a really cool spot! The old spur trail to the summit of Outerson Mountain is now very hard to find, and leaves from a wide spot on the left side of the road just past the hoodoos. Don't bother with this trail; it is rough and the view is limited at best.

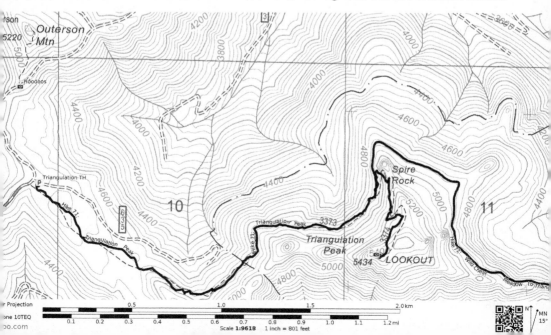

72. WILD CHEAT MEADOW AND TRIANGULATION PEAK

	Wild Cheat out & back	Triangulation Peak out & back
Distance:	5 miles out and back	12.4 miles out and back
Elevation Gain:	1,200 feet	2,500 feet
Trailhead Elevation:	2,959 feet	2,959 feet
Trail High Point:	4,100 feet	5,424 feet
Season:	May- November	June- October
Best:	June- July	June- July
Map:	Green Trails #557 (Mt. Jeff)	Green Trails #557 (Mt. Jeff)

Directions:
* From Salem, drive OR 22 east for 49.2 miles to Detroit.
* Continue on OR 22 for 10.5 miles past Detroit) to a junction with Whitewater Road on your left, where OR 22 curves to the south.
* Turn left here and drive this potholed and occasionally rocky gravel road 3.3 miles to a bridge over Cheat Creek.
* The trailhead is on the left, where the road crosses Cheat Creek. There is room for 2-3 cars here.

Hike: Long forgotten, the Cheat Creek Trail is a gorgeous approach to Triangulation Peak's panoramic views. But get in shape first! The hike is long and steep, poorly-maintained and very hot on summer days. But there is so much to see: tall tall trees, a cascading creek, wildflower-spangled hanging meadows and jaw-dropping views. As I said the first time I wrote about this hike: easy is not always better.

The hike begins beside Cheat Creek at a signboard and wastes no time, climbing steeply into a dark forest of massive Douglas firs. While the trail never approaches the creek, it remains a constant companion for the first 2.5 miles of the hike. On the way up you'll have to climb over many large downed trees, which add to the adventure, and perhaps to your frustration. At 2.4 miles, the trail reaches Wild Cheat Meadow, a verdant prairie that few people take the time to visit. Throughout June and July look for a veritable cornucopia of flowers: paintbrush, lupine, corn lilies, cat's ears, buttercups, yellow monkeyflower and columbine are all very common here. The meadow makes an excellent destination for a moderate hike, as you can easily spend hours exploring the area and cataloging wildflowers.

Hikers continuing beyond Wild Cheat Meadow should look for a red X on a tree on the far end of the meadow. The trail is tricky to follow for the first 0.2 mile after exiting the meadow as it crosses a creekbed amidst blowdown. Keep an eye out here as the trail bends to the north, away from the flats east of the meadow. If you are paying attention you should not lose the trail. Soon you will begin climbing up a rocky stretch of trail that doubles as a creekbed before topping out onto the ridge. Some 2.9 miles from the trailhead, reach a signed junction with the Triangulation Trail. Turn left.

Just 100 yards past the trail junction, look for an opening to your right. Take a minute here

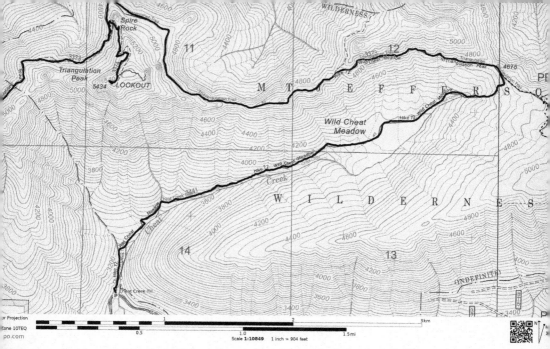

to follow user paths 50 feet to a nice campsite overlooking the Breitenbush backcountry to your north. Back on the Triangulation Trail, the trail is at times very overgrown as it cuts a straight line along the long eastern ridge of Triangulation Peak. You will meet the abandoned Devil's Peak Trail at 0.9 mile from the Cheat Creek Junction. Continue straight on the ridge as the trail begins to open up, passing a series of spectacular meadows as you make your way west. Look for copious quantities of scarlet gilia, red paintbrush, yellow arnica, fuzzy white cat's ears, pink and violet penstemon and blue and purple larkspur. Then turn around: on a clear day Mount Jefferson towers above the ridges behind you, at the end of the Triangulation Trail's long ridgeline approach (and in fact, if you were to follow the trail east from the Cheat Creek junction, you would indeed reach Jefferson Park).

At the final meadow, Boca Cave looms above you, seemingly close enough to make a quick scramble. Don't get ahead of yourself: you still have 1.5 miles to go. Once you've seen the summit ahead of you, it's easy to get summit fever. Instead, the trail passes a needle-like rock pinnacle and enters a dark forest on the north side of Triangulation Peak. This north-facing stretch of the trail is frequently snowy well into June. At 5.2 miles from the Cheat Creek Trailhead, pass under the base of Spire Rock and reach a junction with the popular Triangulation Peak Trail on your left. Turn left here and hike 0.7 mile up to the summit of Triangulation Peak. The lookout here was demolished in 1967 but the view remains. Look north to Mount Hood and south all the way to Diamond Peak, with Mount Jefferson dominating the near eastern horizon.

Before you begin the long hike back to your car, I encourage you to investigate Boca Cave, with its framed view of Mount Jefferson. To find the cave, retrace your steps back from the summit 200 yards to a saddle. Look for user paths branching off to your right here. Make your way down the steep slope here and bend back to your left, traversing the cliff edge 100 yards to the cave. If it is possible to find a more spectacular rest spot than the summit, this is it. Please do not camp here, and please do not disturb anything inside of the cave

Boca Cave and its framed view of Mount Jefferson.

– not only is it federally protected, but it is quite fragile. Do not try to scramble down the hillside from the cave back to the Triangulation Trail – a fall here would be dire. Return the way you came or arrange a car shuttle with the more popular Triangulation Peak approach to the west (see Hike 71).

73. JEFFERSON PARK VIA WHITEWATER TRAIL

Distance: 13 miles out and back
Elevation Gain: 2,300 feet
Trailhead elevation: 4,193 feet
Trail high point: 5,890 feet
Season: July- October
Best: July- October
Map: Mount Jefferson Wilderness (Geo-Graphics)

Directions:
- From Salem, drive OR 22 east for 49.2 miles to Detroit.
- Continue on OR 22 for 10.5 miles past Detroit) to a junction with Whitewater Road on your left, where OR 22 curves to the south.
- Turn left here and drive this potholed and rocky gravel road for 7 miles to road's end at the Jefferson Park Trailhead. There are many places to park but come early – this is an extremely popular hike and the trailhead is often full by mid-morning on summer weekends.
- Leave nothing of value in your car as break-ins have occurred here in the past.
- A Northwest Forest Pass is required to park here.

Hike: There are four ways to hike into Jefferson Park and all of them are beautiful. All four offer vastly different approaches and different views of Mount Jefferson, making all four of them worthy of hiking. The Whitewater Trail is by far the most popular of the four, and is relatively speaking, the least difficult route into the area. If you want to visit Jefferson Park, this is where you should start.

The trail begins by making a steady ascent out of Whitewater Creek's huge canyon. The trail begins in hot, dusty forest regrowing from an old clearcut but soon enters an ancient forest of huge hemlocks. After 1.5 miles, you will reach a junction with the Triangulation Trail at a ridge top. Turn right here and begin a gradual ascent following the crest of the Sentinel Hills. Despite being close by, Mount Jefferson remains mostly hidden behind the trees. If you look closely between the trees, however, you will spot secluded and vivid turquoise Whitewater Lake at the bottom of the valley below; later on, you will glimpse a huge mesa in the canyon below, a formation that separates the canyons of Whitewater and Russell Creeks. At about 4 miles from the trailhead, you will round a bend and reach a talus slope, where you finally come face to face with Mount Jefferson. The view here is magnificent – the eroded, horned, and very complex nature of this old volcano is revealed in all its glory. The Jefferson Park Glacier is the star attraction, tumbling down the slopes of the mountain as it gouges away at the entire north face of the mountain. The Russell Glacier remains mostly hidden, carving its own deep gorge into the mountain's northwest face. Russell Creek tumbles out of the Jefferson Park Glacier, cascading steeply down into its own chaotic, deep gorge. This is one of the finest views of the mountain, and you should spend some time here to fully appreciate it – photos are better in later afternoon, when the sky turns a deep shade of blue on a clear day behind the mountain.

Once you move along the trail, you will re-enter the forest. Cross Whitewater Creek at about 4.5 miles from the trailhead, and soon after reach a trail junction with the Pacific

Mount Jefferson from the Whitewater Trail viewpoint.

Crest Trail, where you turn left. From here the trail is nearly level, passing by small meadows and crossing Whitewater Creek again. It is at this crossing that the beauty of Jefferson Park begins to reveal itself, as the banks of the creek are lined with flowers while Mount Jefferson tantalizes, seemingly hovering above the creek in the background. About 0.6 mile later, leave the forest behind and enter the meadows of Jefferson Park, where the choices for exploration are seemingly endless. The most popular destinations are Bays and Scout Lakes, and both are among the most overused backcountry camps in the state of Oregon. Both lakes are gorgeous and worth visiting, but if you are searching for a picnic or campsite to call your own, head north towards the South Breitenbush River or east towards Russell Lake, where the crowds begin to dissipate. If you avoid Russell, Scout and Bays Lakes you will not see many people and be rewarded with the kind of solitude people assume is not possible in Jefferson Park.

Backpacking in Jefferson Park:
Jefferson Park is among the most crowded backcountry destinations in Oregon. If you wish to camp, plan ahead and check to see if a proposed permit system (similar to the one found at Pamelia Lake) has been implemented. In any case, be sure to camp in designated campsites (marked by a post) or at least 250 feet away from any body of water on bare, non-vegetated surface.

If you visit in July or August, mosquitos are a major nuisance. This is also peak flower season, and the park is extremely crowded. September brings cool weather and less crowds, and best of all, the mosquitos are gone. October brings cold nights and frequent snow showers. The vast huckleberry fields here turn a vivid shade of red, you are more likely to spot wildlife and the solitude is tremendous. You can't beat it if you don't mind the cold.

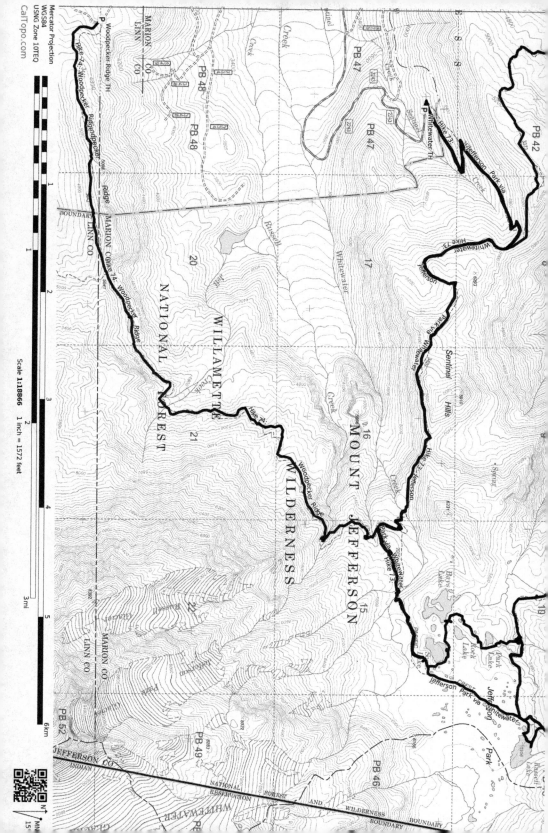

74. JEFFERSON PARK VIA WOODPECKER RIDGE

Distance: 11.2 miles out and back
Elevation Gain: 1,500 feet
Trailhead elevation: 4,478 feet
Trail high point: 5,884 feet
Season: August- October
Best: September
Map: Mount Jefferson Wilderness (Geo-Graphics)

Directions:
* From Salem, drive OR 22 east for 49.2 miles to Detroit.
* Continue east on OR 22 for 11.8 miles to a junction with Woodpecker Road (FR 040).
* Turn left here and drive this narrow and occasionally rocky gravel road for 5.4 miles to road's end at the signed Woodpecker Ridge Trailhead.
* Note: This road receives very little maintenance. The first time I came here a giant boulder blocked the road 1 mile below the trailhead, necessitating an uncomfortable 8-point turn near a cliff edge. Drive slowly on your way up, keep an eye out for rocks in the road and be sure to look for a place to turn around if there is a problem.

Hike: Now, this is a different way to hike into Jefferson Park, one you aren't likely to read about anywhere else. The Woodpecker Ridge Trail is the closest trail to the flanks of Mount Jefferson, and few take the time to hike it. Many who do complain about the steep and rocky first mile, and never take the time to explore the subsequently gentle section of the Pacific Crest Trail north towards Jefferson Park. Overall, it provides a quiet, little-known alternate route into Jefferson Park. Consider: this hike is only slightly longer than the extremely popular Whitewater approach, has less elevation gain (most of it is in the first 2 miles) and offers unique views of Mount Jefferson's west face that no other hike can match. That should be reward enough for most hikers.

Before we get to the hike, there is something else I have to tell you about. Before you reach Jefferson Park, you need to cross Russell Creek. From mid-July to the end of August, the crossing of Russell Creek is difficult and quite intimidating. Though usually tame in the morning, afternoon snowmelt from the Jefferson Park Glacier swells Russell Creek into a raging torrent, one that is extremely dangerous when running high. Absolutely avoid this hike on hot days in July unless you plan on backpacking or establishing a car shuttle – and in that case, plan on beginning your day early in the morning, when the crossing is manageable for most hikers. Or you could just wait until September and October, when the area is deserted and the crossing is generally not difficult at all.

Begin on the rocky, gullied Woodpecker Ridge Trail. This is an old trail, dating back at least to the 1930s, and at times you may wonder if it has been maintained since then. Blowdown is a nuisance, and some of the trees are too large to merely step over. There are compensations, though. Rhododendrons bloom profusely here in July, turning the forest pink. Even better – because you started your hike at an elevation of nearly 4,500 feet, the climbing is mercifully short on this rugged path. Climb up to the top of the ridge, where the trail repents and becomes a gentle forest path. You will then descend somewhat to a junction

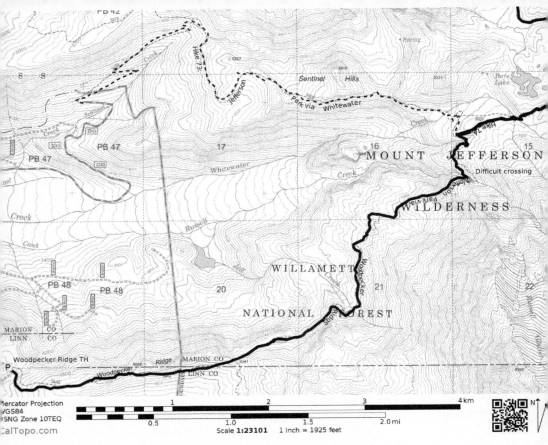

Scale **1:23101**   1 inch = 1925 feet

with the Pacific Crest Trail at just 1.6 miles from the trailhead. Turn left here.

The Pacific Crest Trail is as it is elsewhere – well-graded, well-maintained and very easy to follow. Just 0.5 mile past the Woodpecker Ridge junction, pass a shallow tarn with a gorgeous reflection of Mount Jefferson's summit spires. Pikas meep at you from the rockslide above the lake, warning of intruders. Continue on the PCT another 2.3 miles on the shoulder of Mount Jefferson, hidden out of site behind the ridge above, until you reach the crossing of Russell Creek. You will no doubt hear the creek before you see it tumble out of a deep, rocky gorge below Mount Jefferson's glaciers. The summit spires of the great volcano loom above. Downstream is a narrow, rocky gorge (and below that a large, unseen waterfall). The view here is as intimidating as the crossing (see the photo on page 212).

All things considered, crossing Russell Creek is not that difficult unless the creek is running high. There are often rocks that provide passage with dry feet. If you are not sure of the route across, scramble upstream until you find a wider, flatter spot at which to cross. If you are not certain of your ability to make it across the creek, there is no shame in turning around here. On the other side, look back for a better view of Russell Creek's deep canyon, tumbling out of the glaciers high up on Mount Jefferson. Magnificent, this place is!

From here, continue another 0.5 mile to a junction with the popular Whitewater Trail, where you turn right. Another 0.9 mile of incredible scenery leads you at last to Jefferson Park, where you can choose your own adventure to enjoy this most special of places. Return the way you came, unless you decided to set up a car shuttle.

75. PAMELIA LAKE AND GRIZZLY PEAK

	Pamelia Lake out & back	Grizzly Peak out & back
Distance:	4.4 miles out and back	10.4 miles out and back
Elevation Gain:	900 feet	2,700 feet
Trailhead Elevation:	3,115 feet	3,115 feet
Trail High Point:	3,992 feet	5,795 feet
Season:	May- November	July- October
Best:	May- June	July
Map:	Green Trails #557 (Mt. Jeff)	Green Trails #557 (Mt. Jeff)

Directions:
- From Salem, drive OR 22 east for 49.2 miles to Detroit.
- Continue another 12.1 miles southeast of Detroit on OR 22 to a junction with Pamelia Road (FR 2247) on your left.
- Turn left here, and drive 2.8 paved miles and another 0.8 miles of gravel road to the trailhead at road's end.
- Remember, you need to post your NW Forest Pass here.
- Always have your permit- if you encounter a ranger here they will ask to see it.

Hike: Long one of the most popular places in the Mount Jefferson Wilderness, Pamelia Lake and Grizzly Peak actually pale in comparison with some of the other magnificent hikes in this area. They are, however, beautiful hiking destinations worthy of visiting again and again. The area's popularity precedes it; several years ago, the Forest Service instituted a limited entry permit system, and a few years ago moved that system online. As a result, you will need to get a permit just to do this hike (they cost $6 – get them at http://www. recreation.gov and search for Pamelia Lake). With that being said, the short hike to Pamelia Lake is good for an easy family backpack and the trek up to Grizzly Peak is ideal for a difficult but rewarding hike with a fantastic view at the end.

Begin from the wide and well-graded Pamelia Trail. You will pass through an enchanted forest of green moss and thick Douglas firs and Western red cedar. Along the way, the trail approaches rushing Pamelia Creek several times, offering you a chance to get up close to this lovely torrent. After a half-mile, the trail enters a dusty forest full of downed trees. In 2006, a huge rainstorm caused the remnants of Milk Creek Glacier up on Mount Jefferson to calve off, burying much of this trail in mud and debris. The trail was reopened within a year, a testament to its popularity. It will take a very long time for it to resemble its former self, however; in truth, this hike used to be much better (there are other reasons why as well).

At 2.3 miles, reach a trail junction at the edge of Pamelia Lake. For an easy hike, continue 100 feet to the shore of this shallow lake. Although you are at the foot of Mount Jefferson, you cannot see it from here. You will need to turn right and follow the lakeshore about 100 yards to your right until the mountain comes into sight. This is not the most impressive view of Mount Jefferson; because of where you are on the mountain, it seems foreshortened

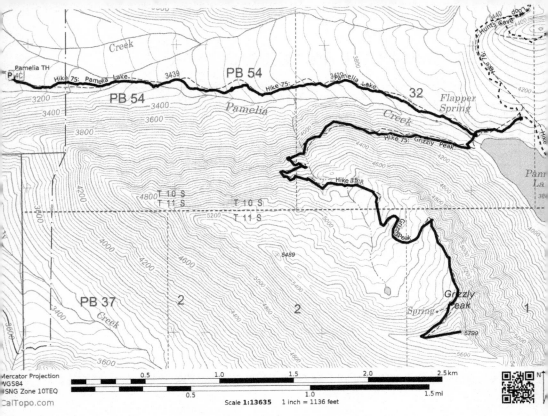

and less impressive than it does from other angles. Just the same, this is a pretty spot. If you have more time, be sure to return to the trail junction and follow the Hunts Creek Trail around the east shore of the lake, passing many springs and excellent campsites. This section of trail is described in Hike 76, Hunts Cove.

To hike to the summit of Grizzly Peak, start at the trail junction on the west end of Pamelia Lake. Turn right (south) on the Grizzly Peak Trail and cross the dry outlet of Pamelia Lake (amazingly, Pamelia Creek disappears underground for about a half-mile before resurfacing not far from the trail). From here, the trail climbs at a moderate grade through a forest of hemlock and pine. Mount Jefferson is visible through the trees on occasion, but otherwise this is a wide and straightforward climb through the woods. At about 2.4 miles from Pamelia Lake (and 4.7 miles from the trailhead), the trail emerges on the long and rocky summit ridge of Grizzly Peak. A quick bash through the trees leads you to an excellent viewpoint down to Pamelia Lake below and out to Mount Jefferson, just across the valley. Keep climbing, as the trail steepens somewhat and becomes more rocky. A few curves around the summit plateau lead you to the summit at 2.9 miles from Pamelia Lake, or 5.2 miles from the trailhead. The view is not as impressive as it once was. Mount Jefferson is still the star attraction, and it seems close enough to touch, but in the past twenty years enough trees have grown in to obscure the once-panoramic view (like so many other peaks, this too was a lookout site). You will need to scramble and bushwhack around the summit a bit to get the view you really want, down to Pamelia Lake and south to Three-Fingered Jack and the Three Sisters. Furthermore, try to hike this trail in July, or after snow starts falling in October; by September, the west face of Mount Jefferson is barren and almost devoid of snow, diminishing the view considerably. Return the way you came.

76. HUNTS COVE LOOP

	Hanks Lake out & back	Hunts Cove Loop
Distance:	12.2 miles out and back	19.8 mile loop
Elevation Gain:	2,100 feet	4,000 feet
Trailhead Elevation:	3,115 feet	3,115 feet
Trail High Point:	5,183 feet	6,015 feet
Season:	July- October	July- October
Best:	July- August	July- August
Map:	Green Trails #557 (Mt. Jeff)	Green Trails #557 (Mt. Jeff)

Directions:
- See directions for Pamelia Lake and Grizzly Peak (Hike 75).

Hike: The rugged trek up to Hanks Lake and into Hunts Cove is one of the most beautiful hikes in the Mount Jefferson Wilderness. Begin by hiking to Pamelia Lake and then traverse the long canyon of Hunts Creek up into spectacular Hunts Cove, where you are greeted by great views of the jagged summit of Mount Jefferson. Be sure you get the required limited entry permit before coming here: the permit is available at www.recreation.gov; search for the Pamelia Limited Entry Area.

The trail begins by following rushing Pamelia Creek as it winds through its demolished riverbanks, a remnant from a massive washout in 2006. After 2.2 miles the trail reaches shallow Pamelia Lake, nestled at the foot of Mount Jefferson. The mountain is out of sight from the trail – for a view, turn right at the lake's outlet and traverse around the lake until the mountain comes into sight. At a junction at lake's edge with the trail up to Grizzly Peak, turn left and hike around the lake 0.2 mile to a junction with the Hunts Creek Trail. Turn right here.

The Hunts Creek Trail traverses around the east side of Pamelia Lake. Cross over several spring-fed creeks to the far end of the lake, a swamp where Hunts Creek empties into Pamelia Lake. Past the swamp, follow the placid creek upstream to a crossing, marked by cairns. Cross the creek on a large downed tree and relocate the trail. From here, begin climbing at a steady pace through deep forest up the rocky slope on the west side of the canyon. Through the trees views begin to open up of the craggy southwest face of Mount Jefferson. At the far end of a switchback near the top of the canyon, turn left at the sound of falling water. Follow a user trail down to a spectacular yet unnamed cascade on Hunts Creek. This wonderful spot makes for a great place to cool off on a hot day. Return then to the main trail, where another switchback takes you to a trail junction with the spur trail into Hunts Cove. Here you are presented with two choices – one a moderate day hike and the other a longer, 2-day backpacking trip.

Whether you are here for a day or a weekend, turn left and hike 0.5 mile into Hunts Cove. The first lake you come to is Hanks Lake, where you will find several excellent campsites. Mosquitos are a real nuisance here in July. While you are here, you can follow social trails

around the lake to its south shore, where you will find an excellent view of Mount Jefferson, just a few miles to the northeast. At the east end of Hanks Lake, reach a junction. Left leads you to Hunts Lake while right leads you steeply uphill to the PCT in about 1.5 miles (this is a useful cutoff if you want to save a couple miles of hiking; it misses some of the best spots on the Hunts Cove Loop, though). If you have the time, take a moment to hike over to Hunts Lake. Though there is no view of Mount Jefferson, the lake is large and tranquil and has several nice campsites. Return the way you came back to the junction after visiting the two lakes.

If you plan on hiking the whole loop, continue right from the junction and begin climbing out of Hunts Cove's basin. The trail switchbacks under a pinnacle at the end of Lizard Ridge and continues uphill, eventually meeting the Lake of the Woods Trail at 8.6 miles from the trailhead (including the trip to Hunts Cove). Turn left here to stay on the Hunts Creek Trail, which continues its ascent to the top of Lizard Ridge. A little under 0.5 mile from the last junction, finally reach the top of the ridge and rejoice: not only is your uphill more or less done, but now begins one of the nicest stretches of trail in the entire Mount Jefferson Wilderness! The next half-mile brings you to the lip of the basin above Hunts Cove, with Mount Jefferson towering above Hunts Cove. After this, the trail passes through the forest until you reach a signed junction with the Pacific Crest Trail at 10.2 miles. Turn left here.

The PCT now passes above Hunts Cove; look for an excellent viewpoint 2 miles from the previous junction. Shortly after this viewpoint, the trail reaches beautiful Shale Lake with its reflection of Mount Jefferson. The lake is a much-loved stopover for PCT hikers and you may have stiff competition for a site in summer months. There are several other small lakes in this area with good campsites; look for social trails to find these lakes. The PCT passes aptly-named Mudhole Lake and continues 4.2 long and fairly monotonous downhill miles to a reunion with the Hunts Creek Trail at the edge of Milk Creek's deep glacial canyon. To finish the loop, you should turn left; before you do, take the time to follow the PCT 100 yards to the crossing of Milk Creek for a great view of Mount Jefferson. From here, return to the Hunts Creek junction and continue straight, now on the Hunts Creek Trail. Hike downhill 0.9 mile to the junction with the Pamelia Lake Trail, and then hike out 2.5 miles back to the trailhead.

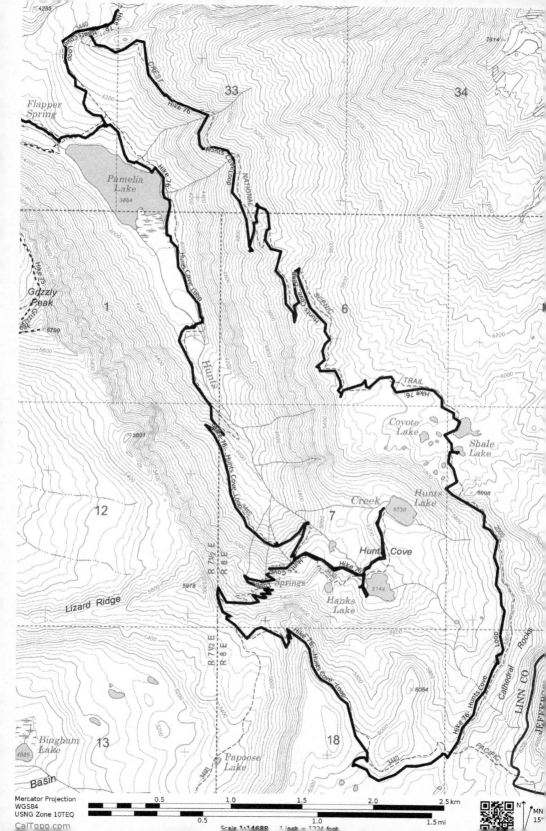

77. BINGHAM RIDGE

Distance: 8.8 miles out and back
Elevation Gain: 1,400 feet
Trailhead elevation: 4,251 feet
Trail high point: 5,519 feet
Season: July- October
Best: July- October
Map: Mount Jefferson Wilderness (Geo-Graphics)

Directions:
- From Salem, drive OR 22 east for 49.2 miles to Detroit.
- Continue east on OR 22 another 15 miles past to a junction with Minto Road (FR 2253).
- Turn left and drive this winding gravel road 5.5 miles to road's end at the Bingham Ridge Trail.

Hike: The Bingham Ridge Trail is another of those lonely Mount Jefferson trails that start high and climb higher, towards the high crest of the wilderness. Few people come up here, and those that do are usually on their way deep into the wilderness. And yet there is beauty to be found on this lonely, fire-scorched ridge. Backpackers can also use the Bingham Ridge Trail as a quiet approach into the interior of the wilderness.

The trail begins with an ascent through a mountain hemlock forest with copious amounts of rhododendrons and beargrass. This first stretch of trail was rerouted in 2014, after I came here on research. The new alignment adds 0.8 mile each way, but is less steep than the old trail. Eventually the trail levels out considerably as you break out into forest burned in the 2006 Puzzle Creek fire. Three-Fingered Jack tantalizes through the burned trees, rising above the charred forests left behind after the Puzzle and B+B Fires.

At 3.7 miles from the trailhead, you reach a junction with the Lake of the Woods Trail. Turn left and begin traversing around a ridge as the trail curves to the north. Before long, you will round a bend and reach your destination: Mount Jefferson, looming over remote, seldom-visited Bingham Basin. This is the first great viewpoint on this hike, and at 4.4 miles from the trailhead, makes the most logical stopping point for dayhikers.

If you insist on continuing, the Lake of the Woods Trail continues 1.9 miles, passing first a pond and then shallow Papoose Lake, to a junction with the Hunts Cove Trail at 6.3 miles. From here, turn right on the Hunts Creek Trail for 1.7 spectacular miles to a junction with the Pacific Crest Trail at 8 miles from the Bingham Ridge Trailhead. Where you go from here is

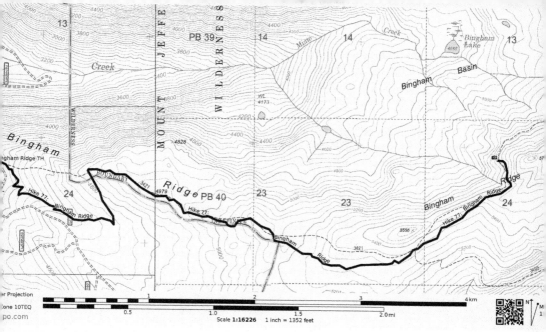

up to you: left leads to Shale Lake, right leads south towards South Cinder Peak and Table Lake; behind you, just 50 yards back the Hunts Creek Trail is the old trail down into Hunts Cove (for more information about Hunts Cove, see Hike 76). The possibilities are limitless, as they say. Just make sure you bring a copy of this book to help you suss out where to go next! If you're just dayhiking, return the way you came.

78. INDEPENDENCE ROCK

Distance: 2.3 mile loop
Elevation Gain: 500 feet
Trailhead elevation: 2,491 feet
Trail high point: 2,921 feet
Season: March- November
Best: March- November
Map: Green Trails #557 (Mt. Jefferson)

Directions:
- From Salem, drive OR 22 east for 49.2 miles to Detroit.
- Continue on OR 22 another 16.2 miles to a junction with Marion Road (FR 2255), just opposite the Marion Forks Restaurant.
- Turn left here and drive this one-lane paved road for about 100 yards to a pullout on your right.
- Look for the trail on the left side of the road here, at a signboard.
- There is a upper trailhead another 0.4 mile up the road, where the loop trail comes down to meet the road.

Hike: This pleasant hike is short on the jaw-dropping scenery for which this area is known, but its season is long and its charm varied. Consider this for a short leg-stretcher if you happen to be in the area, or a Sunday stroll early in the season. This is also a good hike for kids, provided you can keep them away from the cliffs at the top of Independence Rock.

Begin at the first trailhead, where the Independence Rock Trail cuts north into a cool, mossy forest. Before long, you'll enter a recent logging operation where the trail becomes somewhat faint. Continue straight through what remains of the forest, where you will find the trail on the far side. The trail traverses uphill towards Independence Rock via a series of switchbacks, reaching the base of the rock at about 1 mile. An unsigned but very obvious spur leads to the top of the basalt crag, which was was named by John Minto and his survey party when they climbed to this spot on July 4, 1874. The view has changed much since then. Below you are the buildings of the Marion Forks Fish Hatchery, the village of Marion Forks and the long curve of Oregon 22, which parallels the North Santiam River. The rocky summit is fascinating, with tough-limbed manzanita plants dominating the understory. A few huge Douglas firs provide shade on hot days. Visible to the southeast is the tip of Three-Fingered Jack, peeking out over the western ridges of the Mount Jefferson Wilderness.

Return the short distance to the Independence Rock Trail and keep left, angling downhill. The trail has been recently reconstructed following the logging operation that you passed through earlier, and the trail is occasionally a bit faint. You will descend via a series of switchbacks into the same cool forest in which you started this short hike. At 1.9 miles from the trailhead, the trail drops you out on the Marion Road a second time. Turn right and walk 0.4 mile back to your car at the first trailhead.

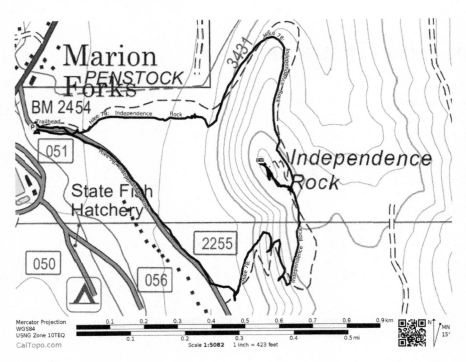

79.   MARION LAKE

Distance: 6.4 miles out and back
Elevation Gain: 1,000 feet
Trailhead elevation: 3,363 feet
Trail high point: 4,231 feet
Season: May- October
Best: May- October
Map: Mount Jefferson Wilderness (Geo-Graphics)

Directions:
* From Salem, drive OR 22 east for 49.2 miles to Detroit.
* Continue on OR 22 another 16.2 miles to a junction with Marion Road (FR 2255), just opposite the Marion Forks Restaurant.
* Turn left here and drive this one-lane paved road for 0.8 mile to the end of pavement
* Continue another 3.7 miles of excellent gravel road to road's end at the Marion Lake Trailhead.
* There are many places to park but come early – this is an extremely popular hike and the trailhead is often full by mid-morning on summer weekends.

Hike: This moderate trek to huge, deep Marion Lake has long been one of the most popular hikes in the Mount Jefferson Wilderness. Hikers flock to this corner of the wilderness in huge numbers all summer, and the lake shows signs of overuse. It is still possible to find solitude here, though; plan on visiting in October, when most of the hikers have gone home for the season and the vine maple around the lake blazes a million shades of yellow, orange and red. Furthermore, intrepid hikers can visit a stupendous waterfall and a fantastic viewpoint of Mount Jefferson to add to the adventure.

Begin by hiking on level trail through a mixed forest of Douglas-fir and Mountain Hemlock. Soon you will begin to parallel trickling Moon Creek on a gentle ascent into deeper forest. Leave the creek and begin a gradual climb in dark, ancient forest. Cross over a few trickles as you switchback up until the trail levels out. Soon you will reach cross the subterranean outlet of scenic Lake Ann. Pass by this shallow lake and continue another 0.4 mile to a junction, the beginning of your loop. Fork to the right here.

Just 0.1 mile later, reach an unsigned trail junction on your right. For a fantastic detour to spectacular Marion Falls, turn right and and begin a gentle climb on an unofficial but obvious trail. Soon you will reach raging Marion Creek. The trail turns right here and follows the creek to the precipice of the falls. Fork to the right here to stay on the social trail, which climbs up and around the cliff edge that holds the lip of Marion Falls. Then you descend steeply down to a viewpoint of the upper tier of the falls, a raging 60 foot plunge into a narrow canyon. Although the trail is obvious, few take the time to hike down here and you may have the place to yourself. A steep, exposed and frightening path continues downstream to a viewpoint of the lower tier of Marion Falls (which is sometimes known as "Gatch Falls", despite obviously being just the lower tier of Marion Falls). Exercise EXTREME caution on this lower path, as it is very steep and very exposed. When you finish, return to the unmarked junction and turn right to continue towards Marion Lake.

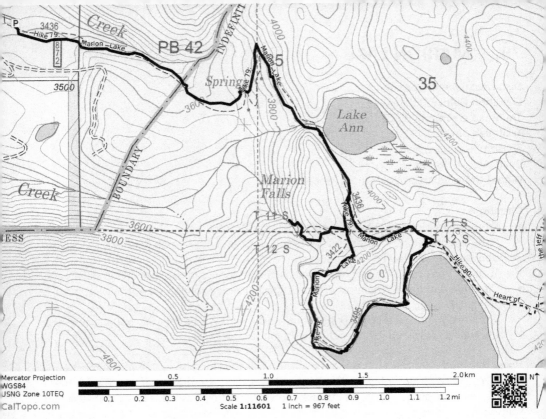

Mercator Projection
WGS84
USNG Zone 10TEQ
CalTopo.com

Scale **1:11601**   1 inch = 967 feet

Beyond the Marion Falls junction, the trail passes a talus slope and then descends slightly to follow Marion Creek upstream. Reach a trail junction at the edge of beautiful Marion Lake at 2.4 miles. At 360 acres and 180 feet deep, Marion Lake is the largest and deepest lake in the Mount Jefferson Wilderness. Once upon a time there were cabins up here, and people would leave boats over the winter for use throughout the summer months. None of this is there now, but the lake remains as beautiful as ever.

For a spectacular view of elusive Mount Jefferson rising over Marion Lake, turn right on the Blue Lake Trail at the bridge over Marion Creek. Cross raging Marion Creek on a wooden bridge and hike up the Blue Lake Trail 0.1 mile to a spot about halfway up a talus slope. Look for a social trail that veers off to the left here, and follow it downhill to lake level. Here you will find a fantastic view of Mount Jefferson, one many people never see. When you are done, return to the junction on the other side of Marion Creek.

Back on the loop, the trail passes several campsites on Marion Lake's busiest peninsula. Stay on the trail here – the steep slopes leading down to the lake are heavily used and, in some places, closed for restoration due to overuse. Views open up to Three-Fingered Jack as you hike around the lake towards its northwest end. At the far end of the lake, reach a trail junction. Turn left on the Marion Lake Trail and hike 2.1 miles back to the trailhead. If you plan on spending the night, remember to camp in designated sites only. Campfires are banned at the lake and will likely be so permanently after a stray campfire started a blaze at the lake in July 2015. There are dozens of campsites along the huge lake, so even on the busiest weekends you should be able to find a site if you spend enough time looking.

80. SOUTH CINDER PEAK AND THE HEART OF THE JEFF LOOP

	South Cinder Peak out & back	Heart of the Jeff Loop
Distance:	16.2 miles out and back	34 mile loop
Elevation Gain:	3,500 feet	7,200 feet
Trailhead Elevation:	3,373 feet	3,373 feet
Trail High Point:	6,739 feet	6,739 feet
Season:	July- October	July- October
Best:	July- August	July- August
Map:	Green Trails #557 (Mt. Jeff)	See map on my website.

Directions:
- See directions for Marion Lake (Hike 79).

Hike: Hike into the volcanic interior of the Mount Jefferson Wilderness on what is the premier backpacking loop in this book. Along the way you'll visit many lakes (including three of the most beautiful lakes in the entire region), pass three cinder cones and a tremendous lava flow and have untold fantastic views of the south side of Mount Jefferson. If you can only do one backpacking trip in the Mount Jefferson Wilderness, make it this one.

Begin at Marion Lake's crowded trailhead. The Marion Lake Trail cuts a wide path through lowland forest before climbing to Lake Ann at 1.2 miles. Continue past Lake Ann another 0.4 mile to a fork in the trail. Keep left here and continue 0.4 mile to a junction on the northwest end of Marion Lake. Keep left again and hike above the talus slopes on the northwest end of this huge, deep lake. Three-Fingered Jack rises above the south end of the lake, offering excellent photo opportunities. At 2.5 miles, reach a junction with the Lake of the Woods Trail. Turn left.

The Lake of the Woods Trail will be your companion for several miles of this trek as it passes through the wilderness. For now, hike north 1.7 miles to a junction with the Swallow Lake Trail in the middle of a large area burned in the 2006 Puzzle Creek Fire. Turn right on this trail and hike uphill through fire-damaged forest until you leave the burn. At 6.3 miles from the trailhead, reach secluded Swallow Lake, a possible camp for the first night of this journey. Though the lake has long been a stopover in the wilderness, few take the time to come here. Beyond Swallow Lake, the trail begins to climb at a very steep grade; over the next 1.4 miles, you will gain 1,000 feet on your way to the crest of the wilderness. When you reach the top, enter a fascinating basin below a small cinder cone. The trail levels out here, entering a huge cinder-strewn plain below South Cinder Peak. As the Swallow Lake Trail curves around the peak, it reaches an unmarked spur trail to South Cinder Peak's summit, marked only by a large cairn. Drop your packs and take a few minutes to climb to the summit where the view is tremendous: below you stretches the southern half of the Mount Jefferson Wilderness, while snowpeaks from Mount Hood to the Three Sisters dot the horizon. For a long but very satisfying dayhike, turn around here.

To continue to the Heart of the Jeff Loop, return then to the Swallow Lake Trail and turn left

The Cabot Lake Trail parallels the edge of the Forked Butte Lava Flow as it heads north towards Mount Jefferson.

to continue the loop. In just 0.2 mile you'll reach a four-way junction with the Pacific Crest Trail and the Shirley Lake Trail. Keep straight here and hike 1.5 beautiful miles downhill on the Shirley Lake Trail to reach Carl Lake at 10.2 miles from the Marion Lake Trailhead. This is the recommended place to camp on Day 1. There are several excellent campsites all around this deep, spacious turquoise lake, as well as several at smaller Shirley Lake to the south.

On the second day, follow the Cabot Lake Trail north out of Carl Lake's basin. This trail switchbacks up a hot south-facing slope before leveling out on the east side of the wide ridge between South Cinder Peak and North Cinder Peak. Pass a junction with the abandoned Sugar Pine Ridge Trail (see Hike 96) and enter a lava-strewn moonscape with excellent views north to Mount Jefferson. The trail passes under North Cinder Peak's cliffs before descending steeply to a junction with the currently-abandoned Jefferson Lake Trail at Patsy Lake. There is a campsite here, but unless you are completely bushed you should keep going towards Table Lake. The Cabot Lake Trail climbs out of Patsy Lake's small basin and then levels out, finally reaching Table Lake at 4.7 miles from Carl Lake (and about 15 miles from the Marion Lake Trailhead).

Although Table Lake is only 4.7 miles from Carl Lake, you should take the time to camp here. Set in a deep bowl at the foot of The Table, the turquoise lake is perhaps the most fascinating place in the entire wilderness- and also perhaps the most fragile. There are several excellent campsites here, enough to hold several groups. Do not establish new campsites, do not camp on the meadows and DO NOT build campfires. The lake narrowly escaped the B+B Fire and has had close calls with two other fires in the last five years. Please respect this beautiful place by treading as lightly as possible. While at Table Lake, take the time to explore the area. One mandatory sidetrip follows the occasionally-faint Cabot Lake Trail northeast for 1.5 miles to its end at a pass next to Bear Butte's pinnacle. Turn right at a sign that reads "viewpoint" and scramble above the pass to an exceptional view of Mount Jefferson, rising above a boggy meadow known as Hole-in-the-Wall Park. The trail once continued down there but is now lost in a maze of blowdown leftover from the B+B Fire.

Upon leaving Table Lake, return south on the Cabot Lake Trail just 0.2 mile to an unmarked junction with a faint trail on your right. This path, believed to be an old Indian trail, cuts a straight line through the meadow and then meanders a bit through a small stand of trees before reaching a gap in between a cinder cone and The Table. If you cannot find the trail, head cross country until you find the gap between the two. The trail passes through the gap, meanders through fields of lupine near a boulder field and then charges steeply uphill to gain the ridge on the south side of Cathedral Rocks. When you reach the top, follow the trail to the PCT, 1.4 miles from the Cabot Lake Trail. If you have the time, take the time to detour a quarter-mile south on the PCT to a viewpoint of Mount Jefferson, The Table and the exact route of trail you just hiked between Table Lake and the PCT. The trail itself is visible, cutting steeply up the green slope on your left. Return to the unmarked junction with the connector trail and continue north a little under a half-mile to a junction with the Hunts Creek Trail. Turn left here.

The Hunts Creek Trail climbs a bit through the forest and then enters open slopes above Hunts Cove. The view of Mount Jefferson here towering over Hunts Cove is jaw-dropping. While you need a special entry permit to visit Hunts Cove (see Hike 76), you do not need one up here if you are just hiking through. At 1.7 miles from the PCT, reach a junction with the Lake of the Woods Trail. Turn left.

The Lake of the Woods Trail descends the heights of the ridge, reaching shallow Papoose Lake at 0.7 mile from the previous junction. You've traveled about 5 miles so this peaceful lake backed by a large talus slope makes a good stop. Beyond Papoose Lake, the trail continues another mile or so to an excellent viewpoint of Mount Jefferson and Bingham Basin. The trail here rounds a corner, passing over some red cinders. You'll have to turn around for the view- don't miss it! The Lake of the Woods Trail then continues 0.7 mile to a junction with the Bingham Ridge Trail. Keep straight here, hiking into the heart of the damage left by the Puzzle Creek fire. In 2 more miles you'll reach Lake of the Woods, where the fire burned hot. While there are campsites in the area, it's not a good idea to camp in fire-scarred forest, as a windstorm could send a tree toppling onto your tent. Instead continue 0.7 more mile to a reunion with the Swallow Lake Trail, and then another 1.7 miles to Marion Lake. At this point, you've covered about 11.5 miles since leaving Table Lake. The trailhead and your vehicle is only 2.5 easy miles away, but if you have an extra night consider staying at Marion Lake. With more time you'll be able to explore around the lake, uncovering viewpoints and taking the time to see massive Marion Falls.

When you are finally ready to leave the wilderness at the conclusion of this backpack, hike downhill from Marion Lake on either trail that departs the lake. On the way down you'll pass Lake Ann, and a little over 2 miles from Marion Lake you'll reach the trailhead and your vehicle.

81. TEMPLE LAKE AND MARION MOUNTAIN

	Temple Lake out & back	Marion Mountain out & back
Distance:	4.8 miles out and back	10.2 miles out and back
Elevation Gain:	400 feet	1,400 feet
Trailhead Elevation:	4,565 feet	4,565 feet
Trail High Point:	4,629 feet	5,329 feet
Season:	June- October	June- October
Best:	June- October	June- October
Map:	Green Trails #557 (Mt. Jeff)	Green Trails #557 (Mt. Jeff)

Directions:
- From Salem, drive OR 22 east for 49.2 miles to Detroit.
- Continue another 20.2 miles southeast of Detroit on OR 22 to a junction on your left with Twin Meadows Road (FR 2261), signed for Camp Pioneer.
- Turn left here and drive this paved and astoundingly well-maintained road for exactly 5 miles to a gate on your left – this is the entrance to Camp Pioneer.
- Keep straight and drive another 100 feet to the trailhead.
- You will need to park on the shoulder here.

Hike: Prepare to be pleasantly surprised! Despite being little-known, this easy to moderate trek through the woods south of Marion Lake is consistently one of the nicest hikes in the entire Mount Jefferson Wilderness. The short and mostly level hike to beautiful and quiet Temple Lake makes for an excellent family backpacking expedition, and the longer hike up Marion Mountain is never difficult, and takes you to a spectacular view of the fire-damaged Mount Jefferson Wilderness.

Begin on the Pine Ridge Trail. Pass Camp Pioneer on your left, a large camp owned and operated by the Boy Scouts. You will need to stay on the main trail and ignore any side trails for the first 0.2 mile, as almost all of them lead to the camp. You will then arrive at a 4-way junction with the Turpentine Trail, which leads south along the fire-scarred western edge of the wilderness to Duffy Lake (Hike 83). Fill out your wilderness permit and then keep straight on the Pine Ridge Trail. You will meander through the forest at a grade that is almost level, sometimes breaking up the monotony with short uphill and downhill stretches. Occasionally you will pass trails on your right – these all lead to a series of lakes south of the Pine Ridge Trail (bring a GPS and explore to your heart's desire). Unless you are prepared to explore, you should stay on the main trail.

At about 2 miles from the trailhead, arrive at a junction with the spur trail to Temple Lake. For an easy hike, turn left here and descend 0.4 mile to the lake. This is a peaceful location: there is a view of the top third of Mount Jefferson, several excellent campsites and even an amateur boat ramp! Whether you are continuing on to Marion Mountain or not, you need to come down to the lake and spend a few minutes!

To continue on to Marion Mountain, return to the Pine Ridge Trail and turn left (east). Be-

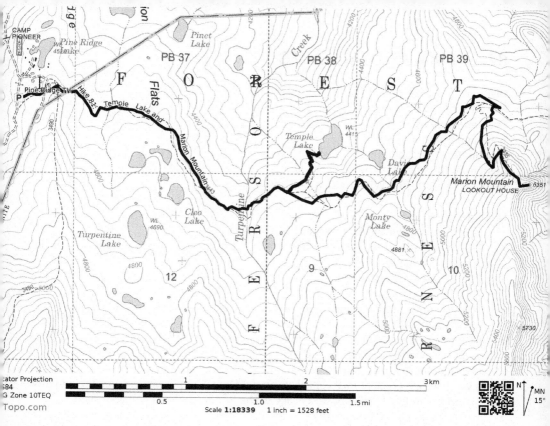

yond the Temple Lake junction, the trail receives less maintenance, so you'll need to step over a few downed logs from time to time. The forest changes too, transitioning to a thinner and more open forest, and eventually into forest that burned in the B+B Fire in 2003. Huckleberries grow in large quantities along this stretch of the trail, so plan a visit in August or September if you want to do some berry picking!

At approximately 4 miles from the trailhead, meet the spur to the summit of Marion Mountain on your right. Turn right here and hike 0.8 mile to the summit of Marion Mountain. The view here is spectacular! To the north, Mount Jefferson rises above huge, deep blue Marion Lake (keen eyes can pick out rafts on the lake and even hikers on trails around the lake). Mount Hood peeks out to the left of Mount Jefferson, immediately to the left of spiky Dynah-Mo Peak. The view extends across the vast, burned interior of the Mount Jefferson Wilderness to Three-Fingered Jack, whose spires loom ominously to the east. The tops of North and Middle Sister peek out to the right of Three-Fingered Jack. Explorations around the summit reveal even nicer views with a bit of effort. Contrary to what the map above says, there is no lookout house - in fact, Marion Mountain's fire lookout was dismantled sometime around 1964.

Return the way you came. On the way back you may be tempted to check out some of the off-trail lakes in the area (there are many), but be sure to bring map and compass or a GPS (or both) to avoid getting lost. The woods here have a uniform quality that makes it difficult to tell where exactly you are without good landmarks.

82.   PIKA AND FIR LAKES

Distance: 1.8 miles out and back
Elevation Gain: 400 feet
Trailhead elevation: 3,962 feet
Trail high point: 4,148 feet
Season: May- October
Best: May- October
Map: Mount Jefferson Wilderness (Geo-Graphics)

Directions:

- From Salem, drive OR 22 east for 49.2 miles to Detroit.
- Continue another 26 miles southeast of Detroit on OR 22 to a junction on your left with Big Meadows Road (FR 2267).
- Turn left here and drive exactly 1 mile to a signed junction with Twin Meadows Road (FR 2257).
- Turn left onto this road and drive 1.5 narrow but paved miles, passing Big Meadows Horse Camp along the way, to a junction.
- Drivers with passenger cars should park here and walk the last stretch, as the road beyond the junction is fairly unpleasant. This adds 1.4 miles to your overall hike but your low-clearance vehicle may actually thank you on the way out.
- If you have a high-clearance vehicle, keep right on FR 2257 from the junction and drive 0.7 rutted and rocky mile past Fay Lake to the Pika-Fir Trailhead on your right.
- There is room for a few cars to park on the shoulder of the road near a signboard.

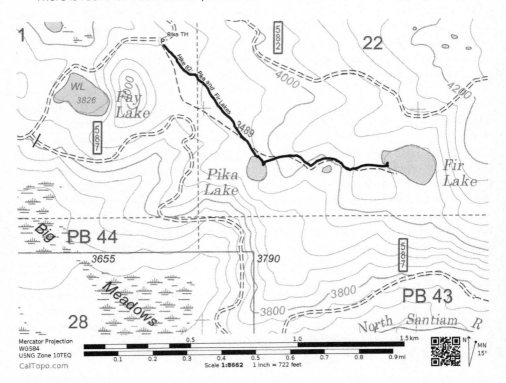

Beautiful Fir Lake on a frosty morning in early spring.

Hike: This short trail to two charming backcountry lakes is a great hike for families with little children, who will love both lakes. While the lakes are devoid of mountain views, they are both quite charming and worth a visit if you happen to be in the area.

Begin at a trailhead just north of Fay Lake. The trail climbs at a slight pace through an older forest of Douglas fir and mountain hemlock before dropping to a boggy crossing of Pika Lake's outlet creek. Reach the lake shortly afterwards. Brush keeps hikers from accessing the shore in most spots. From here, the trail forks to the left, climbs a bit more and drops again to a shallow pond on the right. A third short climb and then descent brings you to cute Fir Lake, backed by a large talus slope. There is an excellent campsite right as you reach the lake, should you wish to spend the night. The trail dead ends part of the way around the lake. You will likely hear pikas at Fir Lake, many more than at Pika Lake. It is speculated that the geographic names board placed the name of Pika Lake in the wrong location. Naturally, sometimes place names just don't make sense!

Truth be told, this area is overflowing with trails; hikers adept at off-trail travel can make all sorts of loops using the roads and trails around here. Most will prefer to return the way they came, however.

If you've got a little extra time, Fay Lake is lovely and worth a short visit. There are a couple of campsites around the lake that have picnic tables, and it is obvious that this area sees considerable use in the summer months.

83. DUFFY LAKE, SANTIAM LAKE AND THE EIGHT LAKES BASIN

	Duffy Lake	Santiam Lake	Eight Lakes Basin
Distance:	7 miles out & back	10.8 miles out & back	16.8 miles out & back
Elevation Gain:	800 feet	1,200 feet	2,500 feet
TH Elevation:	4,008 feet	4,008 feet	4,008 feet
High Point:	4,814 feet	5,188 feet	5,366 feet
Season:	June- October	June- October	July- October
Best:	June- October	June- October	July- October
Map:	Green Trails #557/589	Green Trails #557/589	Green Trails #557/589

Directions:
- From Salem, drive OR 22 east for 49.2 miles to Detroit.
- Continue another 26 miles southeast of Detroit on OR 22 to a junction on your left with Big Meadows Road (FR 2267).
- Turn left here and drive this this paved road for 2.7 miles to a fork.
- Turn left here. The road promptly changes to a mixture of gravel and rough pavement.
- Continue 0.4 mile to another fork in the road.
- Stay left here and drive into the parking lot loop for the Duffy Lake Trailhead.
- There are many places to park but come early – this is an extremely popular hike and the trailhead is often full by mid-morning on summer weekends.
- A Northwest Forest Pass is required to park here.

Hike: When the massive B+B Complex Fire burned a large portion of the Mount Jefferson Wilderness in 2003, it barely spared popular Duffy Lake. You'll see evidence of this fire and other previous blazes on this lovely hike; with some extra energy, you can continue another 1.5 miles to lovely Santiam Lake, nestled at the foot of Three-Fingered Jack. Backpackers and energetic dayhikers can hike north into beautiful Eight Lakes Basin.

Begin by heading uphill into ancient forest on a wide, well-maintained trail. Very soon, you will reach a junction with an older alignment of the Duffy Lake Trail. Continue straight on the main trail and continue a gradual ascent through the forest. Reach a junction with the Turpentine Trail at 1.5 miles; stay on the main trail, which begins to open up as it parallels the North Santiam River. Duffy Butte looms huge ahead of you. After another mile the trail rounds a bend to a crossing of the river, here more like a creek. The ford is not difficult at all, and is usually a rock hop after mid-June in most years. Continue following the river another 0.8 mile to a junction near Duffy Lake (which should be visible through the trees to your left), where you are met with a confusion of trails and a proliferation of great campsites.

What to do? First of all, you should turn left and follow a user trail to the lake. Turn left and hike around the west side of the lake to a view of Three-Fingered Jack, standing tall at the far end of the lake. On your left is craggy Duffy Butte, which burned significantly in the B+B Fire and whose trees stand silver and white, a reminder of the blaze. If you are backpacking here, remember to camp only in designated sites and that fires are banned within 100 feet of the lake. If you are continuing to Santiam Lake, return to the junction south of Duffy Lake.

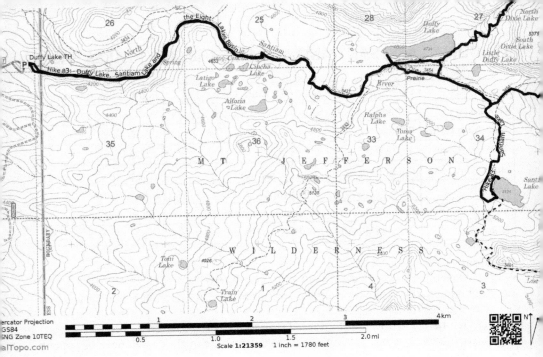

From this junction, continue straight on the Duffy Lake Trail until you reach its end at a junction with the Blue Lake Trail at the far end of Duffy Lake. Turn right here and begin a steady climb uphill on a trail that is at times rocky and rutted. Pass a junction on your right with a cutoff trail back to Duffy Lake; save this for your way back and instead fork to the left on what appears to be the main trail. After 0.5 mile, reach yet another trail junction, this time with the Dixie Lakes Trail on your left. Turn right instead to begin hiking the Santiam Lake Trail. You will climb gradually to another crossing of the North Santiam River, here a mere trickle as it flows from its source at Santiam Lake. Just after you cross the river, reach an unmarked trail junction above Santiam Lake, out of sight but close by on your left. Continue straight and contour around the lake until you reach an open prairie on the south side of the lake. Turn left here and follow user trails down to the lake. Three-Fingered Jack rises over the lake's eastern shore, just a few miles away. There are several great campsites here. Follow user trails left around the lake for more great viewpoints and campsites. When you reach the north end of the lake, you can continue straight on an obvious user trail to return to the trail junction north of Santiam Lake. Given the proliferation of trails, simply following any user trail west from the lake should return you to the main trail. From here, return the way you came; similarly, you can arrange a car shuttle with the PCT Trailhead at Santiam Pass (see Hike 85) or follow the Dixie Lakes Trail to Eight Lakes Basin. The beauty of this area is the great variety of options available to hikers and backpackers.

If instead you'd like to visit the Eight Lakes Basin, instead turn left at the far end of Duffy Lake and hike north on the Blue Lake Trail. The trail climbs 400 feet over the next 0.9 mile to beautiful Mowich Lake. The lake burned badly during the B+B fire, as did all of the subsequent lakes on this hike. There are still some excellent campsites, however. Another 1.9 miles of gradual uphill and then downhill through several pockets of unburned forest brings you to a trail junction at the southern foot of Jorn Lake, the first of the Eight Lakes Basin and 6.5 miles from the Duffy Lake Trailhead. Good campsites abound at the lake

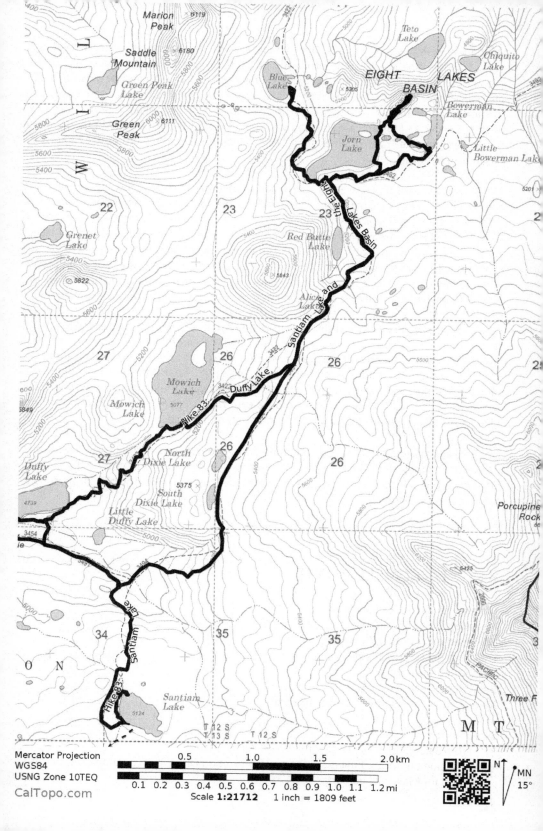

should you wish to stay overnight. Once you've arrived, there is much to see and do! First of all, take the time to hike from Jorn Lake uphill for 0.7 mile to beautiful Blue Lake. There is one excellent campsite at the lake but little else, as the lake is ringed by blowdown left by the B+B fire. Look for the top of Mount Jefferson, rising above the blackened snags on the north end of the lake. The Blue Lake Trail continues north through the burn for approximately 3 miles to Marion Lake. Instead you should return to Jorn Lake, where you meet the Bowerman Lake Trail. For an exciting 1.8 mile loop through the heart of the Eight Lakes Basin, turn left here.

The Bowerman Lake Trail passes through a pocket of unburned forest, passing several great campsites and a few nice meadows for 0.6 mile to the south end of Bowerman Lake. Look for a social trail that heads down to the lake, where you immediately discover a lovely view of Mount Jefferson, framed perfectly by the long curve of the lake. Inexperienced hikers should turn around here, but hikers with off-trail and scrambling experience can follow social trails west from the south end of Bowerman Lake through the maze of ponds and blowdown, aiming for the rock dome that sits between Bowerman and Jorn Lakes. When you reach the base of the dome, scramble up the rocks to the summit. Continue to the far end of the summit where you are met with an unbelievable view: to the north, Mount Jefferson rises over the burned forests of the center of the Mount Jefferson Wilderness. Almost 500 feet directly below you are Teto and Chiquito Lakes. Be careful where you step: the best views are near the cliff edge, where one false step would almost certainly be fatal. From the south side of the rock dome, scramble down to your right, heading in a general southwest direction towards Jorn Lake. When you reach the lake, follow the east shore until you reach the Bowerman Lake Trail near a series of nice campsites. Return to the junction with the Blue Lake Trail and return to Duffy Lake, and then the trailhead.

On the way back you can detour through the burned forests on the Dixie Lakes Trail, which passes the nondescript Dixie Lakes before meeting the Santiam Lake Trail at the far end of a large meadow. This adds another mile to your overall trek but is worthwhile for those who like to make small loops.

84. MAXWELL BUTTE

Distance: 9.2 miles out and back
Elevation Gain: 2,500 feet
Trailhead elevation: 3,766 feet
Trail high point: 6,222 feet
Season: June- October
Best: June- July
Map: Mount Jefferson Wilderness (Geo-Graphics)

Directions:
- From Salem, drive OR 22 east for 49.2 miles to Detroit.
- Continue another 29 miles southeast of Detroit on OR 22 to a junction on your left at a sign for Maxwell Sno-Park.

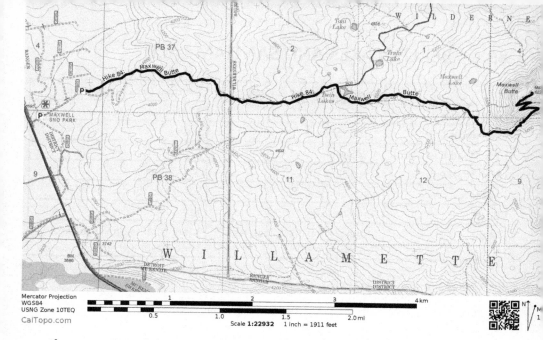

Mercator Projection
WGS84
USNG Zone 10TEQ
CalTopo.com

Scale **1:22932**   1 inch = 1911 feet

- If you are coming from Sisters or Bend, this junction is 2.5 miles after Santiam Junction, and will be on your right.
- Turn left here and park in the sno-park's large parking lot.
- From the sno-park you can drive another 0.4 mile down a rocky dirt road to the actual trailhead, but there is much less parking.

Hike: Maxwell Butte toils in obscurity despite being located only a few miles from both Three-Fingered Jack and Santiam Pass. The trail sees relatively little use and maintenance is infrequent at best. Yet, this is a nice hike to an excellent viewpoint, and at last visit, the trail was in excellent shape. Plan on a visit in July for the best flower displays and views.

The trail begins in a cool forest and is mostly level. At the beginning you will be following cross-country ski trails (you did begin in a snow park, after all), which occasionally branch off to the right and left. You should ignore all side trails, and soon you will enter the Mount Jefferson Wilderness. At about 2.2 miles from the trailhead, meet the Lava Lakes Trail on your left, next to small and shallow Twin Lakes. While left leads to Duffy Lake and the Eight Lakes Basin (Hike 83), the trail to Maxwell Butte forks right. You turn right and continue a moderate ascent up the gentle slopes of rounded Maxwell Butte. As you near the summit, the trail steepens considerably. You will climb a series of switchbacks through open forest, with views to the south amidst hanging meadows. At 4.8 miles, reach the summit and take in the view - it is tremendous! Look north to Mount Jefferson and distant Mount Hood, and the entirety of the Mount Jefferson Wilderness. South is Mount Washington and the Three Sisters. Just a few miles to the east is rugged Three-Fingered Jack, which seems close enough to touch. There are a few remnants left of the Maxwell Butte lookout, which like so many other lookouts in the Pacific Northwest, was removed in the mid 1960s.

Before you begin heading downhill again, follow a short trail to a rockpile on the east end of the summit. The view here is even more impressive, as the mountains are unobstructed and there are views down to Berley and Santiam Lakes (Hike 85). Return the way you came.

85. BERLEY LAKES AND SANTIAM LAKE

	Berley Lakes out & back	Santiam Lake out & back
Distance:	8.2 miles out & back	11.6 miles out & back
Elevation Gain:	1,100 feet	900 feet
Trailhead Elevation:	4,845 feet	4,845 feet
Trail High Point:	5,361 feet	5,416 feet
Season:	June- October	June- October
Best:	June- October	June- October
Map:	Mount Jefferson Wilderness (Geo-Graphics)	Mount Jefferson Wilderness (Geo-Graphics)

Directions:
- From Salem, drive east on OR 22 for 82 miles (or exactly 31.7 miles past the Breitenbush turnoff in Detroit) until OR 22 ends when it merges onto US 20.
- Drive US 20 for 5.4 miles to Santiam Pass.
- Turn into the signed trailhead for the Pacific Crest Trail at Santiam Pass.

Hike: Tucked away less than 200 yards from the Santiam Lake Trail, the gorgeous Berley Lakes are a worthy but elusive destination. For a longer hike, you can continue on to azure Santiam Lake, which has a similarly fantastic view of Three-Fingered Jack but is much easier to find. The trail is dusty and open so be sure to come early on hot summer days.

Begin on the Pacific Crest Trail heading north towards Mount Jefferson (and Canada). The trail cuts through a ghostly forest of snags left by the B+B Fire in 2003. The grade is easy and the trail very well-maintained. Reach a junction with the Santiam Lake Trail in 1.2 miles. While the PCT veers to the right, you will fork to the left to continue on towards the Berley Lakes and eventually Santiam Lake. The trail drops slightly as it follows Lost Lake Creek at a distance and passes through more burnt forest. At 2.7 miles (or 1.5 miles from the last trail junction), reach an unsigned fork in the trail. The safer route stays right on the maintained Santiam Lake Trail, but a left turn leads to adventure – and to Berley Lakes.

This unmaintained trail, likely an old alignment of the Skyline Trail, meanders through a low forest of youthful lodgepole pines as it slowly works its way north. There are a few sketchy spots on the trail but the route is hard to lose, as it continues in a northwesternly direction towards a gap between two unnamed bluffs (for off-trail lovers, Craig Lake is situated in a basin atop one of these bluffs to your left). The closer the trail gets to Berley Lakes, the easier it is to follow. Ascend to a pass about 0.9 mile from where you turned off the Santiam Lake Trail (you are about 3.6 miles from the PCT Trailhead now); behind you, views open up to Mount Washington and the North Sister. Continue straight and drop down to the far shore of Lower Berley Lake at 3.7 miles from the trailhead. Although the Santiam Lake Trail is in fact only 0.3 mile to the east (and only about 500 feet from the eastern shore of Lower Berley Lake), the lakes are much easier to find following the faint trail described above.

Both Berley Lakes were spared in the B+B Fire, and both feature outstanding views of

Three-Fingered Jack appears tantalizingly close at Lower Berley Lake.

Three-Fingered Jack. When the faint trail spits you at the far end of the lower lake, you are delivered directly to one of the finest views in the Mount Jefferson Wilderness! Three-Fingered Jack towers over long, blue and narrow Lower Berley Lake in a most photogenic fashion, and on clear days the lake seems to reflect the blue of the sky in a sublime manner. A nicer spot would be tough to imagine, but then, you haven't seen Upper Berley Lake yet! To find the upper lake, continue past the far end of the lower lake on the same trail, angling to the northwest away from the lower lake. Climb a bit through the forest on an obvious trail, then descend to the Upper Lake, which features several very nice campsites and a similarly great view of Three-Fingered Jack. To return to the Santiam Lake Trail, return to the Lower Lake's viewpoint and follow user trails on either side of the lake 0.2 mile back to the Santiam Lake Trail. Don't fret if you lose the user trail – simply aiming due east on either side of the Lower Lake will deliver you back to the Santiam Lake Trail.

If you don't want to bother with the faint, older trail described above, hike 0.9 mile north of the spot where the trail splits (or 2.4 miles from the Santiam Lake-PCT split) and look for a cairn at a small wash just after the trail descends from a knoll. Turn left here and follow user trails 150 yards to Lower Berley Lake.

From Lower Berley Lake's outwash cairn, the Santiam Lake Trail continues 1.6 miles up a long series of prairies to a junction above Santiam Lake. Turn right and descend a user trail to the southwest end of Santiam Lake. You can follow user trails around Santiam Lake, passing several excellent campsites aong the way to the northwest end of the lake. From here, a short trail leads back to the Santiam Lake Trail. Left leads back to Santiam Pass, while right leads to Duffy Lake (Hike 83). Return the way you came, or the way you wish to return.

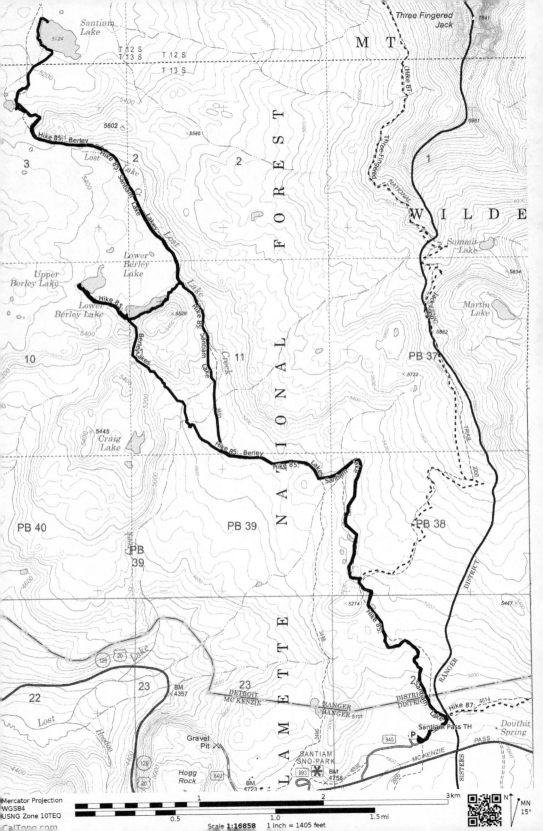

86. GRAND MOUNT JEFFERSON LOOP

Distance: 68 mile loop (53.5 miles without side trip to Jefferson Park)
Elevation Gain: 17,000 feet
Trailhead elevation: 4,845 feet
Trail high point: 6,739 feet
Season: July- October
Best: August
Map: Mount Jefferson Wilderness (Geo-Graphics)

Directions:
- From Salem, drive east on OR 22 for 80 miles to the junction with US 20.
- Drive US 20 for 5.4 miles to Santiam Pass.
- If you are coming from Sisters, drive 20.4 miles west on US 20 to Santiam Pass.
- Turn into the signed trailhead for the Pacific Crest Trail at Santiam Pass.

Hike: Here's a way to impress your friends with an unforgettable loop through the whole of the Mount Jefferson Wilderness. Along the way, this 53.5 mile loop hits almost every scenic high point in the wilderness, passes almost every lake (that has trail access), and delivers you incredible view after incredible view of both Mount Jefferson and Three-Fingered Jack. Take a week off from work in late July or August and tackle this loop- it is among the best in the entire state of Oregon. And as long as you are here, you should add on an additional 14.5 mile out and back trip to Jefferson Park, perhaps the best backcountry destination in Oregon. It simply does not get better than this.

As this is an extremely long trip, I cannot describe every twist and turn: and indeed, that would ruin much of the fun. Many of these trails are described in greater detail elsewhere in this book. What I will instead do is offer a sample itinerary for this challenging and magnificent journey through the Mount Jefferson Wilderness.

Leg 1: Santiam Pass to Wasco and Rockpile Lakes
While you can hike the loop in any direction, it's better to start on the PCT and hike north to Pamelia Lake, then return south on a number of trails that were once part of the Oregon Skyline Trail south towards Santiam Pass. On the first day, you will hike through a seemingly endless forest of snags left after the B+B Fire. Pack lots of water as there is little on this stretch of your trip. Pass a junction with the Summit Lake Trail almost immediately. Stay on the PCT another 1.2 miles to another junction, this time with the Santiam Lake Trail. This is the start of your loop. Keep right to stay on the PCT.

The PCT passes by the west face of Three-Fingered Jack, offering impressive views up to the craggy heights of this heavily-eroded volcano. You will pass directly above Canyon Creek Meadows (see Hike 92) before dropping a bit to Minto Pass. Here, a trail leads to Wasco Lake at about 10 miles from Santiam Pass. The B+B Fire burned most of the area around the lake, leaving far fewer campsites; that being said, the lake is also less crowded now than it once was. If you still have time and energy, continue uphill another 3.2 miles to Rockpile Lake where you will find several nice sites around the lake. This small pool is located at the crest of the Cascades so expect a cold night, regardless of the season. The lake has excellent water in spite of its muddy appearance; tread lightly to help keep it that way!

Leg 2: Rockpile Lake to Pamelia Lake

The second day of your trek takes you along the rugged crest of the Mount Jefferson Wilderness, passing several incredible views north to Mount Jefferson before you descend to beautiful Pamelia Lake, set in a canyon at the foot of Mount Jefferson's west face. Be sure to secure a limited entry permit for the Pamelia Lake area for the day you plan on being there from www.recreation.gov - this permit is required to both visit and camp in the Pamelia Limited Entry area.

Begin at Wasco Lake or Rockpile Lake. If you only made it to Wasco Lake, hike 3.2 miles uphill to Rockpile Lake. Be sure to fill up your water here as there is none for most of the rest of your day. From Rockpile Lake, the PCT drops a bit, passes a junction with the abandoned Brush Creek Trail and then enters a large flats at the eastern foot of South Cinder Peak. At 1.3 miles from Rockpile Lake, reach a 4-way junction with the Shirley Lake Trail (on your right, heading east towards Carl Lake) and Swallow Lake Trail (on your left, heading southwest towards Marion Lake). If you have time and energy, I strongly recommend climbing up to the nearby summit of South Cinder Peak for a panoramic view of the Mount Jefferson Wilderness. To find this view, drop your packs nearby and turn left to hike southwest on the Swallow Lake Trail. After about 0.2 mile, look for an unmarked but very obvious trail heading up the cinder cone on your right. Turn right and climb steeply to the summit of South Cinder Peak, where the view encompasses the entire wilderness. Visible to the south are the Three Sisters and Broken Top. Then return to the 4-way junction and continue north on the PCT.

The PCT continues north along the crest, passing several incredible viewpoints north to Mount Jefferson. The best of these comes at about 3.7 miles north of the 4-way junction, where the PCT curves around a cliff edge. Here Mount Jefferson towers over the rocky, mysterious canyonlands around The Table, offering an intriguing view of the volcanic heart of the Mount Jefferson Wilderness. At 5.7 miles from Rockpile Lake, reach a junction with the Hunts Creek Trail on your left. Continue north another 2 miles to Shale Lake, where you will find several excellent campsites and the last reliable water for several miles. This is the start of the Pamelia Limited Entry Area, so be sure you have your permit with you. From Shale Lake, the PCT continues downhill 4.2 miles to a junction with the Hunts Creek Trail on the south bank of Milk Creek's deep canyon. Turn left here to leave the PCT, and hike downhill 0.9 mile to Pamelia Lake, where you will find many excellent campsites by the lakeshore. Your day's total hike is about 13 miles from Rockpile Lake (this includes the South Cinder Peak detour), or about 16.2 miles if you started your day at Wasco Lake.

Mandatory detour: Jefferson Park

If you have the time and energy, I strongly encourage you to take another night to make the trek north on the PCT to Jefferson Park. The park is perhaps the most spectacular place in the entire wilderness, and the PCT approach from the south is a unique way to visit this special place.

From Pamelia Lake, return to the PCT at Milk Creek. The crossing can be difficult early in the season, so it's a good idea to cross early in the morning before peak snowmelt begins. Continue north on the PCT, passing the Woodpecker Ridge Trail before reaching Russell Creek 2.6 miles north of the Woodpecker Ridge Trail. Fed by melt from Mount Jefferson's glaciers above, this crossing is extremely difficult when the creek is running high; you may need to

Mount Jefferson towers over the mesas and cinder cones in the vicinity of the Table.

make this crossing as early in the day as you can, and barring that, you may need to continue upstream until you find a safe place to cross. From there it is 1.4 miles north on the PCT to Jefferson Park, where campsites are plentiful. Here the north face of Mount Jefferson dominates the skyline, rising above the wildflower meadows and lakes in the park. A more beautiful place would be hard to imagine. As the park is a very popular backpacking destination, be sure to camp in designated spots only and not on the very fragile meadows. Mosquitos are an extreme nuisance in July and early August.

Return to Pamelia Lake to resume your loop.

Leg 3: Pamelia Lake to Marion Lake
Now the loop turns back to the south on what was once known as the Oregon Skyline Trail, the precursor to today's Pacific Crest Trail. Many sections of this trail survive under many different names. You'll begin this leg of your loop on what is officially known as the Hunts Creek Trail.

Hike south 3.2 miles up Hunts Creek's canyon to a junction with the spur trail into Hunts Cove. If you have time, turn left and hike 0.4 mile to Hanks Lake, where you will find nice views of Mount Jefferson from the lake's south shore. Return then to the junction and tackle the switchbacks that lead to the top of Lizard Ridge. After a gain of 900 feet in relatively short order, arrive at a junction with the Lake of the Woods Trail at 1.3 miles from the Hunts Cove junction. Turn right to continue south on the Lake of the Woods Trail (left leads you back to the PCT in 1.7 miles). Continue south on the Lake of the Woods Trail for 2.6 miles to a junction with the Bingham Ridge Trail on your right, not long after you enter terrain burned in the 2006 Puzzle Creek Fire. The last 4.4 miles of this leg are a bit of a slog as the

Lake of the Woods Trail passes through fire-scarred forest. Along the way you pass several lakes and a junction with the Swallow Lake Trail at 2.8 miles before arriving at huge and deep Marion Lake, about 12.3 miles from Pamelia Lake.

There are dozens of campsites at Marion Lake, which is to be expected given how popular the lake is. Your best chance of privacy is to find a spot away from the west end of the lake. As elsewhere on this loop, campfires are absolutely forbidden. Before you leave Marion Lake, make sure you explore! You'll find excellent views of Mount Jefferson, a trail to a massive waterfall on Marion Lake's outlet creek not far from the lake, and much more. More specific directions to some of these spots can be found elsewhere in this book.

Leg 4: Marion Lake to Santiam Pass
There are three ways to get back to Santiam Pass: you can follow the Minto Pass Trail about 3.7 miles back to the PCT at Minto Pass, near Wasco Lake; you can follow the Minto Pass Trail to a junction with the Bowerman Lake Trail, and hike south to Bowerman Lake and then Jorn Lake, where you will rejoin the Blue Lake Trail; or you can follow the Blue Lake Trail to Blue Lake and then Jorn Lake, and then into the Eight Lakes Basin and points south. This is the route I will describe.

From the bridge over Marion Creek at the southwest end of the lake, continue south on the Blue Lake Trail through damage from the B+B Fire for 3.4 miles to Blue Lake. This deep blue lake has only one good campsite but is a worthwhile stop. From here it's 0.7 mile to a junction with the Bowerman Lake Trail at the south end of Jorn Lake. From here, continue south on the Blue Lake Trail another 1.1 mile to a junction with the Dixie Lakes Trail. Right leads to Mowich and Duffy Lakes- a worthy detour- while left leads past tiny Dixie Lakes to a junction with the Santiam Lake Trail not far east of Duffy Lake. Duffy and Mowich Lakes are more interesting (and have excellent campsites) but this route is 1.6 miles longer as it is less direct. The Dixie Lakes Trail heads due south through the burn, passing small Dixie Lakes, for 1.5 miles to its end at a junction with the Santiam Lake Trail. Turn left here and continue 0.9 mile to Santiam Lake, about 7.6 miles from the southwest end of Marion Lake. Set in a shallow bowl, Santiam Lake offers numous campsites and excellent views of Three-Fingered Jack. This is a great place to camp if you wish to prolong your trip.

Beyond Santiam Lake, the Santiam Lake Trail climbs and then descends another 4.3 miles to a reunion with the PCT and the end of your loop. Turn right here and hike 1.3 miles to Santiam Pass, 14.3 miles from Marion Lake and the end of your great journey. The end of a trip like this calls for a celebration- you've earned it!

Photo on opposite page: Mount Jefferson from the south shore of Marion Lake.

SECTION 6: MOUNT JEFFERSON EAST

		Distance	EV Gain
87.	Three-Fingered Jack Loop	23.8	3,000
88.	Blue Lake	1.8	400
89.	Suttle, Scout and Dark Lakes	3.8	200
90.	Round and Square Lakes	5.2	500
91.	Head of Jack Creek	2.6	100
92.	Canyon Creek Meadows	7.5	1,500
93.	Rockpile Lake and South Cinder Peak	15.4	2,900
94.	Carl Lake and South Cinder Peak	10.4	1,400
95.	Table Lake Loop	23.8	3,900
96.	Jefferson Lake Trail and Table Lake	4.2	400
97.	Black Butte	4.0	1,600
98.	Green Ridge	10.8	1,200
99.	Metolius River: Canyon Creek to Wizard Falls	5.2	200
100.	Metolius River: Wizard Falls to Lower Bridge	6.2	200
101.	Metolius River: Into the Horn	20.2	500

The eastern slope of the Mount Jefferson Wilderness and surrounding environs burned horribly in the B+B Fire in 2003. As a result, most of the first ten hikes in this section have long stretches of blackened trail. The fire may have changed the character of these hikes but the area remains extremely beautiful, and you will appreciate the islands of unburned forest all that much more after passing the miles in burned timber. If hot, dusty trail through fire-scarred forest isn't your thing, the Metolius River is a cool oasis that will please pretty much everyone who enjoys the outdoors.

The Wilderness Trails (Hikes 87 and 91- 96) are generally accessible from July to October, as the trails on the western slope are. The Jefferson Lake Trailhead (Hike 96) is accessible much earlier, but no trail suffered worse in the B+B fire; indeed, most of the trail network that once crossed this corner of the wilderness has been lost to impenetrable thickets of snowbrush. The trails along the Metolius have a much longer season, as some of the roads are plowed all winter and others melt out early in the season. The trails near Santiam Pass, Black Butte and Green Ridge are also accessible for much of the year and offer excellent opportunities for snowshoeing and cross-country skiing in the winter.

The roads in this area are in general better than any of the other sections of this book, but some caution is nevertheless important. While most of the roads are good, the road to Black Butte (Hike 97) is fairly rough. One thing that you need to watch out for is deadfall on the roads; with so much burned forest, downed trees are common. You may want to bring an ax or a chainsaw with you just in case you encounter such a problem. Likewise, a small saw is a good idea, as you can saw out deadfall on trails. Some of the trails in this area see only infrequent maintenance, so anything you can do to help is good trail stewardship.

87.   THREE-FINGERED JACK LOOP

	Booth Lake	Porcupine Rock	TFJ Circumnaviation
Distance:	8.4 miles out & back	14 miles out & back	23.8 mile loop
Elevation Gain:	1,500 feet	1,700 feet	3,000 feet
TH Elevation:	4.845 feet	4.845 feet	4.845 feet
High Point:	5,225 feet	6,496 feet	6,496 feet
Season:	June- October	June- October	July- October
Best:	June- October	June- October	July- October
Map:	Green Trails #589	Green Trails #589	Green Trails #589

Directions from Salem / Albany:
- From Salem, drive east on OR 22 for 82 miles (or exactly 31.7 miles past the Breiten-bush turnoff in Detroit) until OR 22 ends when it merges onto US 20.
- If coming from Albany, drive US 20 to Santiam Junction.
- Continue straight on US 20 for 5.4 miles to Santiam Pass.
- Turn into the signed trailhead for the Pacific Crest Trail at Santiam Pass.

Directions from Sisters:
- From Sisters, drive west on US 20 approximately 20 miles to Santiam Pass.
- Turn into the signed trailhead for the Pacific Crest Trail at Santiam Pass.

Hike: Three-Fingered Jack is among Oregon's most photogenic and fascinating peaks. Its crags, striations and spires tantalize all who come to the area. The Pacific Crest Trail and Summit Lake Trails make it possible to circumnavigate Three-Fingered Jack, and while the B+B Fire decimated these forests, leaving behind seemingly endless snags and snowbrush, this is still an excellent loop. Just know going in that the best place to camp is popular Canyon Creek Meadows (Hike 92), which is reached by a short trail from a well-maintained gravel road. Expect crowds near your camp. One important thing to note is that most of this loop has little or no access to running water; be sure to bring lots when you hike here, and filter water at every possible opportunity. It gets awfully hot here in the summer.

Begin hiking north from Santiam Pass on the Pacific Crest Trail. After just a couple of min-utes, meet a junction with the Summit Lake Trail and the start of your loop. As is so often the case, I recommend doing the loop in a counterclockwise direction. Turn right on the Summit Lake Trail (which, I should note, goes nowhere near Summit Lake) and begin hiking in a northeasternly direction. Blowdown has plagued this trail in the years since the B+B Fire, and while the trail was cleared in 2014, you should expect to climb over trees on oc-casion. At 2.4 miles the trail reaches Square Lake, where you reach your first campsites. At the northwest end of the lake, you will reach a junction with the Round Lake Trail. Keep left to continue hiking north on the Summit Lake Trail.

It is obvious that this trail used to be heavily forested. The landscape has greatly changed since then; in place of beargrass and lodgepole pine is the uniformity of snowbrush and snags. Views of Three-Fingered Jack now tantalize above the snags, and you'll get better views as you climb a bit on your way towards the peak. At 4.2 miles, the trail passes Booth Lake. This is a good place to stop, and dayhikers should absolutely stop here. The B+B Fire started with a lightning strike at Booth Lake in August 2003, and few trees were spared in the heart of the fire here. There are few good campsites at Booth Lake.

If you are circumnavigating Three-Fingered Jack, continue north on the Summit Lake Trail. At 1.3 miles from Booth Lake, 5.5 miles from the start of the loop, reach First Creek (you'll know it's First Creek as it is the first creek you cross on this loop). In summer a bouquet of flowers lines the creek, and you'll have the first fresh water of your trip. From the crossing, it is another 2.7 miles to Jack Lake's busy trailhead, where scores of hikers park to visit Canyon Creek Meadows. There are several nice campsites here, as this was a primitive car campground before the B+B Fire. Of course, you probably didn't hike 8.2 miles to camp at a trailhead (at least there's a bathroom!), so you should hike through the trailhead to locate the Summit Lake Trail on the far side. Make Canyon Creek Meadows your goal for the night.

To continue to Canyon Creek Meadows, hike the Summit Lake Trail 0.4 mile to a fork. Keep left, climb uphill and over a ridge into forest that escaped the burn. You'll descend to a junction at the lower edge of Canyon Creek Meadows at 2 miles from Jack Lake and 10.2 miles from Santiam Pass. Turn left here and hike up what is officially an unmaintained trail (but is unofficially one of the best-maintained trails in this area) for one mile until you reach the area around the huge upper meadows at the foot of Three-Fingered Jack's impressive north face. Great campsites abound, so please do not succumb to the temptation to camp on the fragile meadows here (you may see people doing this- feel free to tell them off). The wildflower meadows here at the foot of the mountain are among the most beautiful in the Cascades, with abundant lupine, paintbrush, monkeyflower and many others in all sizes and colors. This is a very popular place, and with good reason. If you have time and energy, be sure to explore the area around the meadows; an unofficial but very obvious trail leads to an overlook of the cirque lake at the foot of Three-Fingered Jack's glacier and then to a saddle directly below the rugged cliffs on the east face of the eroded volcano. This is truly one of the most spectacular places in the Majestic Mount Jefferson Region. For more information about this area, see Hike 92.

To continue on your loop, hike back down to the junction at the lower end of Canyon Creek Meadows and continue 1 mile to a junction with the return trail to Jack Lake. Keep left for 0.7 mile to Wasco Lake, and then continue up to the PCT. Turn left on the PCT and hike 2.8 miles to Porcupine Rock. From Porcupine Rock, the PCT crosses a wildly scenic saddle directly above Canyon Creek Meadows and then heads downhill at a gentle grade through alternating stretches of burned and unburned forest for 7 miles to Santiam Pass. It is worth noting that there is absolutely no water on this stretch of the PCT, so bring as much as you can for this leg of your trek. This stretch of the trail is also highly rewarding as a dayhike in its own right; hiking north on the PCT from Santiam Pass towards Porcupine Rock reveals a series of excellent views of Three-Fingered Jack's south face as well as occasional looks north towards Mount Jefferson. As usual with the PCT, the trail is well-graded and easy to follow. If this is your plan, simply hike north on the PCT for a little under 7 miles until you reach Porcupine Rock's high, exposed pass and outstanding views. Highly recommended!

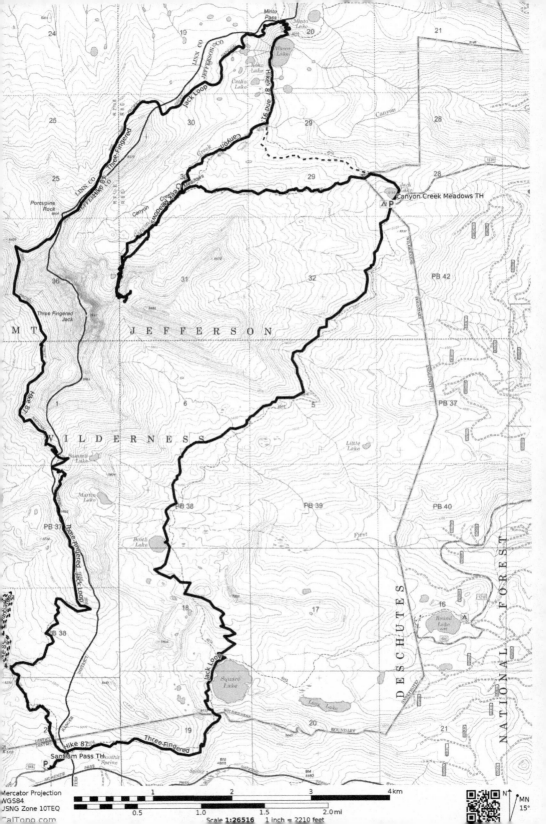

88. BLUE LAKE

Distance: 1.8 mile loop
Elevation Gain: 400 feet
Trailhead elevation: 3,668 feet
Trail high point: 3,724 feet
Season: May- November
Best: May- November
Map: See map on my website.

Directions from Salem / Albany:
* From Salem, drive east on OR 22 for 82 miles (or exactly 31.7 miles past the Breiten-bush turnoff in Detroit) until OR 22 ends when it merges onto US 20.
* If coming from Albany, drive US 20 to Santiam Junction.
* Continue straight on US 20 for 5.4 miles to Santiam Pass.
* Drive US 20 past Santiam Pass for 3.5 miles to a signed turnoff on your right for a fire information kiosk and Elliott Corbett State Park.
* Turn into the lot here.

Directions from Sisters:
* From Sisters, drive west on US 20 approximately 16.5 miles to a large turnout on the left signed for Elliott Corbett State Park.
* Turn into the lot here.

Directions note:
* It is easier to park in this lot, where you will find a large signboard commemorating the B+B fire, which decimated this area in late summer 2003. If you choose to take your chances driving down into Elliott Corbett State Park, drive down gravel road FR 2076 west from the parking lot for 0.7 mile to a junction with FR 200.
* Turn left here, pass a sign that says "Steep Winding Road next 1 and ½ miles" and very carefully drive 1.9 miles downhill on this narrow, winding and occasionally rocky road until it ends at a parking lot near Blue Lake.
* As of this writing, the road is in good shape and any car can manage the drive down, but please see the note below about driving to the lower trailhead.
* Note: There is absolutely no shame in parking at the fire information kiosk and walking the road down to the lake (you will have to do this in the winter). This is what I did – the access road to the lake is narrow, brushy, steep, rocky and subject to occasional washouts that turn the road into a series of deep gullies. Furthermore, turning around is impossible, and if you meet a vehicle, somebody has to back up until you reach the occasional wide spot. Hiking down the road adds 5.2 miles round-trip and 700 feet of elevation gain to your hike. It is not entirely without merit, as you have good views of Mount Washington and the slopes above Blue Lake on your way down.

Hike: A geologic oddity similar to Crater Lake and more than 300 feet deep, Blue Lake will enchant. The lake is almost invisible from every angle until you approach it; the lake is the remains of a collapsed caldera that has been filled in by underground springs. The only problem is how to get close to it! The eastern end of the lake is the property of Caldera, a non-profit retreat, and it has been widely assumed that the lake is entirely on private

property. This is not true, as the western end of the lake is Elliott Corbett Memorial State Recreation Site, but you should obey private property signs where they are posted.

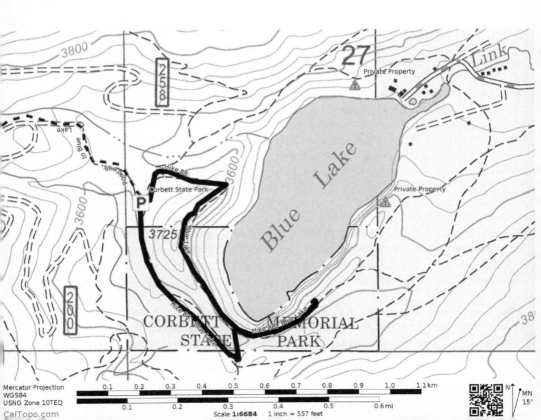

From the turnaround at the end of the road, follow a trail left towards the caldera rim. Although few people take the time to visit, the trail is well-maintained and clearly defined. Soon the lake will come into view, and it is magnificent! The deep blues of the lake are amplified on clear days, and while the blue of Crater Lake is unrivaled, this might be next-best thing. Hike along the trail around above the western end of the lake to a junction. Head straight another 0.2 mile to a knoll above the southern end of the lake, where the steep, red cinder slopes reveal the lake's origin as a volcano. There is a series of rocky bluffs high above the lake that are ideal for rest stops, and you should absolutely stop here. Not long after this spot the trail enters private property.

89.   SUTTLE LAKE LAKE

Distance: 3.8 mile loop
Elevation Gain: 200 feet
Trailhead elevation: 3,444 feet
Trail high point: 3,474 feet
Season: all year (bring snowshoes in winter)
Best: September- October
Map: Green Trails #589 (Three-Fingered Jack)

Directions from Salem / Albany:
- From Salem, drive east on OR 22 for 82 miles (or exactly 31.7 miles past the Breitenbush turnoff in Detroit) until OR 22 ends when it merges onto US 20.
- If coming from Albany, drive US 20 to Santiam Junction.
- Continue straight on US 20 for 5.4 miles to Santiam Pass.
- Drive US 20 past Santiam Pass for 7 miles to a signed turnoff for Suttle Lake on your right.
- Turn into Suttle Lake and drive downhill for 0.3 mile to a turnoff on your right, signed for the Suttle Lake Lodge nad day-use area.
- When you reach a fork after crossing the bridge over Lake Creek, keep right and follow signs to the day-use area.

Directions from Sisters:
- Drive US 20 for 14 miles northwest to Suttle Lake.
- Turn into Suttle Lake and drive downhill for 0.3 mile to a turnoff on your right, signed for the Suttle Lake Lodge nad day-use area.
- When you reach a fork after crossing the bridge over Lake Creek, keep right and follow signs to the day-use area.

Hike: This pleasant loop around beautiful Suttle Lake is an excellent hike in the fall, when the days are short, the leaves turn red and yellow and the motorboats and huge families that overrun the lake in the summer have long since departed. Regardless of the time of year, if you are staying at the Suttle Lake Lodge or one of the campgrounds on the lake, this loop should be mandatory. Of course, if you come here in the winter you may need to bring snowshoes! And if the loop around the lake isn't enough, there are two other lakes you can visit to help fill up your day.

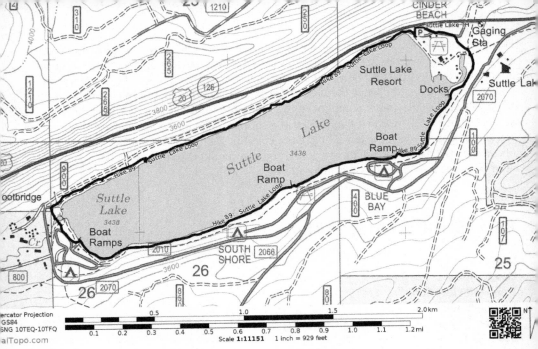

You can begin anywhere along the lake but unless you happen to be staying at one of the campgrounds, I recommend starting your hike at the day-use area on the lake's northeastern shore. The trail leaves from the edge of the day-use area and cuts a path between the lake and noisy US 20. Thankfully, the trail compensates for the noise with great views across the lake. Mount Washington sticks out behind ubiquitous Cache Mountain, and as you work your way around the lake, the mountain will eventually reveal itself. The forest is lovely as well, with a mixture of Ponderosa pine and Douglas fir that speaks to the confluence of eastern and western Oregon you will find here just east of the Cascade crest. Even better, you will pass a few nice beaches along the northern shore that are ideal for picnics, if not a quick swim.

At 1.5 miles, reach Link Creek Campground at the western end of the lake. Follow the trail to a bridge across Link Creek, after which the trail ends at a campground road. Follow the road through the campground to a boat ramp, where you will find the continuation of the trail to the right of a signboard. You will pass through a few campsites before you leave the crowds. The south shore of the lake has no mountain views but compensates by being much quieter. You will pass through Blue Bay and South Shore campgrounds before you reach the eastern end of the lake. Curve to the north, and reach a road bridge over Lake Creek. Take the pedestrian option, and follow signs for the trail through the property of the Suttle Lake Lodge to the day-use area and your car.

If you have more time and want to check out Scout and Dark Lakes, drive out of the lodge and return to the paved road that access the campgrounds. Turn right here and drive 0.9 mile to a road junction. Turn left at a sign for Scout Lake and drive 0.5 mile on FR 2066 to the day-use area at Scout Lake, where you should park. A NW Forest Pass is required here. The lake is extremely busy during the summer but in the fall you will likely have it mostly to yourself. There are no mountain views but the lake is quite pretty as it mostly survived the

Mount Washington rises above Cache Mountain and Suttle Lake.

B+B Fire intact. Walk around the lake to the west on well-maintained trail until you reach the west end of the lake, where you will find a trail that is signed for Dark Lake. Follow this trail over a hill and down into Dark Lake's bowl about 0.5 mile to the southwest, where the trail meets a road near Camp Tamarack. The trail does continue to a remote southern trailhead but you should turn around here. Walking around the lake is discouraged as much of the lake is the property of the camp.

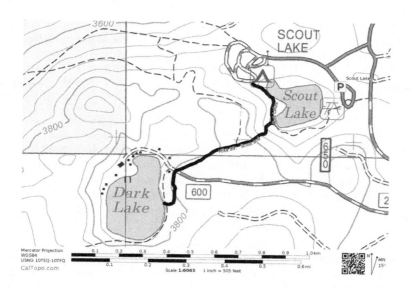

90. ROUND AND SQUARE LAKES

Distance: 5.2 miles out and back
Elevation Gain: 500 feet
Trailhead elevation: 4,320 feet
Trail high point: 4,807 feet
Season: June- October
Best: June- October
Map: Mount Jefferson Wilderness (Geo-Graphics)

Directions from Salem / Albany:
- From Salem, drive east on OR 22 for 82 miles (or exactly 31.7 miles past the Breiten-bush turnoff in Detroit) until OR 22 ends when it merges onto US 20.
- If coming from Albany, drive US 20 to Santiam Junction.
- Continue straight on US 20 for 5.4 miles to Santiam Pass.
- Drive US 20 past Santiam Pass for 8 miles to a turnoff for FR 12, opposite a sign that reads "Mt. Jefferson Wilderness Trailheads." It may be difficult to turn against traffic. The turnoff is less than a mile from the turnoff to Suttle Lake.
- Turn left on FR 12 and drive 1.1 miles to a fork in the road.
- Turn left onto FR 1210, the Round Lake Road, at a sign for Round Lake.
- Drive 5.6 miles of gravel road to a road junction on a hill above Round Lake.
- Turn right at a sign that reads "Christian Camp TH".
- Drive 0.6 mile to the trailhead on your left, just before the road enters the Christian Camp.

Directions from Sisters:
- Drive US 20 for 12 miles northwest to a turnoff on your right for FR 12, signed for "Mt. Jefferson Wilderness Trailheads".
- Turn left on FR 12 and drive 1.1 miles to a fork in the road.
- Turn left onto FR 1210, the Round Lake Road, at a sign for Round Lake.
- Drive 5.6 miles of gravel road to a road junction on a hill above Round Lake.
- Turn right at a sign that reads "Christian Camp TH".
- Drive 0.6 mile to the trailhead on your left, just before the road enters the Christian Camp.

Direction note: FR 1210 south of the camp is terrible- don't drive here from any direction other than the one indicated above. Online maps and GPS units may give you different directions, but the above route should absolutely be the preferred approach.

Hike: Just over two miles from either trailhead (the other is described in the loop around Three-Fingered Jack, Hike 87), Square Lake is a great destination for an easy, enjoyable hike. There is a catch, though: because of where both access trails reach the lake, you'll need to do some work to find the views of nearby Three-Fingered Jack you no doubt seek. Additionally, as the entire route passes through terrain scorched in the B+B Fire, it is a good idea to avoid this hike on hot days as there is very little shade.

The hike begins at a trailhead near a Christian youth camp and charges uphill, switchbacking away from Round Lake at a moderate grade. The next 1.5 miles are somewhat tedious,

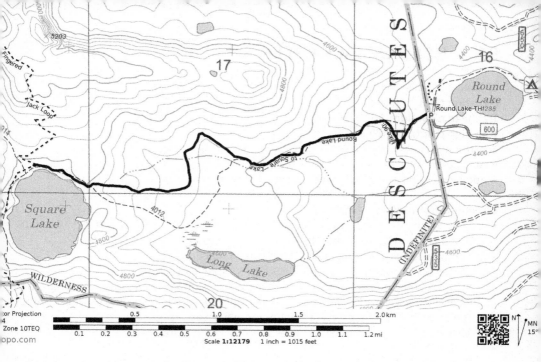

as the trail cuts a line through a forest that was incinerated in the B+B Fire. There are no views, no shade and nothing to look at. Impressive displays of lupine in June and July break up the monotony, but if you come in the fall you'll find yourself wondering how far it is until you reach Square Lake. Additionally, although topographic maps show the trail passing Long Lake, the trail does not in fact go anywhere that lake – don't even bother trying to find it unless you've got lots of time and patience. At a little over 2 miles, reach Square Lake, and note the top of Mount Washington rising above the lake's valley off to the south, At the far end of the lake, the Round Lake Trail ends at a junction with the Summit Lake Trail, which traverses the eastern slopes of Three-Fingered Jack from Santiam Pass to Jack Lake (see Hike 87). In order to find the view of Three-Fingered Jack and the best campsites (and lunchspots), you'll need to make a loop around Square Lake.

Turn south on the Summit Lake Trail from the junction and hike until you reach the end of the lake, From there, look for any number of user trails cutting off to the left. There are no continuous trails around the lake, and you will no doubt find yourself pushing through brush and climbing up and down the slopes above the lake. Before too long, however, the views begin opening up to Three-Fingered Jack to the north. As you make your way around the lake, the going gets easier as well, and you are mostly able to walk around the lake on its rocky beaches (this is easier in the fall). The view of Three-Fingered Jack is outstanding, and there are a pair of excellent campsites on the south shore of the lake that are inviting to backpackers (though I strongly recommend against camping here during times of high wind, as the lake is ringed by dead trees killed during the fire). When you reach the north-eastern end of the lake, make your way towards a quintet of large cottonwood trees on the lake shore, and from here, you will find the trail a few yards away. Return the way you came.

91. HEAD OF JACK CREEK

Distance: 2.6 miles out and back
Elevation Gain: 100 feet
Trailhead elevation: 3,115 feet
Trail high point: 3,226 feet
Season: March- November
Best: March- November
Map: See my website for a high-resolution map of this hike.

Directions from Salem / Albany:
- From Salem, drive east on OR 22 for 82 miles (or exactly 31.7 miles past the Breiten-bush turnoff in Detroit) until OR 22 ends when it merges onto US 20.
- If coming from Albany, drive US 20 to Santiam Junction.
- Continue straight on US 20 for 5.4 miles to Santiam Pass.
- Drive US 20 past Santiam Pass for 8 miles to a turnoff for FR 12, opposite a sign that reads "Mt. Jefferson Wilderness Trailheads." It may be difficult to turn against traffic. The turnoff is less than a mile from the turnoff to Suttle Lake.
- Turn left on FR 12 and drive 1.1 miles to a fork in the road.
- Keep right for another 3.3 miles to a sign for Jack Lake.
- Turn left and drive 0.6 mile of narrow pavement to a bridge over Jack Creek.
- Turn immediately to your left onto FR 1232, which passes the campground.
- Turn another left into the campground, where there may or may not be a sign.
- Drive through the campground to the end of the loop, where you will find the trailhead at a signboard. There is room for 4-5 cars here.

Directions from Sisters:
- Drive US 20 for 12 miles northwest to a turnoff on your right for FR 12, signed for "Mt. Jefferson Wilderness Trailheads".
- Turn left on FR 12 and drive 1.1 miles to a fork in the road.
- Keep right for another 3.3 miles to a sign for Jack Lake Campground.
- Turn left and drive 0.6 mile of narrow pavement to a bridge over Jack Creek.
- Turn immediately to your left onto FR 1232, which passes the campground.
- Turn another left into the campground, where there may or may not be a sign.
- Drive through the campground to the end of the loop, where you will find the trailhead at a signboard. There is room for 4-5 cars here.

Hike: This pretty little hike is ideal for families and perfect for a leg stretcher if you happen to be camping in the very cute Jack Creek Campground. The trail follows glassy Jack Creek, which resembles a miniature version of the Metolius River, through a canyon full of large Ponderosa pines to its springs, where the water seeps directly out of the ground. If 2.6 miles is too much for you or your family, there is a different trailhead further up the canyon that shortens the hike considerably.

Begin from the campground on a wide, dusty trail that parallels the creek at a distance. Though the trail rarely approaches lovely Jack Creek, the creek is always within earshot and adds to the peaceful nature of the scene. Before long, you will begin to leave the pondero-sas as the trail enters forest burned in the B+B fire; indeed, Jack Creek was near the eastern

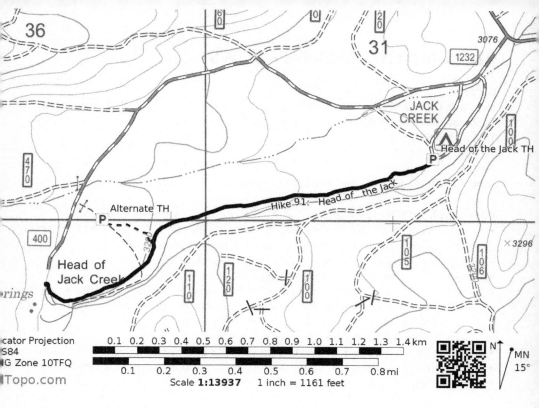

perimeter of the massive fire.

At 0.9 mile, the trail reaches an unsigned junction, where you will find a wooden bench. The trail on your right comes from the more-remote upper trailhead. Keep straight and enter the headwaters of the creek, where it widens and fans out into several different channels. Reach the springs at 1.3 miles from the trailhead, where the creek flows directly out of the slope. There is a sign that reads "End of trail. Please do not disturb springs." Note that the B+B Fire came within 100 feet of the springs- it is amazing to see the contrast the cool forest near the springs and the open forest where the fire burned. After some contemplation, return the way you came.

If 1.3 miles is too far for you or your family to hike, there is another trailhead (but one that requires a NW Forest Pass). To find this upper trailhead, drive past the campground another 1.1 miles on FR 1232 to a fork in the road. Keep straight here and drive another 0.3 mile to another fork. Keep left at a sign for Head of Jack Creek, and drive another 0.2 mile to the trailhead, where you'll find a bathroom and a picnic table. The trail departs from the trailhead and reaches the junction with the bench after only 0.2 mile. Turn right here and continue 0.4 mile to the springs. The round-trip distance of this approach is 1.2 miles, or slightly less than half the distance of the approach from the campground.

92.   CANYON CREEK MEADOWS

Distance: 7.5 mile semi-loop
Elevation Gain: 1,500 feet
Trailhead elevation: 5,151 feet
Trail high point: 6,490 feet
Season: July- October
Best: July- August
Map: Mount Jefferson Wilderness (Geo-Graphics)

Directions from Salem / Albany:
- From Salem, drive east on OR 22 for 82 miles (or exactly 31.7 miles past the Breiten-bush turnoff in Detroit) until OR 22 ends when it merges onto US 20.
- If coming from Albany, drive US 20 to Santiam Junction.
- Continue straight on US 20 for 5.4 miles to Santiam Pass.
- Drive US 20 past Santiam Pass for 8 miles to a turnoff for FR 12, opposite a sign that reads "Mt. Jefferson Wilderness Trailheads." It may be difficult to turn against traffic. The turnoff is less than a mile from the turnoff to Suttle Lake.
- Turn left on FR 12 and drive 1.1 miles to a fork in the road.
- Keep right for another 3.3 miles to a sign for Jack Lake Campground.
- Turn left and drive 0.6 mile of narrow pavement to a bridge over Jack Creek.
- Keep straight 0.7 mile of pavement to a junction on the right signed for Cabot Lake TH.
- Keep straight, now on FR 1234, another 0.7 mile of washboarded gravel to a junction with FR 1235, Bear Valley Road, on your right.
- Keep left and drive 5.1 miles of wide but washboarded gravel road to Jack Lake and the huge trailhead for Canyon Creek Meadows. A Northwest Forest Pass is required.

Directions from Sisters:
- Drive US 20 for 12 miles northwest to a turnoff on your right for FR 12, signed for "Mt. Jefferson Wilderness Trailheads".
- Turn left on FR 12 and drive 1.1 miles to a fork in the road.
- Keep right for another 3.3 miles to a sign for Jack Lake.
- Turn left and drive 0.6 mile of narrow pavement to a bridge over Jack Creek.
- Keep straight 0.7 mile of pavement to a junction on the right signed for Cabot Lake TH.
- Keep straight, now on FR 1234, another 0.7 mile of washboarded gravel to a junction with FR 1235, Bear Valley Road, on your right.
- Keep left and drive 5.1 miles of wide but washboarded gravel road to Jack Lake and the huge trailhead for Canyon Creek Meadows. A Northwest Forest Pass is required.

Hike: Canyon Creek Meadows is one of the most spectacular places in the Oregon Cascades. The massive, heavily eroded wall of Three-Fingered Jack towers over fields of wildflowers, while cascading Canyon Creek is at turns glassy and roaring, providing myriad photo oppor-tunities. This is a magical place, and everyone knows it – the crowds here are formidable throughout the summer. For maximum solitude and maximum wildflowers, try to plan a visit here mid-week in late July or early August, and for the best photos, stay overnight.

The trail begins at the massive Jack Lake Trailhead. There was a campground here before the B+B Fire, and some of the sites remain but they offer little privacy, and the only water

Canyon Creek Meadows and Three-Fingered Jack.

is from the shallow lake. The trail curves around the north side of the lake and sets about a gradual ascent through forest that was incinerated in the 2003 fire. At about a half-mile from the trailhead, meet a junction with the Summit Lake Trail (in fact you've been on the Summit Lake Trail, which traverses the east side of Three-Fingered Jack as described in Hike 87). Turn left and hike uphill, into unburned forest and then downhill into the basin holding Canyon Creek Meadows. At 2.1 miles, reach a junction with the trail into the meadows, beside trickling Canyon Creek. This is where the flower show starts in earnest in the summer – the displays of lupine in the meadows here are among the best in the Cascades.

Just beyond the junction, there is a sign that reads "Trail not maintained". This is to discourage people, but it isn't working – the trail is very much maintained by the hundreds if not thousands of hikers of come up here every summer and fall. The Canyon Glacier Trail ascends into the forest for a bit before opening up into a steep hanging meadow with an excellent view of Three-Fingered Jack ahead. From here you will hike steeply uphill until you reach a junction above the huge glacial outwash plain that is the upper Canyon Creek Meadow. To visit the upper meadow, turn right and descend about eighty feet to the meadow – but let's be honest: since you made it this far, you will almost certainly want to see the unnamed lake at the base of Three-Fingered Jack's glacier. So keep going straight until you see the moraine in front of you. There is a proliferation of trails here but the best and most obvious one shoots for the notch in the moraine. Climb steeply here, passing lots of July and August flowers, until you crest the notch and arrive at a most incredible view: the massive, striated wall of Three-Fingered Jack, with the gorgeously translucent waters of the glacial lake below you. This is the source of Canyon Creek. Try to get here earlier in the season, when the lake is a most beautiful shade of turquoise; later in the summer, the lake

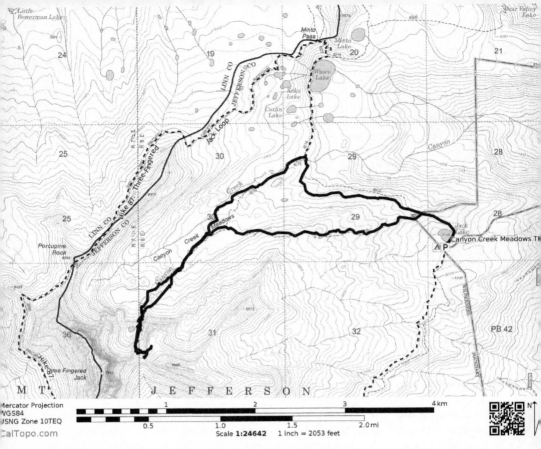

Mercator Projection
WGS84
USNG Zone 10TEQ
CalTopo.com

Scale **1:24642**   1 inch = 2053 feet

turns an unappetizing shade of brown, robbing the scene of some of its majesty. This is an excellent place to stop, should you wish to do so. It is possible to continue to an equally impressive viewpoint below the heavily eroded eastern face of Three-Fingered Jack. All you need to do is continue up this trail above the moraine, always opting for the most obvious trail. Less than a half-mile later and several hundred feet higher, you'll arrive at a small basin directly across the red and brown cliffs at approximately 6,500 feet of elevation, just 1,300 feet below the summit of the mountain. Views stretch south to the Three Sisters and north to Mount Jefferson but the star of this show is the magnificence of Three-Fingered Jack's striated cliffs. Mountain climbers are sighted frequently on the cliffs above, and hikers have occasionally encountered mountain goats in this area – a rare sight indeed!

When you need to turn around, return to the junction just above the upper meadow. From here, drop down into the meadow and drink up the view – it's just as good as the high basin above, but this time you have acres of flowers in the foreground. Do not camp in this fragile spot. You can return the way you came, but I recommend making a short and scenic loop. Follow social trails around the perimeter of the meadow until you arrive at Canyon Creek's slot canyon on the north end of the upper meadow. From here you will follow an obvious trail downhill, paralleling cascading Canyon Creek. The flower displays in this canyon, as they typically are beside alpine creeks, are outstanding. Just a bit later, you will arrive at trail's end at an unmarked and potentially obstructed junction with the main trail into the meadow – making it hard to hike this trail the opposite direction.

Continue hiking downhill until you return to the junction in the lower meadow. You could turn right to hike back to the trailhead here, but I recommend (as does the Forest Service) continuing downhill to make a nice loop. You'll hike downhill alongside Canyon Creek until you enter damage from the B+B fire. After an easy 1.3 miles from the previous junction, meet the Summit Lake Trail again at a sign for Wasco Lake and the PCT just above a falls on Canyon Creek. You could turn left to hike to lovely Wasco Lake but this area was devastated in the fire – unless you want to go swimming, you should turn right to return to the trailhead. The next 1.6 miles cuts through the burn, passing excellent patches of huckleberry until you arrive at the junction where you started your loop. Keep straight here and hike above a half-mile to the trailhead.

93. ROCKPILE LAKE AND SOUTH CINDER PEAK

	Rockpile Lake	South Cinder Peak
Distance:	11.4 miles out & back	15.4 miles out & back
Elevation Gain:	2,200 feet	2,900 feet
Trailhead Elevation:	4,163 feet	4,163 feet
Trail High Point:	6,262 feet	6,738 feet
Season:	June- October	July- October
Best:	June- October	July- October
Map:	Mount Jefferson Wilderness (Geo-Graphics)	See map on my website.

Directions from Salem / Albany:

- From Salem, drive east on OR 22 for 82 miles (or exactly 31.7 miles past the Breitenbush turnoff in Detroit) until OR 22 ends when it merges onto US 20.
- If coming from Albany, drive US 20 to Santiam Junction.
- Continue straight on US 20 for 5.4 miles to Santiam Pass.
- Drive US 20 past Santiam Pass for 8 miles to a turnoff for FR 12, opposite a sign that reads "Mt. Jefferson Wilderness Trailheads." It may be difficult to turn against traffic. The turnoff is less than a mile from the turnoff to Suttle Lake.
- Turn left on FR 12 and drive 1.1 miles to a fork in the road.
- Keep right for another 3.3 miles to a sign for Jack Lake.
- Turn left and drive 0.6 mile of narrow pavement to a bridge over Jack Creek.
- Keep straight 0.7 mile of pavement to a junction on the right signed for Cabot Lake TH.
- Keep straight, now on FR 1234, another 0.7 mile of washboarded gravel to a junction with FR 1235, Bear Valley Road, on your right.
- Turn right and drive 3.8 miles to road's end at a turnaround. This is the trailhead.

Directions from Sisters:

- Drive US 20 for 12 miles northwest to a turnoff on your right for FR 12, signed for "Mt. Jefferson Wilderness Trailheads".

- Turn left on FR 12 and drive 1.1 miles to a fork in the road.
- Keep right for another 3.3 miles to a sign for Jack Lake Campground.
- Turn left and drive 0.6 mile of narrow pavement to a bridge over Jack Creek.
- Keep straight 0.7 mile of pavement to a junction on the right signed for Cabot Lake TH.
- Keep straight, now on FR 1234, another 0.7 mile of washboarded gravel to a junction with FR 1235, Bear Valley Road, on your right.
- Turn right and drive 3.8 miles to road's end at a turnaround. This is the trailhead.

Hike: Rockpile Lake, a small lake set at the heart of the Cascade Crest, was miraculously spared from the B+B Fire in 2003. To get there, however, you'll spend most of your time traversing the green ridges in the heart of the burn. This is a solitary trail and a hot trail, and in spite of all of this, I loved this hike. It isn't for everyone, though; avoid it on a hot day, don't hike it alone, and be willing to turn around if the lack of maintenance spooks you. Energetic hikers can make it all the way to South Cinder Peak, one of the best viewpoints in this part of the Mount Jefferson Wilderness.

Begin at the Bear Valley Trailhead. There is a brand-new signboard, which somehow seems out of place. After just 100 yards or so, reach a junction with the abandoned Minto Lake Trail. The Minto Lake Trail was lost to the elements in the aftermath of the B+B Fire; while I didn't bother following it, it's said to be totally lost and completely impassable. Instead, fork to the right and begin paralleling Bear Valley Road for a stretch (this will be mildly irritating at the end of the hike). Pass a junction with the Metolius-Windigo Trail and keep left, and soon you'll begin a series of moderate switchbacks out of the valley. Enter a pocket of forest spared from the fire, where you should take a moment to enjoy the shade – before long you won't have any for a long distance. The trail then enters the green slopes of the burn zone, where ceonethus (also known as snowbrush) crowds the trail in some places. The views stretch out to the south to Three-Fingered Jack and the Three Sisters as the trail climbs gradually up the slopes of Bear Valley.

Enter the Wilderness at 2 miles from the trailhead. You may see on your map a trail here coming in from a nearby road; this trail too was lost in the fire. At last the trail curves left for good, ascending west through the burn zone towards the Cascade Crest. At about 3 miles from the trailhead, you will enter a small pocket of remnant forest that survived the fire. Although dry, this short section of the hike feels like an oasis compared to everything else around you. Before long you'll be back in the burn zone, where blowdown is an issue. When I hiked this trail, it was clear to me that maintenance stopped around 4 miles from the trailhead. The trail has since been cleared, but expect to deal with blowdown when you visit. After 0.7 mile, you will curve to the right and enter a dead forest of burned trees – it burned so hot here even snowbrush has yet to come back. At a little over 5 miles, you will abruptly enter deep forest, at long last out of the burn zone. Once out of the burn, the trail climbs through a verdant high-elevation forest to Rockpile Lake, where you meet the Pacific Crest Trail on the west side of the lake.

The trail reaches the lake at a litle under 6 miles. There are a few good campsites in the narrow basin that holds the lake, so if you are backpacking look around. One thing to keep in mind is that there is no water anywhere around here other than the lake. If all sites are occupied in the area, you'll need to hike a good distance further to find a spot with access to water. And truth be told, Rockpile Lake is perhaps not a suitable reward for such a long

The Pacific Crest Trail marches north towards South Cinder Peak and Mount Jefferson.

hike. There are few views, and while pretty, the lake pales in comparison to many others in the Mount Jefferson Wilderness. If you are on a dayhike and have some more energy, I strongly recommend continuing to South Cinder Peak's panoramic viewpoint.

From the PCT junction, turn right here and hike around the lake. The PCT leaves the forest and re-enters the burn zone shortly after, where views open north to Mount Jefferson. The red cinder cone to the left of Mount Jefferson is South Cinder Peak, your destination. Continue straight on the PCT, passing a junction with the abandoned Brush Creek Trail and climbing slightly to a high, cinder-strewn plain. Soon you will be parallel to South Cinder Peak, and the trail to the summit is obvious. While you could set off cross-country towards South Cinder Peak, you should continue another 0.3 mile or so to a 4-way junction with the Swallow Lake and Shirley Lake Trails. Once you reach this junction, turn left on the Swallow Lake Trail and hike 0.2 mile to a junction with the trail up South Cinder Peak, marked by a huge cairn. Turn right here and climb steeply up to the summit of South Cinder Peak, where the views are huge – north to Mount Jefferson, south to Three-Fingered Jack and the Three Sisters, and east and west to all points. Look for the USGS marker at the true summit, at trail's end. This is a fabulous spot, and one worthy of a long break. Of course, you have the long trek back to think about – so maybe it's best not to stay for too long.

You can return the way you came, but one way to liven up the trek back is to establish a car shuttle before you even begin your hike. It is very easy and wildly scenic to establish a shuttle to either the Canyon Creek Meadows (Hike 92) or Carl Lake (Hike 94) trailheads, making for a fantastic day of hiking and a much easier trip back. If those options are not available, return the way you came.

94. CARL LAKE AND SOUTH CINDER PEAK

	Carl Lake	South Cinder Peak
Distance:	10.4 miles out & back	14.6 miles out & back
Elevation Gain:	1,000 feet	2,500 feet
Trailhead Elevation:	4,548 feet	4,548 feet
Trail High Point:	5,545 feet	6,738 feet
Season:	July- October	July- October
Best:	July- October	July- October
Map:	Mount Jefferson Wilderness	(Geo-Graphics)

Directions from Salem / Albany:
- From Salem, drive east on OR 22 for 82 miles (or exactly 31.7 miles past the Breiten-bush turnoff in Detroit) until OR 22 ends when it merges onto US 20.
- If coming from Albany, drive US 20 to Santiam Junction.
- Continue straight on US 20 for 5.4 miles to Santiam Pass.
- Drive US 20 past Santiam Pass for 8 miles to a turnoff for FR 12, opposite a sign that reads "Mt. Jefferson Wilderness Trailheads." It may be difficult to turn against traffic. The turnoff is less than a mile from the turnoff to Suttle Lake.
- Turn left on FR 12 and drive 1.1 miles to a fork in the road.
- Keep right for another 3.3 miles to a sign for Jack Lake.
- Turn left and drive 0.6 mile of narrow pavement to a bridge over Jack Creek.
- Continue another 0.7 mile of pavement to another fork, this one for FR 1230. It should be marked for the Cabot Lake Trail.
- Turn right here and drive 6.8 miles of occasionally rocky gravel, ignoring all side roads, until you reach the Cabot Lake Trailhead at road's end.

Directions from Sisters:
- Drive US 20 for 12 miles northwest to a turnoff on your right for FR 12, signed for "Mt. Jefferson Wilderness Trailheads".
- Turn left on FR 12 and drive 1.1 miles to a fork in the road.
- Keep right for another 3.3 miles to a sign for Jack Lake Campground.
- Turn left and drive 0.6 mile of narrow pavement to a bridge over Jack Creek.
- Continue another 0.7 mile of pavement to another fork, this one for FR 1230. It should be marked for the Cabot Lake Trail.
- Turn right here and drive 6.8 miles of occasionally rocky gravel, ignoring all side roads, until you reach the Cabot Lake Trailhead at road's end.

Hike: This moderate hike to scenic Carl Lake is an ideal destination for a moderate back-pack, but is even nicer as part of a longer loop to the north that includes Table Lake and the Pacific Crest Trail (see Hike 95). Even if you don't have the time or the energy to hike to Table Lake, continuing your trek to South Cinder Peak's panoramic viewpoint offers a wildly scenic consolation prize.

Begin on a dusty trail through forest burned in the 2003 B+B Fire. The landscape is eerie,

The tip of Mount Jefferson peeks out over the slopes above deep blue Carl Lake.

with many snags and ghostly trees still standing after the fire – and yet everything seems green due to the incredible amount of snowbrush as far as the eye can see. The trail follows above the burned out canyon of Cabot Creek, offering views north to Sugar Pine Ridge, pointed Forked Butte and Mount Jefferson. The trail abruptly leaves the burn zone at 1.8 miles and soon arrives at an unsigned junction with the short spur trail to Cabot Lake. Fork to the right here and descend a short distance to the brushy lake, set in a viewless, forested bowl. There are few if any campsites here, so it is best to return to the main trail.

From the Cabot Lake junction, the trail begins a moderate ascent via a series of switchbacks for about a mile before leveling off a little over 3 miles from the trailhead. From here, the trail passes a series of ponds and begins climbing again, reaching deep Carl Lake a little over 5 miles from the trailhead. There are a number of good campsites around the lake. Although Mount Jefferson is mostly out of site, hidden behind the ridge to the north, the walk around the lake is wildly scenic. You can follow the sandy beaches along the lake to the north side, where you are forced to hike up onto the rocky bluffs above the lake. If you look down, scratches on the rocks bear evidence of the glacier that scoured out this basin.

If you have the time and energy, you should absolutely consider continuing your hike up to the summit of South Cinder Peak, a trek also featured in Hikes 80 and 93. Set at the very center of the Mount Jefferson Wilderness, South Cinder Peak has an accordingly panoramic view that is worth the long journey. To find the peak, look for a junction at Carl Lake with the Shirley Lake Trail. Turn left here and hike 1.5 miles of moderate uphill to a four-way junction with the Pacific Crest Trail. On the opposite side of this junction, the Shirley Lake Trail becomes the Swallow Lake Trail and continues downhill into the western slopes of the Mount Jefferson Wilderness towards Swallow and Marion Lakes (see Hike 80 for more information). Just a few hundred yards down the Swallow Lake Trail from the PCT, look for the obvious spur trail up South Cinder Peak on your right. Turn right and follow this steep, dusty trail to the summit where the view should exceed even your wildest expectations.

Return the way you came unless you've established a car shuttle with Hike 93 (Rockpile Lake). For more information about the trails north of Carl Lake, see Hikes 80 (Heart of the Jeff Loop) and 95 (Table Lake Loop).

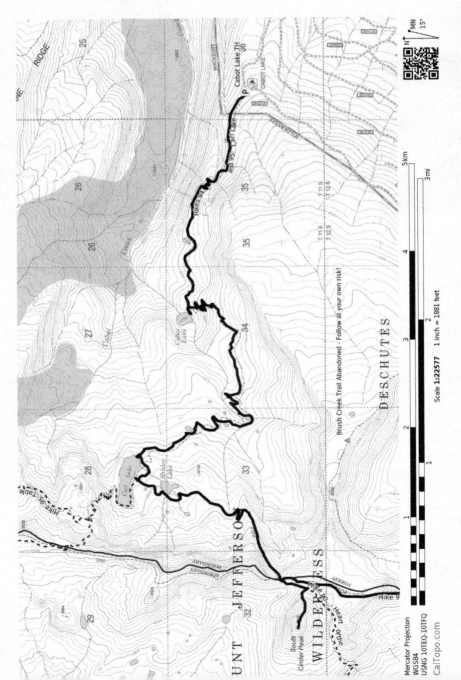

95.   TABLE LAKE LOOP

Distance: 23.8 mile loop
Elevation Gain: 3,900 feet
Trailhead elevation: 4,548 feet
Trail high point: 6,445 feet
Season: July- October
Best: July- October
Map: Mount Jefferson Wilderness (Geo-Graphics)

Directions:
• See directions for Carl Lake (Hike 94).

Hike: This loop encompassing Carl Lake, Table Lake and the Pacific Crest Trail is among the supreme adventures in the Oregon Cascades (don't tell anybody!), providing everything a person could want: gorgeous alpine lakes, outstanding views and ample solitude. The only catch, aside from the length of the trip, is that this area is extremely fragile. Please leave the lightest footprint you can – don't create trails, don't make campfires and don't camp anywhere other than in established sites. This is a special place – please try to keep it that way.

Begin by hiking in a little over 5 miles to Carl Lake (Hike 94). From here, follow the Cabot Lake Trail around the lake, passing a junction with the Shirley Lake Trail. Keep straight around the lake until the trail begins climbing out of Carl Lake's narrow, rocky basin. On a hot day this stretch is punishing, so make sure you take your time (or do it fast to get it out of the way) and rest when needed. Once you top out, the trail arrives at an unmarked trail junction near a pond; this is the start of your loop. Navigation can be a challenge whichever way you go, but for the most direct way to Table Lake, keep straight here. After about a mile, arrive at a junction with the abandoned Sugar Pine Ridge Trail at Junction Lake. Keep straight here. You will soon emerge at the foot of a lava flow, the western edge of the Forked Butte Lava Flow. Indeed, that is Forked Butte ahead of you on the right. This lava flow is believed to be the most geologically recent in this part of the Cascades and has been dated to approximately 4500 BC. The trail curls around the lava, at which point Mount Jefferson appears on the horizon ahead of you to remind you why you came here to begin with. The next mile of trail is among the most spectacular in the state. You will hike directly towards the great volcano as the trail splits the gap between the rugged east face of North Cinder Peak on your left and the colorful twin summits of Forked Butte. A person could spend hours exploring and taking pictures – but there's still more to come.

After this most beautiful pass, the Cabot Lake Trail switchbacks into the basin holding small Patsy Lake, promptly losing 800 feet. This is another good excuse to hike this loop in a counterclockwise direction! At Patsy Lake, meet the Jefferson Lake Trail (Hike 96). There is one excellent campsite here, but the lake is set at the bottom of a narrow basin that sees little sunlight and has no views. The best is yet to come – but you have to work for it! From Patsy Lake, the Cabot Lake Trail proceeds to regain 350 feet in short order on its way out of Patsy Lake's narrow basin. Once the trail levels out, you are at long last nearing Table Lake. Pass a faint trail at a cairn on your left (this trail cuts between an unnamed cinder cone and The Table and is the start of your loop out of Table Lake's basin) and continue 0.2 mile to

Mount Jefferson towers over Hole-in-the-Wall Park, as seen from the slopes of Bear Butte.

Table Lake itself. The trail drops to lake level, passes a spring that gushes directly out of the ground and arrives at the far end of the lake at almost exactly 10 miles from the Cabot Lake Trailhead. There are excellent campsites on the western end of the lake, near the creek that connects Upper Table Lake with Table Lake. There are a few sites on the south side of the lake as well that should provide you with the solitude you seek. Most people who come here backpack – so expect to see at least a few others all the way up here.

Table Lake is an excellent base camp for those looking to explore some of the wonders in this corner of the Mount Jefferson Wilderness. My favorite spot in the area near Table Lake is a viewpoint near the summit of Bear Butte. From Table Lake, continue on the Cabot Lake Trail. There is a confusion of trails here, but continue heading northeast and eventually you will find the real trail. The Cabot Lake Trail crosses a few side creeks and traverse below a rockslide in deep forest until it almost suddenly lurches due north. At this point, enter damage from the B+B fire and climb uphill until the trail levels out at a pass, which you reach at 1.5 miles from Table Lake. A sign on a tree reads "Viewpoint" – turn right here and scramble up to a most incredible viewpoint: Mount Jefferson towering over a deep defile known as Hole-in-the-Wall Park. Few places in the Majestic Mount Jefferson Region can compare. The Cabot Lake Trail does indeed continue down into Hole-in-the-Wall Park but the trail has fallen into such a state of disrepair that it's not worth even attempting. Hole-in-the-Wall Park itself is a boggy marsh without a view of Mount Jefferson- so again, it's not worth it.

There are of course other great adventures to be had in this area, but I will leave it to you to figure out where you want to go and what you want to see – part of the wonderful thing about this corner of the Mount Jefferson Wilderness is that almost anything you do is going to be spectacular.

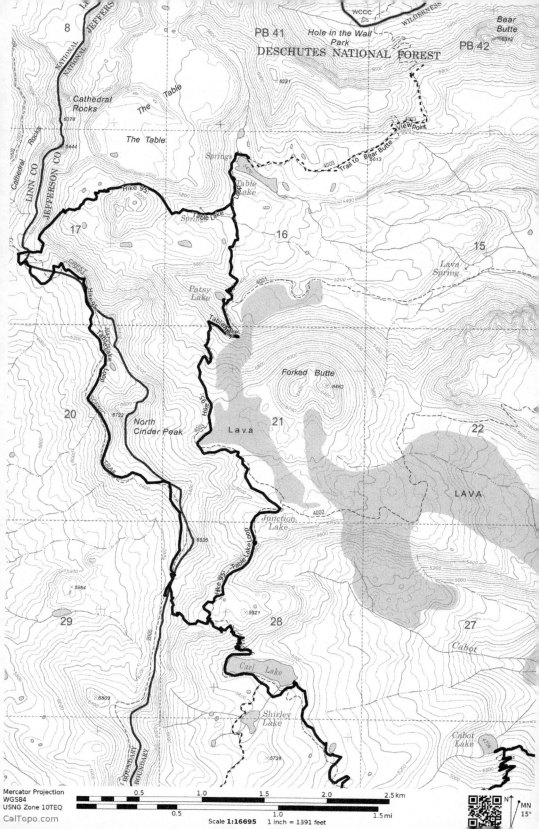

On your way back, it would be oh so easy to just return the way you came (and for those who do not excel at finding faint trails, this is strongly recommended). If you are adept at navigation, I strongly recommend returning on a loop that combines two user trails with a phenomenal stretch of the Pacific Crest Trail. Return to the south end of Table Lake and hike the Cabot Lake Trail back 0.2 mile to an unmarked junction in a meadow (there is usually a cairn but there may not be when you visit). Turn right here and follow a faint trail as it cuts through a meadow heading first southwest and then due west. Within a few hundred yards from the Cabot Lake Trail, this unnamed user trail should be quite distinct. The trail cuts through the forest and wraps around the side of an unnamed cinder cone. If you haven't found the trail yet, the trail splits the narrow gap between the cinder cone and The Table – aim for this spot if you get lost. From here the trail traverses around a couple of ponds and passes several large patches of lupine as it meanders towards the Cathedral Rocks. At the western end of this hidden basin, the trail launches uphill at an extremely steep grade. The misery is short-lived though, and soon you'll be on the ridge above, only a few hundred yards from the Pacific Crest Trail. If you lose the trail up here, simply aiming due west and away from the cliffs will bring you to the PCT. At 1.7 miles from Table Lake, arrive finally at an unmarked junction with the PCT.

The going is now easy for a few miles. The PCT receives annual maintenance and the trail is basically level, giving weary hikers a break. The trail passes a series of fantastic clifftop viewpoints, allowing you to look back to Mount Jefferson and the Table. Keen eyes can spot the Cabot Lake Trail in the valley below in several places. At 2.68 miles from the unmarked junction and at an elevation of 6,223 feet, you should find another unmarked junction on your left. It is not easy to see – look for a cairn and some flagging tape. This trail is well-used but also well-disguised at times. Descend steeply to a campsite, and then pick up the trail ahead of you as it drops at an even steeper clip until you meet the Cabot Lake Trail near a pond just 0.27 mile from the PCT.

If you can't find this spur trail, you will have to continue another 1.6 miles to a junction with the Shirley Lake Trail on your left (see Hike 94); from here, this trail drops another 1.6 miles to Carl Lake, If you have more time and energy I absolutely recommend doing this – but many will opt for the short and steep connector trail given the opportunity.

Once you reach the Cabot Lake Trail, descend steeply to Carl Lake and then continue another 5 miles to the trailhead and your vehicle.

96.   JEFFERSON LAKE TRAIL AND TABLE LAKE

Distance: 4.2 miles out and back (21 miles out and back to Table Lake)
Elevation Gain: 400 feet (2,500 feet for Table Lake)
Trailhead elevation: 3,140 feet
Trail high point: 3,471 feet (5,595 feet for Table Lake)
Season: March- November (July- October for Table Lake)
Best: September -October (July- August for Table Lake)
Map: Mount Jefferson Wilderness (Geo-Graphics)

Directions from Salem / Albany:

- From Salem, drive east on OR 22 for 82 miles (or exactly 31.7 miles past the Breiten-bush turnoff in Detroit) until OR 22 ends when it merges onto US 20.
- If coming from Albany, drive US 20 to Santiam Junction.
- Continue straight on US 20 for 5.4 miles to Santiam Pass.
- Continue on US 20 approximately 11 miles to a junction with FR 14, signed for the Metolius River. Turn left here.
- Drive north on FR 14 for 2.6 miles to a split in the road. While left takes you to the town of Camp Sherman, you keep right here, following the pointer for area campgrounds.
- From this point, drive north on FR 14 another 10.5 miles to Lower Bridge Campground, located on the east bank of the Metolius River where FR 14 crosses the river.
- Continue across the bridge, and the road very quickly becomes gravel.
- Keep right at a four-way junction on what is now FR 12.
- Turn right on FR 1290, now following signs for the Jefferson Lake Trailhead.
- Turn left on FR 1292 for 3 miles to the Jefferson Lake Trailhead at road's end.

Directions from Sisters:

- Drive US 20 for 9 miles northwest to a turnoff on your right for FR 14, signed for Camp Sherman and the Metolius River.
- Drive north on FR 14 for 2.6 miles to a split in the road. While left takes you to the town of Camp Sherman, you keep right here, following the pointer for area campgrounds.
- From this point, drive north on FR 14 another 10.5 miles to Lower Bridge Campground, located on the east bank of the Metolius River where FR 14 crosses the river.
- Continue across the bridge, and the road very quickly becomes gravel.
- Keep right at a four-way junction on what is now FR 12.
- Turn right on FR 1290, now following signs for the Jefferson Lake Trailhead.
- Turn left on FR 1292 for 3 miles to the Jefferson Lake Trailhead at road's end.

Direction notes:

- **Note 1:** You can also drive to this trailhead from FR 12. From the junction with FR 1230 near Jack Creek's car campground (see Hike 90), FR 12 becomes gravel and continues approximately 7.5 miles north to the 4-way junction described above. While this gravel road is in excellent shape and is easy to drive, most will prefer the paved approach.
- **Note 2:** Do not trust online map programs to get you to the trailhead. These maps do not accurately depict the road network in this part of the Deschutes National Forest and thus will give you directions that may be woefully misleading.

Hike: This is a requiem for a wonderful trail, and a hope that it may one day exist again. Before the B+B Fire in 2003, a fantastic loop from Jefferson Creek to Table Lake, and back over Sugar Pine Ridge existed, and was loved by many backpackers and equestrians. The fire burned hot here, and in the aftermath an incredible amount of snowbrush overtook this valley. As a result both the Jefferson Lake and Sugar Pine Ridge Trails were abandoned, so incredible was the damage. Over the past ten years a short segment of the Jefferson Lake Trail has been recovered, and this segment is described below. The Sugar Pine Ridge Trail is likely lost forever.

Begin at the Jefferson Lake Trailhead. The trail immediately descends to a bridged crossing

The Jefferson Lake Trail cuts a path through the Forked Butte lava flow.

of Candle Creek, and then climbs a short ways to a pair of enormous trees. The tree on the left side of the trail is believed to be the largest Rocky Mountain Douglas fir in the country. Take a moment to appreciate how this titan and its only slightly smaller sibling across the trail miraculous escaped the inferno of the B+B fire. As you will see, not all is lost here! The trail parallels Candle Creek through the woods for the next 0.4 mile to a junction with the abandoned Sugar Pine Ridge Trail at 0.5 mile. This lower stretch of trail has spectacular displays of fall color in October. Ignore the junction with the Sugar Pine Ridge Trail and continue straight on the Jefferson Lake Trail. Soon you will emerge from the forest on a jumbled lava flow with excellent views out to Mount Jefferson, just 9 miles to the northwest. The lava is the eastern edge of the Forked Butte lava flow, which dates to 4,500 BC; in geologic time, the lava is quite fresh. Other than a few scattered ponderosa pines and summer wildflowers, nothing grows here. Hikers with children should turn around at the lava flow, as the first mile of the trail is a satisfying adventure in its own right.

The troubles begin once the trail leaves the lava flow. You will skirt the flow for another 0.5 mile or so before the trail begins to slowly enter the snowbrush of the valley. By the 2 mile mark, the trail is quite brushy. At 2.1 miles from the trailhead, pass small Cougar Spring, which flows right across the trail. You should turn around here. Beyond Cougar Spring, maintenance tapers to nothing, and by 2.5 miles the trail is lost in an impenetrable thicket of snowbrush that grows as high as eight feet tall. I cannot be clearer about this: **DO NOT ATTEMPT TO HIKE THE TRAIL BEYOND COUGAR SPRING UNTIL THE TRAIL IS CLEARED, WHENEVER THAT MAY BE. IT IS IMPASSABLE AND YOU WILL GET LOST.**

The trail continued another 4 miles to a junction with the now-abandoned spur trail to Jefferson Lake. Despite its name, there is no view of Mount Jefferson. Beyond the Jefferson

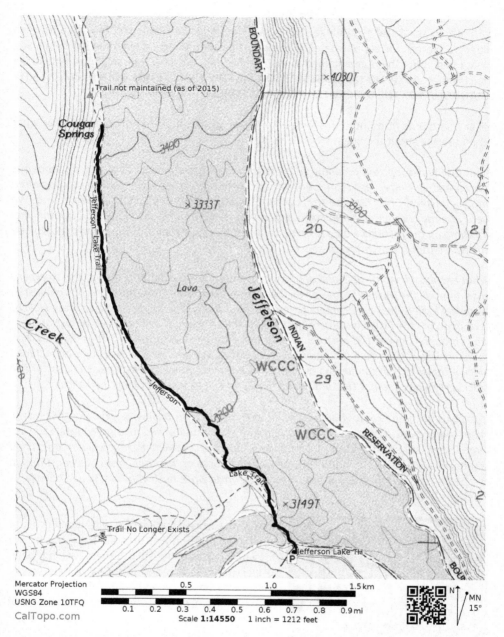

Scale **1:14550**   1 inch = 1212 feet

Lake Spur, the trail continued another 2.5 miles to Patsy Lake, where it met the Cabot Lake Trail 1 mile south of Table Lake (see Hike 95). It will take a herculean effort to reopen the Jefferson Lake Trail, but many who love this area believe the trail can be saved with a lot of work. The Sugar Pine Ridge Trail is beyond saving.

Before the B+B fire, it was possible to make a loop using the Jefferson Lake Trail and the Sugar Pine Ridge Trails. From the junction at Patsy Lake, hikers and equestrians would turn left on the Cabot Lake Trail and hike south 1.9 miles to Junction Lake, where they would turn left on the Sugar Pine Ridge. The Sugar Pine Ridge Trail followed the ridge through older burn areas for approximately 7 miles to a reunion with the Jefferson Lake Trail. See what I said about the unmaintained stretch of the Jefferson Lake Trail: the Sugar Pine Ridge Trail is much worse. **DO NOT ATTEMPT TO HIKE THIS TRAIL. IT HAS BEEN PERMANENTLY ABANDONED BY THE DESCHUTES NATIONAL FOREST. IT IS IMPASSABLE.**

Hiker friend Brad attempted this loop a few years ago. He lived to tell his tale. This is what he had to say about the Sugar Pine Ridge Trail :

"The trail was supposed to follow Sugar Pine Ridge 5 more mile through mostly shadeless burn areas, but after less than a quarter of a mile after the saddle, the trail disappeared into the bushes. Chris had the trail on his GPS, but we still couldn't find it anywhere. We were already committed to going that direction, since turning around to go back the way we came on the first day would take much longer. Or so we thought. The bushes couldn't be any worse that the first day. Or so we thought.

What ensued was the worst kind of bushwhacking I have ever had the misfortune to experience. It made the Bushes From Hell on day 1 seem like a walk in the park. It's like the Bushes From Hell called their big brothers to join them, and their friends, the Hedges From Hell. At certain points the brush was literally impenetrable, forcing us to backtrack to find another way through. I made the mistake of tempting fate by stating to Chris that our situation could be worse. Guess what happened. It got worse. We got into an area that also included blackberry vines that tangled up our feet and legs even more. At least they were the native blackberry vines and not the Himalayan blackberry vines you see along the roadside.

It took us 10 hours to go 4 miles. I don't ever want to go bushwhacking like that again. What started out as an adventure turned into (insert many negative adjectives and cuss words here). When I got home, after taking a shower, I assessed my physical damage. I had scratches all over my arms and legs, as well as bruises on my shins from pushing through the brush. It could have been worse. A sprained ankle while bushwhacking would have been a serious problem."

Brad is a seasoned backpacker with many years of experience both on and off trail. He made it, and not without a lot of hardship. Others have not been so lucky, and Search and Rescue has been called to this area several times as a result of people not heeding warnings about this trail. Don't be one of these people. It just isn't worth it. One day the Deschutes National Forest may reopen the Jefferson Lake Trail. Until then, be content that we still have a couple miles of this beautiful trail open for hiking. If you want to know more about the status of this trail, see my website for updates.

Photo on left: Sign on Sugar Pine Ridge Trail.

97.   BLACK BUTTE

Distance: 4.0 miles out and back
Elevation Gain: 1,600 feet
Trailhead elevation: 4,887 feet
Trail high point: 6,440 feet
Season: June- October
Best: June- October (avoid hot days)
Map: Green Trails #590 (Sisters)

Directions from Salem / Albany:
* From Salem, drive east on OR 22 for 82 miles (or exactly 31.7 miles past the Breiten-bush turnoff in Detroit) until OR 22 ends when it merges onto US 20.
* If coming from Albany, drive US 20 to Santiam Junction.
* Continue straight on US 20 for 5.4 miles to Santiam Pass.
* From Santiam Pass, drive east on US 20 for 14.6 miles to a turnoff on the left for FR 11, also known as Green Ridge Road.
* Drive this paved road for 3.8 miles to a junction with FR 1110, signed for the Black Butte Trailhead.
* Turn left here and drive 4 miles of washboarded and dusty gravel to a junction with FR 700. Fork to the right to stay on FR 1110.
* From here, the road becomes rocky and rough. Drive slowly for 1.1 miles on FR 1110 to the trailhead.

Directions from Sisters:
* Drive US 20 for 8 miles northwest to a turnoff on your right for FR 11, also known as Green Ridge Road.
* Drive this paved road for 3.8 miles to a junction with FR 1110, signed for the Black Butte Trailhead.
* Turn left here and drive 4 miles of washboarded and dusty gravel to a junction with FR 700. Fork to the right to stay on FR 1110.
* From here, the road becomes rocky and rough. Drive slowly for 1.1 miles on FR 1110 to the trailhead. .

Hike: Everywhere you go south of Mount Jefferson, Black Butte's conical silhouette is some-where on the horizon. Set apart and east from the Cascade crest, the view to the top is as magnificent as you would expect; you can see from Mount Adams to Diamond Peak, east to Smith Rock and everything in between. Even better, the view north and south is almost like looking at a road map of the area, something that will appeal to map junkies (like me).

Begin at the upper Black Butte Trailhead and climb at a moderate pace through a forest of old-growth Ponderosa pine. After about a mile, the trail leaves the forest and enters what appears to be an older burn zone, now fully grown in with snowbrush, a plant that is completely ubiquitous in this part of the Cascades. The view opens south here to the Three Sisters, Mount Washington and Three-Fingered Jack. Amazing as it would seem, the views keep getting better as the trail winds around the butte. Looming above you is the lookout tower on the summit, but it will take you some time to get there. The trail winds around the wide mountain and steepens as it rounds the north side of the mountain. Here, the

Above and below: The old cupola building on Black Butte, where the views are fantastic.

views open up to Mount Jefferson, looming over the Metolius River valley to the north. Further in the distance to the north are Mount Hood and Mount Adams, more than 100 miles away. The trail reaches the broad summit at 2 miles, where you meet a trail to the lookout tower on your left. Stay on the trail and leave the lookout tower, which is staffed in the summer, alone. The views up here are magnificent, as you would expect. Follow the trail across the summit to the 1923 cupola building on the west end of the summit. You can then turn and follow user trails to make a short loop across the summit before you start your trek back down. Return the way you came.

It is possible to hike to the summit of Black Butte from its base, not too far from the Head of the Metolius (see page 298 for more information on this cool spot). Doing so requires much more energy of course, as you begin from a much lower elevation. In addition, these trails are not maintained as frequently and occasionally suffer from blowdown. On the other hand, these trails allow hikers to snowshoe to Black Butte's summit in winter, a noble expedition with a huge reward. I did not hike this lower trail and have no directions to offer you - if you want to hike up from this direction, consult the Deschutes Ranger Station for directions.

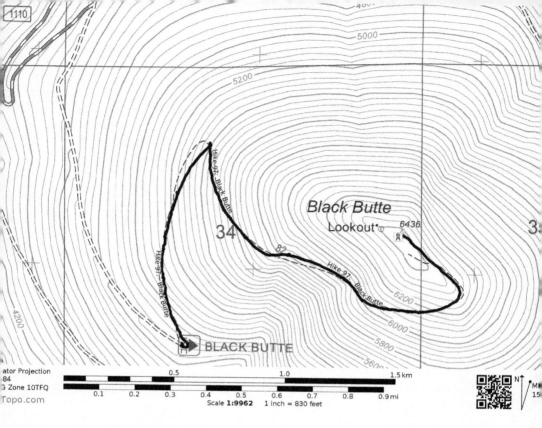

98. GREEN RIDGE

Distance: 10.8 miles out and back
Elevation Gain: 1,200 feet
Trailhead elevation: 3,716 feet
Trail high point: 4,877 feet
Season: May- November
Best: April- May, September- October
Map: See my website for a high-resolution map of this hike.

Directions from Salem / Albany:

- From Salem, drive east on OR 22 for 82 miles (or exactly 31.7 miles past the Breitenbush turnoff in Detroit) until OR 22 ends when it merges onto US 20.
- If coming from Albany, drive US 20 to Santiam Junction.
- Continue straight on US 20 for 5.4 miles to Santiam Pass.
- From Santiam Pass, drive east on US 20 for 14.6 miles to a turnoff on the left for FR 11, also known as Green Ridge Road.
- Turn left here and drive 4.3 miles of paved road to a poorly marked junction with FR 1120 at a curve.
- Turn left and drive 0.9 mile on this red cinder road to the trailhead, at a post marked by orange tape. There is room for a few cars at a campsite across the road.
- The trail departs north from the post.

Directions from Sisters:

- Drive US 20 for 8 miles northwest to a turnoff on your right for FR 11, also known as Green Ridge Road.
- Turn left here and drive 4.3 miles of paved road to a poorly marked junction with FR 1120 at a curve.
- Turn left and drive 0.9 mile on this red cinder road to the trailhead, at a post marked by orange tape. There is room for a few cars at a campsite across the road.
- The trail departs north from the post.
- Incidentally, if you continue downhill on FR 1120 beyond the Green Ridge another 5 miles or so, you will end up at FR 14- the road that follows the Metolius River. The junction is about 1 mile north of the road the cuts off into Camp Sherman. If you are camped or staying in the Metolius area, you can use this cutoff to reach Green Ridge easily.

Hike: Green Ridge is the most eastern ridge of the Cascades in Central Oregon, marking the transition from the high country to dry desert of the high plains. It just feels different here- the ponderosa pine trees and far-ranging views are more like what you would expect further east. The moderate hike over the slopes of Green Ridge is ideal for hikers wanting an earlier-season trip to the mountains. Keep in mind also that this is a multi-use trail, and is heavily used by equestrians and mountain bikers- you should yield to both as you hike this trail.

The trail begins by heading uphill to the north through an open forest consisting primarily of ponderosa pines, with a few incense cedars and Douglas firs mixed in. The understory is primarily snowbrush, but it does not intrude on the trail unlike so many hikes in this area. You will curve around the end of the ridge and continue uphill amongst ancient ponderosas. When you reach the top of the ridge, you will also reach your first good view: here, the trail passes an opening in the trees that looks down to the long valley of the Metolius River and out to Three-Fingered Jack and Mount Jefferson. Less able hikers and hikers with children should turn around here, as the trail ducks into the forest for the next few miles.

Over the next few miles, you will stay in the forest as the trail follows the western end of the long ridge. Along the way you will pass a few roads; keep an eye out for yellow diamonds on the trees to help you on the way. The trail is not always well-defined but as it follows old roads, is very easy to follow. At a little over 4 miles, you will reach the end of trail at a junction with a road. Stay left here to walk the road, which is your route for the next mile-plus of the hike. At a little over 5 miles from the trailhead, as the road curves downhill to your right, look for a faint trail leading to a knoll on your left. Leave the road here and follow faint trail up to a campsite at the knoll. Head left here, towards a rockpile about twenty yards to your left, where you finally get the view you've wanted: here Mount Jefferson towers over the Metolius valley, with Mount Hood peeking out on the right over the peaks of the Warm Springs Reservation. Bring a picnic and soak up the view- you've earned it!

The Green Ridge Trail does continue north but becomes faint and brushy for a spell, then follows logging roads north approximately 4 miles to the Green Ridge lookout tower. The view at the tower is great- but of course, you can drive there, and you can rent the tower (see Appendix 4). Return the way you came, unless you feel like setting up a shuttle.

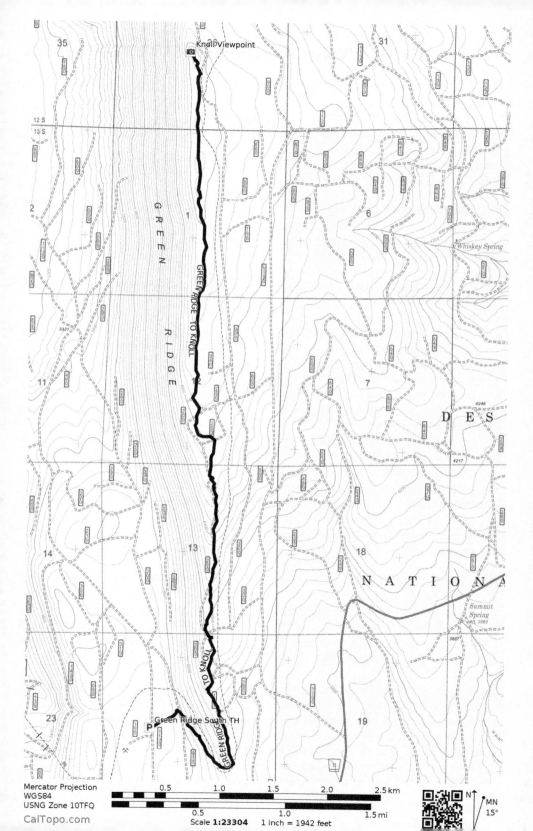

KnollViewpoint

GREEN RIDGE TO KNOLL

G R E E N   R I D G E

Whiskey Spring

D E S

N A T I O N A

Summit
Spring

Green Ridge South TH

GREEN RIDGE

TO KNOLL

35
31
12 S
13 S
2
1
6
11
7
14
13
18
23
19

Mercator Projection
WGS84
USNG Zone 10TFQ
CalTopo.com

0.5   1.0   1.5   2.0   2.5 km

0.5   1.0   1.5 mi
Scale 1:23304   1 inch = 1942 feet

N↑ MN
15°

99. METOLIUS RIVER: CANYON CREEK TO WIZARD FALLS

Distance: 5.2 miles out and back
Elevation Gain: 200 feet
Trailhead elevation: 2,870 feet
Trail high point: 2,887 feet
Season: all year
Best: May- June, October
Map: Green Trails #558 (Whitewater River)

Directions from Salem / Albany:
- From Salem, drive east on OR 22 for 82 miles (or exactly 31.7 miles past the Breitenbush turnoff in Detroit) until OR 22 ends when it merges onto US 20.
- If coming from Albany, drive US 20 to Santiam Junction.
- Continue straight on US 20 for 5.4 miles to Santiam Pass.
- Continue on US 20 approximately 11 miles to a junction with FR 14, signed for the Metolius River. Turn left here.
- Drive north on FR 14 for 2.6 miles to a split in the road.
- Keep straight to drive to Camp Sherman.
- Drive north 2.2 miles to a junction, where FR 1419 turns right towards Camp Sherman.
- Keep straight and drive 3.3 miles on what is now FR 1420.
- At a junction with FR 1420-400, turn right.
- Drive 0.7 mile to the end of the road at Lower Canyon Creek Campground.

Directions from Sisters:
- Drive US 20 for 9 miles northwest to a turnoff on your right for FR 14, signed for Camp Sherman and the Metolius River.
- Drive north on FR 14 for 2.6 miles to a split in the road.
- Keep straight to drive to Camp Sherman.
- Drive north 2.2 miles to a junction, where FR 1419 turns right towards Camp Sherman.
- Keep straight and drive 3.3 miles on what is now FR 1420.
- At a junction with FR 1420-400, turn right.
- Drive 0.7 mile to the end of the road at Lower Canyon Creek Campground.

Hike: With flower-spangled islands, gushing springs and huge Ponderosa pines towering above, the Metolius River is pure magic. Equally magical is the ease of the hikes along the river, making this area a great destination for families and inexperienced hikers. For the best experience, try coming in June and July when the river's scenic islands overflow with a kaleidoscope of flowers, or in October when the vine maple along the river blazes orange and red.

Begin at Lower Canyon Creek Campground. The trail curves around a bend and soon arrives at a viewpoint across the river to a series of cascading springs that flow right into the river. From here, follow the river downstream as it roars through a narrow canyon. Unlike many trails, the West Metolius Trail stays near the banks of the river – this is highly unusual, but then again, because it is entirely spring-fed and has few tributaries, the river rarely floods. At about 1.5 miles, the trail climbs a bit to the bluffs above the river, where you will stay for the rest of the hike. Social trails lead down to exceptional vistas of the river! At about 2

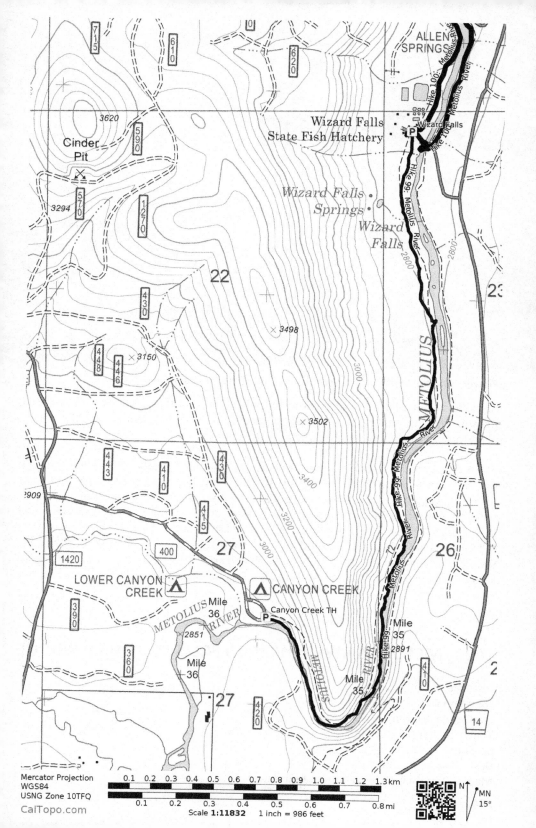

Flowers line the banks of the Metolius River in spring and summer.

miles from the trailhead, pass a series of islands in the river that overflow with flowers in the summer. The contrast of the masses of blue lupine, luscious greenery and the electric blue river provide for outstanding photo opportunities.

At 2.5 miles, reach Wizard Falls Fish Hatchery. Don't look for the falls- the water from the erstwhile creek has been diverted to the fish hatchery. There are picnic tables and tanks full of fish waiting to be fed. From here, you can either return the way you came, or continue on a beautiful 6.4 mile loop along both sides of the Metolius. This hike is described in Hike 100. A car shuttle is also possible; to establish a shuttle, drive back to the junction of FR 1420 and FR 1419 and turn left (east) on FR 1419. Drive 1 mile on this road, heading towards FR 14. When you reach FR 14, turn left and drive 4.1 miles to the turnoff for Wizard Falls Fish Hatchery. Turn left and drive into the Fish Hatchery parking lot.

100. METOLIUS RIVER: WIZARD FALLS TO LOWER BRIDGE

Distance: 6.2 mile loop
Elevation Gain: 200 feet
Trailhead elevation: 2,772 feet
Trail high point: 2,772 feet
Season: all year
Best: May- June, October
Map: Green Trails #558 (Whitewater River)

Directions from Salem / Albany:

- From Salem, drive east on OR 22 for 82 miles (or exactly 31.7 miles past the Breitenbush turnoff in Detroit) until OR 22 ends when it merges onto US 20.
- If coming from Albany, drive US 20 to Santiam Junction.
- Continue straight on US 20 for 5.4 miles to Santiam Pass.
- Continue on US 20 approximately 11 miles to a junction with FR 14, signed for the Metolius River. Turn left here.
- Drive north on FR 14 for 2.6 miles to a split in the road. While left takes you to the town of Camp Sherman, you keep right here, following the pointer for area campgrounds.
- From this point, drive north another 7.7 miles to the signed turnoff for Wizard Falls Fish Hatchery.
- Turn left here and drive across the bridge into the Fish Hatchery, where you will find a small parking lot.

Directions from Sisters:

- Drive US 20 for 9 miles northwest to a turnoff on your right for FR 14, signed for Camp Sherman and the Metolius River.
- Drive north on FR 14 for 2.6 miles to a split in the road. While left takes you to the town of Camp Sherman, you keep right here, following the pointer for area campgrounds.
- From this point, drive north another 7.7 miles to the signed turnoff for Wizard Falls Fish Hatchery.
- Turn left here and drive across the bridge into the Fish Hatchery, where you will find a small parking lot.

Hike: This exceptionally easy hike can be combined with Hike 99 (Lower Canyon Creek to Wizard Falls) for a longer, 12 mile partial loop that will give you a full tour of the Metolius River Canyon. While this hike passes through several campgrounds and is in general not as wild as the upper stretch of river described in the previous hike, this section of the canyon does have its charms.

Though you can also begin the hike at Lower Bridge, I recommend beginning your hike at the Wizard Falls Fish Hatchery where there is considerably more parking. Behind the bathrooms at the fish hatchery, look for a sign that says "River Trail". Once you locate the trail, follow it upstream along a wide stretch of the Metolius. Soon the river curves gracefully around a bend on the opposite side of the river from Allen Springs Campground. This is a magnificent view! Look up the slopes of Green Ridge opposite the trail for signs of the Bridge 99 fire, which burned the slopes of the east canyon wall in the summer of 2014.

The trail cuts back into the forest to avoid some private riverfront property but soon re-emerges on the banks of the river where it threads through several grassy islands. At 3.2 miles, reach the aforementioned Bridge 99, the last bridge over the river before it enters its secluded inner canyon. Cross the river and pass Lower Bridge Campground, where you may use the restroom and fill up on water if necessary. To continue your hike, turn right at a sign for the East Metolius River Trail and begin hiking back upstream.

After a short half-mile, reach Pioneer Ford Campground. Follow the trail onto the campground loop, and continue until you find the continuation of the trail just after site 19 in the campground. Continue downstream, passing by several groves of Ponderosa pine and

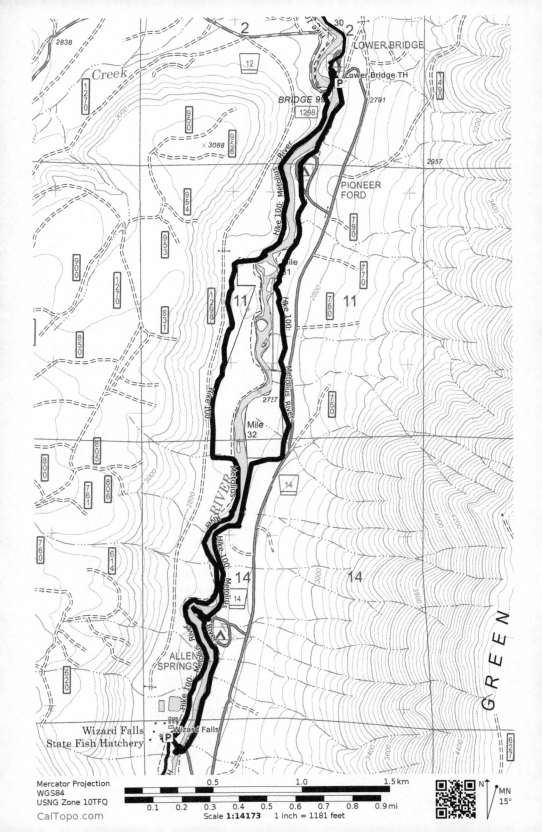

Scale **1:14173**   1 inch = 1181 feet

The graceful curve of the Metolius River near Lower Bridge.

a few parcels of private property (look for signs to stay on the trail in a few places) until you reach Allen Springs Campground at about 5.8 miles. Here the trail seems to end at the pit toilet and picnic table in the campground's day use area; look for a continuation of the trail by following the river past several campsites until the trail becomes obvious. Keep straight from here along the river until you reach the bridge at Wizard Falls, where you must cross the bridge to return to the trailhead and your car.

EXTENDING YOUR TRIP:

The West Metolius River Trail continues along the west bank of the Metolius River another 1.5 miles beyond Bridge 99 to Candle Creek's isolated car campground. If you've got time and energy, this makes for a wonderful addition to your hike. While the Metolius River is always scenic, this stretch of trail is especially scenic as the trail follows the river along several long, graceful curves.

To find the trail, start from the left (west) end of Bridge 99, on the opposite side of the river from Lower Bridge Campground. Follow FR 14 for a few yards until you see the obvious trail dropping back towards the river. The trail stays close to the river for the most part, usually staying about twenty feet above river level. On occasion you drop into a dark forest, but soon you are back near the river. As you near Candle Creek Campground, you will cross Abbot Creek on a wooden bridge and then reach the flats at the campground. Here you can walk through the campground, which is isolated from the other Metolius campgrounds due to its location and approach, to the far end where you find Candle Creek. On the other side of the creek is the Warm Springs Reservation, entrance to which is absolutely forbidden. Return the way you came to Lower Bridge, and then continue your loop from there.

101. METOLIUS RIVER: LOWER BRIDGE INTO THE HORN

	Metolius Camp:	**To Shut-In Trail:**
Distance:	11.2 miles out & back	20.2 miles out & back
Elevation Gain:	300 feet	500 feet
TH Elevation:	2,728 feet	2,728 feet
High Point:	2,728 feet	2,728 feet
Season:	all year	all year
Best:	April- June, October	April- June, October
Map:	Green Trails #558	Green Trails #558

Directions from Salem / Albany:
- From Salem, drive east on OR 22 for 82 miles (or exactly 31.7 miles past the Breitenbush turnoff in Detroit) until OR 22 ends when it merges onto US 20.
- If coming from Albany, drive US 20 to Santiam Junction.
- Continue straight on US 20 for 5.4 miles to Santiam Pass.
- Continue on US 20 approximately 11 miles to a junction with FR 14, signed for the Metolius River. Turn left here.
- Drive north on FR 14 for 2.6 miles to a split in the road. While left takes you to the town of Camp Sherman, you keep right here, following the pointer for area campgrounds.
- From this point, drive north on FR 14 another 10.5 miles to Lower Bridge Campground, located on the east bank of the Metolius River where FR 14 crosses the river.
- Park on the opposite side of the campground access at a small parking area, next to a signboard on the east bank of the river.
- The trail departs from the far end of the campground.

Directions from Sisters:
- Drive US 20 for 9 miles northwest to a turnoff on your right for FR 14, signed for Camp Sherman and the Metolius River.
- Drive north on FR 14 for 2.6 miles to a split in the road. While left takes you to the town of Camp Sherman, you keep right here, following the pointer for area campgrounds.
- From this point, drive north on FR 14 another 10.5 miles to Lower Bridge Campground, located on the east bank of the Metolius River where FR 14 crosses the river.
- Park on the opposite side of the campground access at a small parking area, next to a signboard on the east bank of the river.
- The trail departs from the far end of the campground.

Hike: With its incense cedars, ponderosa pines and yes, rattlesnakes, it may seem like the lower canyon of the Metolius River is a world removed from Mount Jefferson. You might be surprised to discover that this remote canyon is in fact less than ten miles from the great volcano. This canyon, tucked into the mountain's rain shadow, is the true eastern edge of Mount Jefferson country; this is where the Cascades unfurl to the east into central Oregon's high desert. It is a trek that is short on difficulty and long on rewards. Best of all, it is open almost year-round, offering backpackers (at least those with a high tolerance for cold nights) the chance to go deep into the backcountry at times when other locations are

The lower section of the Metolius River is peaceful and remote.

snowbound. More than anything it is a special place, one that soothes the soul even on the coldest and rainiest of days. The only thing about this place that isn't soothing is the presence of ticks throughout the year- this is the only place in the Majestic Mount Jefferson region where they are common, and you should check your clothes and skin from time to time to keep them out of your business.

Begin at Lower Bridge's car campground. While most of your trek will be on the Lower Metolius Road, now closed to vehicle traffic, you should start by hiking on an unofficial trail that parallels the east bank of the Metolius. Look for this trail departing from the far (northern) end of Lower Bridge Campground. A sign on an incense cedar reads: "Hiker Trail". You will follow the trail as it meanders along the river, passing a series of outstanding campsites. The trail seems to end at a debris flow at about 1.6 miles, opposite Candle Creek's campground on the other side of the river. Turn right here and ramble a bit away from the river where you will very quickly intersect the Lower Metolius River Road. Turn left here and continue downstream.

The Lower Metolius River Road parallels the river for nearly its entire length, spending much of the time in the woods out of sight of the river. At 3.1 miles, reach a fork in the road. Keep left and begin one of the best stretches of this trek, where the road passes directly above the river at times. At 5.5 miles, the road passes another series of excellent campsites next to the river. If you are dayhiking, you should turn around here- while the road downstream is beautiful, remember: it's all beautiful. The uniform beauty of this area is one of its charms. If you're backpacking, there are lots of great sites- if this spot is occupied to capacity, keep going downstream until you find one to your liking.

Scrambling up the slopes of the Metolius River canyon reveals great views and almost total solitude. Be careful, though; the slopes are crumbly and finding your way down can be more difficult than finding your way up. It's worth it, though.

Downstream of the campsites, the road enters a large flat beside the river. Believe it or not, you may encounter rattlesnakes here in warmer conditions, and ticks are a nuisance in the spring. Occasional views open up of crags on Green Ridge above. The trail passes directly under one of these crags at 6.5 miles and continues closely following the river to the edge of the Horn, located at about 8.7 miles from Lower Bridge. Here the river bends to the east and begins its end run towards Lake Billy Chinook. Soon after the Lower Metolius River Road passes through a small section of private property; here you are required to stay on the road. At a little under 10 miles, you'll pass another excellent campsite with river access; this is the last campsite before the temporary end of the road, and you should probably turn around here if you haven't already. Keen eyes can spot Gothic Rock, also known as Five-Fingered Sentinel, on the ridge above.

At 10.1 miles, the Lower Metolius River Road ends abruptly at the remote trailhead for the Shut-In Trail. This trail, which more closely resembles a brushy fisherman's path, follows the Metolius River 1.5 miles until the road reemerges. This stretch of trail receives little maintenance and you may need to duck under some deadfall and rock hop in a few places. The nice thing about the Shut-In Trail is that it follows the Metolius quite closely.

Once you are back on the road, you can continue approximately 6 miles further downstream to trail's end near Monty Campground, near Lake Billy Chinook. Most hikers won't want to hike this far without first establishing a car shuttle, a time-consuming endeavor that involves driving an endless series of gravel roads across Green Ridge. Unless you can pull this off, return the way you came from wherever you ended up stopping.

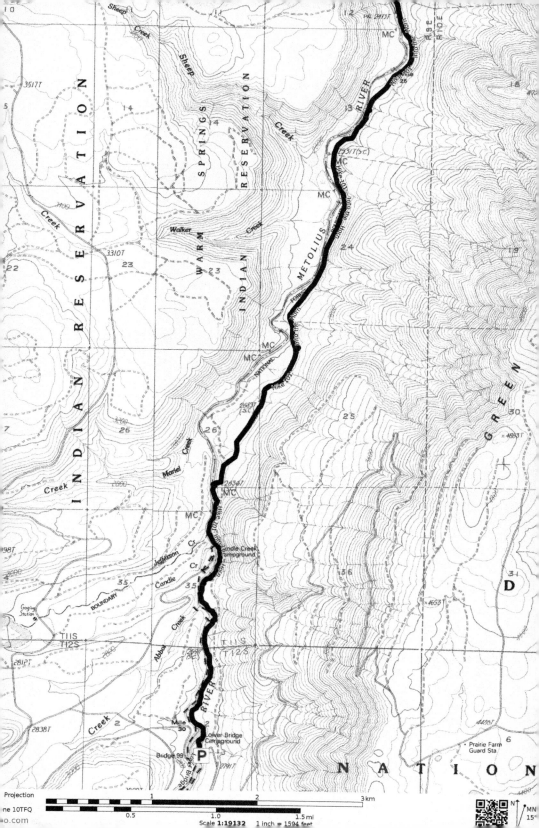

APPENDIX 1: TOP 5 LISTS

Unsure of where to go? Let these lists guide you to your destination!

Best hikes for old-growth forest:
- Hike 7: Bagby Hot Springs and Silver King Lake
- Hike 23: Opal Creek
- Hike 28: Battle Creek and Emerald Pool
- Hike 38: Middle Santiam River
- Hike 46: Echo Basin and Hackleman Grove

Best hikes for wildflowers:
- Hike 2: Rooster Rock
- Hikes 45 and 48: Browder Ridge
- Hikes 63, 70, 73 and 74: Jefferson Park
- Hike 72: Wild Cheat Meadow and Triangulation Peak
- Hike 92: Canyon Creek Meadows

Best hikes for lovers of rushing streams:
- Hike 11: Elk Lake Creek
- Hike 20: Little North Santiam River Trail
- Hike 50: Sahalie and Koosah Falls
- Hike 67: South Breitenbush River Trail
- Hikes 99, 100 and 101: Metolius River Trails

Best hikes for waterfall lovers:
- Hike 21: Henline Falls
- Hike 23: Opal Creek
- Hike 50: Sahalie and Koosah Falls
- Hike 60: Breitenbush Cascades
- Hike 79: Marion Lake

Best hikes for lakes:
- Hike 57: Double Peaks / Timber Lake Loop
- Hike 58: Ruddy Hill / Olallie Lake Loop
- Hike 80: Heart of the Jeff Loop
- Hike 83: Duffy Lake, Santiam Lake and the Eight Lakes Basin
- Hike 86: Grand Mount Jefferson Loop

Best hikes for panoramic views:
- Hike 27: Battle Ax
- Hike 54: Olallie Butte
- Hike 69: Bear Point
- Hike 80: Heart of the Jeff Loop
- Hike 97: Black Butte

Five hikes with lookout towers:
- Hike 3: Pechuck Lookout
- Hikes 8, 9 and 12: Bull of the Woods
- Hike 29: Gold Butte
- Hike 51: Sisi Butte
- Hike 97: Black Butte

Best hikes for solitude:
- Hike 4: Upper Molalla Divide
- Hike 13: Rho Creek and Big Bottom
- Hike 16: Sardine Mountain
- Hike 19: Elkhorn Ridge
- Hike 36: Scar Mountain and the Old Cascades Crest Loop

Best backpacking trips:
- Hike 12: Mother Lode Loop
- Hike 80: Heart of the Jeff Loop
- Hike 86: Grand Mount Jefferson Loop
- Hike 95: Table Lake Loop
- Hike 101: Lower Metolius River

Best fall color hikes:
- Hike 23: Opal Creek
- Hike 49: Clear Lake
- Hikes 51- 63: Every hike in the Olallie Lake Area
- Hike 79: Marion Lake
- Hikes 99, 100 and 101: Metolius River Trails

Best hikes in winter:
- Hike 7: Bagby Hot Springs and Silver King Lake (stop at the river crossing)
- Hike 16: Sardine Mountain
- Hike 20: Little North Santiam River
- Hike 23: Opal Creek
- Hike 49: Clear Lake (you may need snowshoes)

Best hikes for rainy days:
- Hike 7: Bagby Hot Springs and Silver King Lake
- Hike 20: Little North Santiam River
- Hike 23: Opal Creek
- Hike 42: House Rock Loop
- Hike 43: Gordon Meadows

Best hikes for children:
- Hike 21: Henline Falls
- Hike 23: Opal Creek
- Hike 42: House Rock Loop
- Hike 56: Olallie Lake Loop
- Hike 99: Metolius River: Canyon Creek to Wizard Falls

APPENDIX 2: PLACES YOU CAN DRIVE TO

Not every great place in this book requires a hike. There are many fantastic spots that require no effort beyond driving, and are thus open to anyone who can make the drive. Many of these spots are located on the way to trailheads, while a few are detours. Most are accessible by any vehicle, while a few require rugged vehicles with lots of clearance. Be sure to bring your camera and your sense of adventure!

TABLE ROCK AND BULL OF THE WOODS NORTH
* Molalla River Eye: On your way to hikes 1-4, you will pass a rock formation on the Molalla River known as the Molalla River Eye (or the Sundial). This is a popular swimming hole for area teenagers in the summer; expect to encounter teenagers and broken beer bottles. How do you find the Eye? Well, you'll know it when you see it. Look for a pulloff on the left side of the road, not long past where the Molalla Road crosses Shotgun Creek. While you are in the area, you may want to check out Shotgun Falls on Shotgun Creek. Look for a faint trail leading up Shotgun Creek to the two-tiered waterfall.

* The Bridge to Nowhere: Near the Elk Lake Creek Trailhead (Hikes 11 and 12), you'll find the so-called Bridge to Nowhere. The bridge was constructed as the opening salvo of a logging road that would lead up Elk Lake Creek's canyon. Designation of the Bull of the Woods Wilderness in 1984 stopped construction of the road at the crossing of the Collawash River just yards after the confluence with Elk Lake Creek. As a result, an embankment stops the bridge at its far end, giving the place a bit of a post-apocalyptic vibe. To find the Bridge to Nowhere, drive to the bridge over the Collawash 0.3 mile before the Elk Lake Creek Trailhead and instead keep straight on FR 6380. Continue a quarter-mile to a campsite at the end of the road, at the bridge.

OPAL CREEK AND BULL OF THE WOODS SOUTH
* Niagara County Park: If you are traveling east on OR 22, look for a sign marking this small county park. From the small parking lot, a trail drops down a set of metal stairs to a platform above the North Santiam River. Here the river churns through a narrow slot in a most photogenic manner (see photo on opposite page). There aren't too many good places to admire the North Santiam, and this is by far the best. Don't be a fool and wander out onto the rocks, though; people have fallen into the river here. Don't be one of those people.

* Elkhorn Lake: This lovely and peaceful lake is ideal for a quick visit if you happen to be up on Elkhorn Ridge. For more information see Hike 19.

* Three Pools: Now here is one of the most beautiful places in this book, and you can drive right to it. Of course, there's a catch. If you visit in the summer, this is where seemingly all of Salem and the central Willamette Valley meet to go swimming. Can you blame them? Here you'll find the Little North Santiam River squeezing through a series of rock formations, creating three deep, emerald-colored pools. Downstream of the pools, the river appears to be a tantalizing shade of electric green as the clear, deep waters reflect the greenish rocks of the riverbed. So unless you want to go swimming with scores of other people, save Three Pools for the winter- when the place is abandoned. Come in the winter with a tripod and a thermos of coffee for a satisfying couple of hours in this beautiful spot, all by your lonesome. To find Three Pools, drive as to Henline Falls, Henline Mountain and Opal Creek

(Hikes 21- 24), but at the junction of FR 2209 an FR2207, turn right on FR 2207 and drive 0.8 mile downhill to Three Pools. A Northwest Forest Pass is required.

* Sullivan Creek Falls: Further down FR 2207, across the Little North Santiam River and up Cedar Creek, is Sullivan Creek Falls. This graceful multi-tiered waterfall plunges 160 feet to a splash pool beside FR 2207. While the top half of the falls is difficult to see, the lower tiers are extremely photogenic, as the falls cuts through several steep, mossy slots. The falls is located 1.8 miles beyond Shady Cove Campground on FR 2207.

* Cedar Creek and French Creek Road (FR 2207): This is a drive that is as adventurous as most hikes. This 18 mile road, almost all of it gravel, connects the Opal Creek area with Detroit. It's a long drive even as far as forest roads go, and the road is frequently beset by washouts, rockfall, potholes and ruts. You can do the drive from either direction but the best way is to drive from the Opal Creek side, saving the most spectacular (and challenging) driving for the climax. At the junction of FR 2209 and FR 2207, turn right. The road drops downhill for 1.8 miles, passing Three Pools on the way, to Shady Cove's lovely car campground. Here you'll cross the Little North Santiam River and follow cascading Cedar Creek for about 3 miles. Take a few minutes to check out Sullivan Creek Falls at about 2 miles from Shady Cove. Once you cross Cedar Creek, the road climbs considerably via series of sharp switchbacks before leveling out on a narrow precipice over a thousand feed above Cedar Creek. For this reason the 2207 Road is not for the faint of heart. The next several miles are plagued with rockfall, and you may need to get out from time to time to push rocks out of the road. At a little over 8 miles from the Opal Creek junction you'll pass the trailhead for Opal Lake, and in another 2 miles you'll reach the French Creek Ridge at a pass. Continue downhill on a road that hugs a cliff another 3.6 miles to a junction with paved FR 2223. Turn right and drive 4 miles to a junction with OR 22 just west of Detroit.

* Elk Lake: The trailhead for hikes 27 and 28, this beautiful mountain lake is worth a visit in its own right even if you aren't hiking. Make sure to take a few minutes to check out the lake before or after any hike in the area. The best viewpoint is on the lake's eastern shore, where Elk Lake Creek flows out of the lake to start its journey towards the Collawash River. Opposite the bridge over Elk Lake Creek, look for a path heading towards the lake. Here you'll find an outstanding campsite (frequently occupied) and a small beach on the lake, with views west to Mount Beachie and Battle Ax, looming across the other end of the lake.

OLD CASCADES
* Blowout Arm: This suspension bridge passes over a forgotten arm of Detroit Lake, mostly hidden from the public. For more information, see Hike 31.

* Coffin Mountain Viewpoint: On the way to Coffin and Bachelor Mountains, FR 1168 passes a wide spot at a corner with a spectacular view out to the Cascades. Be sure to stop here on the way to or from the area trailheads - and you'll know the viewpoint when you see it. The view opens up to Mount Jefferson and points south.

* Quartzville Creek Road: This scenic 50 mile road connects Sweet Home and Marion Forks, providing numerous viewpoints of both canyon and mountains. For more information, see this link: http://www.blm.gov/or/resources/recreation/site_info.php?siteid=212

OLALLIE SCENIC AREA
* Olallie Lake: Olallie Lake is a great place to visit even if you don't plan on hiking. The best view of Mount Jefferson at the lake is located at the resort, offering people of all abilities the chance to get views better than most hikes. For more information, see Hikes 56- 58 as well as the next appendix for information on how to stay here.

* Skyline Road Viewpoint: Located about a half-mile above Horseshoe Lake, this excellent viewpoint is perhaps the best view of the Olallie Basin there is. The only downside is that the road is so terrible you may be tempted to walk here. From the small parking lot, head uphill to a collection of boulders that offer excellent views down to Horseshoe, Monon and Olallie Lakes, as well as Olallie Butte. You are on the Warm Springs Reservation here so please be as respectful as possible. Sadly there is no view of Mount Jefferson here.

* The Skyline Road: In a truck or SUV this road is a load of fun to drive; in anything smaller it is a nightmare. The Skyline Road was built in the 1920s in an attempt to construct a highway that led from Mount Hood south on the Cascade crest; the builders only made it as far as Breitenbush Lake, and given the terrain in this area, it's easy to see why they gave up. The road is a nightmare to maintain, and the 13 miles or so between Olallie Lake and the snow gate near FR 46 are among the worst roads in the state of Oregon. The best way to drive the road is from Breitenbush Pass to Breitenbush Lake, and then downhill to Horseshoe, Monon and Olallie Lakes. Breitenbush Lake is near the middle of this stretch of road. The worst stretch is the 2.5 miles from the Breitenbush Lake PCT Trailhead down to Horseshoe Lake. Throughout the 13 terrible miles expect boulders, brush, bedrock, ruts and gullies. The Skyline Road is also quite narrow, so meeting somebody going in the other direction is a problem in many spots. Once upon a time we got our little Nissan Sentra through most of this road - let's just say I don't recommend this to anyone who isn't sure they can make it.

* Breitenbush Cascades: This enormous multi-tiered waterfall is reached by a short trail off the Skyline Road. For more information see Hike 60.

* Breitenbush Pass: Though not officially named, where FR 46 crosses from the Mount Hood into the Willamette National Forest (and vice versa) is known as Breitenbush Pass. I've always had a soft spot for the place. Although the view of Mount Jefferson is obstructed by both powerlines and ridges, this is one of the few places around here with a view of the big snowy mountain. Sadly there is no place nearby to get a better view.

MOUNT JEFFERSON WEST
* Roaring Creek: There is a lovely spot on FR 4685 where the road crosses cascading and aptly-named Roaring Creek. Just beyond the crossing is the Roaring Creek Trailhead of the South Breitenbush River Trail. The best place to photograph Roaring Creek is at a campsite on the creek's left bank. This is an excellent place to spend a night in the summer provided you can snag it (not easy). We once spent a night here in the winter, which was like camping inside of an icebox- the creek is a natural refrigerator. See Hike 67 for directions and more information.

* Crown Lake Road Viewpoint: Further up FR 4685, about halfway between the South Breitenbush Trailhead for Jefferson Park and the Crown Lake Trailhead, is an exceptional viewpoint of Mount Jefferson. It is easy to find, as it's the only pullout on the left as you drive up the road. Here you can look across the canyon of the South Breitenbush River to rock formations on Devil's Ridge, and you can follow the canyon to Mount Jefferson's rocky, snowy crest. I once watched thunderstorms swirl over Mount Jefferson from this location (see the photo above), which reminded me of the utility of roadside viewpoints: when you want to observe nature from near the safety of your vehicle, come to a place like this.

MOUNT JEFFERSON EAST

* Jefferson Creek Road: On the way to the Jefferson Lake Trailhead (See Hike 96), FR 1292 passes through a green valley with spectacular views west to Mount Jefferson. The green, of course, is all snowbrush, a tough-limbed shrub that dominates terrain after fires. There are a few pullouts where you can stop to take photos .

* Head of the Metolius: Not far past the Camp Sherman / Campgrounds split on FR 14 is the short trail that leads to the Head of the Metolius River. From the split, fork right and drive a short ways to the turnoff on your left signed for the Head of the Metolius. This is a popular spot. The short paved trail leads to a viewpoint of the Metolius River as it flows out of the ground fully-formed at the foot of Black Butte. You can look downriver to views of distant Mount Jefferson (see photo on the opposite page). This neat little spot is good for a leg stretcher on your way or from some of the other hikes in this area.

* Wizard Falls Fish Hatchery: The trailhead for Hike 100 and an alternate trailhead for Hike 99, this neat fish hatchery is a fun place to hang out. There are tanks of fish to feed, great views of the Metolius at the bridge and good picnic spots complete with tables. There is not, however, a waterfall here. Wizard Falls was located on a nearby creek, but the water has been diverted away to help fill the tanks at the hatchery. It seems to be a fair trade.

* Green Ridge: The lookout tower on Green Ridge is among the most coveted lookouts in the state for those wanting to spend the night. There's no harm in coming up here during the day just for the view, but be sure to give either the lookout staffer or the folks staying here their privacy. For more information, see Appendix IV.

* Gothic Rock: Mysterious and well-hidden, Gothic Rock is also known as Five-Fingered Sentinel. Finding it is a massive pain, as it is located near the Horn of the Metolius at the top of the ridge. I'm not going to give specific directions, but suffice to say you'll find the sentinel by driving past Green Ridge Lookout to the far end of the Horn of the Metolius. Both the pleasure and the pain of this area is navigating the endless gravel roads that lead to the Horn's end.

* Balancing Rocks: I got lost looking for Gothic Rock and wound up here, above Lake Billy Chinook and well east of the eastern border of the territory covered in this book. What I found was worth including here, even if it's several miles east of Green Ridge. To find the rocks, drive FR 11 for 10 miles of pavement and another 10.4 miles of excellent gravel road until you reach a four-way junction with FR 1170, signed for Lake Billy Chinook. Turn right towards Lake Billy Chinook and drive this well-maintained gravel road 4.7 miles to its end at a T-junction just above Lake Billy Chinook. This is, in fact, the same road that leads to the Lower Metolius River Trailhead at Monty Campground described in Hike 101. Turn left here and drive 0.2 mile to an unsigned but obvious pullout on the right side of the road. Here an obvious and well-maintained trail leads to Balancing Rocks, a cool collection of rocks sitting on other rocks that stand above Lake Billy Chinook. Mount Jefferson and Olallie Butte tower over the western horizon. This is a really neat spot in spite of, or perhaps because of its remoteness. You can of course drive here from Madras and Terrebonne, but I didn't come from that direction so I'm not going to give you directions. The sign at the junction near the trailhead said it was 13 miles from Cove Palisades State Park to the junction near the Balancing Rocks Trailhead. In any case, it's a long drive from wherever you started.

APPENDIX 3: CABINS AND RESORTS

It took me three years to write this book, in three whirlwind periods that encompassed June to October of 2013, 2014 and 2015. While most of my trips to the area were dayhikes and others were camping trips, I was very grateful to have several excellent places to stay indoors during my trips to the area.

One thing that makes this area so appealing is in fact the wide variety of cabins, resorts and lookout towers that offer visitors a chance to stay in the area. These cabins and resorts range from rustic spots without electricity and running water to full-scale resorts that cater to a more upscale clientele. The only thing these places have in common, other than location, is the need to reserve as far in advance as possible. These places are popular! These are organized in the order their respective locations appear in the book and prices are as of December 2015.

* **Opal Creek Ancient Forest Center:** Located in the small community of Jawbone Flats, the cabins here have electricity and running water but are otherwise as rustic as it gets. The blessing and curse of this place is the need to hike in more than 3 miles to the cabins; of course, you are less than a half-mile from Opal Pool but you need to get there first. One fantastic way to visit this area is to sign up for the Opal Creek Ancient Forest Center's volunteer weekends, which take place every year in April and November. For a small price you get to spend a weekend in the lodge, eat some of the lodge's magnificent vegetarian cuisine and give back to one of Oregon's most special places. If you plan on staying in the cabins, reserve them as early as possible as they sell out quickly throughout the year. For more information about hikes in the area, see Hikes 20- 26. Cabins start at $100 / night. See http://www.opalcreek.org/ for more information.

* **Clear Lake:** Located near the junction of OR 22, US 20 and OR 126, the Clear Lake Resort is useful for visiting a large variety of places in this book from Iron Mountain (Hike 44) all the way to the east side of the Mount Jefferson Wilderness (Hikes 87- 96). Of course, Clear Lake is also extremely beautiful in its own right, and this is the ideal base camp for expeditions into the McKenzie River area (see Hikes 49 and 50). The resort here is run by Linn County and feels a bit dated. There are rustic cabins without electricity and modern cabins that feature electricity and kitchens. The cabins are cheaper in the winter, too- bring snowshoes for hiking. Rustic cabins start at $64 / night while modern cabins start at $99 / night. See http://www.linnparks.com/pages/parks/clearlake.html for more information.

* **Olallie Lake Resort:** Set on the northern end of beautiful Olallie Lake, the Olallie Lake resort is the ideal way to visit the Olallie area. The campgrounds here are crowded, lack water and give you no shelter against the hordes of mosquitoes that plague this area from June into early August; why not stay in one of the cabins or yurts here instead? The cabins lack electricity, offering instead vintage oil lamps. For heat, there are woodstoves. Staying here is like stepping into the past, and that is one of the primary charms of visiting (that, and the stupendous view of Mount Jefferson across Olallie Lake). The store at the resort offers a nice selection of items you may need for your stay, and has a surprisingly good selection of craft beers. Cabins start at $65 / night while yurts start at $100 / night. Rates are cheaper on weekdays and after Labor Day. See www.http://olallielakeresort.com/ for more information.

Mount Jefferson looms over the docks at the Olallie Lake Resort.

* Breitenbush: The resort and hot springs feel both out of place and out of time, and are all the better for it. Most of the people who visit have no intention of hiking, and are instead here for the various programs as well as to soak in the various pools along the Breitenbush River. The place has a new-age vibe, for better or for worse (depending on your point of view). The pools are wonderfully hot, and you should absolutely expect that most people will soak nude. The vegetarian food in the mess hall is delicious and as healthy as you would expect. Alcohol is expressly forbidden at the resort. Please respect the rules and requests of the resort. If you plan on hiking, the trailheads for Hikes 65, 66 and 67 are within a half-mile of the resort and the trailheads for Hikes 68, 69 and 70 are less than a half-hour away. The only real downside of this place is the cost: cabins start at about $100 a night *per person* throughout the year, and even tent sites cost around $60 per person. Lodge rooms are similarly priced. See https://www.breitenbush.com/ for more information.

* Suttle Lake: This beautiful resort is definitely in the more upscale category, but its charms are numerous and its lodge among the most beautiful in the state. The cabins and lodge rooms are quite spendy, with prices starting around $250 a night- but when you stay here, you'll agree that it's worth it. This is cheaper and less pretentious than nearby Black Butte, and is nicer than most of the places in nearby Camp Sherman. The restaurant has excellent food (or so I'm told), and the lodge is a fantastic place to hang out at night- I once spent an evening in here counting up the various species of animals represented in carvings around the lodge. If your budget cannot afford the modern cabins or lodge rooms, try the rustic cabins. At $100 a night they lack a bathroom, kitchen or television, but they're warm and cozy on cold nights. For directions, see Hike 89. This is an excellent base camp for all of the hikes in section 6 of this book, Hikes 87- 101. As of this writing the resort is now under new management- if you want to visit, look online to see if the lodge has reopened.

APPENDIX 4: LOOKOUT TOWERS

Staying in a lookout tower is among the most rewarding ways to visit the Majestic Mount Jefferson Region. To be able to wake up to a panoramic view, snug in a small building in the middle of nowhere, is as good as it gets. Once upon a time, there were dozens of these buildings scattered throughout the region, and they were manned by young individuals and couples whose job it was to spot fires before they could grow out of control. In the case of Green Ridge, this is still the primary function of the lookout tower. In the 1960s, aerial surveillance began to replace the lookout towers, and most of the towers were either dismantled or burned to the ground (an especially cruel irony). Today, only eight lookout towers remain in the Majestic Mount Jefferson Region; you can stay in the four below while three others (Coffin Mountain, Hike 32; Sisi Butte, Hike 51; and Black Butte, Hike 97) remain active fire lookouts that do not permit visitors. The eighth, the lookout atop Bull of the Woods (Hikes 8, 9 and 11), is in a state of disrepair and is closed to the public. The lookout tower atop Iron Mountain (Hike 44) was dismantled in 2008 as it had fallen into a state of tremendous disrepair and was no longer safe for staffers or visitors.

All information on how to stay in the lookouts is current up to December 2015.

* Pechuck Lookout: This lookout just outside the east edge of the Table Rock Wilderness was lovingly restored by the Sand Mountain Society, an organization that works to restore lookout towers. The cupola-style construction is unique to this lookout, and the building looks absolutely beautiful from the outside. The inside of the lookout is not too spacious, and it does not take long to realize that the lookout is already inhabited. Some won't mind the resident mouse population, but many will. The view at the lookout has grown in as well, with only views north to Table Rock.

Staying at the lookout is first-come, first-served- and the competition is fierce. There is no fee, but come early and plan on sharing the cabin with others (including, of course, the mice). I visited the lookout on a warm day in January of a low-snow year only to find at least ten people either staying in the lookout or hoping to stay in the lookout. Patience is a must here. For more directions and information, see Hike 3.

* Gold Butte Lookout: Gold Butte's lookout tower has one of the most unique views in the Majestic Mount Jefferson Region, and the tower has been lovingly kept up by volunteers. It is a crown jewel of the lookout reservation program. As you might imagine, getting a reservation for this lookout is quite difficult. It took me several months of trying, and only then was I able to book the tower for a Thursday in mid-September. If you want to stay here, be patient and plan ahead. There is firewood and a wood stove, but bring everything else you may need. The lookout is beloved, and with good reason. While there, be sure to check out the visitors log- visitors to the lookout are amazed, amused and awestruck.

The access roads are absolutely terrible, but this does little to discourage people from visiting. Directions to the trailhead are described in Hike 29. To book the tower, head over to http://www.recreation.gov, search for Gold Butte and wait patiently until you have the chance to book a reservation. It may take you awhile to get a reservation, but of course, it is absolutely worth it.

The Gold Butte Lookout Tower has a heck of a great view - if isn't raining.

* Hawk Mountain: Here is one of the best-kept secrets in the Majestic Mount Jefferson Region! It's an easy hike to Hawk Mountain's summit, where the view of Mount Jefferson is stupendous and the flower displays in July and August among the best in the region. The lookout tower is long gone - instead, the building on the summit is the cabin where staffers stayed at night. The cabin is open to the public on a first-come, first-served basis, and is of course free.

When you visit remember that this a restored cabin, one that is as rustic as it gets. There is a rusting cot that would not make for a good night's sleep- bring a sleeping bag. Do not disturb anything, don't break anything and don't be a jerk. Treat this place with the love and respect that it deserves. For directions and more information, see Hike 30.

* Green Ridge: Now we've come to the most popular lookout in the region. The Green Ridge Lookout is staffed during the summer and thus the tower is only available for rent in April and May, and for six weeks in the fall. The view down to the Metolius and out to Mount Jefferson is fabulous, and this is the kind of place that is difficult to leave. Of course, I am not the only person who feels this way. In truth, I never visited the lookout- I tried for three years to get a reservation and failed every single time. On the other hand, a good friend was able to get a reservation at the last minute due to a cancellation. Maybe you'll have better luck than me.

To reserve (or at least try) the Green Ridge Lookout, go to http://www.recreation.gov and search for Green Ridge. What I said about Gold Butte applies twice as much here: it may take months or even years to get a reservation. But it is worth it, or so I am told. For more information and directions, see http://www.recreation.gov as well as Hike 98 in this book.

APPENDIX 5: CAMPGROUNDS

I spent three years writing this book, and over that time I managed to stay in many of the campgrounds that dot the Majestic Mount Jefferson Region. There are lots. I stayed at many more of these campgrounds as a child growing up in Salem, as the Majestic Mount Jefferson Region was my playground. While I don't have the space to describe every campground in detail, I'll at least try to give you an idea about each campground in the area. As it is difficult to find information about some of these campgrounds online, this small guide should help you organize a trip to the area. As always, you are free to stay in dispersed sites in the Majestic Mount Jefferson area; just be sure to bring water, pack out your garbage, bury your human waste and observe fire bans when necessary. And no, I won't tell you where the best dispersed sites are- the joy of finding the good ones is also the joy of keeping them a secret. The campgrounds below are organized in the order you would pass them on the way to the hikes in this book.

* **Molalla River Sites:** This collection of first-come, first-served sites along the Molalla River is convenient for Portland-area campers but lacks many of the amenities associated with traditional campgrounds. Consult the BLM's website and maps for the Molalla Recreation Corridor online for more information.
free / many sites / no water / no toilets / non-reservable / year-round

* **Kingfisher:** This small campground on the way to Bagby Hot Springs is popular and fills frequently over the course of the year. I've never stayed here but the location is great. Sites are reservable on www.recreation.gov.
$21 / 24 sites / water / toilets / reservable / May - September

* **Bagby:** This new campground near the popular trailhead for Bagby Hot Springs (see Hike 7) is as popular as the trail to the hot springs. I've never stayed here before but it seems to be well-maintained and clean. The people currently managing the hot springs are doing an excellent job, and I'm sure that courtesy extends to the campground as well.
$16 / ??? sites / no water / toilets / non-reservable / February-September

* **Little Fan:** This small campground on the Collawash River on FR 63 fills up fast and it can be difficult to get a site here during the summer. The location is very convenient for visiting the nearby Bull of the Woods Wilderness (hikes 6- 12) but the campground lacks charm and can be kind of noisy.
$14 / 5 sites / no water / 1 toilet / non-reservable / May - September

* **North Santiam State Park:** This small and little-known park is located along the North Santiam River on a side road about a half-mile from OR 22, just after the junction with the Little North Fork Road. With only 9 first-come, first-served sites, competition for a site is fierce. There is a small trail network at the park with 2.4 miles of trails that makes for a nice hike mid-winter. I really like this little park.
$10 / 9 walk-in sites / water / toilets / non-reservable / May-September

* **Fisherman's Bend:** I used to stay here often when I was young, and I remember this large and popular campground operated by the BLM with great fondness. It is larger and more modern than most Forest Service campgrounds with electric hookups, flush toilets

and showers. There is also a small trail network. Located near Mill City, the campground is closer to the Willamette Valley than it is to Mount Jefferson but makes for a convenient base of operations if you are visiting the Little North Fork areas. Sites are reservable on www.recreation.gov.
$16 / 63 sites / water / toilets and showers / reservable / May - October

* Detroit Lake State Park: This is the mother of all Oregon campgrounds, the site of some of the most epic parties in the Majestic Mount Jefferson Region. For better and for worse, this is what you get at Detroit Lake. The park leaves some of the sites open year-round, offering camping even in the middle of winter (if you are inclined to do so). In the summer this place is hopping all the time, much to the chagrin of those who prefer a wilder, more secluded camping experience. But you can't beat the location, and the park serves as a good base camp for most of the hikes in this book. Just know that it will be noisy and very crowded. Sites are reservable on http://www.reserveamerica.com
$19 / 300 sites / water / toilets and showers / reservable/ year-round

* South Detroit Lake Campgrounds: If you want to stay at Detroit Lake but don't want to stay at the state park, this series of campgrounds on the lake's south shore may be more your style. Cove Creek, Hoover and Southshore Campgrounds are located on the south side of the lake. Santiam Flats is located along Blowout Road just off OR 22. Piety Island is a small and primitive campground on its namesake island that is only reachable by boat. All of them other than Piety Island are reservable on www.recreation.gov.
$16 - $22 / approximately 100 sites / water / toilets / reservable / May - September

* Bear Creek: This brand-new campground that opened in 2014 offers 15 sites along the Little North Santiam River. Operated by Marion County Parks, this small campground is charming. Information on the campground is hard to come by.
$14 / 15 sites / water / toilets / non-reservable / Memorial Day - Labor Day

* Elkhorn Valley: This campground on the Little North Santiam River 8.5 miles northeast of Mehama offers 23 sites on a first-come, first-served basis. The campground fills fast in the summer and closes early in the season.
$14 / 23 sites / water / toilets / non-reservable / Memorial Day - Labor Day

* Shady Cove: This small campground along the Little North Santiam River is an ideal base camp for trips into the Opal Creek area. Located just across the river from the upper trail-head for the Little North Santiam River Trail, Shady Cove is charming and secluded and everything you want in a campground (don't tell anybody). Best of all, the campground is ppen all year. I spent many a night here in the winter as a child when the camping bug bit my family.
$8 / 13 sites / no water / toilet / non-reservable / all year

* Elk Lake: The road to Elk Lake is awful (see Hikes 27 and 28), something that paradoxically makes Elk Lake's small campground one of the notorious party spots in this book. Avoid holiday weekends here. Elk Lake is beautiful though, and this is the only place to camp on this side of the Bull of the Woods Wilderness. Bring lots of water as there is none at the campground, and be sure to pack out your garbage.
$10 / 17 sites / no water / toilet / non-reservable / June - October

* Cascadia State Park: This park on the South Santiam River has excellent campsites in a lowland environment. For more information see Hike 39.
$17 / 25 sites / water / toilets / non-reservable / May - September

* South Santiam River Campgrounds: Fernview, Trout Creek and Yukwah Campgrounds are located on the South Santiam River. Trout Creek is located directly across US 20 from the Trout Creek Trailhead (see Hike 40). Many sites are situated along the South Santiam River. Sites can be reserved on www.recreation.gov. Smallish Fernview is located directly across US 20 from the Rooster Rock (Hike 40 alternate) trailhead. With only 11 sites and no reservations, competition is stiff to grab a spot. Further upriver, Yukwah offers more sites along the South Santiam in a convenient location.
$ 15 / 53 sites / water / toilets / reservable (except Fernview) / May - September

* House Rock: Set in a classic old-growth forest, this charming and beautiful campground on the South Santiam River is a great place to camp out while visiting the Old Cascades. Some of the sites are on the river while others are on a bluff above the river. The campground is the trailhead for Hike 42. Sites are reservable on www.recreation.gov.
$15 / 17 sites / water / toilets / reservable / May - September

* Lost Prairie: This small campground at Tombstone Pass offers first-come, first-served sites along Hackleman Creek. Expect cold nights up here. The group campsite is reservable on www.recreation.gov.
$15 / 10 sites / water / toilets / non-reservable / May - October

* Coldwater Cove: Situated on the east side of Clear Lake, Coldwater Cove is a popular campground that provides an alternative to staying at the Clear Lake Resort. 13 of the campground's 35 sites are reservable, so plan ahead if you want to guarantee your spot here. The loop trail around Clear Lake (Hike 49) passes right through the campground. The 13 sites available for reservation are found on www.recreation.gov.
$20 / 35 sites / water / toilets / 13 of 35 sites reservable / May - October

* Olallie Meadows: This small campground is away from the lakes in the Olallie Scenic Area and thus is less crowded. This is the trailhead for Hike 52.
$15 / 7 sites / no water / toilets / non-reservable / July - September

* Lower Lake: With only 8 sites, competition is stiff for sites at this small campground. The sites are fairly close together as well, which actually makes this campground ideal for group trips. The campground is not at Lower Lake; you need to hike down the Fish Lake Trail about 250 yards to Lower Lake. As with all other campgrounds here there is no running water.
$15 / 8 sites / no water / toilets / non-reservable / July - September

* Paul Dennis: Located next to the Olallie Lake Resort, this campground offers 17 sites near Olallie Lake's shore. The star attraction here is the view of Mount Jefferson (this is by far the best view of the mountain from a campground). There is no water at the campground though there are spigots at the resort. The access road into the campground is fairly rough, too; any car can handle it, but drive slowly. This is the trailhead for Hike 56.
$15 / 17 sites / no water / toilets / non-reservable / July - September

* Camp Ten: The smallest of Olallie Lake's three campgrounds, Camp Ten is also the first to fill on summer weekends. Camp Ten is located on the Skyline Road about a mile south of the Olallie Lake Resort, along a narrow strip of land between the road and the lake. As with other campgrounds in the area, there is no water.
$15 / 10 sites / no water / toilets / non-reservable / July - September

* Peninsula: The largest campground at Olallie Lake, Peninsula is also one of the busiest. Road access is decent but the road south of the resort along the lake leaves a lot to be desired. This campground burned during the 2001 fire and thus some sites are lacking in shade (and tree cover). The campground is located on the south end of Olallie Lake, on the narrow band of land separating Olallie and Monon Lakes.
$15 / 36 sites / no water / toilets / non-reservable / July - September

* Horseshoe Lake: Maybe the smallest campground in this book, Horseshoe Lake is also one of the prettiest. The road access is terrible but once you get there it's a really nice place to camp. The sites are right on the Skyline Road but there's little traffic.
$15 / 6 sites / no water / toilets / non-reservable / July - September

* Breitenbush Lake: Operated by the Warm Springs Reservation, this campground is a good base camp for hikes 61- 63 but comes with a different set of rules than all other campgrounds. You have to stay in the area of the campground; absolutely stay out of the lake, the area around the lake and stay off the trail network south of the lake- all of these are open only to members of the Warm Springs tribe. The only way to get a view of Mount Jefferson is to go out on the lake in a kayak or canoe. Alcohol is also prohibited. And of course, the road access is terrible. Please be respectful and follow these rules.
free / 20 sites / no water / toilets / non-reservable / July - September

* Humbug: Located 4.5 miles up the Breitenbush River from Detroit, this campground is also the trailhead for Hike 64. There are several very nice sites on the Breitenbush River here, but overall this campground is not as nice as Breitenbush Campground further up the river. Sites are reservable on www.recreation.gov.
$16 / 21 sites / water / toilets / reservable / May - September

* Cleator Bend and Fox Creek: At one time Cleator Bend was a typical campground but is now used for large groups. Located near Breitenbush Hot Springs, this is the best place to stay if you want to visit the hot springs but don't want to pay $60 per person for a tent site at the resort. Nearby Fox Creek Group Camp is only one large flat but serves a similar purpose. Cleator Bend has water while Fox Creek does not, but Fox Creek can accommo-date more people than Cleator Bend. Both are reservable on www.reserveamerica.com.
$40 for Fox Creek; $133 for Cleator Bend / 1 site at each campground / toilets / water / reservable / May - September

* Breitenbush: The nearest campground to Breitenbush Hot Springs, this medium-sized campground is also one of the busiest in this area. Plan ahead if you want to stay here as reservations fill up fast in the summer. Sites are reservable on www.recreation.gov.
$16 / 30 sites / water / toilets / reservable / May - September

* Whispering Falls: Named after a small, seasonal waterfall that tumbles into the North Santiam River from the opposite side of the canyon, this campground is a popular base camp for trips into the Jefferson Park and Triangulation Peak areas. Sites are reservable on www.recreation.gov.
$16 / 16 sites / water / toilets / reservable / May - September

* Riverside: Located 2.5 miles north of Marion Forks on a bluff above the North Santiam River, this is my favorite campground in this area. The sites are relatively secluded and the location, between the Pamelia, Minto and Marion Roads (see Hikes 75- 80) is as good as it gets. Best of all, the campground is reservable, offering the opportunity to plan trips far in advance with the security of knowing you'll have a campsite waiting for you. The sites by the river are nicer; some of the sites are near OR 22 and can be a little noisy. Site are reservable on www.recreation.gov- make sure you search for Riverside at Detroit.
$16 / 38 sites / water / toilets / reservable / May - September

* Marion Forks: This is a forgotten campground hiding in plain sight just a half-mile from the Marion Forks Restaurant. There's no water but the sites are secluded away in a mossy forest and the campground is among the quietest in this area. Highly recommended.
$10 / 15 sites / no water / toilets / non-reservable / May - October

* Lost Lake: This campground on a lake near Santiam Pass is small and noisy, but is very conveniently-located. The shallow lake is marshy and becomes meadow later in the year through a curious phenomenon: a small lava tube drains the water out of the lake in the spring and summer.
$8 / 12 sites / no water / toilets / non-reservable / June - October

* Suttle Lake Campgrounds: There are three campgrounds at Suttle Lake and all three are heavily used in season. Expect crowds and a lot of noise. Blue Bay is the first you come to on US 20, while Link Creek and South Shore are on the other end of the lake from the resort. All three are reservable on www.recreation.gov, and Link Creek has three yurts available for reservation as well.
$18 / 96 sites and 3 yurts / water / toilets / reservable / May - September

* Scout Lake: Just up the hill to the south of Suttle Lake is lovely Scout Lake. The lake is a popular swimming spot for families in summer, but be warned: dogs are not allowed in the adjacent day use area, nor are they allowed in the lake. This is to preserve the purity of the water. Violating this rule is a $100 fine.
$18 - 44 / 1 single site, 6 double sites, 3 group sites / water / toilets / reservable / May - September

* Jack Creek: This campground is well-known but suffers from a bit of an identity crisis. The signs into the campground are gone, the access road into the campground has a few rough spots and there is no water despite being located next to a swift-flowing mountain stream only a mile from its source. Nevertheless, this is the best place to camp in this area and is worth a stop if you are hiking around here. This is the trailhead for Hike 91.
$14 / 16 sites / no water / toilets / non-reservable / April - November

* Upper Metolius / Camp Sherman Campgrounds: There are six campgrounds in the immediate vicinity of Camp Sherman: Riverside, Camp Sherman, Allingham, Smiling River, Pine Rest and Gorge. Many of the campgrounds are oriented more towards RVs, and out of all the campgrounds in the area, only tiny Pine Rest is tent-only. As it is, Pine Rest is also the best of the bunch, offering spacious sites immediately next to the Metolius River. Only Camp Sherman and Allingham have running water, so bring lots of water from home or expect to make lots of runs down to these two campgrounds to fill up your water jugs. Camp Sherman Campground is open all year, with lower rates in the winter. Camp Sherman is the only one of these six that has reservable sites; visit www.recreation.gov to reserve a site.
$12 - 18 / 102 sites / water only at Camp Sherman and Allingham / toilets / non-reservable except for Camp Sherman / May - September except Camp Sherman (year-round)

* Lower Canyon Creek: This small campground is in a great location, situated next to the mouth of Canyon Creek at the trailhead for Hike 99. There is no running water but you can't beat the river access. Due to its small size and great location, the campground fills fast on summer weekends.
$14 / 7 sites / no water / toilets / non-reservable / June - October

* Allen Springs: This campground on the east bank of the Metolius is open year-round, depending of course on snow levels. Hike 100 passes through the campground. Like many other campgrounds in this area, there is no drinking water- you'll have to bring your own or drive up to Pioneer Ford or Lower Bridge to fill up.
$14 / 16 sites / no water / toilets / non-reservable / year-round

* Pioneer Ford: This spacious campground on the east bank of the Metolius is peaceful, and a lovely place to spend a night or four. Hike 100 passes through the campground, offering the opportunity to hike directly from your campsite.
$16 / 20 sites / water / toilets / non-reservable / May - September

* Lower Bridge: Of all the campgrounds on the Metolius River, this is by far the best. The location is fantastic, at the trailhead for Hike 101 with Hike 100 passing by and Hike 96 only a few miles away. Competition is fierce for a site here, so expect this campground to be full and hope to be pleasantly surprised. This is one of the few campgrounds in the area with running water. There are also several sites next to the river, some of the nicest campsites in this book. Don't leave food out here, as the area chipmunks are skilled at stealing campers' food. Store your food properly!
$18 / 12 sites / water / toilets / non-reservable / April - November

* Candle Creek: This spacious campground offers a small number of sites in great solitude, far away from the other campgrounds on the Metolius. The campground is located at the confluence of Candle Creek and the Metolius, down a gravel road near the end of FR 12. There's no water but you can't beat the sites. You can also hike here from Lower Bridge on an easy 1.5 mile stretch of the West Metolius River Trail (see Hikes 100 and 101).
$14 / 10 sites / no water / toilets / non-reservable / May - September

Majestic Mount Jefferson Index

About the author:

Matt Reeder moved from Illinois to Salem, Oregon at age 7 and soon after fell in love with the Majestic Mount Jefferson Region. He spent many summer and fall weekends hiking and camping near Opal Creek and Mount Jefferson and came to know the area very well. He moved back to Illinois with his parents when he was 16, but Matt returned eight years later to resume his love affair with Opal Creek and Mount Jefferson. *101 Hikes in the Majestic Mount Jefferson Region* is the end result not just of three years of constant hiking, camping and research but a realization of a childhood dream.

Matt is the author of *Off the Beaten Trail: Fifty fantastic unknown hikes in NW Oregon and SW Washington*. He lives in old farmhouse in southeast Portland with his wife Wendy. When not on the trail or in the classroom, he spends his free time obsessing about music, following the Portland Trail Blazers and reading voraciously. You can usually identify Matt on the trail by his red St. Louis Cardinals hat, a visible sign of his lifelong love of the 2006 and 2011 World Series Champions.